D0931196

SKYSCRAPER DREAMS

Books by Tom Shachtman

THE DAY AMERICA CRASHED (1979)
EDITH AND WOODROW (1981)
THE PHONY WAR, 1939–1940 (1982)
DECADE OF SHOCKS, 1963–1974 (1983)
SKYSCRAPER DREAMS (1991)

Collaborative Books

THE FBI-KGB WAR by Robert J. Lamphere and Tom Shachtman
(1986)
THE GILDED LEAF by Patrick Reynolds and Tom Shachtman (1989)
STRAIGHT TO THE TOP by Paul G. Stern and Tom Shachtman (1990)
IMAGE BY DESIGN by Clive Chajet and Tom Shachtman (1991)

For Children

Novels:
BEACHMASTER (1988)
WAVEBENDER (1989)
DRIFTWHISTLER (1991)

Nonfiction:
GROWING UP MASAI (1981)
THE BIRDMAN OF ST. PETERSBURG (1982)
PARADE! (1985)
AMERICA'S BIRTHDAY (1987)
VIDEO POWER (with Harriet Shelare, 1988)
THE PRESIDENT BUILDS A HOUSE (1989)

SKYSCRAPER DREAMS

The Great Real Estate Dynasties of New York

TOM SHACHTMAN

LITTLE, BROWN AND COMPANY

BOSTON   TORONTO   LONDON

First Edition

Library of Congress Cataloging-in-Publication Data

Shachtman, Tom, 1942–
    Skyscraper dreams: the great real estate dynasties of New York/
Tom Shachtman. — 1st ed.
        p.   cm.
    Includes index.
    ISBN 0-316-78213-0
    1. Real estate developers — New York (N.Y.) — Biography.   2. Real
estate development — New York (N.Y.) — History.   3. Family
corporations — New York (N.Y.) — History.   I. Title.
HD268.N5S52   1991
333.77'15'09227471 — dc20
[B]   90-25070

              10 9 8 7 6 5 4 3 2 1

                        RRD-VA

            Published simultaneously in Canada
        by Little, Brown & Company (Canada) Limited

        Printed in the United States of America

"City of tall facades of marble and iron!
Proud and passionate city —
Mettlesome, mad, extravagant city!"
                                    Walt Whitman

"Make no little plans. They have no magic to stir men's
blood and probably themselves will not be realized. Make
big plans: aim high in hope and work. . . . Remember
our sons and grandsons are going to do things that would
stagger us. Let your watchword be order and your beacon
beauty."
                                    Daniel Hudson Burnham

"I'd rather be alive at eighteen percent than dead at the
prime rate."
                                    William Zeckendorf, Sr.

Contents

SKYSCRAPER
DREAMS

Prologue

Public and Private Ceremonies

THE MAJOR PARTICIPANTS in the "ultimate power breakfast" event at the Regency Hotel on the morning of Thursday, September 22, 1988, arrived early, and as they entered the dining quarters from the Park Avenue lobby they looked a bit askance at the rapidly rising jumble of cables and paraphernalia of the television crews and public relations people filling the room. Wearing crisp, understated suits and ties, the players avoided the center of the dining area, where lights were being adjusted and microphones tested, and sat at side tables. In front of gilt-edged murals of medieval châteaus, they sipped cups of coffee offered by attendants at silver urns, ate croissants or bagels, salmon and fresh fruit, and talked quietly among themselves. All had agreed to participate in this event, whose purpose was to generate publicity for a charity; even so, the apparatus of hyperbole appeared to make them a bit uncomfortable.

"Third time I've seen you in three days," said Leonard Stern as he shook hands with Lew Rudin. Stern, a small, dark, intense man of fifty with a strong, nasal New York accent, presented a contrast to the tall, bespectacled, affable Rudin, who was ten years older and more relaxed in the public eye. Stern darted about, drawing his own coffee, having short staccato-burst conversations with acquaintances, while Rudin stayed at a side table and let people approach him.

They had also spent time together at Rudin's annual break-the-fast cocktail party and dinner just after sundown at the close of the Jewish holy day of Yom Kippur, held at the Regency the previous evening and reported in the gossip columns. Their other meeting had been a session of the board of trustees of New York University.

Another of this morning's participants, Preston Robert Tisch, a barrel-chested man with a toupee, a few years older than Rudin, had also been present on all three occasions.

All three men were superwealthy — Tisch and Stern reputedly billionaires, and Rudin a member of a family whose Manhattan property was assessed at about a billion dollars. They were sipping coffee together now because of their overlapping, even convergent interests. Jonathan Tisch, Bob Tisch's recently married son and the president of the family's hotel chain, had conceived an unusual event, a game of Monopoly to be played at a power breakfast by his father and friends, true real estate barons — an instance of life imitating a game that was itself supposed to mirror life. The Regency had worked assiduously to become the place for the city's movers and shakers to start their day. This particular breakfast was also billed as part of the celebration of the Regency's twenty-fifth anniversary; later in the week, the hotel planned to hold a nostalgic "1963" costume ball and other galas. But Jonathan Tisch's event needed more than Tisches, so the family reached out to Stern and others. Stern agreed to attend, but only if the game could be played for the benefit of Homes for the Homeless, a charity of which Stern was the treasurer as well as the guarantor of its considerable financial obligations.

Plastic top hats, part of the outfit of the Monopoly game's Rich Uncle Pennybags, were handed out at the door; few guests wore them. The third big wheel, Rudin, was more blunt about his participation in what was taking on more and more the air of a publicity circus as the fifty-dollar-a-ticket audience arrived. "I'm only here because of Bob and Joan," Rudin confided to an observer. "They're lifelong friends." But Rudin wouldn't go so far as to wear the Monopoly tie that had been provided; one of the city's leading boosters, he was sporting a New York Mets tie, for there was hope that the Mets would clinch the National League East title that very evening.

So: the charity to be favored was under Stern's aegis; the setting was a Tisch hotel (which also had a drum to beat); and Rudin seldom missed an occasion to display his civic-mindedness and oblige friends. Calling on one another for this sort of minor favor was expected in their circle, even encouraged. Such mutual obligations and pleasures were, in fact, celebrations of power by the representatives of an oligarchy, a small number of families whose wealth was largely intertwined with the symbols of New York City: Manhattan's crown of skyscrapers.

Paul Goldberger, Pulitzer Prize–winning architecture critic for the *New York Times*, made an unheralded entrance. Clad in a sports jacket, the bearded Goldberger seemed hopelessly tweedy and academic among these titans of business. He had been recruited as a fourth player to add a patina of reportorial respectability so the event would be more than a public relations affair. There were some on the edge of the room who whispered that it was Goldberger's recent article disparaging the taste of Donald Trump that had caused Trump, who had been announced as a participant, to withdraw from this event at the last minute. The true source of the withdrawal — Trump's simmering feud with Leonard Stern — wouldn't become publicly apparent for several months. In any case, comic Jackie Mason, the current toast of Broadway as sole performer in *The World According to Me*, arrived to replace Trump. Adam Moss, editor of what was then a new weekly, *7 Days* (owned by Leonard Stern), thought appropriate this substitution of Mason for Trump: "one media star for another." This weekly had instigated the feud by reporting that purchasers of Trump Tower units were having difficulty reselling their apartments, a notion that had been vehemently denied by Trump and for which he had demanded a retraction, which was not forthcoming; Moss had hoped Trump would appear here, so he could beard the lion. Other reporters and television crews were even more disappointed at Trump's absence.

Intense halogen lights were turned on full for the benefit of the television cameras as the players took their seats around a table in the room's center. Except for Jackie Mason, the participants seemed only to endure the glare, not to enjoy it. A guard arrived with thousands of dollars in crisp new bills — real money to be used by the players — and the fun began. Cameras and reporters formed a ring about the central table that made it impossible for most of the paying guests to see the game. To one side, a nine-foot-square Monopoly board provided a backdrop for opening comments by Robin Leach, host and originator of the syndicated television program "Lifestyles of the Rich and Famous." Leach's gray snakeskin shoes, flamboyantly checked suit, and outspoken Cockney presence captured the crowd's attention. Officials from Parker Brothers, the manufacturers of Monopoly, and some champion players commented on the action, acted as bankers, and kept score.

Cameras recorded Leonard Stern's taking off his jacket and putting on glasses to play, the sweat beading the brow of Bob Tisch, and Jackie Mason's quips: "I'm a homeless, too — I live in a building owned by Lew Rudin."

After buying the Hartz Mountain pet-supply company from his father and expanding its nationwide business, Leonard Stern had weathered a $40-million judgment against the company and masterminded its return to respectability, at the same time diversifying his own operations. His major triumph had been the purchase of the Meadowlands area in New Jersey and its subsequent development as a massive sports complex. He owned the last private townhouse on upper Fifth Avenue, while his former wife remained in residence at the last private townhouse on Park Avenue. With success had come the glimmer of a dream that many men in this room shared: to build a skyscraper in Manhattan, one that would thrust high into the sky and reflect its conceiver's power and sensibilities. The purchase of the *Village Voice* and the backing of *7 Days* had made him, like several other real estate titans, a power in the city's news media. But the sleek black skyscraper around the corner from the Regency, on 62nd Street and Madison Avenue, was Stern's pride and joy.

In their youth Bob Tisch and his brother Larry had scraped together the money to purchase a small resort in New Jersey, then bought and expanded the Loew's chain of hotels and theaters. Using their real estate holdings as a base, they had branched into other businesses: for instance, gaining control of high-flying Philip Morris, whose stock had increased in price eight times during the 1980s. The financial community acknowledged that no men in the country were better at analyzing the finances of a company than the Tisches; as a recent article put it, their heaviest losses over the years had been their hair. Bob had now returned to Loew's from a stint as postmaster general of the United States, and Larry had taken over CBS and become its chairman. Bob's son Jonathan, president of Loew's Hotel, had recently married the daughter of financier Saul P. Steinberg in a fancifully extravagant "billionaire society" wedding ceremony and reception; wags said that the nuptials had had to be approved by the Securities and Exchange Commission.

Lew Rudin had a public image of being less of a buccaneer than Stern or Tisch, perhaps because he had carefully nurtured the position of statesman and spokesman for the industry. The Rudin family had been in New York real estate since the early days of the century and had steadfastly refused to broaden out into other fields, preferring to be very good at what they knew best. The dream of influencing the skyline of Manhattan had been instilled in Lew from an early age: the empire of apartment houses and office buildings that his father, Sam, had begun, and that Lew and his brother Jack had augmented with new towers every few years, placed the Rudins among the largest landlords in Manhattan. There was a Samuel Rudin trophy for the annual New York City Marathon; many policemen wore bulletproof vests purchased with money donated by a Rudin foundation. Thought by some to be a bit enamored of his own influence, and by others to be a soft touch, when crossed Rudin was known for sending the perpetrator a small pillow with the embroidered legend "No Good Deed Goes Unpunished."

Though the players were friends, they were sometimes also rivals. When a choice plot went on the market, each would attempt to outmaneuver the other, without a moment's hesitation or sympathy for the loser in the game. They all regularly applied for construction and mortgage loans from the same big banks, insurance companies, and pension funds, and had to elbow each other out of the way for their share of the financing pie. Their ruthless jockeying was not so much a concomitant of the quest for money — each man had more than enough millions for himself and for several generations of offspring to live in complete comfort; rather, it was the consequence of the desire to erect a skyscraper, to be able to look out one's office window and see a part of the glittering skyline that was one's own.

These men and their peers, some of whom dropped by to gawk at the festivities, shared a love of soaring buildings that was more than an appreciation of their worth as pieces of property. When they had one under construction, these men in conservative suits would not be able to stay in their offices and let the construction managers handle the sites; no, they would find excuses to get out and see how things were going, don a hardhat, ride a rickety construction elevator to a floor that was as yet only a slab between steel beams where the wind could always be felt, pore over a blueprint they'd seen a hundred times before, get concrete dust on their shoes. Before the building officially opened, they'd walk around it or traipse to a spot several blocks away to see how it looked against the backdrop of the other skyscrapers; all told stories about the magic moment when the lights were finally turned on and the building really began to live. In their eyes the skyscrapers of Manhattan were animate jewels that reached for the heavens, crystals that absorbed the sun during the day and shone at night.

The Monopoly game careened on, played at double or triple speed in order not to waste the time of the tycoons — or the press. Rudin was announced to be losing at the halfway mark. Goldberger was in the lead, inciting jocular speculation from the audience as to what chaos might ensue if an architectural critic beat the builders. With an apparent lack of anything better to do, Leach interviewed fellow reporters, even though plenty of guests at the event might have qualified for his program: so numerous were the wealthy among the audience that outside the hotel their waiting cars had caused limousine gridlock.

Samuel "Sandy" Lindenbaum, former city official and one of New York's foremost zoning lawyers, chatted with public relations expert Howard J. Rubinstein; both had clients at the center table and were considered among the most influential men in New York. Over the previous dozen years or so, Lindenbaum had successfully lobbied the city to grant approximately half a billion dollars in tax abatements for his clients. Rubinstein was the city's leading public relations man; few large real estate companies in New York dared to get along without his services. Both men often attended the Regency's power breakfasts.

During the game, Manhattan Borough President David Dinkins, considering a run for the mayoralty, worked the room. As well as any other politician, Dinkins knew that New York depends heavily on the real estate industry. While the interrelationship between big real estate and New York City has always been complex, in the modern era it has become symbiotic. The city government's largest single source of revenue is the real property tax, and Manhattan office buildings provide over one-quarter of the total; levies on big apartment buildings and hotels add another substantial fraction. If real estate occupancy rates go up, so does the city's financial health; if real estate heads into the doldrums, the public treasury quickly experiences a period of lassitude. No aspirant to public office could afford to ignore New York's real estate barons, and not simply because of their possible campaign donations. In this room were some of the major backers of the city's nongovernmental infrastructure: private hospitals, museums, opera and ballet companies, and colleges had become heavily dependent upon the contributions of the real estate barons. In the past month, Leonard Stern's gift of $30 million to New York University's business school had been announced; in the weeks just ahead, a Tisch family gift of $35 million to the medical facility and to other divisions of NYU would be forthcoming. The Rudin family foundations had been contributing substantial sums to NYU for years. All three men donated more than a million dollars a year each to the city's other cultural and civic institutions.

Critics said that such contributions were made only to assuage the developers' guilt. However, in the 1980s the real estate millionaires of New York City had contributed more money to more causes throughout the United States than any other similarly wealthy group in the country's history — more than the robber barons of the Gilded Age, more than the Wall Street wizards, more than the oil-rich Texans. Many of the developers' contributions had been made quietly, without public acknowledgment. This was in accordance with their wishes, but sometimes the lack of acclaim was grating: Donald Trump got as much fanfare out of the monetarily modest act of sending his own airplane to bring a child cross-country to a hospital as did the Milstein family of developers with a gift to Yeshiva University of $35 million.

On *Forbes* magazine's annual list of the country's 400 richest people and families, Manhattan's real estate royalty accounted for the largest single group, about fifty places, and another dozen drew their family's historical source of money from New York's land and buildings. Among the latter were the Kennedys and the Rockefellers. Few realized that Joseph Kennedy, Sr., had made the bulk of his fortune through owning pieces of Manhattan, or that the Rockefellers' incomes derived as much from Manhattan real estate as from their oil interests.

The wealth and power of the families whose members sat at the game board seemed reflected in the demeanor of those who had come to watch: their deference would have befitted courtiers at a feudal manor. Many of the guests were quite wealthy but not yet truly prominent: graying fathers in sedate suits such as the players wore, trailed respectfully by similarly attired sons. "Have you met my son?" one would say to a friend; the greetings were always polite, but the sons were often ignored when business discussions began. Some men in the crowd were accompanied by their wives, elegantly turned out in cocktail dresses and adorned with jewels even at this early hour; the women seemed more like consorts than working members of ruling or aspirant families. These wives —

and these families — had not participated in the wholesale entry of women into the American workplace.

Though the men in the crowd were polished, most lacked the patrician manner of those born to wealth. Self-made, they had earned a place here through years of toil, leasing out offices and apartments, trying to collect back rents in bad years. None had yet forgotten the middle 1970s when New York City itself had been about to go under and many in the real estate community had despaired. Though good fortune had returned — indeed, had multiplied tenfold the worth of their holdings — it had not altered their deliberately understated ways. Though extremely comfortable, their lifestyles were far from ostentatious.

While the players continued rolling the dice, buying and selling cardboard properties, the crowd discussed real estate–related lawsuits. Harry and Leona Helmsley, whose empire was valued above $1 billion, had recently been indicted on charges relating to their alleged conspiracy to evade about $4 million in federal and state income taxes. The older men here, who had done business with Helmsley, whispered the news: "Harry's got Alzheimer's." Though his daily swims might make him fit in body, his mind was no longer sound. "Maybe it's a blessing that he doesn't understand what's happening around him," they said.

In two linked cases that were notorious in the real estate community but had received less public attention, the children of the late Sol Goldman were involved in suits and countersuits with their mother, Lillian, over the correct disposition of the estate. The children of his partner, Alex DiLorenzo, Jr., were similarly embroiled in a court dispute. Young Alex DiLorenzo III was being sued by his brother Marc and sister Lisa, for what Marc called "squandering" the family's holdings through unwise purchases and sales — over $20 million lost in 1988. At stake for each of these families were several hundred New York City properties estimated to be worth between $1 billion and $2 billion. To leave a tangled estate — and to have one's family fighting over it — was every big property owner's nightmare, and even those who hadn't liked Sol Goldman cringed at the thought. The real estaters also shook their heads at young Alex's evisceration of the two major brokerages he had recently acquired, and at the idea that he was reversing the process of evolution that had been followed by his father: instead of continuing to move out of slum housing, he seemed to be getting the family back into it.

In a quarrel even less noticed by the public, but which touched nerves among many in the real estate community, the heirs of Sylvan Lawrence were forcing his brother, Seymour Cohn, to break up sixteen acres of New York buildings worth an estimated $750 million. Lawrence had imprinted on his checks the words, "Real Estate is the Key to Wealth." Why couldn't Lawrence's widow just live off the considerable income from the properties and not diminish the power of the portfolio?

Another topic of conversation was the result of a recent primary election in which one young scion of the oligarchy had actually run for public office. He was Joe Rose, handsome and personable in his early twenties, his jacket slung over his shoulder in the Jack Kennedy pose, a Harvard graduate student and third-generation member of the Rose Associates family. As head of Community Planning Board Five, Joe had come out swinging against development that threatened to get out of hand — an unusual thing for the son of a developer but not, friends said, if you knew the Roses. Joe had done a great deal to oppose putting a tower over St. Bartholomew's Church and to force the city to reconsider developer Mort Zuckerman's plans for huge buildings at Columbus Circle. "Can you believe it? Joe even returned my campaign contribution," said one of the players at the big table, a friend of the candidate's father and uncles. The rejection ostensibly allowed Joe to avoid being seen as unduly sensitive to developers. Rose's opponent had been the incumbent, State Senator Manfred Ohrenstein, who was under indictment for alleged misconduct while in office. All the major newspapers had endorsed the young man, but at the last moment Ohrenstein's flyers and advertisements had painted Rose as a tool of the landlords who would promote development at the expense of ordinary citizens. This tactic turned the tide and Ohrenstein won the primary. It was proof to the real estaters that a virulent antilandlord bias still infected the city.

As the Monopoly game approached its close, special editions of the *New York Post* were passed around the room. Second-generation developer Peter Kalikow, owner of that newspaper, had obliged his friends by printing an edition with green-inked front and back pages featuring the game and portraits of the players. Inside, as in each Thursday's *Post*, was a pull-out section on real estate in which some of the participants regularly advertised.

At 8:25 A.M., the game was declared over, the value of the properties tallied, and Lew Rudin proclaimed the winner. He announced that he was donating his $5,000 winnings to the cause and acknowledged a round of applause. Homes for the Homeless would receive just over $23,000, a very small sum indeed in relation to the wealth represented in the Regency's breakfast room, but everyone agreed that the public relations value outweighed the dollar amount. Rudin earnestly told reporters that his strategy had been conservative, to hold money and resources in reserve while others spent wildly, so he could come on strong toward the end. After the television lights went off, Lew's brother Jack and son Billy ribbed him about giving such a serious answer to a frivolous question.

A week later, at his daughter's apartment, Lew Rudin was playing Monopoly with his six-year-old grandson. The boy was winning, and Lew urged him to sell some properties so that the game and the fun could continue. "No, Grandpa," the boy said, "I never sell any properties. Never!"

"Oh," said Lew, leaning back on the couch, "if your great-grandfather could hear you now!"

That great-grandfather, Sam Rudin, was one of the nominees to join a pantheon that already included members of other families of the oligarchy, such as David Tishman, Percy and Harold Uris, Bill Zeckendorf, and such earlier luminaries as the Astors and Rockefellers. "The Creators of New York" were annually chosen by a committee of the Real Estate Board of New York. At his townhouse a few yards from the Regency, one afternoon in November 1988, Seymour Durst, guiding light of the committee, had coffee served to fellow members as they went through the motions of deciding whom to elect this year.

Durst was in his seventies, a Jewish leprechaun with a wry sense of humor, a widower since 1950, a recluse with thick glasses and omnipresent cigar who considered himself the gadfly of the industry. His townhouse was a recent purchase and completely renovated for his purposes, which had little to do with gracious living: it was filled to the built-in rafters with the most extensive collection of books, postcards, and other materials about New York City ever assembled by an individual. He called it the Old York library as an expression of his belief that New York was disintegrating. The collection had so overflowed his first townhouse that he'd had to move. His initial choice had been a townhouse near his first one, but Durst discovered to his chagrin that it was owned by the Kaufman brothers, another wealthy developer family. The battle over this small townhouse had given fellow builders a good chuckle. On one side was Mel Kaufman, with his cowboy hats and a propensity to put objects such as giant chessboards and soft airplanes on the sides and tops of his buildings; on the other was Durst. The Kaufmans and Dursts had been competitors in the skyscrapering of Third Avenue for the past thirty years, and Mel wouldn't sell the townhouse to Seymour because he thought the canny Durst wanted it for another of his secret assemblages of property. Durst couldn't convince the Kaufmans that he merely wanted the house for his treasures, and eventually settled on his second choice. You could bet that William Kaufman, the founder of the Kaufman family empire who had died at about the same time as Sam Rudin, would have to wait a few years before enshrinement in this hall of fame.

Durst was brilliant as well as eclectic. He fired off missives to public officials and newspapers every week or so, citing statistics on abandoned buildings, low construction starts, and population shifts to demonstrate how New York was going to hell on an express train because builders were unreasonably hampered in their efforts to put up new housing. His letters contained thoughtful discourses on rent control and the nature of real estate taxation. The newspapers printed some but wouldn't accept them all, so he resorted to advertisements. "Resurrect one Moses — or the other," said one of his bottom-of-the-front-page squibs in the *New York Times*. Few people could figure out his linking of the biblical Moses with megabuilder Robert Moses, one of the new group of nominees for The Creators of New York.

Committee member Charlie "Jay" Urstadt, whose cigars vied in length and pungency with the host's, was happy to have this great man of the public sector acknowledged by the real estate community Moses had so often battled. During his years as a housing adviser to Governor Nelson Rockefeller, Urstadt had come to know Robert Moses and lunched with him regularly until Moses's death in the 1970s.

The current chairman of the Real Estate Board of New York, Larry Silverstein, arrived late to Durst's townhouse, but the coffee-sippers were charmed by his delighted appearance. In the past two days the wiry, red-haired, gregarious Silverstein had concluded two enormous deals, and was congratulated on them. Silverstein had finally landed the Salomon Brothers brokerage house as the anchor tenant for his building at 7 World Trade Center — a building that had been substantially empty since his first anchor tenant, another large brokerage firm, had pulled out after the stock market debacle of October 1987. In a second coup, Silverstein had signed an equity funding agreement with a Japanese company for a new project at the corner of 86th Street and Lexington Avenue; he showed the group a new business card he'd had made up with his name in Japanese.

It was a great day for Silverstein and he couldn't stay long, so Durst passed around a hand-painted postcard of the Castle Village apartment complex along the Hudson River in the Washington Heights section of the city, built by one of the Paterno brothers (another nominee) in 1938.

"Castle Village!" Silverstein piped up. "I lived there. Klara and I had our second apartment there, for $250 a month." He gave rave reviews to the complex's X-shaped towers, which allowed each apartment excellent views of the river and the surrounding area.

Aaron Gural, the portly, phlegmatic head of Newmark & Company, a major broker and sometime developer himself, chimed in that he had played at the Castle Village site in his youth; then, it had been a real castle, surrounded by swimming pools, aquariums, and seventeen greenhouses. Gural's cousin, Alvin Schwartz of Helmsley-Spear, was also on the committee, but not present at the coffee party; he was, as Gural put it, "under a lot of pressure" these days since he and Irv Schneider held the day-to-day reins of what had been Harry Helmsley's empire. AS-IS, the acronym formed by the initials of Alvin Schwartz and Irv Schneider, was also the way detractors labelled the duo's management style, with its mistrust of modern office machinery and techniques, and a refusal to spend to upgrade properties while skimping on service. That mold had been set, however, by Harry Helmsley, and not in his dotage either, nor only after he had come under the influence of Leona.

As it often did those days, conversation drifted to reminiscences about Harry Helmsley. At a dinner dance in the Rainbow Room atop Rockefeller Center, he'd stood at a window gazing outward to the skyline that blazed with the lights of a hundred skyscrapers, until another guest asked what he was doing. "Just taking inventory," he'd responded with a twinkle in his eye. Or how about the time Helmsley had refused to take a test for licensing real estate brokers who'd begun their business careers prior to the time the city had started to license brokers? "Who in this city could test me?" he'd rhetorically asked. "I know more than any of 'em." Those who knew best agreed that he *had* known more than any other broker. The developers were sad about Harry, whose current difficulties only contributed to the public's willingness to believe the worst of landlords and developers. Nobody understood them but their own.

Before the meeting broke up, the staff coordinator for the Real Estate Board of New York's hall of fame asked the men if they had any suggestions for a place in which to put the display, which was expanding yearly. All the men in this room were interested in history, and specifically in the history of their city and real estate's role in it, but currently their exhibit was on temporary view in one of the halls of the Pan Am building. Though it celebrated the great developers of New York and was sponsored by men who controlled in one way or another a hefty fraction of Manhattan space, the exhibit had no permanent home. It was a tenant without a lease.

The dinner for the first night of Passover — the Seder — in the spring of 1989 was a black-tie affair for the Rose family, as had been their tradition since the 1920s. Heading the contingent were eldest brother Frederick, sixty-six, Dan, sixty, and Elihu, fifty-seven, with their wives and children and grandchildren. Fred was known among the children (and business associates) for the origami totems that he liked to fold and give away. They were made from freshly minted dollar bills — Stars of David, birds, anatomically correct walruses. Dan, father of Joe the would-be politician, was a widely read man with a taste for fine wines and foods. He had once arranged the food and libations for a dinner at the New York Public Library that paid homage to the feast mounted by Talleyrand for Metternich at the Congress of Vienna in 1814, then gave a witty speech suggesting that modern summits should discuss "sauces along with satellites and mousses along with missiles." Elihu was an amateur military historian who sometimes took sabbaticals from the firm to lecture at universities around the world; he was just back from Australia. To friends of the family, he seemed more professorial than most academics.

Two of the three elder Rose brothers lived within a few blocks of one another, near Fifth and Park avenues in the East Eighties; their apartments, like many inhabited by families of the skyscraper builders, were eight or ten rooms on a high floor or in the penthouse; the elevator whisked guests directly into the foyer, as if it were a private mansion.

The Roses' annual Seder was a private affair, though a few people from outside the family were present, usually more than the single required non-Jewish participant, often as not culled from the boards on which the three brothers sat — Lincoln Center, the Metropolitan Museum of Art, Rockefeller University, Yale University, the Federation of Jewish Philanthropies, and the Council on Foreign Relations, to name just half a dozen.

Shortly after this Passover dinner, Rose Associates quietly began a massive conversion of more than 3,000 apartments to cooperative and condominium status. This sell-off, which might realize $270 million for the family, would take the Roses almost entirely out of the ownership of Manhattan luxury apartments.

Were the Roses getting out of New York? Were Fred, Dan, and Elihu planning to retire? Not likely on either count, as the ruling generation of Roses were all energetic, healthy, and committed to New York's cultural well-being. Fred and his wife, Sandra, for instance, had just quietly donated $15 million for a new arts building at Lincoln Center, with the stipulation that the donation not be made public until the building was ready for occupancy. Dan and Elihu and their wives had each donated a million more. But perhaps the Roses had a glimmer of the approaching downturn in real estate that would deeply affect the fortunes of New York and its builders.

"We'd hoped to keep places like 333 West 57th Street in the family forever," Fred later explained, "but with rent control, anti-warehousing legislation, and the like, we have to sell now." Besides, the Rose brothers' interests had outgrown Manhattan apartments. After twenty years, the firm was reaching the culminating stages of developing Pentagon City, near Washington ("riches beyond the dreams of avarice," as Dan quoted from *Ali Baba and the Forty Thieves*). Dan was also about to be named developer for Penn's Landing, a billion-dollar project in downtown Philadelphia, more evidence that greater opportunities beckoned outside Manhattan. Fred announced that as chairman of the firm he was initiating a policy of granting the summer off to anybody who had been with Rose Associates more than fifty years. As the only qualifier, he intended to spend the summer working on the new building for Lincoln Center. "The world needs a Lincoln Center more than another shopping mall," he later said.

There were more subtle reasons for the Roses' maneuver: this was not the 1940s and 1950s when the three brothers had each in turn willingly acceded to parental wishes and come into the family firm. Fred's son Jonathan, in his thirties and the bearded founder of a jazz record company, had been induced into the firm mainly by promises of being able to develop projects of his own. "A Jewish father can refuse his son nothing," Fred would joshingly tell everyone, but the knocking of heads among so many fathers, sons, uncles, nephews, and nieces was inevitable. The Roses had always prided themselves on working hard to prevent interfamilial strain, but how many skyscraper dreams could coexist in a single company? "We debate issues of freedom and structure all the time," Jonathan allowed. Money had to be provided for his projects and for those of his cousins among the third generation. And one consequence was the fact that the Rose family was changing the nature of its half a century of involvement in Manhattan's skyline.

Near the Candy Kitchen in Bridgehampton, during the last two weeks of August 1989, one member of the governing council of the Real Estate Board of New York (REBNY) would bump into another — buying a paper, going off the diet for an ice-cream cone, or just having a coffee at the counter to get away from a house full of friends or relatives — and joke that they ought to hold governing-council meetings of REBNY in the coffee shop, since everyone who counted was in the Hamptons at the same time anyway. Members of the Rose, Rudin, Tishman, Tisch, Resnick, and Stern families, as well as several other major players, all had homes in the Hamptons — large, comfortable, well sited, and not quite so understated as their New York apartments. In the Hamptons, they had a tendency to sprawl. Men who knew to the dime how much a square inch of Manhattan was worth took being out in the country as occasion to buy adequate acreage to encourage flights of imagination by their architects, to put in private tennis courts and pools that overlooked the ocean. Moreover, on the tennis courts and at the obligatory cocktail parties each weekend, the members would see one another as much as they did while in the city.

Business never seemed to stop, even during vacations. Hampton phones would ring with the details of another deal, another hitch or triumph in the financing. "Couldn't they just forget about business for a while, play golf or tennis or get in the boat or lie on the deck and soak up the sun?" asked a woman who'd spent time at several developers' summer homes.

In the party chatter of the tycoons this summer were hints of the coming crunch in real estate, the signs of which were already apparent but whose potential impact was overwhelmed by the optimism characteristic of eternal salesmen. In the Hamptons, the preferred subject of summer speculation was politics. The real estate barons were concerned not so much about who would become the mayor of New York but whether they could contribute early enough, and in a significant enough manner, to the winner's campaign. In the high-stakes world of developing Manhattan skyscrapers, good relations with city hall were an absolute necessity. If you weren't on the victor's train before it left the station, you might not be assured of a cordial reception for your new projects from a politically sensitive bureaucracy.

The Democratic race had narrowed to the incumbent, Mayor Ed Koch, and Manhattan Borough President David Dinkins. Only a few in the fraternity had contributed to front-runner Dinkins, a courtly black who had been in city government for many years, and even those who had anted up for Dinkins had covered themselves by also contributing to other candidates. Even fewer had sent significant money to the campaign of one of their own, Richard Ravitch, whose family had been builders for generations and who had erected several important skyscrapers in Manhattan. The gravel-voiced Ravitch was known as a brilliant manager; he was a former chairman of the Metropolitan Transportation Authority, of the state's Urban Development Corporation, and of the Bowery Bank. Most of the real estate men conceded that of all the candidates he would make the best mayor. Close friends such as the Roses were backing him, and young Tom Tisch held a high position in Ravitch's campaign — but still, business was business, and as a man who had never held elective office Ravitch didn't stand a chance. "I don't like throwing money down a sewer," Aaron Gural grumbled when Ravitch called personally for a contribution. He'd sent a token amount anyway, for old times' sake; he was sure Dick understood his position.

Just after announcing formally his intention to enter the contest for mayor, Dinkins ran a television advertisement in which he stood in front of WorldWide Plaza, a residence and office complex nearing completion just west of the Broadway theater district. (Bill Zeckendorf, Jr., whose famous name made him the most visible of the men who had developed the complex, must have loved that, the fraternity members chuckled.) In the commercial, Dinkins said that some of the apartments inside WorldWide Plaza were selling for over a million dollars, but that as borough president he had managed to force through laws that made the developer set aside 132 units in the complex to be sold or rented at much lower rates. "So if you're looking for a million-dollar co-op," Dinkins continued, "maybe Ed Koch is your man. But if you're looking for something a little more reasonable, my name is David Dinkins and I'm running for mayor."

Dinkins's characterization of Koch wasn't entirely fair, for the mayor had also supported the inclusion of lower-priced rental units in new luxury projects, but in general Dinkins was on target in painting Koch as the candidate strongly linked with, if not provably beholden to, the developers. No question about it: the twelve Koch years had been plated with platinum for the real estate operators and developers of Manhattan. During Koch's reign, the city government had continuously and vociferously encouraged the development of new skyscrapers as pump-primers for the local economy by regularly providing tax breaks and other incentives. Mostly as a consequence of these actions, the city witnessed a construction boom the likes of which had not been seen in Manhattan since the 1920s, the fervid era when the city's core of great apartment houses had been erected. How well the Koch administration had played to the developers' needs was depicted starkly in a New York State Controller's report studying ten of the dozens of projects that had gone up in Manhattan in the previous five years. The controller's office fumed that the city's "bulk for benefits" program had permitted developers of those ten projects to add an estimated $100 million in value to their edifices in return for making only about $5 million in improvements to New York City's subways and other public facilities. No public outcry was raised against this twenty-for-one equation, and the controller's report was soon forgotten because the city as a financial entity had become addicted to the revenues brought in by new skyscrapers.

If any demonstration of the city's dependence was needed, it surged to the fore in this last week before the primary as opponents of a massive, recently approved complex at Columbus Circle sued to stop the city from selling the site to developer Mort Zuckerman. Some $247 million from that sale was to have been paid to the city during the current year, and more later. Should the transaction not go through before the end of 1989, the city would have a serious budgetary shortfall and might be forced to lay off thousands of municipal employees. Any further shortfalls in the next mayor's budget would bring calls to raise revenues by raising real estate taxes; that, of course, would be felt in a big way by all these party-goers. The last time New York City had drastically hiked real estate taxes was in 1972–73, and many in the real estate community saw that rise as a major factor in precipitating the city into near-bankruptcy in 1974–75. Could such a pattern be repeating itself? "When things get tough, they sock it to the real estate owners," one party-goer opined. "We're an easy target. After all, we can't pick up our property and take it somewhere else."

Not many developers personally loved Ed Koch — a difficult man with an ego the size of Central Park — but most had contributed repeatedly to his election campaigns (some up to the $50,000 limit) because doing so, they felt, was a business necessity. In the previous mayoral election years of 1977, 1981, and 1985, the real estate fraternity had been the single largest group of contributors to Koch's campaigns. Now he was seeking an unprecedented fourth term. But all through the winter and spring, Koch seemed a sure loser. His abrasive personality, coupled with a backlog of scandals involving close political allies and cronies, seemed certain to defeat him. Only a handful of loyalists contributed during the early months. Needing money to run advertisements on television, the Koch campaign was forced to borrow from several wealthy men, including Larry Silverstein; when challenger Dick Ravitch announced in a press conference that Silverstein's company had recently received a favorable ruling from the city on a large new project and raised the question of a possible connection, the Koch campaign returned the Silverstein loan even as both Koch and Silverstein issued denials of a quid pro quo or impropriety.

During August Koch began to surge in the polls, and many builders and owners came forward eagerly and openly to support him. New campaign-financing laws made it impossible to offer the sort of large personal contributions that the mayor had collected from real estate men during his previous campaigns. Now the individual limit was $3,000, but contributors were allowed to bundle their money with that of friends, relatives, and colleagues, and submit these checks as a package. A bundler expected that his package would total a dollar amount large enough to be noticed. Prominent bundlers for Koch included Jerry Speyer of Tishman-Speyer and several other members of the Tishman families and their partners; William Zeckendorf, Jr., and the Stanton and El-maleh families allied with him in the recently opened WorldWide

Plaza; and leading officers of other real estate empires such as Bernard Mendik, the Fisher brothers, the Rudins, and several of the Roses. Now that the real estaters had divined which way the wind was blowing, they would help make it into a gale.

In late August, black teenager Yusuf Hawkins was killed by young white men in Bensonhurst, and many real estaters became alarmed, both personally and professionally. The incident seemed to polarize racial tensions in the city and to signal that the closing days of the mayoral campaign would be more influenced by the respective races of the candidates than by any of the issues. Since the time of New York's near-default, an ad hoc group led by banker Felix Rohatyn, municipal union consultant Jack Bigel, Teamsters Local 237 President Barry Feinstein, and Lew Rudin had been meeting on an irregular basis to discuss city problems. These men, white and Jewish as were the vast majority of real estate barons of the city, were concerned that racial harmony be restored, and believed continued silence might implicitly condone racial attacks. Hampton and Manhattan telephone wires heated up as they assembled an impressive list of "business and labor leaders" (most of the former connected to real estate) to append their names to a full-page advertisement in the New York newspapers calling for swift justice for the murderers and for "all New Yorkers to join us in making clear that racial hatred and bigotry are intolerable and must stop now and forever."

Though undoubtedly heartfelt, the advertisement was dulled because it appeared on Sunday, September 3, the same day the *New York Times* ran an article listing many of those same signers as contributors to the Koch campaign in its closing days. Overshadowing both items was that day's editorial, a somewhat unexpected endorsement of Koch for reelection — surprising, because the paper had repeatedly slammed the mayor for the scandals that had embroiled city hall since 1986. With a sigh of relief, the Labor Day cocktail-party standees agreed that the *Times*'s seal of approval would ensure Koch's reelection.

Just a few days earlier, on August 30, a jury of what Leona Helmsley's attorney insisted were *not* her peers had convicted the hotel queen on thirty-nine counts of federal income-tax evasion and associated crimes. The president of the Helmsley and Harley hotels had illegally deducted from her income as "business expenses" costs ranging from the installation of a dance floor over a pool at the Helmsleys' country home to such small things as lingerie and makeup. All had been billed to company accounts and covered by false invoices. She had been indiscreet and arrogant enough to say to an employee, "Rich people don't pay taxes — the little people do that"; now she might well be on her way to jail. Most real estate men and their wives took some delight from Leona's squirming, for she had often been rude to them in the days when Harry had been healthy and the Helmsley empire had been at its height. Even so, there was worried comment that the public's focus on the Helmsleys' practices did not augur well for others in the industry. The publicity implied that all real estate people engaged in similarly larcenous practices. The party-goers knew that most big players were aboveboard; they might be ruthless, but they weren't fools.

Before and during the trial, when the Helmsleys had been in the spotlight, virtually no one in real estate had been willing to comment to reporters about Harry or Leona except Donald Trump. Despite his money and celebrity, Trump was not part of the ruling group; members of the fraternity respected his deal-making abilities, but in their eyes he was not a *mensch*, the Yiddish word for a man of good character. This judgment did not come from his being Gentile — Harry Helmsley wasn't Jewish either, but Harry had made it a point to come to their dinners, to fraternize, to give to their charities. Their main complaints about Trump were the shallow nature of his commitment to the future of Manhattan and his personal viciousness. The major cultural and civic institutions of the city had seen relatively little of Trump's supposed fortune. It was completely to be expected of Trump, real estaters heatedly agreed, to have written Leona letters calling her a disgrace and then released these to the press together with selected interviews emphasizing the notion that because he loved Harry, he was sick at what Leona had done to the wonderful old guy. Trump was good at kicking someone when he was down; witness, they said, his humiliation of Merv Griffin in an Atlantic City casino deal, his lawsuit against his father's old friend and architect Phil Birnbaum, his full-page advertisements in all the New York City papers that made a rabble-rousing call for reinstatement of the death penalty after a white female jogger was attacked in Central Park. (The Rudin-Rohatyn group's plea for a calmer city may have been made partially in response to Trump's earlier ad.)

Everyone had to admit that Trump was a master at throwing sand in the public eye. Through adroit pronouncements he focused attention on a forthcoming television game show bearing his name and his plans to build the world's largest yacht and a 150-story tower — while behind the scenes he maneuvered projects that would augment his wealth at the expense of others. When Trump had erected his Trump Tower edifice at the corner of Fifth Avenue and 56th Street, he had made use of a tax-abatement program designed to encourage low- and middle-income housing. Many people, including Ed Koch, had been outraged that this program had been usurped to support luxury units, but Trump won his abatement in court. Then, after having lured buyers to the tower's 283 luxury condominiums on the basis that the units were partially exempt from property taxes, Trump turned around and tried to force those condo owners to bear a higher share of the building's real estate taxes than they presently paid, in order to remove some of the burden from the tower's commercial establishments. Trump Tower's condo owners were incensed, and so was the city's finance department.

In a second maneuver that had tongues wagging, Trump was trying to take what he styled the development rights on nineteen acres of piers and underwater portions of the seventy-six-acre parcel he had assembled on the Upper West Side of Manhattan, along the Hudson River, and transfer them to the onshore portions. Should this transfer be permitted, he would be able to build perhaps as much as seven times more apartment and office space on his site than city zoning laws would usually permit.

The real estate community knew, however, that Trump was "exposed" by these big projects and by the Taj Mahal casino he was erecting in Atlantic City — he had money at risk and being drained from him each day. Some understood what the public was not yet ready to believe, that Trump was rapidly going broke. While Trump held the former Penn Central railyards on the Upper West Side but was unable to build, he had to pay out millions each year in taxes. In his time, Bill Zeckendorf, Sr., had had the same city-sized dream for these yards and had been bled dry by holding the area. Insiders were certain that Trump's planned 150-story tower would never be built.

More talk at Labor Day parties was fueled by the feud between Trump and Leonard Stern, the focus of that week's cover story in *New York* magazine. Stern had financed a documentary about Trump made by an independent producer — it was supposed to be a pilot for a series about movers and shakers. While the documentary was being taped and edited, Trump gathered information that in his view demonstrated it was going to be biased against him. Then, Trump had carefully but casually dropped a bombshell by telling a reporter for the *Daily News* that the second Mrs. Leonard Stern had repeatedly asked him for a date. Reading the story, Stern's immediate reaction was a promise of strong legal retaliation. The press hastened to point out that while Leonard Stern was short, dark-haired, and Jewish, Alison Stern was tall, blonde, and non-Jewish — in those categories, physically similar to Trump. To get at Stern and the documentary, the reasoning at the Labor Day feasts went, Trump had held very few playable cards; Stern had plenty of money — money more solid than Trump's — and no deals were hanging between the men. Canny guests surmised that Trump had concluded Leonard might be vulnerable to a calculated yet unprovable allegation against Alison that would provoke Stern to threaten legal action. That threat would demonstrate what Trump had really been trying to prove: that the bankroller and guiding spirit of the documentary was biased against him and therefore the product could not be fair and ought not to be shown in public. Further, should the tape be broadcast anyway, Trump would already have established a basis for a lawsuit of his own that could charge Stern, the documentary's production team, and the broadcast entity that aired it with defamatory practices. Small wonder that no television network, station, or syndicator seemed willing to touch the tape.

It was of some satisfaction to the big real estaters that Trump's marriage seemed to be rapidly heading toward dissolution, and further consolation that Trump was being deliberately excluded from consideration as a buyer in one of the biggest deals ever made in New York, the pending sale of Rockefeller Center. His brassy style and the questioned worth of his holdings were considered by the center's controllers unsuitable to bid for ownership of Manhattan's most famous cluster of buildings.

In a massive transaction made public at the end of October 1989, the Mitsubishi Company of Tokyo bought control of the greatest single complex of Manhattan skyscrapers ever completed, Rockefeller Center. The $846-million sale came almost precisely on the fiftieth anniversary of the opening of the center on November 1, 1939. At a stroke, the most identifiable, lucrative, and architecturally distinctive group of New York skyscrapers fell under the ownership of a foreign entity. So symbolic of New York and so

American were these skyscrapers that many people were outraged to learn they had been sold to foreigners; those who commented were perhaps unaware that the other prospective major bidders had been Deutsche Bank and Olympia & York, a Canadian company. Real estate billionaire Sam LeFrak, who also owned shares of the Rockefeller Group, pointed out that the Japanese had snapped up "the biggest bargain in the world." The purchase followed the historic pattern of Manhattan real estate: trophies went to those who could afford them best, and the Japanese currently had deeper pockets than anyone else.

Aside from a wish to sell at the top of what was already being understood as a declining market, the major reason for the sale was to raise cash for eighty-eight Rockefeller descendants through a tremendous infusion into the trusts from which they derive income. Middle-aged, fourth-generation Rockefellers were saddled by financial obligations, according to the *Wall Street Journal*, and those of the fifth generation were said to be "eager for cash to finance their business efforts." To squeeze more money from the properties, the buildings had been refinanced in 1985 by taking a $1.3-billion mortgage on most of the rentable space, then selling off shares in that mortgage and in the company, as well.

Truth was, the sale signaled the complete end of Rockefeller dominance in New York real estate. Though the family had participated in the building of many colossal monuments — the United Nations complex, Lincoln Center, and Rockefeller University, to name the most prominent ones aside from Rockefeller Center — it no longer held together as a business entity. Without business clout, or with that power divided among eighty-eight pairs of hands, there would be no cultural and political puissance, either.

Social observers wondered: with the Rockefellers dispersed and their major income-producing property in the control of the Japanese, what family or families would now be dominant? Who would really matter? There had always been ruling families in the city, starting with the Astors in the early days of the United States, and these families' power was inextricably intertwined with their control of the lion's share of the island of Manhattan.

PART ONE

ELEMENTS OF THE DREAM

Chapter One

The Sixth Sense

EVERY WEEKDAY MORNING during much of the last quarter of the nineteenth century, John Jacob Astor III strode the seven blocks from his mansion at Fifth Avenue and 33rd Street to his offices at 21–23 West 26th Street. Tall, erect, with the bearing and mutton-chop whiskers of a Victorian gentleman, Astor was well known on these streets. Shopkeepers set their watches by him, as they had set them by his father when he had made the daily pilgrimage from home to business. A small bronze plaque identified the Astor Estate; no further display allowed the casual passerby to learn that the modest structure contained the nerve center of the family's $100-million holdings in Manhattan, the most highly valued collection of real estate in the Americas. Astor's agents, wearing derbies and round-cut jackets, constantly shuttled in and out of the stone building on errands to the myriad properties. Behind payment windows with curving bars, a dozen clerks accepted the coins and notes of renters, or receipts and money from agents as the latter returned from making their collections. Upstairs, ledgers were inscribed and plat books (describing the city's plots) examined.

A few blocks away, at 9 West 17th Street, the brothers Robert and Ogden Goelet presided over a similar edifice and a similar set of Manhattan property holdings amassed by earlier generations of Goelets. Uptown were the discreet headquarters of the Beekman estate, the Rhinelander estate, and the offices of the legatees of the Lenox farm, all of which owned considerable fractions of the island.

John Jacob Astor III, dean of these old, property-rich families and known as the Landlord of Manhattan, was less a human being than a granite icon who happened still to be made of flesh and bones; his dignity, his rectitude, his proper charities and perfect homes in Newport and on Fifth Avenue, his painstaking, unimaginative manner had become the subject of legend. Few had ever heard him laugh. Although the *New York Herald* admired him as "the ideal landlord [whose] property was well kept up," the adulation was not universal, for the *New York Times* wrote, "He loses no opportunity of raising his rents, never repairs a street if he can help himself and takes good care to do less for his tenants than any landlord in the city." In fact, he was neither the perfect landlord nor the devil his detractors limned, but an owner who reflected the canons of property of his day.

He relied on a trio of lawyers who seemed to have served his family all their lives and his. The most interesting one was Charles F. Southmayd, about whom the English poet Matthew Arnold swore that he had strayed out of a Dickens novel. Southmayd's law partner wrote that Charles displayed a character trait central to a true understanding of real estate: "a sixth sense — the sense of property."

He shared this sense with John Jacob III, and it is this sixth sense that underlies the many tales of accumulation and enterprise in this book. In Southmayd, a modest property owner, we see it raw, unadulterated by other passions or even by the softening touch of the wealth that John Jacob III enjoyed. Southmayd spent all his life defending the Astor holdings and had no other interests, not even a family or a predilection for sports or gambling; women he considered an expensive, only occasionally necessary luxury. For fifty years of life as a mature man Southmayd did not change his style of dress or ride the elevated railway or mechanical elevators; he trusted only his own feet or horse-drawn surface lines.

Southmayd's understanding of the sixth sense had been put to its greatest test during the Civil War, when an income tax had been levied by a strapped federal government. For an Astor who was then the largest taxpayer in the country, Southmayd prepared a case against what the Astors — and the Beekmans, Goelets, Rhinelanders, et al. — considered a dastardly attack on the foundation of their wealth. Southmayd's brief decried the income tax as an assault upon their right of property, one that would steal the fruits of one man's labor and apply them for the benefit of another man who had been less enterprising. In the U.S. Supreme Court, Southmayd's arguments were advanced in such an eloquent manner by another of the partners that the Court declared the income-tax law

unconstitutional. For the remainder of the century, this ruling pro-
tected the Astors and fellow property owners from a levy that today
we would consider trifling, 1 or 2 percent of annual income.

In the 1890s the Astor properties were all over Manhattan. If
one read the plat books from south to north — as the settling of
Manhattan had proceeded — the first properties could be found
honeycombed through the twisting byways of the Wall Street area.
In Greenwich Village, still below the part of the island where streets
began to be numbered, the Astors were landlords on Bleecker,
Bowery, Barrow, Broome, Grand, Greene, Greenwich, Houston,
and Hudson. Moving northward, their listings dotted the island
from river to river: parcels on Avenue A, First Avenue, Third
Avenue, Fourth Avenue, Park Avenue, Madison Avenue, Fifth
Avenue, Broadway, Sixth, Seventh, Eighth, Ninth, Amsterdam,
Tenth, and Eleventh avenues. On the numbered streets the Astors
owned properties along Third, Fourth, Fifth, Sixth, Seventh,
Eighth, 11th, Little West 12th, 13th, 14th, 15th, 16th, 17th, 18th,
19th, and 20th streets, and more on 25th, 26th, 27th, 29th, 30th,
33rd, 34th, 35th, 36th, 39th, 40th, 41st, 42nd, 43rd, 44th, 45th,
46th, 47th, 48th, 49th, 50th, 51st, 52nd, 54th, 55th, 56th, 74th,
75th, 76th, 79th, 90th, 91st, 92nd, 93rd, 94th, 95th, 96th, and on
various widely separated streets from 107th to 185th.

On a former strawberry patch in what came to be known as the
Lower East Side, the Astors had erected hundreds of tenement
houses in which tens of thousands of immigrants existed at the
poverty level. They had also created big business blocks from Wall
Street up Broadway for nearly two miles. The Astors' experience
in squeezing profits from these buildings was the foundation of later
and taller aspirations. A skyscraper is a building designed for the
central purpose of making money. The key, the Astors learned,
was density. And it was most pointedly on display in the biggest
money-maker of all the Astor holdings, the hotel known as the
Astor House, which had been the pride and joy of the first John
Jacob Astor in the 1830s.

As every New York schoolchild learns, the twenty-two-square-mile
island of Manhattan was bought by Peter Minuit of the Dutch West
India Company from a tribe of Native Americans in 1626, for beads
and wampum whose equivalent (in the Spanish milled-silver coins
then in general use) was $24. To characterize the deal in later terms,
it provided the first New World evidence that a sale of real estate

takes place only when buyer and seller disagree on the true value of the property being conveyed. Natives undervalued the island, viewing it as a forest from which most game had already been hunted out and whose subsurface bedrock rendered it unsuitable for farming. The Dutch saw it as one of the greatest natural ports on the globe, a fine base from which to conquer the New World — but made sure not to display their true evaluation by employing the classic tactic of refusing to overpay.

Various governors of New Amsterdam granted large farming tracts on Manhattan Island to prominent families, and similar grants were given by the English after 1664, when they captured the colony and renamed it New York. By the Revolutionary War, the Beekmans, Lenoxes, and Rhinelanders farmed hundreds of acres of Manhattan. Francis Goelet and his son Jacobus, French Huguenots from Holland, began to buy, and their holdings were augmented by the purchases of grandson Peter. Claes Martenszen van Rosenvelt, founder of the Roosevelt clan, held title to a farm between what later became 23rd Street and 34th Street, from Park to Sixth avenues. Other large owners were Lispenards, Schermerhorns, Cuttings, and Brevoorts. These families only held on to their land; development fell to newer immigrants.

In 1789, the year of George Washington's inauguration as our first president, the twenty-six-year-old German immigrant John Jacob Astor took some profits from his small fur business and bought from his brother Henry two lots along the Bowery Road. During the next two years Astor paid a total of $7,000 for several more lots: they were the purchases of a small-time merchant diversifying his holdings. Fifteen years later, when Astor was still a relatively minor merchant, he heard the news that John Jay had persuaded the British to sign a trade treaty and remove their troops from the Northwest Territory. Astor remarked, "Now I vill make my fortune in de fur trade" and proceeded to do just that. In five more years he was worth $250,000 and enjoyed steadily increasing revenues from furs and from packet trade with China. Ill-mannered in society, fierce in business, with a heavy German accent that would not fade, Astor was roundly despised and feared. In this, he was not unique: others had as much money and as few manners. What distinguished Astor from other rich men was that sixth sense. In Astor it took the form of being possessed by a vision no other men with money shared, a conviction as to the extent and vitality of Manhattan's future.

Manhattan was then a city of 60,000 souls clustered near the southern tip of the island, its crowded streets full of trash and stinking from sewage that ran in unraked gutters. Astor looked beyond the garbage and envisioned a developer's paradise. Of an evening or on weekends, he would climb on his horse and ride north; a half-mile from his home he would leave the city's bustle behind and enter open country — dirt paths, green fields, and hillocks that boasted occasional, isolated mansions with Ionic columns and neoclassic porticos owned by long-resident families. Sometimes he rode along the Hudson River road through what had been the King's Farm and had since become the property of Trinity Church.

Trinity Church's spire rose at the intersection of Wall Street and Broadway. The Episcopalian sanctuary was the favored house of worship for presidents and governors, but it was in a cash crunch. A legislature imbued with the need to separate church and state had devised a scheme to ensure that Trinity remained poor and to prevent it from gaining the power that revolutionaries believed would attend the possession of riches: though Trinity owned land that reached almost from its adjacent graveyard north through the sylvan groves of Greenwich Village, it was constrained by the legislature to receive an annual income of no more than $12,000 from that tract. The church had to lease its lands at ridiculously low rentals.

Aaron Burr headed a 1797 legislative committee appointed to look into the church's affairs. Burr found that church and state had been nicely separated by the legislature's maneuver, and took advantage of inside information to obtain for himself the lion's share of Trinity's 465-acre Mortier lease. Abraham Mortier had been paymaster general of the British forces in North America; though he was a casualty of war, the lease that bore his name was still valid. This document allowed the holder to pay Trinity a mere $269 per year for the next sixty-nine years. Burr re-leased portions of it for thousands of dollars. By 1803 the profligate Burr, then vice president of the United States under his rival Thomas Jefferson, was supporting so lavish a lifestyle that he was forced to sell 241 lots of the Mortier lease (and his own mansion, Richmond Hill) to John Jacob Astor for $62,500 in cash. Astor had a downtown home and had already begun a country estate at Hellgate (on the East River at what would become 86th Street), so he leased Burr's home to New York's governor, George Clinton. Two years later, Clinton was vice president of the United States and also found himself strapped for cash. He deeded Astor 243 lots in Greenwich Village in exchange for $75,000.

After Burr killed Alexander Hamilton in a duel, he had to sell more of the Mortier lease to Astor. Later, Astor cut out the middleman and negotiated with Trinity Church directly to buy additional land. In just four years he paid $300,000 for Manhattan real estate — an amount exceeding what had been earlier estimated as his total net worth — and considered the money well spent. He also knew he would shortly have even more money to spend, because President Thomas Jefferson's Louisiana Purchase had just doubled the area from which Astor's agents could harvest the hides of beaver, mink, and fox.

In 1807 some of the city's most astute men were called upon to design a plan for future development in Manhattan. Simeon deWitt, Gouverneur Morris, and John Rutherford labored four years and birthed a plan to introduce order into the chaos of an unplanned city. This plan also imposed the hand of man rather definitively on the island's topography: modern architectural critic Rem Koolhaas suggests that "through the plotting of its streets and blocks [the plan] announces that the subjugation, if not obliteration, of nature is its true ambition." Starting from a point one and a half miles above the twisting byways of the existing city, the commissioners plotted a grid of 12 arrow-straight avenues to run north and south, and 155 equally rigid streets to course east and west — this, to regulate an area then composed mostly of open farmland, swamps, and rock. Further reflecting the age's thirst for rationality, the commissioners decreed that these avenues and streets would be numbered rather than named, and that each of the approximately 2,000 blocks within the grid would be of about uniform size and hold dozens of lots 100 feet deep and as small as 25 feet wide. No circles, ovals, stars, or broad boulevards deflected the grid, for the commissioners were concerned with "convenience and utility," arguing that a city is "composed principally of the habitations of men, and that strai[gh]t sided, and right angled houses are the most cheap to build and the most convenient to live in."

The authors of this plan were aware that it would sound outlandish. They wrote, "For some it may be a matter of surprise . . . [and] a subject for merriment that the Commissioners have provided space for a greater population than is collected at any spot this side of China." The commissioners hoped their design would facilitate the "buying, selling and improving of real estate." Despite the commissioners' wish not to "furnish materials to the pernicious spirit of speculation," the 1811 plan did precisely that. In fact, the plan made Manhattan safe for development.

To John Jacob Astor, the commissioners' triumph was a blueprint of where to buy and hold on to establish wealth. It reinforced his general strategy: to buy land at wholesale prices and make money from it, in the smallest units possible, at retail prices. Astor preferred to purchase unimproved land rather than lots already graced by buildings. He seldom sold. Rather, he would lease his parcels for a period of twenty-one years — a practice common in his native Germany. Leaseholders would then erect buildings and make nice profits, but when the lease expired all their "improvements" belonged to Astor unless the leaseholder was able to convince him to renew the lease, which he would do only at a much higher fee. Astor sold one house in lower Manhattan to a merchant for $8,000; the man crowed, thinking he had beaten Astor because he knew the house would increase in value by 50 percent within a few years. "Very true," Astor responded. "But with your $8,000 I'll buy eighty lots above Canal Street. By the time your lot is worth $12,000, my lots will be worth $80,000."

Astor's estimates were accurate, because the city kept flowing inexorably northward. Even disaster fueled its expansion. Greenwich Village was a country hamlet with low rents until a typhoid epidemic drove merchants to hurry their families to the spot for relief from the disease-haunted streets further south. When the Village filled up, development edged further north. Districts changed character by degrees. An old block might originally have been made up of single-family dwellings; as the city expanded, the owners of those homes moved into more comfortable housing to escape the business district. The downtown homes they left behind metamorphosed first into boarding houses and later, as demand grew, became stores and small business entities. When such old buildings were demolished — by act of nature or hand of man — it then was possible to erect larger buildings devoted solely to the commercial purposes of tenants willing to pay higher prices for the space than previous ones. After one fire leveled Wall Street, new stone buildings went up that the *New York Herald* called "great, gaudy, splendid, Corinthian, scheming, magnificent, and full of all kinds of roguery."

Visitors lambasted New York as the filthiest, least distinguished city of its size in the world. Slaughterhouses, glue-works, and distilleries gave off noxious odors in all parts of town except those inhabited by the very wealthy; one tourist labelled New York's conditions "nearly medieval." Even so, the value of each Manhattan lot increased yearly. An enormous jump in Manhattan property prices, for instance, attended the 1825 opening of the Erie Canal, which connected New York by water to the Great Lakes and the fertile plains of the Midwest. New York surpassed Philadelphia and Boston to become the commercial and social capital of North America.

In this city that considered itself devoted almost exclusively to business, government seemed to work most efficiently when asked a favor by the landlords. Astor, Stephen D. Beekman, and other members of the old families regularly obtained grants of unused city land, then convinced the city to put in sewer pipes that enhanced the value of their lots and even petitioned the city to repay them for the dirt taken from their lots when a street was graded. They also bought "water lots" (swamplands) from the city, which would drain and fill them in at low cost. Charitable and educational institutions were also the recipients of municipal largesse: for one dollar each, an asylum for the "deaf and dumb" was granted lots between Park and Fifth avenues at 49th and 50th streets, a Roman Catholic asylum for orphans was given a plot between Madison and Fifth avenues at 51st and 52nd (providing the land would always be used to care for orphans), and the Free Church of St. George was awarded a site on Fifth Avenue between 54th and 55th streets. In settlement of a small debt, the state granted Columbia College the land between Fifth and Sixth avenues from 49th to 51st streets.

In 1830, with $2 million, John Jacob Astor was the wealthiest man in the New World. His son William Backhouse Astor — steady, solid, educated at the best universities in Germany, then apprenticed to his father in managing some upstate lands — was heir to a considerable estate of his own from Astor's brother Henry, and had recently joined the Manhattan business. On one of Astor's properties at Lafayette Place a lessee had constructed the Vauxhall Gardens, home of outdoor celebrations in the city for two generations. William Astor tore it down and built a red-brick house for himself and a neo-Florentine house faced with granite for a sister, separated by some of the trees and gardens from the old pleasure area.

The 1832 death of John Jacob Astor's firstborn, a daughter named

Magdalen, began a series of deep family hurts. A second child, Astor's namesake, was incompetent if not insane. In 1834 Astor traveled to Switzerland, to the sickbed of his most-loved child, Eliza, already in a final illness, and then returned home to more bad news. William boarded the boat to tell Astor that his wife Sarah was dead. So copiously did the seventy-one-year-old man weep at the news that even the ship's passengers, who had come to dislike Astor for his attempts to bribe the captain to return to port during a storm, were touched.

In the weeks following his wife's funeral, Astor tidied up the affairs of the American Fur Company and sold it. His employees were in the process of pulling down an entire block of older buildings opposite St. Paul's Chapel, to clear space for the Astor House. The planned hotel's importance was underscored by Astor's willingness to spend his money for it. During construction, diarist Philip Hone called it a "*palais royal* which will cost him five or six hundred thousand dollars," more than Astor had ever spent on a building. It had taken him years to assemble the block front; he paid about $15,000 each for most of the houses. In Manhattan's first recorded case of a holdout, former neighbor John G. Coster refused to sell until Astor agreed to let mutual friends fix the value of Coster's home and add $20,000 to that figure. Astor could only have countenanced this bad deal because his hunger for the hotel was so keen.

As Astor grew infirm he became obsessed with the financial health of the estate that would survive him. Both William and grandson John Jacob Astor III joined him in the business. One beautiful spring day, a visitor chanced upon the three generations of landlords in their offices on Prince Street, doing a menial task. When he asked why they had not gone outdoors on such a lovely day and turned over this routine job to underlings, old Astor replied, "When we do it ourselves it is done right."

In 1836, when the hotel was complete and functioning, Astor and William did go outside one day, to City Hall Park to gaze at their enormous structure on Broadway. With its myriad and various-sized windows, dozens of haphazard chimneys, sprawling levels, and makeshift appearance, it was a mess in architectural terms — a squat, ugly, six-story pile of bricks, undistinguished except by its bulk. Yet it was that very thing desired by all Manhattan builders: attractive to renters. Guests considered the Astor House luxurious, with seventeen bathrooms (complete with free soap) to serve 300 bedrooms. Its lobby featured bootblack stands and an arcade for shopping, and it was situated at the very center of the teeming, still-young metropolis. At two dollars a day per overnight lodger, Astor knew it would be a great money-making machine. In a tender moment while standing in the park, Astor told William he would convey its title to him for "one Spanish milled dollar, and love and affection."

In this gesture, as in so many other facets of his life, John Jacob Astor set the mold for Manhattan real estate barons to come. He demonstrated that though he had one face for his tenants, his competitors, and the public, he reserved quite another, a more humane and loving visage, for his family.

When Alexis de Tocqueville traveled through the United States, he noted a lack of those rich and cultured enough to support civilized pursuits. By the 1840s, a complement of suitably wealthy men had emerged in America, most of whom resided in New York and controlled large sections of Manhattan's real estate. To show off both their wealth and their culture, in the 1840s the Astors, Goelets, Rhinelanders, Beekmans, Roosevelts, and their set built townhouse mansions that were the equal of those in Paris or London: six-storied, stone residences with plate-glass windows, silvered door handles and bell pulls, spacious entrance halls laid with tessellated marble, and stairs and balustrades carved of polished dark woods. The rooms were furnished in what one visitor called "the old baronial fashion," with satin and velvet draperies, Arminster carpets, inlaid marble tables, and Parisian mirrors. These mansions had running water on each floor, an amenity not shared by most of London's townhouses. "The luxury of this city is prodigious," wrote William Makepeace Thackeray on visiting New York.

While guests at John Jacob Astor's frequent feasts ate oysters, turkey, quail, and beef, because of his own failing health the great man ate less and less, until he was reduced to taking sustenance only from the breast of a wet nurse. Walt Whitman watched one winter day as Astor emerged from his home at Hellgate: "a bent, feeble but stoutly-built very old man, bearded, swathed in rich furs, with a great ermine cap on his head, led and assisted, almost carried, down the steps of his high front stoop (a dozen friends and servants, emulous, carefully holding and guiding him) and then lifted and tuck'd in a gorgeous sleigh, envelop'd in other furs, for a ride."

By 1847 the eighty-four-year-old Astor could no longer take rides, and for exercise was tossed about in a blanket. A mutual friend informed Dolly Madison that Astor "may linger on awhile longer, but can have no pleasure in life. I am told by those that know him best that his relish for wealth is as keen as ever. That gone, he is gone." Astor inquired of one of his agents if a certain tenant had yet paid her back rent. The agent protested that the woman was in dire straits and needed time; Astor insisted she render the money. Learning the story, Astor's son William counted out coins from his own pocket for the rent. The agent conveyed the money to Astor without revealing its true source. "I told you she would pay it," Astor crowed.

John Jacob Astor died in the spring of 1848, leaving a $20-million estate, almost all of it income-producing property that was steadily appreciating in value. His will set aside for charity only a few hundred thousand dollars, a miserly 2.5 percent of the greatest fortune on the American continent. Most of that went to found the Astor Library. His secretary, Joseph Cogswell, had bought 100,000 books for Astor over the years, but during his lifetime the old man had refused to put up a building for them. The bequest was not enough to establish a permanent residence for the tomes, but William agreed to foot the bill — as his father had expected him to do.

A quarter of a century later, William Backhouse Astor, in his eighties, was almost retired in favor of his heir, John Jacob Astor III. "William will never make money," his father had said, "but he will keep what he has." In his tenure as head of the estate, William managed only to double its size, a growth rate of between 2 and 3 percent a year, compounded. Father Astor's prognostication proved insightful; moreover, it characterized the lives of many other second-generation real estaters from that day forward. For these heirs it was not a matter of having been born with silver spoons in their mouths, but rather that the nature of their tasks differed from the tasks of the founders. Whereas John Jacob had taken great risks in Manhattan property and reaped an enormous fortune, William was constrained by that very fortune from being equally daring. The first Astor had had nothing to lose; the second, everything.

In the 1870s the Machine Age drastically altered the American landscape by encouraging the growth of extremely large cities. Five major technologies provided the impetus. Before this time, a city's size was effectively limited by proximity to its supplies of food.

Refrigeration allowed the transport of perishable meats and vegetables from remote sources, and new harvesting techniques increased the quantities of grains available to supply the cities and
reduced the amount of labor necessary to produce them. The telephone and the electric light transformed prior understandings of
both distance and time, and enhanced the possibilities of doing
business from a single commercial center. Lastly, Elisha Otis's
elevator, introduced at New York's Crystal Palace Exhibition, permitted cities to expand in the one direction they had never before
conquered — upward, toward the sky. In 1874, for the first time,
a building in Manhattan reached a height greater than that of the
spire of Trinity Church; it was called the *Tribune* building, and
had a slender clock tower not unlike that of a church.

The opening of a cleared Central Park in the early 1860s had
produced flurries of speculative building activities on both sides of
Manhattan above 59th Street, and several daring builders decided
to place their bets on an innovation that would become the hallmark
of New York living from then on: the apartment house. One series
of connected "French flats" surrounded a courtyard at 72nd Street;
the building was so far from civilization it was named the Dakota,
after the then-current locale of Wild West novels.

Luxurious apartment houses were coveted by the city's burgeoning upper middle class — so much so that they returned developers nearly 30 percent a year. Apartment-house builders rushed
to put up residences in clusters around the new elevated railway
stations at 72nd, 81st, 93rd, 104th, and 125th streets, enhancing
the value of the many Astor properties nearby. Such cooperation
between the family and the city government — or, as some
charged, such collusion — continued to be a factor in the growth
of Astor wealth. Mayor Fernando Wood had been in the pocket of
the Astors. His protégé, Tammany boss William M. Tweed, looted
the city of $30 million in thirty months, a fleecing swift and large
enough to raise a public clamor for an investigation. John Jacob
Astor III was chosen to head a citizens' committee to look into the
matter, an appointment tantamount to asking the velvet glove to
scrutinize its own iron fist. So embedded in the Tweed Ring mach-
inations was Astor's committee, through providing money for political campaigns and accepting low city assessments for the
members' real estate properties, that its report was nonsense. After
examining Tammany Hall's books, Astor announced, "We have all
come to the conclusion and certify that the financial affairs of the

city . . . are administered in a correct and faithful manner." When the real facts came out, Astor was chastised but suffered no financial consequences.

The extremes of wealth and poverty that have characterized New York throughout its history were particularly apparent in the Gilded Age. Each week *Harper's* and *Frank Leslie's* would print artists' conceptions of the stark contrasts to be seen everywhere in Manhattan — the rich family in front of a huge fireplace with a marble mantel, contrasted with a homeless family arranged for sleep next to the steam grate of an office building. Vast differences frequently were noted between Fifth Avenue's "patrician velvet" and neighboring Sixth Avenue's "plebeian corduroy." Fifth Avenue was a boulevard of mansions, from the Astor enclave near 34th Street to the Vanderbilts in the 52nd Street area up to Andrew Carnegie's home on 90th. In the late afternoon the millionaires' carriages could be seen returning along Fifth from races in the park — a series of broughams, landaus, clarences, and phaetons bearing men in long coats and fine boots and women whose blue veils floated from their tall silk hats. As a contemporary noted, Sixth Avenue featured "the carts and vans, the five-cent cars, the workmen's [elevated] trains, the street-stalls and lager-beer saloons, the odor of fish, and cabbage, and stale tobacco, the bars, the butchers, the democracy of Sixth Avenue." That democracy extended to the Hudson River on the west and dominated east of the Park Avenue railroad tracks, in clusters of immigrant shantytowns from 42nd to 110th streets. The Astors owned property throughout these slums.

The Astor Library was the most important cultural institution nearest to the major ghetto, the Lower East Side. Partly through William Astor's efforts, by 1875 the Astor Library with its quarter of a million books was the largest collection on the continent; those at Harvard and at the Library of Congress were less comprehensive. But the Astor Library, said the *Times*, was "a sadly impecunious establishment," inadequately heated and lit, that permitted very few people to study its books and spent only $5,000 a year on new acquisitions. William learned a bitter lesson: charitable gift-horses are often looked at askance, the more so when the horse-givers are very rich.

Perhaps this sentiment informed William as he made out his will, which upon his death in 1875 contributed the same amount to charity as John Jacob's will had done in 1848 — and even less when considered as a percentage, since the fortune had doubled. No other rich families clucked at this niggardliness, for the Astors, Rhine-landers, Beekmans, and Goelets supported no organizations that channeled funds (or even soup) into the hands or mouths of poor people. At the time, social theories frowned upon direct transfer from rich to poor. New York had more millionaires than any other city in the United States but, a study found, they were the least generous of America's wealthy, more miserly than the upper classes of Baltimore, Philadelphia, and Cincinnati. Having made a great deal of money from the growth of the city, the aristocracy of New York seemed interested solely in itself. Mark Twain observed the old families "stunned and helpless under the new order" that had made fortunes from the exigencies of the Civil War and America's thrust to the west; they found themselves "supplanted by upstart princes of Shoddy, vulgar and with unknown grandfathers."

This self-absorbed focus was epitomized by the refusal for some years of *the* Mrs. Astor — Caroline Schermerhorn Astor, wife of William Backhouse Astor, Jr. — to allow into her 34th Street mansion and her fabled evening galas Mrs. Alva Vanderbilt, whose husband was looked down upon because he was in trade. To celebrate the exclusivity of her Patriarch Balls, Caroline's sycophant Ward McAllister created the notion of the Four Hundred, supposedly the number of revelers that could fit comfortably into Mrs. Astor's ballroom. No Jews, Catholics, or railroad men could dance on her floors. Many didn't care, because Mrs. Astor's mind proved to be as narrow as her guest list. Contemporaries recalled her grand fetes as dreadfully dull and the artworks that crowded her walls as mediocre.

Then came a family imbroglio of the nonsensical sort that often befuddles the rich and especially the idle. William Backhouse Astor had two competent sons: William Backhouse, Jr., married to Caroline Schermerhorn, and John Jacob III, married to a neighbor, Charlotte Augusta Gibbes, of whom a contemporary wrote that she was "a brilliant woman full of social and intellectual attainment," whose guests at tea included artists, writers, and people from the theater. Caroline was so domineering that her husband spent his time out of town; he left the overseeing of the Astor properties in Manhattan to his brother, John Jacob III. Since neither John Jacob III nor his wife, Charlotte Augusta, had much interest in high society, Caroline was able to become known as *the* Mrs. Astor. John III was content to wield the real power; during his fifteen-year tenure, the Astor properties quadrupled in value to what Southmayd (his fellow possessor of the sixth sense) estimated at just under $200 million — bettering greatly the rate of increase achieved by his father and bringing the fortune to massive size.

Charlotte Augusta, never very healthy, died in 1887, and her husband, John Jacob III, went into severe decline. At this precise moment, their son William Waldorf Astor brought his new bride up to Newport, where the wealthy had erected a series of country homes whose grandeur was unrestricted by the confines of Manhattan's street grid; each "cottage" was more beautiful than the next because the millionaires spent freely to outdo one another. William Waldorf Astor was a distinguished man, a former state senator, minister to Italy, and the author of two novels. He was astounded to learn that, in Newport, letters addressed to "Mrs. Astor" were all delivered to his Aunt Caroline and not to his wife. He became enraged, since by the logic of primogeniture he was now *the* Mr. Astor and believed that his wife had sole right to receive mail addressed to "Mrs. Astor."

To take revenge on his aunt, William Waldorf ordered his parents' home on Fifth Avenue and 33rd Street torn down and an enormous hotel erected. The Waldorf would engender so much traffic that Caroline's adjacent home would be deprived of sunlight and privacy, and also would suffer as the neighborhood was overrun by trade.

When it comes to real estate, the great stories are all personal — but also all business. In this instance, William Waldorf found a sound economic reason to underpin his vengeance: guests who let rooms by the night paid in the aggregate even more than those who rented tenement rooms by the month. The Goelets were also building hotels. Astor-related families such as the Roosevelts, Rhinelanders, and Cuttings were selling off their properties at good prices and moving further from the bustle and noise of a city rapidly filling with immigrants.

The plans for his own hotel laid and his father dead, in 1890 William Waldorf Astor and his family moved to England, where he continued to oversee the family's Manhattan estates by mail. Faced with the possibility of living next to the overbearing hotel, Caroline folded her tent. She commissioned a neo-Italian palace for the corner of Fifth Avenue at 65th Street, a Victorian monument of grand proportions — one half for her, the other for her son John Jacob Astor IV. A partition between the two halves could open on special occasions to form one enormous ballroom into which many more than 400 would be able to fit. It was a pretty solution, and by moving so far up the avenue Caroline leap-frogged the Vanderbilts and others who still lived in mansions around 57th Street. But her nephew's slap in the face was the beginning of her social end. Her son ran away with a Philadelphia beauty, her daughter was embroiled in a divorce scandal in which intimate letters were published in the newspapers, and her guest lists sputtered rather than sparkled. Finally Caroline's former home on 34th Street was torn down to build a hotel that at first competed with the Waldorf but was then joined to it to form the center of Gay Nineties society, the Waldorf Astoria.

The 1892 will of William Backhouse Astor, Jr., provided $450,000 for the Astor Library, virtually the same amount his grandfather had left it in 1848. This stingy bequest ended the library's independence. Within a few years, the Astor Library's collections merged with those of the Lenox and Tilden foundations to become the basis for the New York Public Library. The building itself remained. What could be done with it? Trustees somewhat belatedly discovered that the group of citizens who had been most avidly reading its books were the tides of European immigrants that had begun to lap at the gateway of New York. This informal alliance between the leading family of old New York real estate and the group that was to provide the greatest of the New York real estate fortunes in the new century was later made formal as the Astor Library became the headquarters of the Hebrew Sheltering and Immigrant Aid Society.

Chapter Two

The White City

O N ASTOR PLACE in Chicago, on a cold, overcast Sunday in December 1891, the most distinguished architects in the United States gathered at the home of John Wellborn Root. Guests at tea included Frederick L. Olmsted, the designer of New York's Central Park, and his partner, interior designer Ogden Codman; the principals of the McKim, Mead & White firm responsible for many of New York's most famous public buildings; the equally well known George B. Post and Richard M. Hunt, the latter currently fashioning Mrs. Caroline Astor's new Fifth Avenue residence, and pairs of architects from Boston and Kansas City. All were the guests of Root and his partner, Daniel Hudson Burnham. In a few years the United States would commemorate the 400th anniversary of the arrival of Christopher Columbus in the New World. A spectacular setting surrounding a lagoon off Lake Michigan had been chosen as the site of the celebration. Burnham, Root, Olmsted, and Codman had worked on preliminary sketches for some months, in hope that the Columbian exhibition would be an unequalled artistic experience for the expected millions of visitors. There had been doubts. Just yesterday, on a windswept pier overlooking the foam-encrusted lake, the Boston man had asked Burnham, "Do you really say that you expect to open this Fair by '93? I don't think it can be done."

"It is already settled," Burnham had said, and later in the evening he had pleaded eloquently for the help of all the architects. He was persuasive, and the architects pledged their efforts with gusto. They conveyed their enthusiasm to Root on Sunday but did not stay long, as Root and his wife, Dora, were ill. Root returned the courtesy by personally seeing the visitors out to their carriages —

without benefit of an overcoat. The next morning, his doctor diagnosed pneumonia, and by Thursday Root was breathing far too rapidly.

"You won't leave me again, will you?" Root asked his partner, who had been shuttling back and forth to the fair site.

"No, John, I will stay," Burnham answered, but momentarily went into another room to see how Dora was doing. An instant later, Root's aunt came in and informed them that Root had just died.

Into the evening, Burnham sat on the dark upper curve of a stairway. His loss was of such proportions that many years later he would still not be able to speak of it to his son. That troubled night Burnham's despair was cosmic, a rebuke of the heavens. He paced and shook his fist and mumbled loud enough to be overheard, "I have worked. I have schemed and dreamed to make us the greatest architects in the world. I have made him see it and kept him at it — and now he dies — damn! damn! damn!"

John Jacob Astor had set the style for the landlords of New York. Daniel Hudson Burnham would serve as the model for the business-oriented architects who came to be most influential in building the early skyscrapers in Manhattan. "He was one of the handsomest men I ever saw," wrote Paul Starrett, an assistant in the design office. "He had a beautifully molded head, a great crown of dark brown hair that curved low over his broad forehead, a thick reddish moustache above his powerful jaw, a quick, direct glance out of his deep-blue eyes. . . . It was easy to see how he got commissions. His very bearing and looks were half the battle. He had only to assert the most commonplace thing, and it sounded important and convincing." The residence Burnham set up on the site of the Columbian Exposition, his son later wrote, was so large that "he seldom went to the big cafeteria below, for his old colored servant Jackson looked after him. . . . The room had a huge fireplace, for he loved an open hearth, and there, he often gave suppers." Burnham's gourmet tastes expanded his waistline, which he attempted to trim by smoking cigars, drinking Vichy water, performing calisthenics, fencing, and working out with a personal trainer — whom he prevailed upon for a special rate, on the basis that he was buying several hundred workouts at a time. His manner was labeled by friends as baronial, by critics as feudal and imperious.

After he failed the entrance exam at Harvard, his father, president of the Chicago Mercantile Association, obtained for him an apprenticeship with architect William LeBaron Jenney, who championed many new building techniques. After quarreling with Jenney, Burnham took off for the silver fields but struck no paydirt. Humbled, in 1871 he allowed his father to intercede with another architectural firm, Carter, Drake & Wight. It was a good time to be an architect in Chicago. When Mrs. O'Leary's cow kicked over a lantern, the resulting fire consumed thousands of old structures and $200 million in property. Disaster begat development. In the Carter, Drake & Wight office, Burnham first met John Wellborn Root, who had earlier been apprenticed to James Renwick, designer of New York's St. Patrick's Cathedral, and to the architect of the great railroad terminal at Madison Square. Burnham and Root admired one another and shared interests in Wagnerian opera, the "organic" nature theories of John Ruskin, Ralph Waldo Emerson, and Viollet-le-Duc. Root was more the scholar and artist, shy and unambitious. Burnham could imagine grandiose projects and talk convincingly about them. The salesman and the artist, the man of action and the man of thought, Mr. Outside and Mr. Inside: these paired descriptions all attempt to characterize the distribution of tasks and talents that enliven a partnership whose whole is greater than the sum of its parts. Each pair of labels was applied to the combination of Burnham and Root.

Poet Harriet Munroe, Root's sister-in-law, argued that in the early years Burnham's influence "saved Root from dilettantism, held him to a definitive purpose, and helped to keep him confident in spite of tardiness of fortune." Burnham, she wrote, had "initiative, strength of will and a certain splendor of enthusiasm which captured men and held them while his partner was amply content to sit in the inner office, aloof from the boresome talkers and do his work." Root's mind, Munroe thought, "was of the Shakespearean type: it could build temples, towers and palaces on a hint; but it craved the hint as Shakespeare craved the plot, for the starting point of his dream." Burnham supplied those hints, sketching out ground and floor plans for Root, serving as editor and critic of Root's designs, offering suggestions that Root at first rejected, then almost always embraced.

The partnership of Louis Sullivan and Dankmar Adler paralleled theirs; Sullivan was the artist, Adler the older, steadying hand and liaison to the outside world. Visiting Root one day, Sullivan reported that he observed John "in his private room at work designing an interesting detail of some building. He drew with a rather heavy, rapid stoke and chatted as he worked. Burnham came in. 'John,' he said, 'you ought to delegate that sort of thing. The only way to handle a big business is to delegate, delegate, delegate.' John sneered. Dan went out, in something of a huff." Burnham explained to Sullivan that he was "not going to stay satisfied with houses; my idea is to work up a big business, to handle big things, deal with big businessmen, and to build up a big organization, for you can't handle big things unless you have an organization." Sullivan later quoted the statement to deprecate Burnham, but it is at the core of Burnham's business philosophy.

Burnham's tenets probably reflected his first blush of involvement with Peter and Shephard Brooks, Bostonians who wanted to put up office buildings in Chicago. Burnham saw in the Brooks brothers his own path to the future. For them, in 1882, he and Root first completed a structure named the Montauk, a large, rectangular, solid block that was the first building to be properly called a sky-scraper. Ten stories tall at a time when the highest a building might reach (aside from the occasional bell or clock tower) was six stories, it seemed to contemporary observers to stretch to the top of the sky. "What Chartres was to the Gothic cathedral," wrote a breath-less admirer, "the Montauk Block was to the high commercial build-ing."

Chartres cathedral is beautiful; the Montauk was impressively practical. Access to its floors was by elevator; had there been no elevator, there would have been no occasion for ten floors. Peter Charndon Brooks had demanded, in letters to Burnham, "A plain structure of face brick . . . with flat roof. . . . The building throughout is to be for use and not for ornament. Its beauty will be in its all-adaptation to its use." There should be "no projections on the front (which catch dirt), and the less plumbing, the less trouble." He advised putting in wiring for electric lights, which had replaced gas jets in Boston but not yet in Chicago, but vetoed Root's plans for plate glass on the front of the urinals and tile on the facade above the first floor. "Strike it all out," he ordered.

To most architects at that time, specific direction from a client, no matter how wealthy or erudite, was anathema; many would have considered Brooks's letter an invitation to resign the commis-sion. To Burnham, this attitude was nonsense. His ambition, and Root's willingness to be directed by it, were a good fit for Brooks's pragmatic insistence on the Montauk's "all-adaptation to its use." Burnham & Root liked the Montauk well enough to move their offices to the new building, though there are stories of Root disparaging the building to a friend. The Brooks brothers commissioned two more Chicago skyscrapers from the team. The 1886 Rookery was blocklike in the manner of the Montauk but more highly decorated, with turrets and mock battlements around the crest and an atrium lobby framed by steel trusses. Burnham & Root promptly transferred into offices there, and in 1891 moved again into the third Brooks building, the sixteen-story Monadnock Block. This is considered John Wellborn Root's masterpiece, admired by latter-day critic Paul Goldberger as "smooth and clean in a way that must have appeared startling to nineteenth century eyes. The walls are thick and heavy at the bottom and then, as if to express the diminishing weight they bear as they rise, they taper to thinness . . . [and] serve to emphasize verticality."

Skyscrapers, the new buildings being designed by the Chicago architects, were seen by contemporaries as distinctly American. European cities calculated what increasing the height of commercial buildings would mean to their low-lying cities — and shuddered. London, Paris, and other European capitals passed edicts to limit the height of structures, and builders made few objections to those limits. When building-height limits were proposed in the United States, entrepreneurs cried foul. They argued that restricting height would impinge on their property rights. Such limits, they also said, would crimp their First Amendment rights to free expression. Similar arguments were then being advanced against the first traffic lights, which, opponents insisted, restricted the right of pedestrians and passengers in horse-drawn and machine-driven vehicles to freely express themselves by crossing streets at any time, regardless of danger. Believing that concern for public safety must override individual expression, municipal officials were able to successfully legislate traffic lights into existence, but for many years were unable to set limits on the height and bulk of buildings.

That was just fine with those who commissioned the new skyscrapers, the evolving big corporations. American business was in the throes of creating enormous corporate entities through combines, trusts, and forced mergers. Big businessmen came to believe that their corporate headquarters ought to be physically located in, and symbolized by, buildings that were technologically innovative, mirrored their own amassing of ever-larger and more prestigious commercial enterprises, and arched as high as possible into the sky.

*   *   *

For young Chicago architects such as Burnham, Root, Adler, and Sullivan, each new building was an opportunity to push the limits of design and construction. Technological breakthroughs were being made almost daily in metal framing, fireproofing, new ways to use heating and lighting, and in a whole new technology that architects had never previously considered: bridge design. Previously, a building was constructed as if it were a giant jigsaw puzzle — first you laid the outside wall, then went inside to do the detailed work. Using a steel skeleton — almost a bridge stood on end — permitted a complete reversal of this process. You put the structural elements inside the building, before doing the walls, which could be later "clad" or finished with masonry and windows. Burnham hired a bridge engineer to advise him on skeleton-making.

Architects also searched for a style appropriate to the new buildings. Later, Louis Sullivan would articulate an aesthetic that became the credo of modern architecture, avowing in a famous magazine article that "form ever follows function." Long before that article, at the time of the Montauk, Rookery, and Monadnock, Root and Burnham were pressing much the same point. "A building designated for a particular purpose should express that purpose in every part," Root wrote; the architect must first ascertain the conditions "essential to the function which a house is to perform; and the force with which that function is expressed measures its value as a work of art." Burnham reminded a merchants' club, "Beauty has always paid better than any other commodity, and always will." As the skyscrapers went up, newspapers and magazines began for the first time to refer to the commissioning businesses as *institutions*, a word previously applied only to nonprofit groups or government branches, and one that pleased the sponsors since it encouraged public approbation.

While Burnham and Root embraced their corporate clients, Sullivan moved toward an opposite stance. "Problem," he later posed in his article on the artistic possibilities of the skyscraper. "How shall we impart to this sterile pile, this crude, harsh, brutal agglomeration, this stark, staring exclamation of external strife, the graciousness of those higher forms of sensibility and culture that rest on the lower and fiercer passions?" His answer: reject ornament and strive for simplicity, grandeur, and a form that was itself an expression of height. Sullivan's aesthetic would become the basis of America's architecture for the next half a century. But Sullivan himself was not afforded many more opportunities to turn theory into structure, especially after the mid-1890s, when he split with Adler, the buffer between Sullivan's prickly genius and the firm's clients; alone, he received fewer and fewer commissions. Sullivan's rejection of business intertwined with antipathy toward Burnham. "During this period," Sullivan later wrote, "there was well under way the formation of mergers, combinations and trusts in the industrial world. The only architect in Chicago to catch the significance of this movement was Daniel Burnham, for in its tendency toward bigness, organization, delegation and intense commercialism, he sensed the reciprocal workings of his own mind." To Sullivan, Burnham's embrace of business was the mark of an artist who had sold out.

To handle the expanded workload of the Columbian Exposition, Burnham took on many draftsmen, among them Emery Roth, who had recently won a design competition even though he was not yet twenty and had never attended an architectural school. The Hungarian immigrant was a romantic young dandy, cocky as only a youth who has successfully managed to survive alone in a friendless world could be. Winning the design competition was his ticket into Burnham's atelier, and working on this classical exposition was as if he had gone to heaven. Previously apprenticed for no salary to a small-minded architect in a small town, he was now earning forty-five dollars each week (ten times the average national wage) in the bosom of a most prestigious firm and on the project of a lifetime. Roth was delighted to make detailed plans for copies of the Roman Temple of Vespa and the Greek Choragic Monument of Lysicrates, and then to have these structures built — even if one wound up as a refreshment stand selling chocolate candies. While on the job, he took time to study avidly not only the firm's comprehensive architectural library but also the personality traits and styles of Burnham and the other charismatic architects, and later displayed his own versions of their personal flair and elegant manners.

Among the other apprentices was Paul Starrett, who resembled Burnham more in background and physical appearance than did the small, dark Roth. Big, broad-faced, and fair like his five brothers, he followed several of them as apprentices to "Uncle Dan." The sons of a midwestern minister turned lawyer and a pioneering newspaperwoman, the Starretts all had building work in their blood. Their father had constructed his own church, been part of the team that had erected the first building at the University of

Kansas, and had put up his own stone home. As they came of age, each boy left college to take up an apprenticeship with Burnham. The most iconoclastic was Ted, who seemed congenitally incapable of taking direction for very long and who by the time of the exposition had fought with Burnham and resigned. The once-tubercular Paul stayed with Burnham, who noticed that he was hanging around construction sites taking notes on the engineering aspects. Observing his meticulous ways, Burnham said, "You have a genius for organization and leadership." He advised Paul to concentrate on those skills. Paul did well enough so that after Root's death, he was put in charge of construction of two of the fair's larger buildings.

Late one Saturday afternoon, when everyone else at the fair's architectural headquarters had gone home, Roth was left alone in the drafting rooms. Richard Morris Hunt, the nation's most distinguished architect, arrived out of breath in desperate need of immediate assistance on details of the Administration Building. Under Hunt's direction, Roth prepared sketches and scale drawings, then volunteered to stay all night and construct a new plaster model of the building, which sculptor Karl Bitter needed to place eight bas-reliefs. The next day, as Bitter worked with wax, Roth noted that the figures would be in shadow almost all the time if they were attached to the building and suggested that they might appear to better advantage if they were free-standing. "Out of the mouths of babes," the sculptor muttered, and sited the figures forward of the building. Hunt gave Roth a note promising him a job in New York once the fair was completed.

Hunt's Administration Building was one of a half-dozen exhibition halls, pavilions, and a triumphal arch that became known as the Court of Honor. These white, neoclassic buildings surrounded a lake-size reflecting pool in which stood a huge statue, *The Republic*. Each building was colonnaded or domed or adorned with a peristyle worthy of a national monument, and they presented a stunning, palatial panorama unrivalled since the heydays of Athens and Rome. "It was the sheer beauty of its ensemble, rather than the wealth of its exhibits, that made this exposition so remarkably significant in its effect upon American civilization," a contemporary wrote. The White City's majestic public structures gave impetus to the "city beautiful" movement in which large municipalities first considered the notion of city planning, and smaller towns reserved acres for central squares and graced them with neoclassic court-houses and county seats.

Vagrants and homeless people, refugees from one of the worst economic depressions ever seen in the United States, had already taken up residence in the fair's abandoned, vaulted halls when a fire destroyed most of the Court of Honor near the end of 1893. Augustus Saint-Gaudens's statue *Diana* was taken to New York and placed in the cupola of McKim, Mead & White's "garden" at Madison Square.

Burnham was invited to New York for a sumptuous dinner in his honor at that site, given by Hunt, McKim, and other eastern architects who had been skeptical of Chicago's (and Burnham's) ability to pull off such a huge undertaking. The major artisans of the Gilded Age all attended this tribute: Saint-Gaudens, William Dean Howells, historian Charles Eliot Norton, conductor Walter Damrosch, and designer Louis C. Tiffany sat comfortably among business tycoons. Burnham was presented with a massive loving cup of solid silver. In a gesture worthy of a baron, he filled it to the brim with wine and passed it so that each among the mighty could take a sip and be cheered by the others as he did so.

"Make no little plans," Burnham would later say in a valedictory, "they have no magic to stir men's blood and probably themselves will not be realized. Make big plans: aim high in hope and work. . . . Remember our sons and grandsons are going to do things that would stagger us. Let your watchword be order and your beacon beauty."

In the years following the Columbian Exposition it was Burnham, rather than the other distinguished architects of the fair (who were actually far better and more imaginative designers), whose vision informed the designing of tall business buildings. Burnham, his associates such as Charles Atwood and Ernest Graham, his son, and his "nephews" — Roth, the Starretts, Henry Bacon, and other former apprentices — adhered to his understanding of the inter-relationship of big business and the possibilities for new buildings as they designed and supervised the construction of ever-larger skyscrapers.

Chapter Three

Within the Pale

IN ORDER to make palatable to the Russian masses his marriage to a young consort, on March 1, 1881, Tsar Alexander II secretly signed a draft of quasi-democratic constitutional reforms proposed to him by his liberal mentor, Mikhail Loris-Melikov, and planned to announce these advances when he made his new marriage public. But later that same day, the terrorist group People's Will, after having failed in three previous attempts (by bullets, by derailing his train, and by blowing up the Winter Palace), succeeded in killing the tsar with a bomb. His assassination set off a chain of events that transformed the character of the Russian empire and led to a massive emigration that affected the future of New York City.

Alexander III, according to even his friends the most stupid, ignorant, and narrow of the Romanovs, was implacably committed to orthodoxy in religion and autocracy in government. Days after his father's death, he canceled the Loris-Melikov reforms and enthusiastically endorsed the measures of the procurator-general of the Holy Synod, Constantine Pobyedonostzev, a zealot whose deeds and words evoked comparisons with the Spanish Inquisition. Pobyedonostzev publicized the fact that the assassins of Alexander II included a single Jew, Hesia Helfman, a minor plotter among scores of socialist and idealistic non-Jews. Seizing upon the supposed Jewish character of the assassins, a secret league of noblemen called the Black Hundreds began a series of pogroms against the several million Jews who lived in what was known as the Pale of Settlement.

The Pale was officially begun by Catherine the Great in 1792, principally to consolidate and make easier her rule of areas won from Poland, but also to protect Moscow tradesmen from undercutting by Jewish entrepreneurs who sold their goods at lower prices. Pales were a medieval concept; the appellation derived from the Latin word *palus*, or stake. The English settled the Irish "beyond the pale," and had imposed a similar cordon in northern France. The Russian Pale's 386,000 square miles encompassed most of Poland, Lithuania, Estonia, and the Ukrainian portion of Russia, extending to the borders of what was then the Austro-Hungarian empire. Only a minor fraction of the Pale was considered choice or fertile, and many of its small towns were historically poor. Half the Jews in the world lived there, and were habitually subject to harsh laws, such as a conscription act that functioned like a scythe, removing young Jewish men from the community for a period of twenty-five years.

In 1881, the signal for the onset of violence was a sustained whistling, a sound Jews soon came to fear. An aroused peasantry, abetted by police who looked the other way and by militia without orders, smashed Jewish businesses in 200 localities from the Baltic to the Black Sea. Raping hundreds and killing thousands, the attackers instilled terror. During the pogroms, Gentiles in the Pale, who outnumbered Jews ten to one, placed Russian Orthodox icons in their windows and painted crosses on their doors and gates to steer mobs away from their homes. Pogroms soon inflamed larger cities and other Eastern European countries. In Warsaw, the cause of a church fire in which twenty-nine people were trampled to death was falsely laid to Jewish pickpockets, and Warsovians stoned Jews in the streets. In Hungary there was the Tiszaeszlar Affair, a "blood libel" case in which Jews were accused of ritual murder and subjected to anti-Semitic excesses.

In Russia, the government officially blamed the Jews for "injurious activities which, according to local reports, were responsible for the disorders." Ultraconservatives urged continued pogroms to divert the Russian masses from discontent with the central government. Visitors from abroad were appalled. Michael Davitt, an Irish leader, witnessed a pogrom in progress in a middle-sized city:

From their hiding places in cellars and garrets the Jews were dragged forth and tortured to death. Many mortally wounded were denied the final stroke. . . . In not a few cases nails were driven into the skull and eyes gouged out. Babies were thrown from the higher stories to the street pavement. . . . Jews who attempted to beat off the attackers were quickly disarmed by the police. . . . The local bishop drove in a carriage and passed through the crowd, giving them his blessing as he passed.

Counselor Pobyedonostzev ("victory-bearer") became known among the Jews as Byedonostzev ("misfortune-bearer") for a series of May Laws in 1882 that severely hampered Jews' ability to live, work, and prosper within the Pale. No longer could Jews move from town to town, contract to own land in most areas, seek or receive credit from banks, or practice many professions. If a Jewish artisan left his old village for seasonal employment in a larger town he would be prevented from returning home. Peddlers who habit- ually traveled from town to town showing their wares on successive market days were barred from the circuit. Old Jewish soldiers were denied pensions; Jewish doctors were forbidden to have non-Jews as patients; Jewish industrialists and their workers were nearly taxed out of existence. When asked what would happen to the Jews as a result of these restrictions, Pobyedonostzev said, "A third will be converted [to Christianity], a third will emigrate, and the rest will die of hunger." His predictions were chillingly accurate. Shortly, tens of thousands of Jews began to migrate to the West, mostly to the United States, until very near a third of those who had lived in the Pale were gone. Of the remaining Jews, half did perish of starvation. As for the last third, abject poverty and the determi- nation for change that repression engendered eventually brought them to participate eagerly in the 1917 revolution that instituted the Communist state.

Most Jews from the Pale settled in New York City. There, within the space of only a single generation, Russian-born Jews and their sons began to permeate the city's building industry and, to a degree far exceeding that of any other small group of people, to shape the city's skyline. Tishmans, Roses, Rudins, Urises, Dursts, Horo- witzes, Ravitches, Minskoffs, Lefraks, Milsteins, and their like all originally came from the Pale, and most emigrated to America between 1881 and 1905. Moreover, their embrace and domination of the real estate and building industries was directly linked to experiences and attitudes carried with them from the Pale.

Retroactive romanticization has colored our usual understanding of what life was like in the *shtetls*, the Jewish portions of towns in the

Pale. Contributing to the haze is the view unforgettably crystallized in Sholom Aleichem's description of a semirural enclave:

> Stuck away in a corner of the world, isolated from the surrounding country, the town stands, orphaned, dreaming, bewitched, immersed in itself and remote from the noise and bustle, the confusion and tumult and greed, which men have created about them and have dignified with high-sounding names like Culture, Progress and Civilization.

This passage well conveys the attractive, mystic quality of many small towns, but its acceptance as a complete picture of life in the Pale obscures the more painful aspects. Far from being idyllic, existence for the Jews of the Pale was poverty-stricken and terrifyingly constrained. The inability to own any meaningful tract of land kept Jews rootless. Confiscatory taxation deprived small Jewish merchants of the opportunity to accumulate capital that could enlarge their businesses and enable them to enter the realm of the more privileged. Most Jews lived crushed together in small spaces, eight and ten to a room in the cities, several families under a single roof in the rural villages. Whereas the preponderance of Gentiles within the Pale were farmers who lived in rural communities, Jews, prevented by law from farming, became artisans or engaged in small commerce. Artisans (tailors, butchers, candlestick-makers, leather-shapers, printers) were often forced to work and live alone in a city where their wives and families were forbidden to join them. A Russian study in 1849 showed that only about 3 percent of the Jews had accumulated more than enough kopeks to see them through a bad winter.

Even the repressive government learned that despite restrictions, Jews were quite successful in whatever field they entered. Census-takers and tax assessors documented that Jewish middlemen got better prices for their products than did neighboring Gentile farmers (and consequently that small villages in the Pale were better off than those just outside it), that Jewish artisans were steady and prolific producers, and that Jewish peddlers or proprietors of small shops made a living even when Gentile establishments couldn't stay in business. For the past thousand years emperors and kings had encouraged Jews to settle in their domains in order to exploit this sort of commercial acumen and enliven the economy. During the nineteenth century, occasional Russian bureaucrats would admiringly cite the figures of the tax assessors and suggest that if Jews were dispersed more evenly throughout Russia, Gentiles would benefit; such recommendations were routinely brushed aside.

The most comfortable profession for Jews was as *arendators*, or middlemen. Working for absentee landlords, these men reaped considerable profits for the owners. The *arendators* kept only a fraction of the rents and fees for their own use, but bore the brunt of anger of the peasants, who felt manipulated by the rich. Virtually all commerce touched the *arendator's* hands. Often, in a village, in addition to collecting rent for the landlord, he ran an inn for travelers where liquor was distilled and dispensed, he was the purchasing agent for grain-buyers in distant cities, and he operated the village store, which sometimes also served as a local bank. The *arendator* operated as a landlord and was a figure of envy to many Jews in the Pale.

Other Jewish occupations were admired for the qualities they seemed to produce in their practitioners. Artisans and itinerant peddlers enjoyed a modest but real sense of independence; they had a trade, and what money they made depended in large measure on their own industry and ingenuity rather than on the whims of employers. Also admired was their capacity to land on their feet after a fall. If you could not change directions or occupations, or were so spendthrift that you did not invest your capital wisely toward that inevitable day when things would change, you would submerge forever in dire poverty. Such were the vicissitudes of life within the Pale for Jews that artisans and peddlers were quite often wrenched out of one occupation and forced into another: during a famine year the butcher became a leather worker, the candlestick-maker took to the road to peddle an accumulated overstock, and the innkeeper evicted by a landlord took his few kopeks to Odessa, where he opened a small shop. Peddlers and artisans shared an unquenchable optimism that served as an antidote to the gloom about them. This attitude was so prevalent that it could be satirized by a contemporary Yiddish writer:

Certainly [the economic situation] is bad! . . . Well, God will help anyway. Things will be a little pinched; we shall eat a little less, somewhat less of this, a trifle less of that. No matter! . . . Along comes a cold wet autumn, strongly intimating that they can no longer remain outdoors; so they bundle together, as is, in make-shift lodgings. Cramped a bit? Never mind, as long as they are cramped together.

While Western European Jews blended into the non-Jewish populations of Germany, France, Denmark, and other countries and became somewhat assimilated, Jews of the Pale were forced into a pattern of life that many observers described as medieval and which, in turn, fostered an older style or orthodoxy. In the Pale, Jewish men continued to wear caftans and caps and refused to cut their beards or sideburns, though these practices had died out elsewhere in Europe. The religion of the Jews in the Pale was orthodox, severe, and all-encompassing, the fiat of rabbis whose authority extended from the spiritual realm into every corner of daily life. Precisely 248 "do's" and 365 "don'ts" proscribed the Jewish day, shaping and hemming in activities from hand-washing to preparation of food to proper paths of study and proper times to have sexual relations with a spouse.

The tremendous hold of the rabbis on the communities was a mixed blessing for the Jews. On the positive side, their insistence on continual study resulted in males who were trilingual — able to read Hebrew from their sacred texts, to speak and sometimes write in Yiddish, and invariably to converse with local Gentiles in the language of the area (Russian, Polish, Estonian, and so on). To be trilingual was to exhibit a certain suppleness in dealing with the world. Another plus: the rigidity imposed by the rabbis ensured that Jews would give preference to the *maarufia*, other Jews who were their suppliers. In terms of later behavior in the New World, one of the most important concepts reinforced by the rabbis in the Pale was *tzedaka*, which obligated everyone in the community to help the less fortunate. If a man had enough to eat — and sometimes, even if he were starving himself — he must give to coreligionists or be ostracized from the community.

Tzedaka was linked to the great emphasis on study throughout life in the Pale. The ultraserious boys became men who venerated learning. Entire communities looked up to those who devoted themselves to the pursuit of the knowledge encapsulated in the Talmud and its myriad commentaries. After work, and in every spare hour, the good Jewish laborer or merchant would try to do what the perpetual student did all the time. From the smallest village to the great towns of Odessa, Kiev, and Vilna one could find in every community men who performed no commercial work but who fulfilled a great service of studying and thinking about the Talmud and its lessons on how life was to be lived. In a Yiddish phrase, such a man was a *luftmensch*, one who lived on air. Indeed, these dreamers seemed filled with air, adept in the use of their imagination, their minds aloft in ennobling thought while the rest of humanity toiled below, a sentiment expressed in one of their poems:

> High above aspires my being
> Up into my land of dreams
> Where source of thoughts fresh and mighty,
> Reason flows in purest streams.

Luftmenschen were given sustenance by the community and considered evidence of its erudition and spiritual worth. In many places they formed an important axis with a community's more well-to-do merchants. The bond holding these two sorts of men together derived their strength from both parties' essential agreement on life's general direction and on the division of labor each would pursue in the mortal sphere. Merchants toiled so sages could imagine; perpetual students cogitated and advised *arendators*, peddlers, and artisans so that glory and meaning could be infused into the lives of all. The dreamer, believing himself unable to accomplish what merchants did in the sphere of business, looked at the successful merchant and marveled; the merchant, believing himself capable of lofty thoughts only once in a while, celebrated the thinker for dazzling mental acrobatics and did not disparage a *luftmensch* who could not (or would not) even provide for the roof over his own head. Between the merchant and the dreamer there formed an unshakable bond of mutual respect, admiration, and need. This axis worked well in its original environment and would not lose its power when its practitioners transferred to the New World.

On the negative side, enforced religiosity perpetuated a climate we would today label fundamentalist, featuring a determined resistance to and intolerance of progress and change. During the reign of Alexander II, many Jews in larger cities and towns embraced the governmentally sanctioned notion of "Russification," a rubric under which Jews would assimilate and be valued within the larger Russian society, where their religion would become merely a private matter of choice. The lure was more places in the universities and a loosening of the restrictions on travel and types of employment. The new ways were championed among the Jews by a movement called the *Haskalah*, which was the progenitor of two distinct and important strains of thought. As Zionism, it led to a slow but steady emigration of Jews to Palestine — the Rose family, once of Poland, emigrated to New York in 1870 but was later drawn to Palestine; the Lefraks went directly there before Harry came to New York. The second strain, socialism, led to unions of artisans and agitation for a system of more democratic governance to replace the tsars.

Jewish defenders of the old ways believed Russification would turn Jews from the paths of righteousness, and held off Russification through the 1870s. Once pogroms began, many Jews who had embraced assimilation rejected it and began to emigrate.

Most left with little more than the clothes on their backs and arrived in New York with an average of about twenty dollars in their pockets. Their actual savings had probably been higher, but most had spent it to get out of the Pale. When a child of draft age emigrated, parents who stayed behind were subject to a fine equal to several years' earnings; no matter, many parents paid the fine to ensure a child's freedom. In the 1870s Louis Jay Horowitz's father moved from Czestochowa, 150 miles southwest of Warsaw, across the border into Germany to escape having to spend a quarter of a century in the military. In the early 1880s Louis, nearing draft age, left for the same reasons — and his grandparents paid the same sort of fine — and so he could be reunited with his father. Most emigrants left as families. Fifteen-year-old Lewis Rudinski left the Lithuanian area of Veluzun in 1883 with his parents and came to New York by way of the northern route, through Germany. Julius Tishman, a young man from Minsk, a city in the more central Russian area of the the Pale, emigrated by similar means with many family members.

In the southern portions of the Pale, escaping Jews went first to the Galician town of Brody. Galicia was even more wretched than the neighboring Pale, but French, British, and German Jewish organizations had representatives there to help Jews cross the Atlantic. A man from the Alliance Israelite Universelle found the streets of Brody jammed: "From early morning until late at night," he reported home, "French delegates were surrounded by a crowd clamoring for help. Their way was obstructed by mothers who threw their little children under their feet, begging to rescue them from starvation." The French transported refugees to Germany and the Germans sent them on, either by steamship directly, or by rail and ferry to London where English helpers booked them on steamers for the New World. Most assistance to emigrants came from European Jews, prominent among them the Baron de Hirsch and the Rothschild family; aid from earlier waves of German Jewish emigrants to the United States, who had now become wealthy department-store and banking families, was sparse. Western Europe had already been emptied of those who wished to go to the New World, so steamship companies lowered their rates to attract the new wave. Steerage passage across the Atlantic from Hamburg cost thirty-four dollars — twenty-five dollars from Liverpool. In many instances, even these modest amounts were paid by the Jews of France, Germany, England, and Denmark. The Swigs from Byelorussia, the Crowns from Latvia, and similar families who would later achieve great wealth arrived penniless in New York in the 1880s. Emigration fever spread out from the Pale to encompass other Eastern European Jews; in 1884 thirteen-year-old student Emery Roth left Hungary alone and (as he later wrote) "ashamed to tell [my schoolmates] that I was going to America," since "the need to emigrate is a confession of poverty, a disgrace no one — at any rate, any boy — will confess to."

For Jews who remained in the Pale, living conditions worsened as smaller towns shriveled and inhabitants were forced into larger enclaves. A visitor to Berditchev, near Kiev, saw 30,000 Jews newly piled in on top of 60,000 others, "one of the poorest populations anywhere in Europe. . . . The whole place, with its filthy streets, its reeking half-cellars under the overhanging balconies, and its swarming throngs of unwashed, unkempt wretches, packed into the narrow thoroughfares on the lookout for food, made a picture scarcely human." Though the pogroms eased somewhat after 1883–84, misery increased apace through the rest of the decade.

Oppressed Jews everywhere, at all points in history, have given special significance to Passover because of its resonance with their own travail; the celebration of the escape of the ancient Jews from Egypt was widely known even among Gentiles as the most important annual spiritual event for the Jews of Russia. Thus, Jews were particularly shocked by the government's announcement, on the first night of Passover in March 1891, that within the next few months those few Jews who had by their artisanry or expertise in medicine or law earned the right to live in Moscow would be permanently expelled from the new capital, and that even greater restrictions would be placed on Jews throughout the Pale and the rest of the Russian empire.

Shortly thereafter, the tide of Jews from the Pale coursing toward New York swelled to a flood.

After voyages lasting up to six weeks that left steerage passengers reeling with seasickness, immigrants were herded from the ships directly onto a small outcrop of rock located only a few dozen yards from Manhattan's southern tip, near Wall Street. On it was an old circular fort known as Castle Garden. "For about a week," a recent immigrant reported, "they kept us in this Hades where we had to sleep on the floor [of the courtyard, packed in] under the open skies, which is not comfortable at any time, particularly when it rains. . . . Castle Garden [is a] Gehenna through which all Jewish arrivals must pass to be cleansed before they are considered worthy of breathing freely the air of the land of the almighty dollar." Actually, immigrants were checked for inoculations and to determine whether any had trachoma, glaucoma, or other diseases that would make them a burden to the United States. As the number of immigrants increased in the wake of the 1891 expulsion laws, the questioning at Castle Garden and its successor gateway Ellis Island became tougher. Gentile agents unfamiliar with Eastern European patronymics also shortened or altered Jewish names or recorded the hometown as the family's American moniker.

Newly named, immigrants were released into the city. At the ramp, they were met either by representatives of organizations devoted to finding shelter for them, by relatives or *landsmen* from their old villages who had preceded them here, or by predators who would pretend to such associations and then bilk the immigrants of what little they possessed.

Each section of Eastern Europe had a new home ground on the Lower East Side of Manhattan. Hungarians clustered about Avenues A and B, on the numbered streets above Houston; Galicians lived to the south and Rumanians a bit to the west; and "Central Pale" Russians, Poles, Lithuanians, Estonians, and Ukrainians stretched along the largest area, from Grand Street to near City Hall. Recent immigrants, faced with a world quite different from what they had known, wished to be near people and institutions that they understood, and so had limited choices as to where to live. The Tenth Ward, the central area of the ghetto, became packed with 500 inhabitants per acre, nearly 3,000 per block; as Arnold Bennett remarked, "The architecture seemed to sweat humanity at every window and door."

The center of this transplanted *shtetl* was Rutgers Square, at the corner of Ludlow and Hester Streets on the Lower East Side, where stood the *Khazar Mark* or Pig's Market, an absurd name for the crossroads of an immigrant culture whose dietary laws forbade them to eat pork. Nonetheless, at the *Khazar Mark* at 8:00 A.M. every morning of the workday week, a large crowd of new and recently settled Jewish immigrants from beyond the Pale would gather — enough people to make this the most crowded and voluble street corner in an overpacked and noisome city — and make the economic transaction that was at the heart of their new lives.

The *Yidn*, as the Eastern European Jews were known (because they spoke primarily Yiddish), came to the *Khazar Mark* to collect as many pounds as they could shoulder of unfinished men's and women's garments that they took home to airless, nearly lightless tenement apartments and sewed together. One of every three immigrants from Eastern Europe toiled in New York's garment industry; for many recent arrivals, the "home work" given out next to the *Khazar Mark* was the only employment they could consistently find. The garment industry was New York's largest employer and the largest manufacturer of clothing in the entire United States. It was then dominated by the *Yehudim*, the German Jews who had been in the United States since the 1840s and who by the late 1880s had become prosperous. German Jews did not think highly of their coreligionists, calling them Asiatics and Orientals, stigmatizing and disparaging the newcomers' generally more fervent religiosity and lesser degree of sophistication. This was not simply the usual disdain of the insider for the outsider: as an official of a German-dominated emigrant-relief fund wrote to the Alliance Israelite Universelle, "Please bear constantly in mind that the position of the Jews in America is not such that they can well afford to run any risk of incurring the ill-feeling of their fellow citizens." The *Yehudim* worried that the caftans, medieval manner, and desperate poverty of the *Yidn* would grate on the Gentile majority and create a backlash of anti-Semitism that would affect all American Jews, including themselves. Anti-immigrant legislation was being debated in Congress, and articles in such staid periodicals as the *North American Review* echoed Pobyedonostzev about the source of the pogroms:

> Bitterness produced by the exactions of the Jew, envy of his wealth, jealousy of his ascendancy . . . were the motives of the people for attacking him. . . . The explanation of the

whole trouble, and of all the calamities and horrors attending it, past or to come is that the Jews are . . . a parasitic race [who] insert themselves for the purpose of gain into the homes of other nations. . . .

Faced with anti-Semitism from the Gentile majority, the *Yehudim* — once inhabitants of the Lower East Side, now moved uptown — kept their social distance from the recent wave of immigrants and only grudgingly funded some charitable assistance for them.

But the *Yehudim* had no qualms about employing the newcomers in the clothing industry, though they generally did so by means of intermediaries who insulated the owners so that they did not have to know about the low wages and deplorable conditions endured by the sweating *Yidn*. "Contractors" were awarded a fee only on the finished goods they delivered, which encouraged them to pay as little as possible to the actual sewers and pressers of garments. Most intermediaries were themselves Eastern Europeans, a fact noted by contemporary Isaac Rubinow in an early study. "Almost every newly arrived Russian Jewish laborer comes into contact with a Russian Jewish employer," he wrote, just as "almost every Russian Jewish tenement dweller must pay his exorbitant rent to a Russian Jewish landlord." Many *Yehudim* owned buildings in the ghetto, as did the great landlords such as the Astors, and all had need for Yiddish-speakers to deal with the tenants. *Arendators* from the old country — or those who knew from the *arendator* example that to become an agent was to prosper — fought to get these jobs, even as they acknowledged that their payment was wrung from the sweating brows and backs of their fellow immigrants. In every ghetto the world over, at every time in history, no matter what the race, color, or creed of the inhabitants, exploitation has been rampant. Though the new *arendators* were vilified, most ghetto dwellers understood that, just like everyone else, the agents were doing what they had to in order to get by.

Of the hundreds of thousands of immigrants, only a handful became powers in real estate. A clue to the selection process exists in a division noted between types of clothing workers. "Happy were they who knew a trade in the old country," Bernard Weinstein later wrote in a memoir of the labor movement, for "the tailors, the joiners and other artisans would obtain employment very quickly. But the bulk of the Jewish immigrants had no vocation." No *precise* vocation, that is; census studies show that more than 50 percent of all Jewish immigrants were trained, though not in a particular craft. They possessed white-collar skills such as the ability to read and write, an adroitness with numbers, managerial acumen, and a mind-set they adapted readily to various office and sales tasks. This bifurcation of training produced a strange paradox. Artisans could obtain employment quickly but ran into difficulties later. Statistical studies of the immigrants show that all too often such people remained for decades in those lower-level artisan jobs, whereas those who were forced to scrounge in the needle trades viewed such jobs as only temporary expedients to keep body and soul together, and schemed to find a way past them. On the Lower East Side it was said that the man who had a trade kept it all his life, but the man who had no trade was more likely to become a millionaire.

The potentially extraordinary man also separated himself from the bulk of those arriving from the Pale by his avoidance of the old ways. Michael R. Weisser's investigations document that about half of the "greenhorns" from the Pale formed or joined a *landsmanshaft*, a benevolent society composed of people from their old neighborhoods in Eastern Europe, at some time during their lives. But, as Weisser points out in his study of these "brotherhoods of memory," the strength of these organizations was also an expression of their members' weaknesses:

> Politically conservative and culturally backward, if [the *landsmanshafts*] helped an immigrant to retain his sense of the past, they did very little to prepare him for the challenges of the future. . . . People who joined a landsmanshaft and kept it at the psychic core of their existence were at the same time rejecting the larger society and resisting its opportunities for assimilation.

As Weisser documents, those who carried the *shtetl* with them and let it be their world in America as it had been in the Pale turned out to be the ones least likely to make advances in wealth and status.

The division between the old ways and the new was a wedge separating Louis Jay Horowitz and his father. They had quarreled on the voyage to New York, but on landing went to live together with one of their *landsmen* from Poland, a music-hall manager; there were ten people in the apartment. Soon, the unskilled sixteen-year-old had an argument with his father, found housing elsewhere, and began working as a "cash boy" for a clothing store, taking customers' money to the cashier and returning with change. Horowitz was so poor that he had to stub out his cigarettes several times to make a ten-cent pack last a week, and such a greenhorn that he had to be shown how to eat corn on the cob, sold everywhere on the streets. Transferring to a shoe store, he worked his way up from stock boy to salesman, in his spare time spending every extra cent on attending the theater. Then his estranged father, mired in a job from which there seemed no escape, begged his son to get into real estate, even if he himself could not. Louis talked his way into a position with a man named Pretzfelder who bought and sold leases in the ghetto and near Wall Street; the old German and the young Pole couldn't convince the telephone company to put a telephone in the brokerage office, but they could use a pay phone in the hall. Shortly, the $3-a-week stockboy was a $40-a-week real estate man.

The adaptable man: Abraham E. Lefcourt came from a Russian Jewish family, even though he'd been born in Birmingham, England, in 1877; his family emigrated to the Lower East Side in 1882 and were poor as temple mice. As soon as he was able, Abie made a living on the streets, selling newspapers, shining shoes, and doing odd jobs. But whereas most Delancey Street paperboys were content with one or two routes, Lefcourt, on obtaining another regular job, paid other boys to deliver papers for him so he wouldn't lose that income. It was the act of an entrepreneur, one he repeated in his career in the garment trades. Starting as a bookkeeper for a dress firm, he worked his way up to salesman in the boondocks territory of Missouri. If he could sell shoeshines he could sell anything; Lefcourt grew successful enough to buy the company when the manufacturer retired. The head of his own enterprise, he felt he'd earned the right to outdistance his childhood nickname and to be known to friends as A. E. Now he was ready for real estate.

Adaptability was essential for upward mobility. So was a thirst for learning. Two favorite haunts of Russian immigrants were the Cooper Union Library — "the most beautiful building upon which America can take pride," a Yiddish-language memoirist recalled — and the Astor Library next door, which in the period after its exclusivity had been assailed and before it merged with the New York Public Library was open from eight in the morning until ten at night. Immigrants loved these institutions that, alone among the libraries of the city, allowed even penniless tenement dwellers to come and read in their collections. James B. Reynolds, head of the University Settlement House, which succored many new immigrants, wrote of the Russian Jews' "intellectual avidity . . . intensity of feeling, high imagination . . . with an utter disregard of the restraining power of circumstance and conditions . . . a character often full of imagination, aspiration and appreciation." Scratch a Hester Street peddler and you would find a Talmudic scholar; listen in on the talk of young women sewing shirt pieces together in a Rivington Street sixth-floor walk-up apartment and you would hear spirited socialist discourse. Hutchins Hapgood pinpointed the source of the immigrants' intensity:

> Certainly few of us can feel as keen a joy as falls daily to the lot of the picayune merchant of Hester Street who feels himself about to rise in the exciting world of America, and sees the old limitations of his race removed, and, behind the old barriers, a broad, fascinating field of commercial activity. . . . The dominant effect of the life [in the ghetto] is that of business — eager, militant business.

New York was in the throes of an expansion in commercial activity that created tremendous opportunities. Banking resources and the number of manufacturing plants in the city more than doubled in a decade, while those in the country as a whole rose only 10 percent.

Immigrants took most of the new jobs that expansion created, but the nature of that growth, coupled with what newspaper want ads regularly referred to as a "Christians only" policy, directed Jewish mobility away from mainstream channels. Insurance companies, for instance, were in the process of erecting the tallest skyscrapers ever seen in New York; just then their largest source of money was the premiums paid by immigrants, and all the companies pursued the new immigrants to buy policies and had collection agents continually knocking on doors throughout the ghetto. But Jews were not hired by insurance companies for anything but collection jobs. Nor were Jews employed by most of the large corporate businesses that were in the process of setting up national headquarters in Manhattan. As a consequence, upward progress from the ghetto had to rely on individuals' own initiative. Entrepreneurial immigrants began their own businesses, while the rest took positions within industries that already succored them, such as clothing, metalworking shops, cigar-rolling factories, and printing plants.

On the whole, the immigrants' upward mobility was so pronounced a phenomenon in New York that it staggered statisticians, who learned that in New York, much more so than in any other American city, both Jewish and Italian immigrants were moving beyond blue-collar jobs at the rate of 37 percent in a single decade. Very quickly, one in three peddlers became a shop owner; one in three sewing-machine operators became a clerk in the front office or an agent who had groups of sewing-machine operators working for him; one in three masons became a building contractor.

After the first decade in the New World, though, the records of the immigrant groups diverged, and the disparity provides a clue to the motivations of the men who would found real estate dynasties. During the first ten years after passage to America, about one-third of each ethnic group moved out of manual labor into the middle class; during the second ten years after arrival, many more Jews from the Pale than Italians found their way into the middle class. Citing these figures in a landmark study, Thomas Kessner concludes that Italians' "ambitions were geared to the short range" because they were economic migrants, "birds of passage" who came only to find work, interested in accumulating money in order to return to their native country rather than in permanently settling in the United States. Jews had absolutely no wish to return to the Pale. Because their flight had been spurred by the "determined persecutions of an antagonistic officialdom," Kessner writes, "their departure was therefore stamped with finality, and they carried with them few nostalgic recollections of a beloved mother country." Once here, Jews "thought in terms of the long range." While Italian males most often came to this country alone and left wives and children behind, Jews came in family groups and did not have to send most of what they earned back to the old country, nor did they have to put aside money for passage home, as did many Italians. Jews also brought their *luftmenshen* with them, whereas other contemporaneous immigrant groups left their intellectuals in the old country.

Those Italians who did put down roots in the United States, an industrial commission found, characteristically moved "to the suburbs and became property owners in Long Island City, Flushing, Corona, Astoria, etc." While more than 20 percent of retired Italian clothing workers bought homes in the suburbs, less than 10 percent of similarly retired Jewish clothing workers did the same. Sociologists attributed the Italians' pursuit of a home of their own to nostalgia for the family farm in Italy. Conversely, almost no Jews had been farmers in the Pale; most had lived in cramped, apartment-like residences all of their lives, whether in small villages or in great cities. Living on the Lower East Side, while painful, did not induce as many Jews as Italians to dream of a quarter-acre home and garden plot. Jews who could afford to leave behind the awful Lower East Side tenements moved to larger rental apartments. Because they didn't use their savings as a down payment for a home, they were able to accumulate capital for investment.

The brightest and most ambitious of the *Yidn* knew they had to do three essential things: first, get out of manual labor; second, be a *balabos for sich* (literally, a "person for himself," or a "man without a boss"); third — and perhaps most important — use their capital to build a business, not just to ensure a comfortable home for their old age. Julius Tishman, still a teenager in the 1880s, accumulated money by working on the Lower East Side in what was known as the dry goods industry; by the middle of the decade he had opened the first department store ever seen upstate, in Newburgh, New York. By 1890 he had married Hilda Karmel, fathered his first child, and moved back to Manhattan to use his department-store profits to enter the real estate business, while his cousins, also from Poland, found their way into the clothing business. Lewis Rudinski arrived from Lithuania in 1883 knowing no English and without a trade. He took odd jobs and by the end of a decade had married and opened a small grocery on the Lower East Side. Soon he was thinking about buying a piece of property.

Many Jewish families in what Moses Rischin calls "the promised city" could get by on the work of the father of the family; but they had not come to America only to survive — they had come to get ahead. Jewish women accepted the indignity of sewing sleeves on shirts at home to make a few dollars a week, or suffered loss of privacy by taking in boarders to keep down the family's overhead costs. Everything in their lives contrived to push these particular families to accumulate capital: the persecution they had escaped, the bad conditions they learned to endure, the deep-seated optimism, the suppleness of mind that allowed them to search out schemes for advancement, the desire for independence, the bent toward intellectual pursuits and scholarship that had fewer accredited outlets here but whose power could be turned to the making of money.

Contemporary immigration researcher Robert Foerster noted and encapsulated in a single sentence another trenchant factor that informed the immigrants' lives: "A too facile assimilation to established ways may even make profit less easy." Isolation enforced by the immigrants' Old World ways and predilections produced what another observer called "ruthless underconsumption." By refusing to spend disposable income to buy the sort of goods that already assimilated Americans considered important, those who did not fall into the trap of keeping up with the Joneses were able to retain more dollars. A "sweater" family often accumulated up to thirty dollars a month, Jacob Riis wrote after years of observing the ghetto, "and in a few years will own a tenement somewhere and profit by the example set by their landlord in rent collecting. It is the way the savings of Jewtown are universally invested."

The hunger for land ownership born of deprival in the Pale became transmuted not to the simple buying of a suburban home but to the desire to own commercial real estate of the sort that in the future would reward the owner and his family with mansions. It was obvious even to the inhabitants that New York's tenements sweated profits as well as humanity — 10 to 20 percent return on investment each year. The *Jewish Daily Forward* often published stories carrying the message that the *Yehudim* had prospered after moving to the Upper East Side because they retained title to the brownstones and tenements that they had earlier worked so hard to buy, and that they now rented out for good profit. The saying went that the distance between Rivington Street (home of the *Yidn*) and Lexington Avenue (where the prosperous *Yehudim* now lived) was ten years. Real estate was the key to wealth; philosopher and mayoral candidate Henry George had declaimed his theories about that connection to the ghetto, and the Lower East Side had responded by giving him more votes than any other candidate in the race, even Teddy Roosevelt.

America was in the midst of one of its occasional orgies of celebrating rich men. Current newspapers were full of reports about the spectacular amounts of money being made by the "Standard Oil" crowd. For the most part, the immigrants considered those Gentile millionaires as remote from them as the tsars in the Kremlin once had been. But not always.

One day in the 1890s, a strange and luxurious automobile pulled up at the Lower East Side retail grocery of Lewis Rudinski and out stepped John D. Rockefeller himself. A vicious price war was then going on between Rockefeller's companies and other sellers of heating oil, which in the ghetto could be bought at such shops in small quantities; Rockefeller was asking shopkeepers not to switch to the competition but to stay with Standard Oil. Rudinski nodded, and asked Rockefeller where he lived. The millionaire said he lived on 54th Street. Rockefeller got back in his car and left for the next stop, but Rudin remembered 54th Street. He didn't have enough money yet to buy property, but when he did, he wished to buy on 54th Street.

As the ghetto bulged and expanded northward, more tenements could be erected. Young Julius Tishman saw his opportunity and plunged in, applying his accumulated capital from the Newburgh store to the building of 519 East 13th Street, a six-story tenement indistinguishable from a thousand others on the side streets just off avenues A, B, C, and D. Abraham Cahan, pioneering editor of the Yiddish-langauge newspaper *Forward* and a Russian immigrant himself (class of '82), noted a widespread phenomenon:

> Small tradesmen of the slums, and even working men . . .
> investing their savings in houses and lots . . . [becoming]
> builders of tenements or frame dwellings, real estate specu-
> lators. Deals were being closed and poor men were making
> thousands of dollars in less time than it took them to drink
> the glass of tea or the plate of sorrel soup over which the
> transaction took place.

This was especially true in the upper Manhattan district known as Harlem and, thanks to an expanding public transportation system, even north of Manhattan's boundary, the Harlem River, in the green fields and beautiful hills of the Bronx. Whole-acre lots were selling for mere hundreds of dollars each in the Bronx, whereas a 25-by-100-foot plot in lower Manhattan could go for thousands. To the shrewd immigrant businessman it was obvious that many from the masses who had been cramped in the great ghetto would want to live in such verdant areas as the Bronx, just as soon as they escaped poverty. The Bronx was so beautiful and slow-paced that you could jump off the horse-car line, pick huckleberries from an adjoining field, and climb back on — hence the nickname, the Huckleberry Line. And the commute from the Bronx wasn't very long or arduous. Manhattan-bound men could take one of several railroads that served the Bronx "villages," or even the horse-car line to 129th Street and Third Avenue, where they could catch the elevated and go downtown.

After the Brooklyn Bridge opened in 1883, directly connecting the Lower East Side with a still quite green Brooklyn, even greater opportunities came knocking. In 1885, an elevated railway opened that enabled people to travel from further within Brooklyn to the bridge; soon the trains were handling a million passengers annually. In one decade, 1880–1890, the population of Brooklyn increased by 40 percent to 840,000, and Brooklyn became known as Manhattan's bedroom.

After five years of working with the old German real estate agent on Wall Street, Louis Jay Horowitz knew what he had to do. Brokering lofts and tenement apartments would never make him rich. He must create property. The dream had been in his mind for years; he didn't know when, precisely, it had come upon him, but for several years he had been accumulating money toward the day when he could build his first structure. It wouldn't be a skyscraper — that took serious money — but it would be his own. He bought a lot in Brooklyn Heights for a few hundred dollars, shelled out $2,000 more of his own and $7,000 borrowed from friends, and started construction on a six-floor apartment building. It had to be completed by October 1, which had replaced May 1 as moving day. By that date Horowitz also had its twelve apartments fully rented for an annual income of $3,840. At that rate, in three to four years the building would pay for itself and continue to bring in profits. So obvious were "the numbers" on his six-floor building that Jay was able to sell it, pay off his loan, recoup his $2,000, and reap a $5,000 profit. Horowitz celebrated with a first-class crossing to Europe. What sense was there in having money if it couldn't be enjoyed? But he couldn't sit back and simply live the good life, for a newer dream seized his mind: to make a larger building.

PART TWO

REACHING FOR THE SKY

Chapter Four

Converging Streams

JOHN JACOB ASTOR and his set of old families controlled the land; Daniel Burnham, his apprentices, and his spiritual offspring provided the main architectural imagination and construction expertise; a set of immigrant developers typified by Jay Horowitz contributed the entrepreneurial urge. Just before the turn of the twentieth century these three streams began to converge in ways that led to the first great phalanx of Manhattan skyscrapers.

Some sections of the Lower East Side had a density of 986.4 people per acre, far greater than in the slums of London. The ghetto was riddled with "contracted quarters, lack of family privacy, and promiscuous toilet arrangements, inviting moral deterioration; lack of light and air, and of sanitary accommodations, insuring a large death rate . . . a disgrace to humanity," concluded the *New York Times*. Philosophers of social change argued that the poor would be more moral and less criminal if they lived in better housing. Following this reasoning, projects such as the City and Suburban Homes blocks on the Upper East Side received funding from a consortium of wealthy families who agreed to limit their annual return on capital to 6 percent. On their other current investments — the Astors' upper-Broadway luxury apartment buildings, or the Cuttings' commercial buildings along 42nd Street — they were making 20 to 30 percent.

Meanwhile, the ghetto was actually losing population as its inhabitants prospered. "The formation of a well-to-do class in the midst of the Russian Jewish colony has been a very interesting phenomenon. The general improvement in the character of the stores, the sudden appearance of a dozen or more commercial banks, the well-furnished cafés . . . all tell eloquently of this growth," said contemporary observer Charles Bernheimer. As they readied themselves to move out of the ghetto, Lower East Siders believed that the proper antidote to walking up six flights to a railroad flat with long, narrow rooms and no view was to ride an elevator up to a comfortable, square-roomed apartment whose windows looked out onto green. New apartment buildings were being built weekly. In Harlem, Abraham Cahan remembered, the corner of Fifth Avenue and 116th Street "usually swarmed with Yiddish-speaking real-estate speculators."

Among them were the brothers Leo and Alexander Bing, both widely read, cultured, fastidious, and intelligent young lawyers. Like many who became developers, they exuded a quiet confidence and favored a conservative appearance; they learned early that trust was more easily given by the financiers if the seekers were not too flamboyant. Under their three-piece suits with high collars, the brothers concealed progressive sentiments. Alexander was much taken with the City and Suburban Homes model for development. Using their legal knowledge, the Bings formed a syndicate of investors to buy land along Broadway near intersections where subway or elevated lines were being constructed, resell the plots to builders, then provide them with loans for construction. The brothers had not yet caught the fever of pursuing real estate as a route to satisfaction. Their temperatures rose when they crossed paths with Hungarian immigrant Emery Roth.

Roth's letter from Richard M. Hunt had indeed secured him a job in the Hunt firm on his arrival in New York, and when Hunt died, a job in the atelier of Ogden Codman, another figure from the elite, Protestant, old-money crowd once dominated by Caroline Astor. Codman, for instance, collaborated with Edith Wharton on a book about designing interiors and she, in turn, located her novels in homes with interiors that seemed to have been decorated by Codman. Roth judged Codman to be only a dilettante in architecture. Roth was "wrestling with the Angel of the Big City," in off-hours spending time with sculptor Karl Bitter, who posed him for figures on the doors of the remodeled Trinity Church. In 1897, for $1,000 (most of it borrowed), Roth bought the practice of two retiring Hungarian architects. At the time, most architects obtained work through family and social connections; active solicitation was considered uncouth. Roth had only an extended family in the form of the Hungarian Jewish émigré community. He went to the Café Boulevard, a Second Avenue institution featuring gypsy music; there, for ten cents, you could sip coffee, munch *kipferl*, and talk Magyar. One conversation got him the contract to renovate the café. Then a café habitué introduced him at other shops that needed renovations, and the Boulevard's owner asked him to redo a summer hotel in Arverne, which led to commissions in Edgemere and Far Rockaway.

Desperate for more work, Roth submitted plans to speculative builders in the hope that, if they were accepted, he would receive the architect's fee. "I was . . . ambitious but also quite gullible," wrote Roth. "Some real estate agent would put me to work on the pretext that he had a builder, then would use my sketches to promote a sale and even the consummation of the sale was no assurance that my plans would be used." Most of these "tough hombres . . . bought plans as they did bricks or lumber, as cheaply as possible." But at least they bought them!

At the turn of the century, Roth began to see some of his designs realized and himself acknowledged as the designer. He created fanciful Belle Epoque versions of the sort of buildings already the fashion in middle-class neighborhoods in Paris: the seven-story Saxony Apartments at 82nd and Broadway, and the Hotel Belleclaire, a ten-story multiple residence at the corner of 78th and Broadway. The Belleclaire featured Italianate bay windows and an ornate limestone facade; its luxurious apartments felt like personal castles. The Belleclaire attracted the admiration of Leo and Alex Bing, who had run into a problem. A speculative builder to whom they'd sold a parcel on 136th Street had submitted plans they considered inferior; the Bings asked Roth to alter these so that more money could be made.

Roth's design, created in a few days, enabled more rentable rooms to be built in the same space and also beautified the building. After this first joint project, the Bings decided to skip the middlemen and develop properties themselves. They turned the entire block of 137th Street between Broadway and Riverside Drive into a spanking-new complex that rented out in record time. Thus began a grand marriage between developers and an architect that would last for the next forty-five years and create many of the jewels of New York's skyline. In Roth, the Bings found a supple artist who understood the business side of making an edifice; in the Bings, Roth discovered an integrity in their work, as well as in their business methods, that assured me — at a time when I sorely needed such assurances — that square dealing rather than cunning leads to success. In those first years, I was often confronted with situations that required a subtlety I totally lacked for matching the shrewd and at times unscrupulous practices that faced me. It was like a breath of fresh air to transact business without the fear of being taken advantage of.

In the Bronx, the seat of the action in the real estate business was East 149th Street, along which builders, contractors, brokers, carpenters, coal dealers, and tradesmen were so crowded that many had to share offices. The Bronx was booming, especially after construction began on the Grand Concourse, a stately boulevard originally conceived as a speedway leading from the overcrowded streets of Manhattan to the verdant parks of the Bronx. The borough became a hatching ground for many future skyscraper builders, such as Fred F. French, one of four children of a cigar-maker. French grew up in the Bronx, attended Horace Mann school on a science scholarship, spent a year at Princeton, and labored as a cowboy, ditch digger, and railroad worker before returning to New York. Tall, broad, and physically imposing, he found a job as a timekeeper on a construction site. French had to be forceful, as the job entailed not only watching the hours but keeping construction workers from taking advantage of the management.

When French's employer laid him off in 1907, it was a moment of crisis of the sort that every tycoon later recalls with relish for having surpassed it: "I was broke — actually penniless, and had nothing in view. To collect my scattered wits I sat down in City Hall Park, weak with hunger and fatigue. The only person I could think of to ask for aid was Andrew W. Edson of the Board of Education. By a tremendous effort I managed to walk up to 59th Street and caught Mr. Edson just as the office was closing.

" 'May I borrow $500, Mr. Edson?' I asked.

" 'What security have you,' he queried.

" 'Nothing but my personal note,' I answered, and he drew out his checkbook.

" 'And pardon me, Mr. Edson, but could I have $10 of that in cash?' I added, remembering my empty pockets. The amazing good fortune to have $10 with me with which to relieve an empty stomach made me lightheaded. I walked to the Savoy Hotel and ordered one glorious meal. My delight in the food was complete; but the amount of the bill consumed my $10 and I had to walk back to my room near 116th Street."

French used the $500 to renovate his childhood home, then mortgaged it and used the resulting cash to erect others. Within a few years, he moved his operations to Manhattan. An eccentric even then, French refused to own a car, wouldn't attend the theater, didn't drink or play cards; the only vice he allowed himself was a cigar now and then, perhaps in memory of his father.

In the Brownsville section of Brooklyn, newspaper editor Cahan recalled, the gathering spot was a café on Pitkin Avenue, where "houses were bought and sold over a cup of coffee." In Brooklyn, as in Harlem and the Bronx, the most prolific of the speculative builders were immigrants from the Pale — often pairs of brothers or brothers-in-law.

Looking back at who became successful, it becomes apparent that these Russian immigrants had more characteristics in common than their area of origin. Most had arrived with their families, rather than alone as most Italian and Irish immigrants did, and they had emigrated when they were between the ages of ten and twenty. A builder's age at the time of transit seems to have been the key determinant. Sociologists have long argued that a person's most impressionable years are those between the onset of puberty and the early twenties; attitudes formed during those years dominate for the remainder of a lifetime. Collateral accounts of Jewish immigrant culture reveal that males who were over the age of twenty at the time of arrival in New York generally led very different lives compared with younger boys — they immediately became burdened with grown-up responsibilities and later were less inclined to court risks in business. A willingness to live with risk is critical to high-stakes real estate endeavors. Older immigrants didn't have it; neither did those who were younger than ten when they emigrated, for they tended to spend their time and energies assimilating into the mainstream of American culture. Those between ten and twenty at time of passage had persecution seared into them in the Pale and in the New York ghettos, but not deeply enough to undercut their optimism. They became the group most likely to succeed.

Evidence of the initiative and personalities of the forefathers of the great real estate dynasties in this early time is hard to find, and much cherished when unearthed. Dan Rose unfolds an old letter on the character of his grandfather Joseph, who was so interested in world affairs that he often neglected his business for great thoughts. Dick Ravitch pulls out of his briefcase a clipping from a New York newspaper of 1903: side-by-side advertisements quietly solicit business for the competing iron-mongering firms of Joseph Ravitch and Harris Uris, located on neighboring side streets of the Lower East Side. Joseph Ravitch came from Russia at age fourteen in 1888; Uris, from Latvia at about the same age and time. Big, burly men who in an earlier day might have been village black-smiths, Ravitch and Uris supervised small iron foundries that made manhole covers and elevator doors. Decades later, Harold Uris would have one of his father's ironwork implements made into a desk; Dick Ravitch would come across a sidewalk grate on the Lower East Side with his grandfather's name on it, and pay for its removal and transformation into an office table.

The surge in elevated train stations, as well as the need for railroad lines to be sunk below the streets, created demand for iron products. The first subway in Manhattan opened in 1905; in 1906 Joseph, David, and Abraham Ravitch incorporated and moved their business to Long Island City, where they opened a foundry that became the largest maker of structural steel in the New York area. Harris Uris took more spacious quarters near the East River on 26th Street; his new foundry concentrated on ornamental iron work — grills, fire escapes, highly decorated and fireproof elevator doors.

The elder sons of Julius Tishman the tenement-builder, Simon Chanin the painting contractor, and Lewis Rudin the grocer all entered college in the years between the turn of the century and the onset of the Great War. Schooling was a privilege and a reward for industry that Jewish families coveted and which had been denied to them in the Pale. The decisions to send the sons had little to do with the young men; rather, they reflected the fathers' dreams for the future.

Lewis Rudin had dropped the "ski" from his name, become a ladies' coat manufacturer, and by 1903 had put aside enough money to make a first investment. Recalling that Rockefeller lived on 54th Street, Rudin asked a broker to find him a property to buy on that street. The broker suggested a well-built tenement on Lexington Avenue at 54th, but didn't bother to explain to Rudin that although millionaires lived on 54th west of Park Avenue, the avenue itself was a huge railroad cut, lined with factories such as that of the

F. & M. Schaefer Brewing Company and various piano-makers. East 54th was literally on the wrong side of the tracks, part of an uptown ghetto.

Rudin didn't yet have enough capital to transfer his expertise from the cutthroat garment business to the equally tough and speculative trade of builder, but cloak-and-suit executive Abraham E. Lefcourt did. A. E. had become the sort of bantamweight, cock-of-the-walk dandy made famous by Broadway song-and-dance man George M. Cohan — the poor immigrant boy from the Lower East Side who propelled himself up in the world by fierceness and charm. Though a small man, Lefcourt had phenomenal energy that he attributed to his swims in the ocean; he was a member of the Polar Bears of Long Beach, who dipped into the waters daily no matter what the temperature. Sentimental about his youth, as were many of the builders, Lefcourt kept as his lieutenant one of his childhood friends. A. E. became a leader in the Cloak, Suit and Shirt Manufacturer's Protective Association and spent most of his time trying to abolish sweatshops and smoothing relations between garment-center employers and employees. (The increased militance of garment workers was due to the latest wave of immigrants, tempered in the fire of socialism in the Pale, who joined the American trade-union movement more readily than their predecessors had.) Lefcourt erected a twelve-story loft at 48 West 25th Street, some garment-makers moved in, and Lefcourt had both a success and a revelation. Clothing-makers had to concoct a new line twice a year; if consumers hated it, a manufacturer could go out of business in a few months despite having had years of profitability — but there was a business that didn't have to be reinvented twice a year in order to make a great deal of money: real estate.

Jewish entrepreneurs built in the garment center because they could not get into the game of erecting grand hotels and office blocks. They lacked access to large amounts of capital and credence within the rather tight circle of the wealthiest and most influential businessmen in the city. They had to settle for putting up modest apartments in outlying areas and lofts in the garment center, while the largest residential and hotel buildings continued to be constructed by the old and moneyed families, and the tallest skyscrapers by the well-established, mostly Gentile business institutions.

These factors were constraining Louis Jay Horowitz, one among the downtown Brooklyn real estate crowd that gathered along

Joralemon and Court streets. At the turn of the century he was still in his twenties and just back from that vacation to Europe he'd awarded himself after his first small triumph. To realize his second dream — a new building on Brooklyn Heights several times larger than the small unit he'd already built and sold — he desperately needed private financing. Bank financing was available only to men willing to mortgage their own homes in order to get money for their projects, a requirement that underscored the risky nature of speculative building. Horowitz had no home to mortgage, so for financing he had to go to Venette F. Pelletreau, whose offices "had the atmosphere of a small bourse," Horowitz later wrote. Many builders shuttled in and out. Pelletreau loaned them money and then was delighted if they defaulted, for then he could foreclose and take possession of the buildings, which were worth more than the loans. Horowitz borrowed some money from Pelletreau and cadged additional funds from a wealthy druggist. Construction proved remarkably easy, and once again Horowitz won a triumph. But having climbed into the foothills he could see the true size of the mountain he wished to scale: creating bigger and better buildings, perhaps even a skyscraper. He received an offer too good to refuse and sold his second dream for $125,000.

Had Horowitz been able to pocket all that money, he might have been tempted to retire and spend his time attending the theater. But he was unable to get hold of the $125,000 all at once: as partial payment Horowitz was forced to accept some lots of questionable worth on Brooklyn's Ninth Avenue. That, combined with his urge to leave his mark on New York, impelled him to keep building to try to turn his profit into actual cash. "In the protean way of my craft," he wrote, "I had slipped my various possessions into the transaction so that practically my entire fortune had taken the shape, for the time being, of those Ninth Avenue lots." This mode of behavior crystallizes the experience of skyscraper builders of New York from that day forward: each new building is facilitated by the previous one, but to erect it one must throw nearly all of one's resources into the fray.

The immigrant Russian-Jewish builders, still small scale, were in direct competition with the longer-established, predominantly non-Jewish speculative builders who had been constructing in New York since the Civil War. Anglo-American contractor and owner Philip Braender of 125th Street completed 1,500 private homes and apartment units before the turn of the century; Francis Crawford put up dozens of houses from West 72nd to West 89th. For two generations, they and their brothers-in-mortar had covered Manhattan with brownstone row houses. They started as artisans, then crossed over into development; they built small, and they built well, but they worked alone and seldom brought in sons or brothers.

Absence of continuity was one reason their firms didn't survive into the twentieth century. They also disappeared because their capacity to build the sort of big towers on which empires could be based was limited by their finances. Those Brooklyn banks that were then squeezing Jay Horowitz's competitors by making them pledge their own homes as collateral had nothing on the banks of a slightly earlier era, which frowned on loaning money for any speculative building projects, regardless of how they might be secured. Most Anglo-American builders were forced to borrow from wealthy individuals — and by 1900 wealthy people had stopped lending their money to small-timers and were using it to erect edifices of their own. So in the building frenzy, the Anglo-American builders fell behind. But the immigrant community provided its own builders with more backing, because its lenders were just as hungry as the builders. Minor *Yidn* capitalists were just emerging, eager to lend to a Jay Horowitz or a Julius Tishman or a Leo Bing. Any smart man could see that an investment in a building was sure to return a quick gain far in excess of what a Jew could earn by putting his money in a bank.

Anglo-American speculative builders were also more set in their ways. Well past the time when six-story brownstones and small groups of flats were profitable, they continued to erect them; the immigrants plunged into the substantially higher-risk multiapartment buildings and reaped bigger profits that fueled the growth of their enterprises. The upstarts' products cost less because they were able to hire cheaper labor, semiskilled Jews who had been systematically excluded because of their religion from the established construction guilds. Faced with applications from the recent immigrants, one Irish-dominated guild established a $100 initiation fee to join its ranks and be allowed to work on certain building sites. This fee was considerably beyond the means of those who stood to make $5 a week from construction work. So you could find a surprising number of nonunionized Jewish carpenters, masons, and painters. In the Pale, many had been scholars who hadn't had to support themselves. Now they did, and they worked extra hard for canny Jewish contractors who sent them home at sundown on Friday and paid them for an extra half-day rather than working them on Saturday, as was the industry norm.

When he commenced his third building in Brooklyn, Jay Horowitz decided the project was larger than he could supervise by himself. Old real estate hand Clarence H. Kelsey suggested he hire Ted Starrett's firm, Thompson-Starrett, to construct it for him. Ted was the combative genius of the Starrett clan of Chicago, five brothers who had become mainstays of the two largest construction companies in the country, and who were going head to head just then in the building of the biggest skyscrapers in New York.

Ted was "explosively quick to anger," a friend later wrote of him, "but the flaming wrath of the moment died out as quickly as it had blazed forth." Once he'd worked for Burnham, and quit with much rancor and vituperation. He'd done the same two more times with another employer, Harry Black of the Fuller Company. Black was dynamic himself, stumpy, with piercing blue eyes and dark hair; having married George H. Fuller's daughter, he had the personal drive to take over the reins and transform the company from a $50,000-a-year private concern to a public corporation with stock worth $15,000,000. Even after he'd fired Ted, Black recognized him as a talent who would be good to have in his company — if he could be controlled.

Black's interest in Ted was raised again when Ted's younger brother Paul walked into his office. After the 1893 Columbian Exposition, on Burnham's behalf, Paul supervised the work of a contractor whose efforts were so inadequate, Paul later wrote, that they "awakened in me the idea of becoming a builder." However, as a nonarchitect Paul felt he'd never really get his hands on a building if he remained in Burnham's office. So he crossed the street to Fuller and asked to see Harry Black, "a business genius, a gambler, a financial juggler . . . [whose] contradictions had me baffled." Black offered Paul Starrett less money than he was currently paid by Burnham, but the chance to realize his dream — to be wholly in charge of a new building. Paul seized the opportunity. Black sent him to Baltimore and Washington, D.C., to erect new skyscrapers; in a year, he was making more than he ever would have with Burnham. It was then that Black called Ted and offered him a job at Fuller, too.

"Human nature," Ted Starrett later wrote, "is a vast bundle of inconsistencies and follies," and he knew that he was, too. Though wary of Black, Ted agreed to go to New York to work for the

Fuller Company because in the 1890s New York had surpassed Chicago in constructing large numbers of skyscrapers. The arrangement lasted two years. In 1900, the hot-tempered Ted walked out on Fuller for the third time, also leaving brother Paul in the lurch, and formed a new company with a partner. With good financial backing and Ted's expertise, Thompson-Starrett quickly became a major force in New York. Ted then convinced his other brothers to come and work for him; once they were in his employ, he proceeded to dominate them.

Craftily, then, Black decided to move Paul Starrett from Baltimore to New York as head of construction. A race was on to put up the highest skyscrapers in Manhattan, and Black the businessman wanted Paul at Fuller to beat out Ted at Thompson-Starrett. Black stoked the fires of their rivalry. Paul later wrote, "The competition for jobs and the speed on jobs — for which [Ted] and I were largely responsible — were killing, the more so that our competition with each other was in a certain sense unnatural and unfraternal."

One year an insurance-company monument would take the height lead; the next year the new home of one of New York's newspapers; the third, another insurance company; the fourth, another newspaper. Manhattan used four times the electricity of London and handled more money daily than Paris. A French novelist likened its skyscrapers to human beehives, connoting the admirable "tireless forward" attitude of New York. To a British journalist, Manhattan's towers cried aloud of "struggling, almost savage, unregulated strength. Nothing is given to beauty; everything centers in hard utility. It is the outward expression of the freest, fiercest individualism. The very houses are alive with the instinct of competition." Expatriate novelist Henry James, returning home after many years, complained that the skyscrapers stuck out, "extravagant pins in a cushion already over-planted"; and to H. G. Wells, who had imagined many futures, Manhattan's skyscrapers were "tall irregular crenellations, the strangest crown that ever a city wore. They have an effect of immense incompleteness . . . a threatening promise." Russian revolutionary Maxim Gorky likened the skyscrapers to the uneven teeth of a capitalistic shark.

Words were coined in various languages to describe the buildings that were becoming the symbols of New York: in French, skyscrapers were *egratineurs de ciel;* in German, *Himmelskratzer;* in Italian, *gratticieli;* in Spanish, *rascielos.* Europeans recognized the skyscraper as alien to their own culture and quintessentially American, expressing what they found most appealing about America: freedom, unlimited space, an abundance of natural resources, monetary wealth, and a belief in the positive aspects of the future. Bill Starrett, the first historian of tall buildings, called the new crop "completely American, so far surpassing anything before undertaken in its vastness, swiftness, utility and economy . . . [that they have become] the cornerstone and abode of our national progress."

George Fuller had recently died, and Harry Black considered himself the equal of the newspaper publishers and insurance company chieftains who were commissioning the buildings that his company was constructing. If they could have an edifice, so could he; it would be a celebration of his importance. For the tower that would celebrate himself, Black bought the best site in Manhattan, a triangular spit of land at the intersection of two of the most famous avenues in the world, Fifth Avenue and Broadway, which crossed at 23rd Street. To design the Fuller Building, Black hired the most distinguished architect he knew: Daniel Burnham.

Just then Burnham and his retrograde classicism were triumphant as Louis Sullivan retreated into drink and bitterness. Uncle Dan was an adviser to the president, the leader of the American Institute of Architects, the redesigner of San Francisco and Manila, the architect of dozens of buildings in various stages of completion — among them the great Union Station in Washington, D.C. "Burnham was accustomed to be a Czar on his buildings," Paul Starrett recalled, while Black, "who had quite as much ego as Uncle Dan, wanted to decide every disputed point himself. I was caught between them." Black would want a particular schedule adhered to; Burnham would imperiously refuse to bind himself to it. Burnham threatened to resign; Black, to sue. Starrett tried to keep construction on schedule and on budget during their tiffs, walking a high beam between two monumental egos.

When finished in 1902, the triangular building was a marvel — not the tallest building on the skyline but the most striking, an elevated palazzo with French Renaissance details, covered by curlicues and stone filigree work. Critics thought it overdecorated but crowds in the streets loved its shape, twenty stories high though only six feet wide at the apex of the triangle. Alone and isolated it stood, with no other tall buildings nearby, and attracted hordes of sight-seers. The wind would whip around it and swirl women's skirts away from their legs; policemen chased male oglers from the site with the admonition, "Twenty-three skidoo." Observers groped for a phrase by which to convey the Fuller Building's beauty and attraction: it was a giant wedge, a ship's prow, an arrow pointing up Fifth Avenue in the direction of the growth of New York. Finally it was likened to the shape of an iron used to press clothes, and became known as the Flatiron Building. Ascending to the stratosphere of the imagination, it became an icon, the most famous building in New York, the focal point for painters and photographers striving to convey the spirit and triumph of modern man.

Black proved that this was a dream project rather than a practical one by refusing to sell the Flatiron for a million-dollar profit. Instead, he installed the Fuller Company's headquarters on a high floor, whence Paul Starrett could look out across Madison Square and see an old acquaintance — Saint-Gaudens's statue *Diana*, once at the 1893 Columbian Exposition, now residing in the cupola of Madison Square Garden. New projects awaited: a store for Macy's at 34th and Broadway; a home for the *New York Times* at 42nd and Broadway.

Meanwhile, in Brooklyn Heights, Thompson-Starrett was completing that midsize apartment house for Louis Jay Horowitz. On the site daily, often without an overcoat, Horowitz developed quick consumption — tuberculosis. His mother had died of it at an early age and Horowitz worried that he, too, would succumb. Therapy consisted of doses of creosote, six meals a day, and the fresh air of the Bergenstock in Switzerland. On his return Clarence Kelsey informed him that Thompson-Starrett was in trouble, for Ted Starrett's genius did not include keeping a tight rein on expenses. Instead of simply purchasing the granite for a new building, the impatient Starrett had had the company invest in a granite quarry in Vermont, which soon became a major money drain. In another bad deal, he had accepted some "painfully slow-selling junior securities" in exchange for construction work. Kelsey and a Standard Oil man had invested heavily in Thompson-Starrett, and their investment was at risk. These same men had been impressed by Horowitz; in five years, with ventures that increased steadily in size, he had increased his fortune from a few thousand dollars to hundreds of thousands. That sort of acumen and continued growth emboldened the investors to ask Horowitz to enter Thompson-Starrett to ride herd on Ted. Kelsey was a powerful figure; in addition to being tied to the Rockefellers, he had political clout with Vice President William Howard Taft and access to the wealth of the Du Pont family. Horowitz realized that if things broke right, he could shortly become head of Thompson-Starrett. He waited for Ted to make an unforgivable mistake.

"There is great dissatisfaction [with the progress on Union Station]," Burnham wrote to Ted Starrett. "It will not avail your reputation to explain afterwards that legally you are not to blame for delay. What the heads of great corporations look for in a man is success under difficulties, and nothing goes with a worse grace than constant explanations of failures. This is a very big man's job. It cannot be handled by anyone except the boss." Starrett complied, but he was burning himself out; approaching forty, to his brothers he seemed much older. One day Ted called Horowitz into his front office, leaned back in a chair, and said, "You are very smart. I am just wondering if you won't prove too smart for me." Horowitz protested his loyalty, but shortly thereafter, Ted decided the time had come to reconcile with brother Paul.

Paul, too, was under pressure, because he'd listened to the siren voice of Harry Black. It was the era of the formation of such giants as U.S. Steel, and selling stock seemed a wonderful way to find money for real estate. That there were attendant dangers never entered Black's head. To form the largest real estate stock company ever assembled, called United States Realty and Construction, Black and James Stillman of the First National Bank combined the Fuller Company with a brokerage and a bond firm; the capitalization was $66 million, of which, the *New York Evening Post* wrote, "One half . . . is pure water and wind." The wind was the product of such directors as a former Tammany mayor and a well-known stock market manipulator, but the company also had more solid board members such as steel magnate Charles M. Schwab, railroad builder Cornelius Vanderbilt, and banker Henry Morgenthau. These men frequently played poker and baccarat together for high stakes, and — just for fun — sometimes tried to ruin one another financially. They double-crossed Black and insisted on someone else as president. The new company's first large endeavor involved paying $4 million to combine two sites adjacent to the Trinity Church graveyard near Wall Street, then getting the city to agree to move a street out of the way in order to construct two tall, incredibly narrow skyscrapers that featured light blue Indiana limestone, bronze, marble, gold leaf, and stained-glass windows. U.S. Realty did well with these buildings, but soon became overextended at just the moment in 1907 when both business and real estate values in New York took a nosedive. The plummeting of U.S. Realty stock ruined Paul Starrett, whom Black had advised to invest heavily in the "sure thing."

It was then that Paul got a phone call from brother Ted. "Look here," said the elder brother, "why don't you come over and join me?" Paul deduced that Ted's "nerves were shot" and that he was "failing," and considered his options. Together the brothers went to see Clarence Kelsey, who was enthusiastic and offered Paul the same salary as at Fuller, plus a share in the profits. In his mind, Paul conjured up "a happy picture of us five Starretts working side by side all through the years to come, a big team, each contributing to make the name Starrett synonymous with good building." But the next day, at lunch, Ted told Paul that upon joining the firm he would have to acknowledge Ted as the boss.

"Oh, no," Paul demurred. "We're going to work together. I know just as much about building as you do. In some ways, I may know more."

"You know more than I do?" Ted responded, eyes flashing, face flushed.

"Yes, in some ways I think I do."

The brothers were silent for a few moments, but Paul concluded that "a mental gulf had yawned between us" because Ted didn't want to recognize that his younger brother could possibly have grown up. The deal was called off — to the immense relief of both men — but afterwards they became better brothers. "Our failure to come to terms in a business way seemed to put us on more intimate terms personally."

Seeing how near he had come to losing Paul, Black made him president of Fuller, while Black worked solely on the U.S. Realty side. But when Horowitz and his backers in Thompson-Starrett learned that Ted had been unable to lure their chief competitor into the fold, Ted was finally removed and Horowitz awarded complete direction of the company.

Perhaps that freed Ted's mind for bold thoughts, for shortly, in a Sunday supplement article, Ted Starrett, the leading building contractor in New York though not an architect of note, proposed a skyscraper that would be 100 stories tall. He drew a design for it, an inelegant though lofty box whose foundations went deep into the earth and whose crown was in the clouds. Starrett envisioned it containing "the cultural, commercial and industrial activities of a great city," with factories at the bottom, office businesses on the next levels, residences in the middle floors, and a hotel above them. Each section would be separated by public plazas. The twentieth story would be a general market, the fortieth a cluster of theaters, the sixtieth a "shopping district," and at the very top would be "an amusement park, roof garden and swimming pool." People would be "shot upward" by elevators "with the rapidity that letters are sent across the Brooklyn Bridge." The climate would be controlled so that Manhattanites would have no need of going to Florida in the winter or to Canada in the summer. "Step by step we have advanced from the wooden hut to the 30-story skyscraper," Starrett wrote. "Our civilization is progressing wonderfully. . . . We must keep building and we must build upward. . . ."

Ted Starrett's grand vision provoked a good deal of talk and commentary, but the idea was too outlandish for most. Only the constructing fraternity understood that all anyone now needed to realize a 100-story building were some technological advances. The leap of faith had already been made.

Chapter Five

Horizontal to Vertical Monuments

THE DEATH of Miss Elizabeth van Beuren in 1908 occasioned the removal of the last live cow from Manhattan, the one she had tethered behind her rococo mansion at the edge of her family's holdings at Union Square. That cow gone, and stone dwellings already emplaced on virtually every block from Manhattan's southern to northern tip, it was clear that Manhattan would nevermore be a village and that it was a moment for departure from the patterns of the past. The old landowning families switched to putting up splendid hotels. There were two by Vanderbilt, two by the Astors, and the Goelet family's Ritz-Carlton Hotel, among others.

It was the era of monumental public and semipublic edifices — such as the great, vaulting spaces of Pennsylvania Station, a spectacular McKim, Mead & White design. A broker who was the brother-in-law of President Theodore Roosevelt accumulated the land for the railroad, then 393 small buildings, mostly tenements, were pulled down. No outcry was raised about the displacement. Such removals were commonplace: 21,000 buildings were demolished in Manhattan between 1898 and 1908. Most plots, it was pointed out, had been built over three times. The New York Public Library, whose grand marble facade rivaled that of Penn Station, was under construction at the site of the old reservoir, between Fifth and Sixth avenues from 40th to 42nd streets. Grand Central Station was rising two blocks east. For years, traffic was snarled as trucks and wagons hauled immense granite blocks and marble columns for the library and the station. These three edifices were the last horizontal monuments of the era before the Great War, each covering several square blocks but rising to only modest heights.

Down by Wall Street, a new breed of building was soaring. The most gracious vertical monument was 149 Broadway, the Singer Sewing Machine Building designed by Ernest Flagg. The lower part was a bulky French Renaissance jewel box, above which a set-back, slender, terra-cotta and brick tower rose forty-seven stories. Its elegant Victorian lobby featured colored marble, bronze, and glass-saucer domes. The world's tallest building in 1908, it was higher than most existing skyscrapers by several hundred feet and was even forty feet taller than the Washington Monument in the nation's capital, which scandalized some people. The tower's crown could be seen from many vantage points in Manhattan, in Brooklyn, and from across the Hudson in New Jersey. The Singer had not even been completed when construction began on another bulky-base-and-slender-tower edifice that exceeded it in height, the 700-foot Metropolitan Life skyscraper at Madison Square, for which Napoleon LeBrun drew up plans shortly before his death. Immediately, there were announcements of plans for still larger structures.

Civic boosters thought the battle of the skyscrapers a great thing for New York. Not everyone agreed. Structures such as A. E. Lefcourt's recent loft building, the Fifth Avenue Association testified to a city commission, "are crowded with their hundreds and thousands of garment workers who swarm down upon the Avenue during the lunch hour . . . and as work ends at the close of the day, thousands of these operators pour out upon the sidewalks within a short space of time, and congest the side streets with a steady stream of humanity" that made women shoppers avoid the retail area. The association wanted the size of loft buildings limited, a position opposed by the makers of garments and the owners of midtown property. Hundreds of hearings were held in schools, lodge halls, and open-air parks around the city to allow concerned citizens to have their say. Advertising campaigns popularized the theme, "Shall We Save New York?" One broadside put all the complaints in a single jawbreaking sentence, saying the city must be saved from "unnatural and unnecessary overcrowding, depopulated sections, from being a city unbeautiful, from high rents, from illy-distributed taxation."

Like most commissions, the panel listened more attentively to experts and the representatives of pressure groups than it did to the man in the street. In this instance, however, *vox populus* had a distinguished champion, architect Flagg. The son of a cleric turned artist, he had also been a speculative builder. To qualify for the Beaux Arts, the bearded and cantankerous Flagg had had to falsify his birthdate. Later, Stanford White kept him out of the American Institute of Architects for twenty years, though Flagg had designed the entire campus of the United States Naval Academy at Annapolis, several other schools, and the Corcoran Gallery in Washington, D.C. From an initial adherence to the neoclassicist impulses of Burnham, Flagg had matured and warmed to the ideas of Louis Sullivan. "How can a building whose height is out of all proportion to the width of the street . . . and which has greed written all over it, be a work of art?" Flagg charged. Light and air were precious aspects of a city's space that must be preserved; his own slender Singer tower did not overly burden the skyline, he said, but unnatural boxes that directly rose to such heights without the upper stories set back would overpower the streets. Builders angrily responded that they were forced to erect the largest structures possible because land costs in Manhattan were so exorbitant that on most sites only a tall building made economic senses. Restricting height would be tantamount to restricting the profit not only of the builders but of the businesses in the new structures — in short, it would infringe on the right to property. But this was not the 1860s, and an echo of Southmayd's appeal on the Astors' behalf could no longer prevail. Reformers were enacting the first national income tax — one the Supreme Court would declare constitutional — and the national mood was to compromise between property rights and the public good.

Fortunately for Flagg's notions on the shape of future skyscrapers, the next building to challenge the heights was the Woolworth tower. Dime-store magnate F. W. Woolworth was a little man, and like many men of short stature an admirer of Napoleon. In his office, he would stand in front of a portrait of the emperor and Josephine in their coronation robes so the comparison could easily be made. His flair for the dramatic was also on display in his mansion at Fifth Avenue and 80th Street, where he would play a huge organ for his guests, looking for all the world like a figment from *The Phantom of the Opera*. To celebrate himself, one thing had been missing: a skyscraper in Manhattan. He wanted something striking, elegantly beautiful, and very tall — akin to an entire city under one roof and his name. His empire of stores, which had revolutionized American marketing, might eventually fade from the scene, but a stone monument to himself would endure for the ages and be a great advertisement for the company. Woolworth was willing to spend a considerable fraction of his fortune to realize this dream. He commissioned Cass Gilbert, an admirer of European palaces and churches, and Gilbert's design was breathtaking — a Gothic cathedral writ large. Its base would be a solid twenty-nine stories in the shape of a U, a base larger than any of the previous generation of skyscrapers; the front part of the U served as the pedestal for another twenty-nine stories, shaped into a tower that was slightly set back once and then a second time before arching to the pinnacled crown that would make it, at 792 feet, the tallest structure in the world. Terra-cotta buttresses that resembled those of Paris's Notre Dame and plenty of gargoyles emphasized the feeling of a cathedral, as did two dozen entranceways cast by the Tiffany Studios in polished steel and gold, and elevator doors that resembled bronze confessionals. Eager to get going, Woolworth had the foundations done before hiring a firm to construct the building itself. Unfortunately, the foundations were executed badly.

Only slightly chastened, Woolworth invited Paul Starrett of Fuller and Jay Horowitz of Thompson-Starrett — separately, of course — to look at the work already done and bid to construct the rest of the building. Despite his association with Burnham, Starrett was not a diplomat. Outraged at the sloppy foundations, he blistered Woolworth's ears with his opinion, in construction-worker language. By contrast, Horowitz had become accustomed to the ways of the wealthy; he rode horses in Central Park in the mornings, and arrived at Woolworth's office in a chauffeured car. His private evaluation of the foundations was as bad as Starrett's, but he deduced that, like Napoleon, Woolworth would admit neither failure nor defeat. To belittle the foundations would label Woolworth a fool, so Horowitz said all could be fixed with the application of money, and won the contract. Woolworth wrote a check on his personal account for the entire cost, $13.5 million.

Translating Gilbert's designs into the world's tallest skyscraper was a complex task. Routes had to be surveyed so that hauling steel to the site would not cave in the roads; special elevators, scaffolds, and hoisting engines had to be machined. The building's water and sewer system would be larger than that of a small town, and its pipes big enough for a horse-drawn carriage to drive through. Its generating plant could provide enough electricity for a city of 50,000. On misty mornings during construction, the upper half of the steel skeleton disappeared in the clouds. When completed, the Woolworth Building was acknowledged as a masterpiece, the greatest expression of height yet raised anywhere. "Imperturbably august . . . it storms the sky," the *New York Times* said. Gilbert wrote that its Gothic style "gave us the possibility of expressing the greatest degree of aspiration . . . the ultimate note of the mass gradually gaining in spirituality the higher it mounts." Horowitz would wander into the cruciform lobby to gaze upward at the gargoyles of himself, Gilbert, and Woolworth that decorated the ceiling. President Woodrow Wilson pushed a button in the White House to first turn on all its lights. The Episcopal bishop of New York called the building "The Cathedral of Commerce" and suggested that the country's fascination with commerce had produced "gratifying benefits" as well as a "succession of [skyscrapers] without precedent or peer" in Manhattan; of these, the Woolworth Building was the queen, acknowledged as such "by those who aspire toward perfection, and by those who use visible things to obtain it."

No sooner had Horowitz finished the Woolworth than architect Ernest Graham asked him to accompany him to the office of General T. Coleman Du Pont to talk about a new project. This meeting was a turning point for builders and big buildings in New York, for its outcome would affect all of Manhattan from that day to this.

Du Pont, of the Delaware clan, was a contemporary of John D. Rockefeller who had used a leaf from the Standard Oil book in helping his cousins take the family chemical firm public in 1902; in 1915 he sold his shares to concentrate on real estate and duck hunting. He began the meeting by asking Horowitz to "take a card, any card" from a pack. Horowitz did, and was next fooled into accepting a match that wouldn't light. Du Pont was addicted to practical jokes: exploding cigars, rubber candy, a cigarette case that when opened released a serpent made of springs.

The third man at the conference, Graham, was Daniel Burnham's official successor. Burnham had recently died of diabetes. In his last years, a biographer suggests, Burnham had become "an artist in businessman's vestments." In this meeting, Graham seemed a businessman in artist's garb. After reeling off numerical projections of the building's income, Graham outlined a plan that would have Du Pont put up nothing but his name, yet emerge with the ownership of the structure to be erected on the site of 120 Broadway, where a fire had recently destroyed a venerable old building that belonged to the Equitable Life Assurance Company.

Horowitz panned the project, saying that the building could not be erected for the sum Graham proposed, nor would it bring in the rents that Graham envisioned; furthermore, he didn't think the public would buy the bonds that Graham would have Equitable sell to finance the building.

"You don't seem too optimistic," the architect scowled.

"You say our setup is not right," the general opined between card tricks. "Perhaps you will tell me what is right."

Horowitz did some calculations and informed Du Pont that rather than putting up nothing but his name, he'd have to provide $10 million to construct the building. Even more important, the proposed skyscraper would have to be substantially enlarged in order to make it profitable. Du Pont had no objections to spending his own money and thought the larger building might be a good idea. He then wondered if a larger building were possible on the site. In answer, Graham did what Burnham himself would probably never have agreed to do: design a structure too large and bulky to be graceful or interesting, but which was big enough to satisfy the financial requirements of the business transaction. Graham's plan called for two huge boxes connected at the base to make a single building that looked like a double stack of corrugated-iron filing cabinets. The new Equitable would not be as tall or graceful as the Woolworth but it would be the largest office building in the world, with an enclosed street for a lobby, flanked by an arcade of shops, restaurants, and services for the 16,000 people on the upper floors. Beautifully wrought entrance arches, extensive wood carvings, bronze castings, and other decorative touches in all the public areas and in the more expensive office suites would make it a lovely building at street level.

The problem was that from across the street, or from any vantage point above street level, Graham's plan for 120 Broadway was a design disaster. It would rise straight up from the edge of the property line to a height of thirty-nine stories, with no setbacks. For all the Woolworth's height, its tapering design produced a "multiple" of less than twenty times the land area in rentable space. But 120 Broadway would be just bulky boxes and yield a multiple of thirty-nine; it would loom over its neighbors, casting nearby streets and smaller buildings into almost perpetual shadow.

Neither investor Du Pont nor contractor Horowitz nor architect Graham voiced any objections, for this was a business deal. Just before construction, the owners of a building that would be affected by the Equitable's bulk came to Horowitz to suggest that Du Pont forgo putting it up and instead make the property into a park. Horowitz laughed, waved his cigar at them, and said that if they were so determined to have a park he'd arrange for the general to sell them the site (at a modest profit) and they could plant it with flowers themselves. The visitors had no such idea, and construction proceeded without further incident. The Equitable at 120 Broadway opened in 1915.

After its opening, however, there was considerable public outrage at its sheer size and light-diminishing bulk. Shortly, the arrogance of 120 Broadway tipped the scales in favor of what city planners and Ernest Flagg had long advocated. The result was passage of New York's — indeed, the country's — first real zoning resolutions. Commercial interests were given plenty of latitude, but both business and residential areas would henceforth be subject to height restrictions. The most severe of these covered Brooklyn and Queens; in effect, the 1916 regulations all but forbade tall office towers in those boroughs, which were thus pushed even further toward becoming bedroom communities. The absence of the same sort of restrictions simultaneously encouraged the building of office towers in Manhattan and discouraged almost completely the construction of residences in downtown and midtown areas zoned for business. This divide between bedroom and workroom districts would continue to deepen for the next three-quarters of the century. From 1916 forward, virtually all of New York's skyscrapers would be built in Manhattan.

Nothing as offensive as 120 Broadway would ever again be designed, but the solution adopted was a compromise. Had Flagg's idea been followed completely, we would see a uniform cornice line, with vistas like those along Parisian boulevards, punctuated here and there by churchlike spires — beautiful, but completely unadaptable to the technology and economic exigencies of later years. Modifying Flagg's basic notion, the zoning code decreed that the height of new buildings must be in mathematical proportion to the width of the streets they faced. Setbacks were required every few stories, so that as skyscrapers rose they would grow slimmer and cast smaller shadows. Since streets and avenues were of varying widths, the exact floor at which setbacks would begin varied accordingly. New skyscrapers also were forbidden to occupy every square inch of their sites; builders had to make structures that took up less space and had smaller multiples than 120 Broadway. The goal was to force new buildings to resemble the elegant Woolworth rather than the crass Equitable. The Singer already belonged to the past.

When it became obvious that some sort of zoning regulations were going to be passed, most building firms shelved their plans, unwilling to begin a structure that might have to be modified radically to conform with the new codes. Construction came to a halt. Ted Starrett, the dynamo of earlier years, fell so idle that he began a series of articles for a building-trades magazine that became a valedictory. Perhaps mindful of the battles among his own clan and their clashes with the outsiders Black and Horowitz, who had taken over what once had been solely Starrett enterprises, he wrote, "They say that each man whom Fate or Providence has marked for a life of responsibility is given to the feeling that his work and life are harder than that of men in other walks of life. . . . I claim that if John D. Rockefeller had tackled the building business instead of the oil business he would have quit early or died of exhaustion long before he reached his goal." A few months later, Starrett was dead at age fifty-two, of what his brother Paul thought were the consequences of exhaustion. By then it was 1917 and the United States had become a combatant in the Great War that had already embroiled England, France, Belgium, Germany, Austro-Hungary, and Russia. When war was declared, the government requisitioned all steel and none was left over for building new skyscrapers.

Chapter Six

Fathers and Sons

IN THE SUMMER of 1918, architect Emery Roth lay in a hospital bed in New York City, his eyes covered with gauze after an operation for glaucoma, uncertain if he would ever see or work again. One eye was already beyond saving. He had had a difficult ten years. Right after the Panic of 1907, many client builders had gone bankrupt or used the panic as an excuse not to pay for the services he had rendered. In 1914, when war was declared in Europe, there was a run on Jewish banks in New York as recent immigrants rushed to withdraw money to help relatives in the Pale; some banks closed, and Roth lost more in commissions due. There was a shortage of building materials, and none at all after the United States entered the fray in 1917. In the hospital Emery's wife, Ella, tried to gloss over the worst of the news from the Great War, then at a low ebb for the Allies. Ella became concerned that the hospital was not sanitary and insisted that Emery return home to Washington Heights, where she was able to save the second eye. While Roth recuperated, seventeen-year-old Julian took a job at a Duesenberg automobile plant in New Jersey, and fifteen-year-old Richard worked four hours a day as a plumber's helper. "It was a far cry from going to Ethical Culture and Fieldston," Julian remembers seventy years later.

After the war ended, and as a consequence of the unfulfilled demand of the war years, there began a boom of great strength and duration. At last, Emery Roth became one of the most prolific architects of high-rise apartment buildings in Manhattan. After returning to complete their education — Richard as an architect, Julian, a businessman — the boys joined the firm that had been proudly renamed Emery Roth & Sons.

Emery moved his offices next door to those of his principal client, Bing & Bing, and acted as in-house architect. During the war, Alexander Bing had been a housing consultant to two government agencies. He dreamed of following the path of the limited-return City and Suburban Homes Company and became the spearhead of the City Housing Corporation, which produced a sprawling complex of one- and two-family homes and apartments in Sunnyside, Queens. Leo Bing split with Alexander in this era because he had a different objective: housing for profit. "That is good architecture," Leo told Roth, "which people are willing to pay for. To erect a building, however well it conforms to the standards of design, that does not produce the maximum of income is, to that degree, poor architecture." Every year, Roth would design a building or two (or sometimes three) for Bing & Bing, now Leo's company, in every district from Greenwich Village to Washington Heights, from simple dwellings to palatial hotels and apartment houses.

In 1920, the state legislature decided to stimulate the creation of badly needed apartments by granting tax exemptions for new housing; New York City followed suit and released such housing construction from real estate taxes for a period of ten years. Also, the state legislature for the first time allowed life insurance companies to invest in housing. In the first year that these new laws came into force, 24,000 residential buildings were begun, nearly three times as many as in the previous year.

That boom enabled the first productions of families who would later come to prominence in the skyscrapering of the city, and who created solid foundations for their empires in this era. The outer boroughs were hospitable to small-time development: you could start from next to nothing and create a building, then use the equity from it to put up others.

Harry Lefrak was one of those outer-borough denizens. Born in the Pale, he traveled in the *Haskalah* movement with his parents to Palestine for a time, and in 1900 arrived in New York at age fifteen with four dollars in his pocket. He shoveled snow, ran errands, and worked as a glazier on the Lower East Side, removing glass from abandoned factory buildings and reselling it. He became a producer of glass, working with the artist Louis Tiffany. Lefrak made enough money to buy a 120-acre farm in the Williamsburg section of Brooklyn, and moved his family to its old Dutch farmhouse. In 1916 he used ten acres of the farm to build small houses along DeKalb Avenue — stores with three rooms in the back and apartments upstairs. He sold these and used the money to build more, then graduated to building dozens of walk-up row houses at a time. Samuel, his only son, remembered the boom days of the 1920s: "After dinner, [my father] would clear the table, and open up blueprints. He'd point and ask, 'What's that? And that?' So when I was eight years old, I could read a blueprint." While Harry Lefrak built up whole blocks of Brooklyn, Queens, and the Lower East Side in the 1920s, Sam attended public schools and, later, Erasmus High. Sam had initially wanted to be a dentist, but his left-handedness would have meant expensive customized equipment; also, he later said, "I began to wonder if I wanted to spend the rest of my life staring into other people's mouths."

In the years just after the Great War, teenager Fred Trump, son of a Swedish immigrant, worked as a "horse's helper," assisting the carts that hauled construction wood up hills in icy weather, before training as a carpenter. Indefatigable and smart, in a year or two Fred had absorbed enough to begin his first one-family home in Queens in 1923. He was just seventeen at the time, so young that his widowed mother had to sign documents and contracts for him. In six years, he'd completed hundreds of modest homes and small developments in Queens; in 1929 he moved up to more-luxurious mock colonial and Tudor homes.

Joseph Rose's youngest son, David, was born in Jerusalem while his family was on an extended visit to his grandparents, who had built several stone houses in the old quarter of the city. On returning to New York, Joseph Rose ended up in the men's-overalls trade. He was known for his wide-ranging reading, and people would ask him about world affairs, not about his business, which suffered because of his other interests. In classic Yiddish terminology, Joseph was a *luftmensch*; "On his deathbed, he was learning Greek," a grandson recalls. Though separated in years, his older and younger sons, Samuel and David, were very close. Sam was a doughboy and a cartoonist for *Stars and Stripes*, the army newspaper. After the end of the Great War, he remained in Europe to study art at the Sorbonne. Something of a *luftmensch* like his father, he nonetheless concluded that he did not have what it took to become a great artist and must find some way to make a living. David attended City College.

Both young men had their father's restless intellect; in those years, it was a question of where and how to put it to work. Sam went into fur tanning with some war buddies; Dave took odd jobs in merchandising but wasn't happy with them. One of the Rose sisters had married a man who was making a fortune in ice cream and who had begun to invest in real estate; the ice-cream man hired Dave to keep an eye on the construction of a couple of buildings for him. Though not trained as an engineer, Dave's mind was well attuned to structural-engineering concepts, and he took night classes in construction. Then, with the conviction of one who has watched others do things inadequately and knows he can do better, Dave told his brother-in-law that he ought to put up the buildings himself rather than just invest in other people's dreams. "Dave offered to personally oversee the construction, and to do it less expensively and with greater quality than you'd get from builders who weren't family," Fred Rose recalls. For the brother-in-law, it was a no-lose proposition.

After a building or two, Dave decided he could do the same thing for himself, if he had financing. He convinced Sam and his partners in the tanning business to back him. Over the next several years Dave Rose erected one or two buildings a year, principally small apartment houses in the Pelham Parkway section of the Bronx, gaining experience and confidence with each new project and involving Sam more and more. Sam still kept the fur business, but the building opportunities were too good to pass up. If you picked the right spot to build, the Roses, Lefraks, and Trumps reasoned, you could hardly go wrong.

The fourth of the nine children of Lewis and Rachel, Sam Rudin left City College in 1918 because his father was ill and he had to take over the ladies'-coat firm in the garment center. His girlfriend, May Cohen, saved enough money from her job to provide the down payment for a modest house in the Throg's Neck section of the Bronx. "Every weekday, Dad would take the Tremont Avenue trolley to the El, then transfer to the train for the ride down to midtown Manhattan," his son Lew remembers; in the early 1920s Sam realized that the transfer point he used every day might be the ideal spot for an apartment house, since people wanted to live near good transportation. After the elder Rudin died, Sam bought a lumber yard near the El and was able to finance the construction of a building that had apartments on the upper floors and shops at street level. When the building's lights went on, Sam Rudin experienced a thrill that surpassed any previous successes in business. He had created a solid structure that soon filled with people about whom he felt positively paternal. He stepped off the El several times a week to visit Westchester Square and make sure everything was going smoothly. Thereafter, Rudin kept one eye on ladies' coats and with the other looked for places to build.

The better opportunities came to those young men who had been through college and who now entered the building-trades–related businesses run by their fathers. These individuals were able to leapfrog the outer-borough stage and get right to building in Manhattan itself.

During their youth, red-haired Percy and Harold Uris would visit their father, Harris, at his ornamental ironwork factory near the East River at 26th Street, or go to sites where Harris's men were working — the Goelets' Ritz-Carlton Hotel, Police Headquarters, the 71st Street Armory, various elevated stations throughout the city — and gawk at the construction. Red hair often connotes hot tempers, but the Uris brothers were seldom riled. Percy, the more cerebral, went to Columbia Business School and received his degree in 1920. Ordinarily, a father wouldn't listen to someone who hadn't yet worked for a living — but educated sons, fathers came to believe in this era, knew things they didn't. Percy Uris convinced Harris to go in a new direction by pointing out that, though the risk was greater in speculative apartments, there was more money to be made building than in contracts for ironwork. Sure enough, after successfully completing their first such speculative apartment houses, they had as much business as they could handle. Harold was at Cornell during these years, studying to be an engineer, then a profession of nuts and bolts. When he graduated, he took the overnight train down from Ithaca and didn't bother going home — he just walked directly into the office at six o'clock one morning and went to work. The eager younger brother was welcomed because he was desperately needed in the management of a growing business.

Similarly, Joseph Ravitch, rival ironmaster to Uris at the turn of the century, took a new direction in 1925 when his son Saul and son-in-law Saul Horowitz came of age. Ravitch had been developing buildings, including some of those Park Avenue apartment houses everyone seemed to want. He incorporated HRH, a separate construction firm that soon branched into property management.

Why did the sons of Ravitch and Uris enter the family businesses when the sons of Anglo-American builders such as Philip Braender or Francis Crawford did not? Upon entering the usual family firm — manufacturing, retailing, accounting, stock brokering, even a trade such as masonry or carpentry — a son would toil for many years in the shadow of the father-founder, possibly for a deliberately low salary. Only upon reaching middle age might the son be allowed to take over the business, which in the interim between his youth and that time would not have grown much larger. A few years later the grandson of the founder would reach working age, and the recently elevated father would then try to impose the same sort of apprenticeship upon him. Knowing this pattern, so many second- and third-generation sons of Americanized families deliberately sought to escape their families' businesses that in the decade of the 1920s small manufacturing and retailing units began to disappear for lack of management continuity.

Immigrant builder families saw the process and requirements of succession differently. For them, taking in a son at an established business provided both a spur and an opportunity for expansion: the business now had to be made large and profitable enough to support two families, but there would be two people, rather than one, to supervise the myriad concerns that came with the territory of speculative building. Just as important, the father could trust that second person implicitly. What if there were more than one son? The Anglo-American tradition of primogeniture forced many younger brothers to stay away from family firms or relegated them to permanent secondary roles. Immigrant speculative-builder families welcomed younger sons. Fathers knew they were excluded from the choices open to others, such as a career in the management of an insurance firm (to give an example of a leading Manhattan industry that employed no Jews in upper-level positions); moreover, the fathers presumed that the entry of these younger sons would provide additional resources for growth.

The pattern was easiest to see in the Tishman family. Father Julius had put up his first tenement on the Lower East Side in 1898. In 1909, eldest son David graduated from New York University law school and joined his father; he had already been working with Julius, off and on, for years. Though David took time out to earn a master's degree in law in 1910, he was clearly a man intent on enhancing a business and thrilled by real estate. Tall and soft-spoken, he seemed patrician even then. His abilities were so evident that in 1912 Julius appointed him vice president of Julius Tishman & Sons; by the end of the Great War, David was firmly in charge, though Julius remained as titular head.

Five Tishman brothers were spread out in age over a fifteen-year span, and the firm eventually absorbed them all. Louis came in soon after David, upon receiving his law degree from Columbia. Louis and David were close friends as well as brothers. Drafted during the Great War, Louis was the only officer of his regiment to survive a series of engagements on the battlefield, during which he was permanently injured by mustard gas; he returned to the firm just after the war. A second set of sons, Paul and Norman, graduated from Ivy League colleges in the early 1920s and came to the firm as well. "Paul was the only real character in the family," his nephew John remembers. "The rest were just businessmen, but Paul was an artist." An engineer, carpenter, and sculptor, Paul delayed his entry into the firm until he had taken postgraduate studies at the Massachusetts Institute of Technology. Julius started him off at the traditional journeyman position — as a timekeeper on construction sites, working up toward superintendent of construction. Norman, more drab and stolid but a better salesman and more at ease dealing with clients, was directed into leasing and management.

Five sons are never equal in talent. David became the undisputed leader, while the four others found things to do — an easy task in a growing company during boom years. If any of the others minded this arrangement, none took action to change it. The usual way of families was to close ranks around problems and to carry laggards, if necessary. Survival of the fittest was for animals; Jewish families wanted all their members to make a living.

As the sons swelled its ranks, Julius Tishman & Sons charged to the forefront of the speculative builders of the era, rapidly constructing apartment houses on the Upper East Side of Manhattan, the first at 125 East 72nd Street. They built smaller edifices on the Upper West Side but concentrated on Park Avenue, erecting seventeen solid, comfortable buildings along Park Avenue and its side streets from the Seventies to the Nineties — more such apartment houses than any other individual or firm. The uniform cornice line of these Park Avenue multimansions was the striking heritage of Ernest Flagg's ideas, embodied in the zoning rule that a building's height must not exceed the width of the adjacent street or avenue.

In the mid-1920s, the Tishmans seemed to be doing everything in real estate, and in every section of Manhattan. In 1927, they bought and sold sites and buildings, some they had constructed and some only purchased, in Greenwich Village, along Park Avenue, in midtown, on the Upper West Side, and on the Upper East Side. In addition, they brokered an apartment house on the Grand Concourse and the Driscott Estate in Scarsdale. Their money did not sit very long. Five days after getting $3.5 million out of a project at 78th and Park, they bought a site at 83rd and Park, for which they paid out three of those millions.

When a financial analyst warned that New York was being overbuilt, Louis Tishman was the designated industry respondent, writing in the *New York Times* that the problem really was "a lack of judgment as to where to build." He decried men who followed "sheepwise some bellwether who has beaten a trail into a section of Manhattan where his perspicacity and ability have enabled him to forecast future requirements." In another article, Louis tried to justify the new, high level of rents in apartment buildings: construction costs, he reported, were twice what they had been at the start of the Great War, four times what they had been in 1902 — and so rents had to be higher than in the good old days. A few months later, the authority was David Tishman, contending in the *Times* that it was not architects who were to blame for colorless modern buildings, but builders who wanted to cut corners; on one of the typical Park Avenue apartment houses, "it would have cost the builder a matter of only $12,000 additional to have produced a building that would have been as desirable architecturally as it is practical and well planned." Contradicting himself a few lines later, David warned that "the owner of a building intended for business should not be compelled to rear a classic temple." Later in the year, David got hot under the collar about individual property owners who stood in the way of progress by refusing to sell — for reasonable prices — when someone wanted to put up a big building. For example, there was an unsightly fish store on Park Avenue between 83rd and 84th, a grocery store in the way of a Tishman assemblage on 87th and Park, and a group of dilapidated buildings preventing progress on another Park Avenue corner. David's solution: "What I have in mind is a commission or authority empowered to intervene when . . . the refusal of an owner to sell or improve creates a status that is of more importance to the city than it is to the individual." Since the city benefited from larger buildings, it ought to insure that small-fry would not unreasonably stand in the way of progress. Tishman's attitude showed how firmly he was enmeshed in establishment ways.

David moved his family from 1060 Park Avenue to a penthouse

duplex at 1095 Park, just above 86th Street, whose rooms became a showcase for the most tasteful and expensive 1920s modern decor available. He may have sounded in his business pronouncements like an Astor or a Goelet, but the Tishman brothers' Ivy League degrees, their ability to handle millions gracefully, and their quiet, polished manners made them more compatible than any of the other immigrant builders with their real models, the elite among earlier generations of American Jews such as the Lehmans and Seligmans, *Yehudim* families heavily involved in stock brokerage.

The city itself was undergoing an upheaval, extending the reach of urbanization through water, sewer, power, telephone, and subway lines. Railways, once elevated, were being submerged beneath the streets. When an elevated spur came down, light and air were revealed where before there had been only constant noise, shadows, and ashes. In 1923, Harris and Percy Uris learned of the imminent dismantling of the Sixth Avenue elevated spur at 57th Street, bought a piece of property on the northwest corner, and put up a "taxpayer," a building just large enough (one or two stories) to bring in sufficient money to cover the annual taxes on the site, so that it wouldn't drain money. Three months later, the spur was torn down and the Urises' property shot up in value even more than they had expected. So manifest was the increase that Uris commissioned Emery Roth (in association with another architect) to design the fifteen-story, 100-suite Buckingham Apartment Hotel for the spot, then pulled down the taxpayer so construction could begin at once. Even Roth was flabbergasted. "Probably no other city than New York would furnish [so conspicuous] an example of such rapid progress in real estate values," he told a Hungarian émigré magazine.

Soon, in addition to his steady work for Leo Bing, Roth was functioning as the main architect for Uris and for Sam Minskoff, another Russian immigrant who had begun as a plumber. What these men liked about Roth was his sense of what was important to a builder. Mies van der Rohe, the great German architect, once told a client that he didn't care what the builder did with the interior of a project they were erecting so long as the builder left him free to work the exterior shape, which van der Rohe viewed as a huge sculpture. Of course, Roth was concerned with the exteriors of his buildings and enamored of fanciful decorations and crowns that would be striking when viewed against the sky, but his specialty was floor plans and interior layouts that maximized the builder's monetary return for the square footage. "I argued and stood up for my theories of layout and design, but adapted them to the requirements and at times to the notions of my clients, and thus established a workable middle course," he later remembered. Among his innovations in this era was enclosing a building's ugly water towers in masonry, with Italianate designs echoing details used on the lower elements of the building. These cost extra money, but Roth convinced builders that they added beauty. "I had a stout ally," he recalled, "that quirk in human nature that takes pride in creating. The most hardened money grubber is not entirely free of it." In time, the masonry-enclosed water tanks became known among his detractors as Roth's Towers, but he took satisfaction from observing that other architects (such as his rival, Rosario Candela, who worked mostly for Italian immigrant builders like the Paternos) were being asked by their clients to make similar towers atop their own buildings.

In 1924, Minskoff commissioned Roth to design a building at the corner of 101st Street and Broadway, and in it Roth included a beautiful though not extraordinarily opulent three-bedroom penthouse apartment for his own family. He acquired a car and a chauffeur, and began dressing in a stylish, almost grand manner that befitted an artist who worked comfortably with businessmen, and which might have delighted Daniel Burnham.

By the standards of the day — being refined with each passing year — Roth's own apartment was less luxurious than many offered by the Bings, Urises, Tishmans, Minskoffs, Paternos, and Campagnas: eleven-room simplexes with three terraces; duplexes and triplexes with dozens of rooms. These were really individual mansions within an apartment-house structure. Each large apartment had its own entrance (the elevator opened directly into the vestibule of the apartment) and many amenities that gave it the feeling of a home — twelve-foot-high ceilings, fireplaces in several rooms, intricate masonry work, built-in wood paneling, multipaned and filigreed windows, and separate accommodations for maids and butlers. Zoning regulations encouraged the creation of many terraces for a building, so that a number of these great apartments had their own gardens. For those who didn't want cooking smells to sully their apartments — a common plaint among the well-to-do — new buildings offered a restaurant on the premises, available to tenants and situated next to a richly appointed lobby suitable for showing off to guests. Uniformed doormen, concierges, mail and message services, and facilities for laundry and cleaning became standard in the new apartment houses. Within a few years, Hollywood's movies took as their definition of American elegance a Manhattan apartment with a living room spacious enough to accommodate a grand piano, and a terrace that overlooked the glittering skyscraper skyline.

The number of wealthy people who could afford such Manhattan apartments was growing rapidly; the residents of the upper-class districts of the island paid more in federal income tax than did all the people in all the states west of the Mississippi River. In the 1920s, New York housed 10 percent of the country's inhabitants and sustained 20 percent of the country's residential construction. Along Park Avenue from just north of Grand Central Station to the low Nineties, new luxury apartments rose steadily; they were unornamented above the third floor, because designers believed that renters preferred the plain style. This stretch of Park Avenue was the wealthiest highway in the world, home to 5,000 families, of which at least 2,000 were millionaires who spent $150,000 a year to live in Manhattan.

A survey found that 80 percent of the speculative builders in the city were Jewish, although Jews made up only 40 percent of the 10,000 builders in the metropolitan area. The immigrants' domination of the field worried some; the new chairman of the board of the United States Realty and Improvement company called the "foreign element . . . a disturbing feature in real estate today." Thirty years earlier, he huffed, "under no circumstances would a foreigner own or operate property," but now "there are probably more foreigners in the real estate field . . . than native-born."

In a curious twist, the prevailing current of anti-Semitism actually proved a boon to the immigrant builders. "Restriction, Convenience, Service," read an advertisement on a Fifth Avenue bus for a modest housing complex in Jackson Heights (Queens), in which Jews were not allowed to rent. The idea of restrictions was challenged in court, but Judge Burt Humphrey ruled that the renting agents did indeed have the right to refuse to allow on the developer's private property any individual or group they wanted to exclude. Along upper Fifth Avenue, the Vanderbilts and other extensive property owners refused to sell to Jewish builders and it was generally understood that Fifth and the lower reaches of Park Avenue were Christian enclaves. (Exceptions proved the rule: the

German-Jewish Schiffs lived on Fifth Avenue, but most of the other *Yehudim* did not.) At the same time, the great residential thorough-fares of the Upper West Side — Central Park West, West End Avenue, and Riverside Drive — came to be thronged with Jews able to afford large, comfortable apartments for themselves and their families. Immigrant builders could take greater risks erecting buildings on such streets. They could apply grandiose architectural touches to their facades and use the finest workmanship because, in offering apartments to Jews, they were assured of a group of upwardly mobile people, restricted from renting elsewhere, who were eager to sign rental agreements for luxury buildings even before construction was complete.

It was an exciting time to be a builder. Nothing could be more American than to tame a plot of land and erect on it a pioneering structure, to take part in what America prided itself on doing best — inventing the future and making it solid. In New York City, the country's financial and commercial capital, no one thought that houses of an earlier era, or even structures from more recent times, ought to be preserved. The inevitable triumph of bigger-and-better-and-newer was considered the main responsibility of a forward-looking society. To tear down the old city and replace it with a better one was tantamount to civic duty.

In the 1890s Mrs. Caroline Astor had been forced to move from Fifth Avenue at 34th Street because of the advent of the Waldorf-Astoria. In the late 1920s that grand hotel was sold and demolished to make way for something new. A few blocks uptown, on the northeast corner of Fifth Avenue and 43rd Street, a Civil War–era Moorish temple capped by twin towers housing the Emanu-El con-gregation was torn down and the site sold to a former immigrant house-painter who was now a builder, Benjamin Winter (class of '82). In partial payment, Winter offered another site he had acquired and razed, Mrs. Astor's now-old mansion at Fifth Avenue and 65th Street. The congregation determined to use it to put up a new temple.

Temple Emanu-El, at Fifth Avenue and 65th Street, was planned to be the largest, most costly, most beautiful temple in the New World. It also would be almost solely the temple of the *Yehudim*, those uptown Jews of German extraction who had long since be-come part of the upper crust in Manhattan, though they still were excluded from a few civic and charitable institutions. Emanu-El was a "reform" congregation whose liturgical practices were attuned to Jews who wished most of all to be Americans; bar mitzvahs were not offered, for they were considered part of a barbaric tradition to be left behind; services were conducted for the most part in English. The rabbi of another reform temple shortly to be absorbed into Emanu-El expressed the prevailing *Yehudim* view on this most sensitive of issues: "Judaism must drop its orientalism, and become truly American in spirit and form. . . . It will not do to offer our prayers in a tongue which only few scholars nowadays can understand. We cannot afford any longer to pray for a return to Jerusalem. It is a blasphemy and lie upon the lips of every American Jew." *Yidn* congregations scattered throughout the Lower East Side offered prayers in Hebrew and were considerably more orthodox in the form and content of their worship. Ghetto-dwelling Jews from the Pale were usually not comfortable in reform congregations, nor German Jews in orthodox ones, but *Yidn* and *Yehudim* were drawing together slowly in other ways.

Years earlier, in the last third of the nineteenth century, with the patrician example of wealthy Christian men before them, the leaders of the *Yehudim* created some general-welfare agencies and institutions. Mayer Lehman of the brokerage firm was known to walk the wards of Mount Sinai Hospital, watching the doctors and nurses as closely as he watched investments entrusted to him; for thirty-five years Jacob Schiff was president of the Montefiore Home for Chronic Invalids, and it was said that he knew all but the most transient patients personally. Similarly, clothing magnate Isidor Straus was involved with the Educational Alliance, and Morris Loeb with the Hebrew Technical Institute. Each autonomous institution attracted a small clique of wealthy donors. *Yidn* charities had a different structure. Starting in the seventeenth century, there had evolved in the Pale the *kehillah*, an autocratic form of government led by an executive body drawn from the wealthy and the learned, whose main charitable concerns were voluntary welfare organizations. The *kehillah* style of organization was reprised in New York in the creation of a loose network of independent welfare agencies and institutions serving the ghetto areas. Beth Israel Hospital was formed so that the *Yidn* need not travel uptown to the *Yehudim*-controlled Mount Sinai, where no Eastern Europeans were employed on the medical staff. The new *Yidn* institutions were roundly criticized by uptowners for duplicating the services of their own agencies, for perpetuating what uptowners saw as the ghetto's self-segregation through insistence on using Yiddish, and for isolating needy Jews from the mainstream of American civilization. Louis Marshall, a corporation lawyer, expressed the prevailing annoyance at proliferating downtown charities:

> A number of men get together. Because a certain person was not admitted into an institution, in five minutes, they decide that a new institution is necessary. They raise a few thousand dollars. Then they decide they will appeal to the public. Who is the public? They go to Mr. Schiff and ask for a contribution; they go to Mr. Lewisohn and ask for a contribution; they go to Mr. Felix Warburg and ask for a contribution. I tell you there are some of us whose backs are being broken under the ever-increasing burden. It is time to call a halt or else the entire charitable system of New York will go bankrupt.

On September 1, 1908, New York's police commissioner, Theodore A. Bingham, published an article in which he stated that 50 percent of all of New York's criminals were Jewish and that the Jewish community itself perpetuated criminal activities. The hesitancy of most uptown Jews to respond instantly to this hyperbolic insult galvanized downtown Jews, who formed an association called the New York Kehillah; a strong link to the uptown Jews was forged when Judah Magnes, rabbi of Temple Emanu-El, became a leader of the new group. Magnes agitated for a federation of all the Jewish charities, already the norm in other American cities, even though this idea was opposed by prominent members of his own organization as too ethnic in nature and inevitably tainted with downtown, pro-Zionist, Orthodox ideas. Magnes convinced Schiff, Warburg, and Cyrus L. Sulzberger, and then even Louis Marshall came around.

The turning point came in 1914, just after war was declared in Europe, and there occurred that run on the ghetto banks that practically bankrupted Emery Roth. The New York State Banking Department closed four banks, stunning 50,000 depositors and immobilizing $11 million in savings. Magnes and Marshall interceded with the banking department and involved the New York Kehillah in the solution to the problem. The difficulties of Europe's Jews during the Great War and the need to succor them further impelled uptown and downtown Jews to cooperation. On January 1, 1917, the Federation for the Support of Jewish Philanthropic Societies was declared in operation, with Warburg as its president. Only three of thirty-eight trustees and four of fifty-four constituent agencies were from the Eastern European groups.

During the ensuing Communist revolution in what had been the Pale, the plight of the Jews remaining there grew dramatically worse — in the Ukraine, called the Flanders of the East after the site of the Great War's bloodiest battleground, 200,000 Jews were killed, 300,000 orphaned, and 700,000 made homeless in 1919–1920. Their misfortune galvanized American Jews to raise $30 million on their behalf.

Earlier in the annals of American philanthropy, the general public was seldom solicited; for any good cause, only a few wealthy donors were approached. The Jews of New York, trying to promote their new federation, decided to eschew private donations and set out to wring the most money from the largest number of people. Federation organized its fundraisers along industry-group lines rather than by neighborhood or social group. Most real estaters knew one another because of the constant deal-making in the industry, so their group of potential donors had particular coherence; because the group and the field itself were fiercely competitive, it also had a culture of mutual challenge that fed into Federation's style of publicly announcing each donor's pledge. To a greater degree than the men of any other industry, real estaters joined the ranks of Federation. David Rose became interested in the Technion Society, Joseph Durst got involved in the Hebrew Free Loan Association, and the various fathers and sons of the Uris, Ravitch, and similar clans interested themselves in Federation's other individual agencies. Julius Tishman was instrumental in the founding of Sydenham Hospital and brought his eldest son into the work; soon David Tishman was president of Sydenham. As the Lehmans had nurtured Mount Sinai Hospital, the Tishmans now took Sydenham under their wing.

Using the *Yehudim* elite as a model had unforeseen consequences. After several fabulous years in the mid-1920s, David Tishman was chafing. The Tishmans controlled assets worth $21.5 million (though most buildings were, of course, mortgaged). They still had to borrow heavily to do business. Construction and completion loans were accepted as necessary, but having to approach a lender for money to tie up a site was the tactic of small-fry, and the Tishmans were no longer a small firm. David became convinced — by people he admired, members of the Lehman Brothers firm — that the answer to his problems was to take Julius Tishman & Sons public. "Dad was sold a bill of goods on a stock offering," his son Bob later recalled. Going public was very much in keeping with the spirit of the times, when many companies were using the stock market as a way to raise cash. The persuasive salesman was either Robert Lehman, who served on several corporate boards with David, or Philip Lehman, the acknowledged genius among the Lehman cousins, the underwriter of many ventures in this era, and a man who consistently helped find financing for the sort of firms other banking and brokerage houses would not touch — textile and clothing manufacturers, for instance. Tishman would have been aware of what Philip Lehman had done for Julius Rosenwald in enabling the expansion of Sears, Roebuck through a public stock offering. The Lehmans were a generation and more ahead of the Tishmans in terms of wealth, financial sophistication, and societal position. Not for a moment could the scion of a *Yidn* family believe that, in this delicate matter of financing a family company, the scion of a *Yehudim* family would lead him astray.

Yet this is precisely what happened. In early 1928, the firm reorganized as Tishman Realty & Construction, Inc., with 400,000 shares of stock, of which 50,000 were offered for sale to outsiders at an opening price of $33; the rest of the shares (and control of the company) were retained by Tishman family members. After the transformation from a privately to a publicly held company, the Tishmans were employees of their firm and not the sole owners. David Tishman became president; Julius, chairman of the board. Very soon after the stock was issued, the Tishmans realized that the decision to go public had been a mistake. The offering had produced only between $1 million and $2 million in working capital — a lot of money for an individual in those days, but not very much for investments in buildings. For example, the Tishmans had to spend $3 million for their building site at 83rd and Park. David reported to stockholders that, in the nine months since the offering, gross rentals were up 62 percent, mostly as a result of reduced vacancies, and that six buildings with a market value of $12 million were under construction. By year's end, the stock was paying $5.41 in dividends for each share. The stock duly went up in price as it was supposed to — a year after being offered at an opening price of $33, it sold at $58.

During this ebullient period, on January 8, 1929, young Norman Tishman exchanged wedding vows with Rita Valentine in the Crystal Room of the Ritz-Carlton Hotel. January 8 was chosen because on that date in 1914 Norman's older brother David had married Ann Valentine, Rita's older sister. At the 1929 wedding, Ann was matron of honor. Receptions followed at 1070 Park, home of the Valentines, and 1095 Park, home of the Julius Tishmans.

An undercurrent of dismay was kept from the wedding guests, but was becoming more apparent to Tishman executives each day. Despite steady growth, the company did not display the sort of bottom line that usually generated a stock price expressed in terms of high multiples of a company's annual sales or profits. Profits were good, but a real estate company's profits are not the benchmark of its health — its cash flow and the worth of the properties it controls are the proper measures, and these are not always reflected in the net income from rentals and sales. That meant the stock could not continue as a highflier for very long. Being public contained another trap: should any Tishman relative who owned stock try to sell any substantial number of shares to outside interests, control of the company could slip out of the family's hands. Therefore, many in the family were unable to realize gains from the company's new configuration. The launching of Tishman Realty & Construction had put the Tishman family into a box from which escape would be difficult.

Chapter Seven

Grand Schemes

IN 1925, a real estate broker took builder Fred F. French to the slaughterhouse district, near the East River on the 42nd Street transverse. French had come a long way since the days when he'd borrowed $500 from a friend and renovated his childhood home in the Bronx. Now he was a well-known builder, distinguished and nearly bald at forty-one. Prospect Hill was filled with dilapidated two- and three-story homes and slaughterhouses whose stench sickened those not inured to it. Other builders, shown the area, had shaken their heads and walked away. It had promise, but was so filled with individual owners and so far away from Park Avenue, where those able to pay high rents currently lived, that it seemed unworkable.

French thought it might be right for his "angels." In 1921 he had conceived what he modestly labeled The French Plan. Prior to that time, investment in real estate had been limited to individuals possessed of great cash reserves and the nerve to risk their money in ventures that might or might not pay off handsomely someday. French wanted to tap the masses of people who had much less money than a Vanderbilt or an Astor but who nevertheless were willing to take some risks with their savings. His investors were like the so-called angels who pooled their money to back Broadway plays, but his owned real property. "Never before, as far as we know," French wrote, "has the man with $100 to invest been given the same terms as the man with $100,000 . . . to participate in the erection and ownership of income producing buildings and obtain their rightful share of the profits." Actually, the $100 investor didn't get as good a deal as the $100,000 man — small investors never do — but the idea of buying a foothold in what had been the province of the very wealthy was attractive. The sale of shares was used to cover the costs of the building beyond a 50 percent mortgage, and French vowed to take no money from the property until he had repaid shareholders their original stake, plus 6 percent a year. After that, he would own the buildings on a fifty-fifty basis with the shareholders.

French had been raised as a Protestant, and among his beliefs — communicated to his phalanx of salesmen (of stock and of buildings) every morning — was that Jesus Christ was the best salesman of all time. French's favorite text for salesmanship was "Knock and it shall be opened unto you" (Matthew VII:7; Luke XI:9), which he interpreted as meaning that the salesman should knock until the door was opened, "and if it isn't opened pretty soon, kick down the door." In his office he hung photographs of Theodore Roosevelt as a big-game hunter, and photos of himself in similar heroic costumes. French's exuberance was camouflage. The only reason for a builder to give up 50 percent of the owner's share of a building was his inability to obtain equity financing from an institutional lender. Sometimes those institutions could be downright unimaginative, leaving a cherished project to languish for lack of money. Builders felt that if they could only bring a project on their own to the point of takeoff — say, when construction was beginning and prospective tenants were already signing up — they could prove to a big lender that their dreams were worth backing.

Thus, with a large stake of investors' money, when he saw the Prospect Hill site, French was emboldened to envision a grand project. For some time he had contemplated creation on a scale not earlier imagined for Manhattan: a city-within-a-city, where he could control the siting of all buildings, the vistas, the flow of traffic. He would transform this riverside district of abattoirs into a city on a hill, an enclave of the middle class within walking distance of the business district near Grand Central Station. It would have a skyscraper hotel, many high residential buildings, a park, a large garage, a generating plant, a swimming pool, and an eighteen-hole golf course. All interior streets of the complex would be closed, or roadways submerged and sidewalks elevated so pedestrians would not be bothered by automobiles and trucks. "The surest way to solve the traffic problem," French wrote, "is to eliminate it."

French put a real estate brokerage firm on a budget and a schedule, and brokers set out to assemble the parcels in great secrecy and haste, fearing that if word leaked out among the owners prices would soar and the project would become economically unfeasible. To talk owners into selling, brokers brought turkeys to families and stayed until the birds were cooked and eaten as Sunday dinners. One owner wanted the broker to find a home for his dog before he'd sign on the dotted line. Another wished to remove the bathtubs before leaving; no one could ever figure out why. Rumors circulated that oil had been struck below a slaughterhouse, that the tract was being assembled by Vanderbilt, by Rockefeller, by Bing & Bing, by the railroad. In thirty-five days, at a cost of $7.5 million, the five-acre assemblage was complete, and French announced that a $100-million complex would rise on the site. To finance construction of this development that would house 10,000 people, he would offer stock to the public "on the French plan."

The offering was well subscribed, and construction began on what French called Tudor City. The name, and the details of the buildings, show an interesting interplay between the builder's vision and the aspirations of those whom he expects to be its renters. The Tudor era in England was long gone, but Americans currently held a great admiration for England because during the Great War, the British had defended civilization before the United States entered the fray. French sought to capture the yearning for a touch of class that had translated into Anglophilia. Tudor City boasted apartment houses named the Windsor, Haddon Hall, Hatfield House, and mock-period details such as heraldic devices above doorways and cornices. Many people signed up to rent in advance of completion. Financial success seemed assured. But French still couldn't find an institution to give a mortgage — not even to absorb half the costs (the usual mortgage was 75 percent of completed value). He had to continue to fund the project from investors' money.

Nonetheless, he went ahead with another, more personal dream, a skyscraper in midtown on Fifth Avenue. He did it partly because he liked the site and the idea of erecting the first big building on Fifth Avenue, and partly because he loved the alliterative possibilities of "The Fred F. French Building, Five-fifty-one Fifth Avenue at Forty-fifth Street." In connection with this edifice, French set the path for future real estate deals in another, less savory way: he was the first builder in modern times to buy political influence to further his projects. Beset by zoning difficulties, French was in danger of not being able to complete his namesake project in time for the fall renting season; should he not open it by then, he might have to carry the unoccupied building for another whole year, at tremendous cost. So he telephoned a former secretary of the New York County Republican Committee and said he was prepared to pay to expedite the decision of the Board of Standards and Appeals, the municipal body responsible for granting zoning variances. For $35,000, of which $25,000 went to a law partner of a former Tammany Hall leader and judge, French was able to get an "interpretation" of the zoning laws funneled to the board, which used it to rationalize a quick decision favorable to him. Later, French estimated that the maneuver saved him more than $150,000.

French was given to symbolism and had a feeling for the occult. The thirty-eight-story skyscraper bore mosaics with secret patterns and hammered-bronze panels on the ceiling and sides of the lobby; more strangely decorated bronze panels adorned the elevator doors and the entrance; the lobby mailbox sported bronze griffins. The French Building exterior was distinctive, with dozens of setbacks (because a pyramid was out of the question) leading up to a sunburst mosaic on its crown. Woven into the multicolored faience decorations near the top of the building was the head of Mercury, messenger of the gods, who was said to be "spreading the message of the French plan."

A more sociological French plan was also taking shape. In 1929, he visited the heart of the Lower East Side, a twenty-five-square-block area between the Manhattan and Brooklyn bridges full of squalid tenements unchanged since the heyday of immigration. Worst was the "Lung Block" bounded by Hamilton, Cherry, Catharine, and Market streets, whose nickname derived from the high density of tuberculosis victims who had lived in its cramped, unsanitary quarters. French envisioned cleaning up New York's hellhole by razing this enormous area and replacing tenements with modern high-rises, affordable by residents. This complex wouldn't have a golf course, as Tudor City did, but it would raise the poor's standard of living. Four dummy corporations began the assemblage. This time, the fear was that if prices rose, French would not be able to charge very low rents for what he styled New Manhattan. Brokers signed covenants constraining them from discussing any details with "man, woman or child, wife, friends, business associates, or even officers and directors of the French companies," except for a small circle of those allowed to share this most grandiose of French's dreams.

*   *   *

Henry Mandel began to build modestly at the same time and in the same manner as French — a two-story building at 96th and Broadway, in 1904. A typical son of an immigrant, stolid and square-built, Mandel started as a bookkeeper in a plumbing company. Moving up, he cultivated two distinguishing traits: a passion for horseback riding and a penchant for political infighting. His grasp of the political dimension was apparent in his first big deal, which involved the most desirable site in mid-Manhattan, a city-owned plot at Pershing Square, along Park Avenue just southeast of Grand Central Station. At an initial auction in 1920, no bidders could be found for the property, because real estate operators believed that a quasi-public charity, the Victory Hall Association, was going to use its mandate to have the state condemn that plot for a memorial to the fallen of the Great War. Mandel found out that wasn't so, and his syndicate offered the municipal agency selling the plot $2.9 million. Others would have paid more, but Mandel's quick action prevailed and enabled him in a single transaction to elevate himself to the ranks of the biggest real estate players in town. On the site, in 1923, he built an ornately detailed, twenty-seven-story skyscraper. In another ingenious transaction, Mandel purchased old trolley-car barns on Fourth Avenue and 32nd Street and convinced the city to extend the designation of Park Avenue several blocks south of 34th Street so that he could name his new building One Park Avenue.

With each new project, Mandel's vision broadened. Whole districts of New York, he said, were ripe for renewal. He recognized "the next great step in the development of Manhattan" as the "transformation of obsolete areas . . . into elevator apartments of the home-garage-and-garden type." For ten patient years he accumulated land along Seventh Avenue between 14th and 23rd streets — half the frontage in this half-mile-long area — on which he planned to create a new, medium-rise, residential district. Despite his political savvy, he couldn't get an entire area's zoning designation changed. Mandel did start two buildings, but nine more sets of blueprints lay gathering dust on the shelves of the city licensing agency.

While waiting, he built several hotels of the small and elegantly serviceable type he himself favored as living quarters: the Lombardy on East 56th, the Tuscany on East 39th, and the Brittany on 10th Street and Broadway, as well as a luxury Park Avenue apartment house that offered thirteen-room duplexes. He was also involved in a modest building at Union Square, and in a dozen others. At times it seemed as if Mandel made a specialty of paying a lot for old buildings, demolishing them, and putting up less distinctive structures. A cry was heard over his razing of the Schermerhorn home on University Place and 12th Street, one of the last remaining gracious nineteenth-century residences of the city's founding families.

As the seminal year of 1929 began, Mandel announced plans to offer ordinary investors a chance to ante up as little as $100 apiece per share, in the manner of the French plan, to raise $10 million for new buildings. He did not say so yet, but he had amassed four city blocks along Ninth and Tenth avenues between 23rd and 24th streets for his own city-within-a-city. London Terrace's fourteen high-rise apartment buildings would rival Tudor City in population density, if not in transplanted suburban ambience.

Demolition of eighty old homes at the London Terrace site began in the spring of 1929, but in June Mandel ran into a holdout who knew how to use publicity. Mrs. Alice T. "Tillie" Harte ran a boarding house on 23rd Street called the Clement Moore, named after the bishop whose classic Christmas rhyme had popularized the modern conception of Santa Claus. She told the newspapers it was the bishop's own house that tradition-wrecker Mandel was seeking to destroy. It wasn't, and the impasse was solved by the application of extra money, but the incident further damaged Mandel's reputation. Construction began. "Live Like a Prince at Popular Prices," the London Terrace advertisements read; "Swim before Dinner."

Real estaters gossiped that success had gone to Mandel's head and led him into marital troubles: Bertha, his wife of many years and the mother of his sons, was objecting to his pursuit of Nola Locke, a younger woman, and might soon sue for divorce. In the community of Russian-immigrant builders, family harmony was highly prized and divorces were almost unknown.

French and Mandel were extremely active skyscraper dreamers during this era, but the most energetic and productive of them all was A. E. Lefcourt. In 1912, Lefcourt had erected the first loft building north of 34th Street on the West Side. During the war years and early 1920s, he divided his time between real estate and his duties as head of a cloak-and-suit-manufacturers' association. He claimed the role of peace negotiator but was really an advocate for the owners, who wanted workers to return to the sweaters' practice of piece work. "The business ruin that weekwork has brought to the industry," he fumed, "only piece work can restore. . . . The slacker, the shirker and the professional leech that has wound his tentacles on the industry, sucking its very life blood . . . will be forced to earn what he produces." His harangues contained the gunpowder of persuasion but the unions refused to be cowed, and the owners eventually agreed to guarantee a week's pay for a week's work. In the manner of all politicians who, when beaten, survive by embracing the winning principle, Lefcourt then took credit for ridding New York of sweatshops by inducing manufacturers to leave old buildings and take up sanitary quarters in his new ones.

On his forty-sixth birthday in 1923, Lefcourt made a big decision. Convinced that all the "needle trades" would eventually relocate to the West Thirties, he wanted to be the one who moved them, and decided to devote all his time to building to make that happen. His dreams were on the scale of French's and Mandel's: all three were acting as city planners, aiming to transform whole sections of the island, not merely to put up a loft or two. Such was the cachet associated in the public's mind with being a builder in those days that broad plans were applauded and even expected of them.

Mortgaging his $10 million in properties to the hilt, Lefcourt bought the major block fronts along Broadway and Eighth avenues from 36th to 39th streets and began to put up $20 million in buildings especially designed for the garment industry, the first one named the Lefcourt Clothing Center. Because of his close ties with the garment industry and his great charm as a salesman, he succeeded in establishing new centers for boys' and men's clothes, millinery, accessories, and women's dresses in his various buildings. F. W. Woolworth, the would-be Napoleon, had put up one building with his own name on it. A. E. Lefcourt wouldn't stop at just one. In the next half a dozen years he expanded beyond the garment center, erecting midtown office buildings and naming them after himself — the Lefcourt Colonial, the Lefcourt Empire, the Lefcourt Madison, the Lefcourt Manhattan, the Lefcourt Marlboro, the Lefcourt National, the Lefcourt Normandie, and the Lefcourt State — skyscrapers of middle size, from fifteen to forty stories high. He formed his own construction company and had enough work to keep it very busy. Shortly, if a plot was sold in Manhattan and mystery surrounded the actual buyer, the first thought in everyone's mind was that it was another deal by A. E.

Lefcourt's eagerness to pay top dollar for the best lots was a trap, and one into which many other builders wandered, although none would then have admitted it. If a particular corner of Broadway or Fifth Avenue was considered hot or particularly desirable, as reflected in its new cost of $2 million (double the previous price of sale), builders would do their sums and find that the figures mandated a $5-million, thirty-six-story skyscraper with close to half a million square feet of rentable space to provide a rate of return that would retroactively justify the plot's inflated purchase price. Lefcourt and a dozen other builders paid too much for such sites and felt themselves forced to put up buildings that were too tall, even though a shorter building might have made more sense in the long run. Lending institutions were avid partners in this recipe for trouble; rather than casting wary eyes on funding new skyscrapers, they allowed builders to construct as grandly as they desired, in the belief that the value of the land and its improvements would continue to rise. Few plots were passed up because they were too dear; rather, if the price was high, that fact alone would often engender a bidding frenzy. Thanks to enthusiastic thinking on the part of builders and lending institutions, in the 1920s skyscraper construction went on as if New York had a never-ending, insatiable requirement for new offices and apartments.

The opening of the Lefcourt Normandie was especially thrilling to A. E., who gushed, "I remember so clearly the days when I stood on this corner selling newspapers, and little did I think that the day would come when I would own such a valuable piece of property." It became an industry joke that Lefcourt would soon run out of sites at which he had once sold newspapers or shined shoes.

When the press of Lefcourt's business kept him from his regular dips in the ocean with the Polar Bears of Long Beach, he managed a midday swim in a regular pool to keep fit. Married for some time, he had a son and a daughter. On the occasion of Alan's bar mitzvah in 1925, Lefcourt announced that he was going to deed the boy the $10-million building he planned to erect at 34th and Madison, a site purchased from the William Waldorf Astor estate. Within months, Alan was dead, victim of an influenza epidemic. Grieving, Lefcourt scrapped his plans for a skyscraper on the site and erected instead a modest eight-story building; over its entrance he placed a head-and-shoulders bust of his son.

Some said that Lefcourt never recovered from this terrible blow.

That seems unlikely, as he soon went forward with many new projects. "I still want more of the thrill of accomplishment," he told a reporter. "If something should happen tomorrow to sweep away every dollar I have in the world, I don't believe I would be frightened. . . . I could rebuild my fortune in half the time it has taken me to make it."

As Lefcourt built, he invariably had to tear down old structures — the Normandie Hotel; the equally ancient Marlborough Hotel; a famous old theater on 39th Street; the old Consolidated Stock Exchange on Broad and Beaver streets; and the first fashionable cooperative apartments ever erected in Manhattan, the "Spanish flats" on Central Park South. He bought from the Rhinelander estate the old family holdings at Washington Square that constituted the beginning of Fifth Avenue, but ran into stiff community opposition to tearing down the dignified old brownstones that still ranged, unbroken, along the Square, and could not build. He also got the blame for pulling down the old Temple Emanu-El on the corner of Fifth Avenue and 43rd Street, but could have pleaded not guilty on that count. In a transaction typical of those frantic years, Ben Winter had sold the site to investor Joseph Durst, who was in the process of demolishing the old temple and planned to put up a thirty-two-story building there when, in 1927, Lefcourt offered him the highest price per foot ever paid for a large parcel of Manhattan real estate, $370. The price demonstrated that the deal involved something more precious to the great builders than money: ego. Lefcourt overpaid for the site because, he said, he had wanted all his life to own a corner on Fifth Avenue. He tore down the rest of the temple and erected the tallest building on Fifth, the forty-story skyscraper at number 521, designed by Shreve, Lamb & Harmon.

While constructing 521, Lefcourt formed a holding company for five of his fifteen buildings, and through Lehman Brothers offered 100,000 shares to the public. In no time at all, the shares were selling for $30 to $40 each; part of the attraction was that the holding company would also participate in future Lefcourt buildings. Then he opened the Lefcourt Normandie Bank and formed a stock-selling brokerage, Normandie National Securities, which specialized in the highest-flying stocks of the day, those of banks (including Lefcourt's own). General Realty & Utilities, which had absorbed Thompson-Starrett and had two Tishmans as directors, bought a lot of Lefcourt stock.

In early 1929, Lefcourt reached what he, his clients, and his competitors considered the pinnacle of success. As had become his custom when one of his new buildings opened, he sat in his office on the top floor of the twenty-three-story Lefcourt Marlborough at 1351 Broadway and accepted the congratulations of delegations from various civic and fraternal organizations — even a group of garment workers, who now accepted him for having ended the sweatshops. From his office, Lefcourt pointed out to visitors every one of his twenty-four buildings, their distinctive crowns peeking up above most of the other structures in Manhattan. They were said to be worth $100 million, thus placing him among the largest landlords in the city and squarely in the ranks of its wealthiest men. Surrounding his desk were framed tributes from civic groups. On his desk was that day's editorial in the *New York Times* characterizing him as "The east side bootblack and newsboy, who as a man . . . finds himself the head of a great banking institution and the master of many skyscrapers." Pausing during a meeting with a delegation, he took phone calls from politicians in several states (he was also currently erecting the tallest building in New Jersey). As these visitors, clippings, plaques, and phone calls attested, Lefcourt was not only enriching himself, but also enriching the community.

An expanding ego is never truly gratified. Lefcourt bought an old two-story taxpayer on the corner of 49th Street and Broadway, and in October 1929 announced for that site the tallest building in the world, at least fifty feet taller than the thousand feet of the recently announced Empire State Building. Attaining the height championship was written into Lefcourt's contract with his major tenant. "New York's Mount Everest," the papers called his attempt, never doubting that Lefcourt could pull off this daring feat of construction and noting that, as every schoolchild in the city was taught, any hill exceeding 1,000 feet earned the right to be called a mountain.

Mandel, Lefcourt, and many other immigrant builders of the era found support for their dreams in what had become a phenomenon in banking, known as the Bank of the United States. It had been opened by Russian immigrant Joseph Marcus on Orchard and Delancey in 1907, with a picture of the U.S. Capitol and other props around the premises to induce customers to think of it as a government depository. By 1923 the bank's assets had jumped to $45 million and Joseph Marcus had all but given way to his son Bernard

Marcus, and Saul Singer, formerly president of a garment-manu-
facturers' association and the chief promoter of a cooperative venture, the Garment Center Capitol Building. While the elder Marcus
had been a legitimate banker, Bernie Marcus and Saul Singer were
pyramiders, creating an empire from a base of the only bank that
really served Jewish New Yorkers. Bank of U.S. had half a dozen
offices, including one in the garment center, and also was heavily
involved with many of the *Yidn* builders, contractors, and real estate
investors. Marcus and Singer brought in as fellow directors Irwin
Chanin, David Tishman, and Joseph Durst, all of whom took seats
on the board's real estate committee. Each had loans outstanding
from the bank, as did Lefcourt, Mandel, and a number of other
players.

Joseph Durst, the man who sold the former Temple Emanu-El
plot to Lefcourt, made his first real estate investment in 1915, using
the money he gained when a partner bought his interest in a children's clothing firm. Shortly, he transferred his expertise to a position as executive vice president of Capitol National Bank, which
made garment-center loans. Garment firms and their suppliers were
cash rich at some times of the year and cash poor at others. Capitol
National offered loans to regularize their income. It also made
construction loans to cooperative alliances in the garment trades
and to independent builders erecting lofts and offices in midtown.
For the immigrant builders, Seventh Avenue was as enticing a
boulevard as the residential West End Avenue, and for the same
reason — lowered risk because so many Jews needed space near
their brethren. In the 1920s density in the blocks west of Fifth
Avenue from the Twenties to the Forties grew from 55 firms per
block to 706. In 1927, Capitol National was sold to a bigger bank,
Manufacturers Trust, and Durst walked away with enough money
to devote himself full time to real estate investments. It was also
at this time that he accepted a post as a director of Bank of U.S.

In the fall of 1927 Marcus and Singer, not content with owning
a very profitable bank, formed a securities affiliate, the City Financial Corporation (CFC) that could buy and sell stocks. CFC's
first capital offering was greatly oversubscribed, a display of the
confidence depositors and investors had in the bank. In December,
Marcus and Singer borrowed money from their bank to speculate
in CFC stock. Similar pools were manipulating many issues traded
on the New York exchanges; the practice was not quite illegal. The

pool pushed CFC stock so high that Marcus and Singer were able to take over the Central Mercantile Bank through an exchange of stock, bringing Bank of U.S. assets to $60 million and sending CFC's per-share price through the roof.

With proceeds from these transactions, Marcus and Singer established twenty dummy corporations that made highly questionable loans to builders. Morris White, the builder of the Fifth Avenue Hotel at Ninth Street and the White Hotel, owed the bank $540,000 and could not pay the interest of $10,017; he was allowed to borrow an additional $1,356,270, unsecured by any collateral, and then to add the interest due on the earlier loan to the principal he had to repay. Abe Adelson, creator of Two Park Avenue and of the Film Center on Ninth Avenue at 44th Street, owed $250,000; he was given a second loan of $400,000, which he used to pay off the first one. His credit reaffirmed, Adelson then was able to borrow an additional $500,000.

Such big loans had to be approved by the board of directors during regular monthly meetings. The setting was the elegant conference suite of the bank's new offices at 44th Street and Fifth Avenue, nestled between French's edifice at 45th and Lefcourt's at 43rd. This was the site of the old Delmonico's restaurant, the center of society in the 1890s; recently, Jacob Ruppert, the brewer, had spared no money on the details of the building. He hadn't had to be chintzy, because Bank of U.S. had thoughtfully loaned him enough money to construct the surroundings for what would be their executive offices. Monthly directors' meetings were called for the end of the business day, when many of the directors could be assumed to be tired. Marcus and Singer ran these sessions in a deliberately chaotic manner aimed at depriving the directors of any incentive to learn the details of what was happening. Directors were arrayed around a large conference table in a way that prevented the formation of groups that might question the proceedings. The late-afternoon sun reflected off the table's long, polished surface, obscuring documents that lay on it. The large second-floor windows that allowed the directors to overlook busy Fifth Avenue were left open to bring in the considerable traffic noise. Many big loans were made to directors themselves, and this promoted laxity. When loans such as White's or Adelson's came up, they were either lumped with other expenditures to disguise them, or directors were told that bank officials had already agreed to them and were urged to rubber-stamp their approval. Marcus and Singer even hired a particularly fast-talking man to read the minutes at a rate of more than 300 words per minute.

In January 1929, Singer and Marcus paid $19 million to buy an Upper West Side bank whose own accounting showed it was worth only $6.4 million. In May 1929 they made a similar deal for the Municipal Bank and Trust Company of Brooklyn, another predominantly Jewish enterprise with its own securities affiliate, Municipal Financial Corporation. Many directors of Bank of U.S. were shortly awarded shares of stock as thanks for their part in the two-bank deal. Joseph Durst's no-cost shares were equivalent to a gift of $24,000; Irwin Chanin's were worth the same amount.

That summer Marcus and Singer went one step further and offered the bank's 440,000 depositors an opportunity to buy shares of the bank's stock — for a limited time only, in limited quantities, for the bargain-basement price of precisely $198. The directors were not consulted about the sale. Buyers were told that if the shares went down in value within the year, the bank would repurchase them. The offering was a great success and the price of the bank's stock went up, so everyone was happy.

By acquisitions and as a consequence of the run up in stock prices, in mid-1929 Bank of U.S. had grown to fifty-seven branches, with deposits of $220 million and resources of $314 million — in terms of depositors served, the largest bank in the country. Even more important for our story, it had become a crucial financial resource for big real estate. What the builders didn't know (but Singer and Marcus did) was that their institution was in trouble. Marcus pleaded with state examiners not to tell the public that $70 million of the bank's money was tied up in real estate; if depositors knew, he said, there would be a run on the bank. He promised to seek more financing, and the examiners said nothing publicly.

In the fall of 1929, Irwin Chanin and his architectural associate Jacques Delamarre were in the midst of overseeing the installation of the steel superstructure of the Majestic Apartments on 72nd Street at Central Park West. Some of Chanin's loans on the project came from Bank of U.S. — which was also backing nearby rival apartments under construction by Joseph Ravitch. Unlike Chanin, Ravitch was not a director, but the relationship of Ravitch's firm with the bank was so close and financially intertwined that newspaper reports mistakenly assumed that the HRH companies (one for construction, the other for management) were subsidiaries of the bank. Great excitement surrounded HRH's two large projects, dubbed the Beresford and the San Remo, both designed by Emery Roth to replace old hotels along Central Park West. So great was the promise that Marcus and Singer thought about issuing bonds on these properties, an action that might assuage the New York State bank examiners.

During the decade, Emery Roth had been steadily perfecting his craft in commissions for such apartment buildings as One University Place (Uris) and 1125 Park Avenue; such fine hotels as the Dorset, the Drake, and the Alden (all Bing & Bing); and hotels for other developers such as the Warwick, the Beverly, the Oliver Cromwell, and the great Ritz Tower Hotel on 57th Street and Park Avenue. Despite the degree to which he was responsible for creating the Manhattan skyline, when he applied for membership in the American Institute of Architects he (like Ernest Flagg) had been initially rejected. His lack of formal training, his Jewish religion, and his willingness to cut rates for speculative builders were all cited as reasons for the denial. Only a persuasive appeal by Thomas Hastings, who had worked with Roth on the Warwick, obtained his AIA membership. That battle won, and at the apex of his artistic powers, Roth designed for HRH the striking facades and spacious appointments of the Beresford (Central Park West between 81st and 82nd streets) and the San Remo (Central Park West between 74th and 75th streets).

The $5-million Beresford was the largest apartment building in the world, the equivalent of a square city block in size and resembling from afar a medieval fortress, romantic and almost over-powering. Facing the Museum of Natural History — another castle — across 81st Street and Central Park to the east, Roth's most characteristic building commanded spectacular views of the Manhattan skyline. Its three entrances and three separate lobbies served what were actually three sets of apartments; setbacks at the tenth, fourteenth, sixteenth, and eighteenth floors created dozens of terraces; the whole was crowned by three baroque, hexagonal towers with pyramidal roofs and green copper lanterns. Brass elevator doors in the lobbies were decorated with the Latin motto *Fronta Nulla Fides*, "place no trust in appearances." Contradicting this warning were the surrounding spectacular public spaces: dragons and bears on the doors; walls and floors covered with more varieties of marble (beige, green, oxblood, terrazzo squares, chevron patterns, mosaics) and more of it, than most vaulted banks; lobby windows of art glass depicting medieval scenes. Upstairs were 172 apartments, many designed to the specifications of their tenants — several sixteen-room duplexes, a dozen of ten rooms, and one eight-room gem that took up one tower and three levels below it. All had the high ceilings, generous entrance hallways, marble fireplaces, ceramic tile walls and floor for the kitchens and baths, clever pantries, room-sized clothes closets, and extra quarters for maids and butlers that had come to be the measure of luxury.

The Beresford, fully rented from the day of its opening, encouraged in late 1929 the beginning of construction on the $4-million San Remo. Though a little more modern in appearance than the Beresford, the San Remo, with 122 apartments, would match its sumptuousness, with marble lobbies, ornate details, and an inner courtyard. The San Remo's main distinction was dual, separated towers rising for ten floors above the seventeenth floor and containing apartments whose windows on four sides would make them unrivalled in providing tenants with light and air. They would be the ultimate in Manhattan apartments. Above them, Roth placed near-replicas of the Choragic Monument of Lysicrates, the fourth-century B.C. Athenian treasure he had re-created when he had worked for Burnham on the Columbian Exposition nearly forty years earlier.

From the thousands of people made newly wealthy by the economic crescendo there seemed to be a thundering demand for such opulent, palatial apartments. These conditions, the artistry of the architect, the experience of the builder, and the financial muscle of Bank of U.S. combined to produce two of the most splendid apartment buildings of an era filled with many competing splendors. The Beresford and San Remo were the greatest of their time — and, because of the economic plunge the country was shortly to take, they were also the last of their line.

In the fall of 1929 the line between dream and reality in regard to business skyscrapers was far from clear. Many men had big plans and were determined to win the height race. Lefcourt was but one of them; newspapers liked to point out that he and his major rivals — John J. Raskob and former governor Al Smith, for example, or Henry L. Doherty — had all been raised poor on the Lower East Side, and thought it wonderful that they should now be competing for the championship of the world.

That same season, the only thing certain about the Raskob-Smith

Empire State Building was that 700 workers from Paul and Bill Starrett's firm were tearing down the Waldorf-Astoria Hotel that occupied the site. The Shreve, Lamb & Harmon plans went a step beyond Lefcourt's National and called for many more floors. A contemporary study warned that the plans might also be uneconomic; it said that economies of scale mandated an ideal size of about sixty stories and that buildings higher than that might devote too much floor space to elevator shafts and suffer a net loss of valuable rental area. The Empire State was designed to have more than eighty stories.

Other builders also disregarded the supposed limit imposed by economies of scale. Paul Starrett's employees were demolishing and clearing the site of the Bank of Manhattan Trust Building to rise at 40 Wall Street; Doherty was in the midst of plans for 60 Wall Street; automobile magnate Walter Chrysler had already started work on his 42nd Street skyscraper. Raymond Hood announced plans for a 150-story building. "The formulas that the present building laws allow to use for steel would enable you to build a tower 7,000 feet high. The elevator companies are ready," Hood explained.

The designs for all these megaliths had been waiting for expression in steel since 1922, when Hood and John Mead Howells had won an important competition sponsored by the *Chicago Tribune* for a design of their new office tower. They took the prize with a plan reminiscent of the Woolworth Building, though more bulky. But great excitement attended some of the runner-up entries in that competition. Eliel Saarinen's idea for a sleek, sculpted building with a set-back, central tower was praised by Louis Sullivan from his retirement. Along with other European entries, such as that of the Bauhaus's Walter Gropius, the Saarinen idea provided American architects and builders with possibilities for skyscrapers that did not have to repeat the Gothic extravagance of the Woolworth Building. Of nearly equal influence to the *Tribune* competition entries were renderings by artist Hugh Ferriss (in association with architect Harvey Wiley Corbett) made to demonstrate the types of "massing" of towers and proportions mandated and encouraged by the new zoning laws; these brooding, monolithic sketches resonated with echoes of the paintings of the Cubists and Futurists, and with the sets designed for Fritz Lang's nightmarish film, *Metropolis*. The New York Telephone Building on Barclay and Vesey streets (1926) seemed a monolith out of Ferriss's dark vision.

A third influence was the 1925 Paris Exposition Internationale des Arts Decoratifs et Industriels Modernes, which spawned the Art Deco style, seen at its best in Two Park Avenue, commissioned by former milliner Abe Adelson and designed by Ely Jacques Kahn with jazzy leitmotifs, zigzag and geometric patterns done in pastel colors to festoon the outside walls and the lobby. The *New Yorker* critic Lewis Mumford liked Two Park and Barclay-Vesey, expressions of modernity that were superior to most of the other modern skyscrapers, which, he complained, had been "born old." He much preferred "the unbroken planes of the Barclay-Vesey Building" to the "ornamental tricks" of previous classics such as the Woolworth tower. Skyscrapers were a modern form and ought to look modern, rather than like some oversize version of an outdated palace or church.

The first of the great cluster of skyscrapers built at the end of the 1920s opened in 1929, diagonally across from Grand Central Station and taking up half the block along Lexington Avenue, 42nd, and 41st streets. At the opening ceremonies of the 680-foot-tall Chanin Building, next to a model of the new edifice, Irwin and Henry Chanin posed holding a model of their first structure, a small two-story frame home in Bensonhurst. Irwin's dream, as befitted the man who had designed Broadway theaters and hotels, was that of a theater for business. The Chanin Building combined height, drama, and utility. Ninety feet lower than the Woolworth tower, its fifty-six stories boasted more commercial floor space and were encased in a design (by Irwin Chanin and Sloan & Robertson) that married Saarinen's ideas to the sort of striking, patterned terra-cotta decorations of the French and Lefcourt skyscrapers a few blocks away on Fifth Avenue, and of Two Park Avenue. As the tallest skyscraper north of Wall Street, the Chanin Building attracted a lot of attention. Casual visitors were mesmerized by the "footlights" — the intricate detail that ran about the base of the building, just at eye level — or were fascinated by the "orchestra pit," a bronze-dominated lobby. Irwin's headquarters, on an upper floor, contained a private bath of etched glass with geometric patterns that he delighted in showing off. The ground level was used to bring in the "audience": it included a bus station. There was even a theater-within-the-theater on one of the high floors. His creation was as modern as Chanin himself and a reflection of his belief in the style and substance of the Jazz Age, inscribed with bold, bronze letters on the facade that said: "New York: City of Opportunity."

As the inevitable crash approached, in October 1929, the superstructure of the Chrysler Building was mounting higher daily on the diagonally opposite corner of 42nd Street and Lexington Avenue from the Chanin skyscraper. The Chrysler, in turn, was in direct height competition with 40 Wall Street, many miles downtown; on a clear day, workmen on the uppermost platforms of both buildings could see one another, even though the two skyscrapers were four miles apart. When the Chrysler Building was announced as going for 925 feet, the builders of 40 Wall Street made their plans to go up to 927 feet. The architects of the two buildings were former partners and bitter rivals; Chrysler's William Van Alen had a surprise for 40 Wall Street's H. Craig Severance and was waiting for the moment to spring it. The surprise was an extension of the tower, assembled inside the Chrysler, which when affixed to the spire made the Chrysler the height champion of the world. We now consider it the most beautiful of skyscrapers; then, it was thought to be only the most eclectic, with its upper story "hubcap" design and triangular windows, gargoyles that resembled 1929-model hood ornaments, lobby of red African marble, and elevator cabs that each boasted a differently patterned wood inlay.

The Chrysler was soon eclipsed by the 1,250-foot Empire State Building. Breaking the thousand-foot mark was the construction equivalent of breaking the sound barrier, and produced as many gasps of astonishment and warnings of impending apocalypse. From a five-floor base, the tower rose steadily with several setbacks to the level where most other surrounding buildings of the time stopped, and then pushed upward in straight, unbroken lines for fifty more stories until a final series of setbacks and a circular tower emboldened the crown. Having striven mightily to make the tower fit within the old and newly modified zoning laws, William Lamb of Shreve, Lamb & Harmon also managed to make the Empire State Building a startling exhibition of grace wedded to great size. Bill Starrett was in charge of its actual construction and considered the Empire State the culmination of his and all of the Starrett brothers' careers. Within the next two years, Bill and Ralph died, victims of overwork as Ted had been. Paul's nemesis Harry Black died, too, by his own hand after reverses suffered in the stock market crash, and Louis Jay Horowitz retired, so that all the players in the battle of Thompson-Starrett versus the Fuller Company in the construction of the skyscrapers of the 1920s were now gone.

It was fitting that the Empire State Building was the Starrett brothers' last effort, since it supplanted the old Flatiron Building, which the brothers had helped construct in an earlier era, as the symbol of New York City. The Empire State was the largest, the tallest, had used the most concrete and steel — was the utmost in any category one chose to name and, therefore, the perfect icon of what both residents and visitors believed to be the spirit of Manhattan. But by the time it was completed and ready for business, in 1931, the country had been plunged into depression. New York's business was already in the grip of paralysis; much of the magnificent structure could not be rented, and the building was transformed into a symbol of another kind, as it came to be derisively nicknamed the Empty State Building.

Even the devastation of the economy could not keep hordes of visitors from making a pilgrimage to this most grand expression of height. They rode the superfast elevators to the top and focused its telescopes. It was not the sight of distant horizons that enthralled, but the "canyons of steel," a phrase just entering common usage. Millions gaped from the observation tower at the Chrysler and Chanin towers, along 42nd Street and west to Fifth Avenue where the sentinels of French, Mandel, and Lefcourt stood guard. Even visitors knew or learned these names and something about their great builders, men universally admired for moving America in a new direction. Many exclaimed, in awestruck terms, that you had to be up in the clouds with these skyscrapers to comprehend their striking beauty and magnificence. Further uptown, the telescope brought into view the castle-like apartment houses of Central Park West, Roth's Beresford and San Remo, and Chanin's Majestic Apartments. Everyone knew these names, too, along with those of the other targets of the telescope, the Flatiron, the Woolworth, the Singer, and other towers of what now seemed an earlier age. How old-fashioned these cathedrals seemed now, and how swiftly they were being upstaged by 40 Wall and 60 Wall and other new downtown behemoths.

When the building boom of the 1920s was done, New York was defined fully by its skyscrapers. There were more of them in Manhattan than anywhere else in the world — the vast majority of all that had ever been built — and 216 of them were between 25 and 102 stories tall. Manhattan was a tall building, a giant arrow of business and modernity forever aimed at the sky.

Chapter Eight

Metropolitan Square

IN HIS YOUTH, before the turn of the century, John D. Rockefeller, Jr., could watch the sun set over the Hudson River from the bedroom of his father's house at 2 West 54th Street, just off Fifth Avenue. In the mid-1920s, the Rockefeller clan still lived along the south side of West 54th — the elderly founder at 2, Junior (now in his fifties) at 10. Junior's art collection, including seventeen fabulous medieval tapestries, had grown so large that he had taken the whole of number 12 to house it. But he could no longer see sunsets over the Hudson, as elevated trains along Sixth Avenue blocked such views, and the area had become considerably less exclusive. This bothered Rockefeller, a square jawed, ascetic-looking man with long hands and wire-thin eyeglasses. When plans were announced to build two hotels on the block, he became alarmed. Emery Roth, coarchitect of both the Warwick and the Dorset, remembered that Rockefeller "fought so hard and spent so much money to preserve against both business invasion and apartment houses" on his block. But the hotels went up, and Rockefeller considered moving the family elsewhere.

Rockefeller had been fascinated by building projects all his life. Currently he was helping to restore colonial Williamsburg, developing hundreds of townhouses on his father's old estate outside Cleveland, and starting on the Cloisters, a medieval castle on the north end of Manhattan. He was also the major force behind construction of Riverside Church, a Gothic-inspired cathedral in Morningside Heights whose twenty-four stories contained office space for many ecclesiastical and social welfare organizations. Rockefeller's lifelong interest in social uplift was also translating into construction of the Paul Laurance Dunbar Houses in mid-Harlem.

These took the City and Suburban Homes model a step further: the apartments were to be sold as cooperatives to provide solid homes to a thousand families.

For all these projects, Rockefeller was far more than a signer of checks. He was happiest, aides said, when knee-deep in blueprints. He carried in his back pocket and frequently used a four-foot-long folding ruler. At a banquet dinner, he leaned over and whispered to a prominent builder, "You know, I envy you. Yes, I envy you. You have built great monuments to leave behind you." Considering Rockefeller's own substantial accomplishments in building, the extreme of modesty encapsulated in this statement must also sum up one of the world's largest inferiority complexes, the consequence of a lifetime spent struggling to emerge from the shadow of his father. The Founder was nearly ninety, still hale and vigorous; through his efforts the family's worth had risen to $11 billion in an era when there were no other American billionaires.

So wealthy were the Rockefellers that they were virtually in a social class by themselves; Junior had few friends among the Vanderbilts, Morgans, Goelets, or Astors. Perhaps that was why, when the Metropolitan Opera project — with a board composed of members of those families — was first broached to him, Junior thought he might be being played for a sucker.

The project (if not the approach to Rockefeller) was the idea of *Yehudim* financier Otto Kahn, who loved opera and had chosen to bestow his ardor and largesse on the Metropolitan. The opera's site at 39th Street and Broadway had become too cramped, and too much in the middle of the booming garment center for some of its patrons. Kahn's idea was to build the Met a home on a new site that would also include commercial space, the rent from which would help offset the deficits he and other wealthy patrons were being asked to defray. In February 1927 Kahn bought a large plot between Eighth and Ninth avenues on 57th Street, two blocks west of the other musical center, Carnegie Hall, and commissioned Benjamin Wistar Morris to design a twelve-story office and studio building around the opera. The plan was beautiful, dynamic, even visionary, but it ran into opposition from Goelet and Vanderbilt, who didn't consider 57th Street a proper surround for their cultural outings. Wistar tried again with a design for another site Kahn bought, on 63rd and Broadway. Again, no approval. Then a real estate agent for Columbia University suggested the opera might sit in what the school called its Upper Estate, between 48th and 51st streets and Fifth and Sixth avenues. That appealed to Kahn. But the Upper Estate was honeycombed with 200 leases, subleases, and complicated rights transfers. Settling them all and buying them out would be a very expensive proposition. That meant even more emphasis on the setting for the jewel, the business buildings that would surround the opera.

The Upper Estate had been established in one of those gifts of land from government to private charitable institutions made in New York before the Civil War. As with many other land grants, Columbia's had been conveyed along with a condition, in this case that the school move its operations to the site. Such a move was never made; its only remaining legacy was the orientation of St. Patrick's Cathedral, placed so that it would face onto what had been expected to be gardens gracing the campus.

The original approach to Rockefeller was a request that he join Kahn and other patrons of the Metropolitan Opera, who would together lease the Upper Estate, donate part of it for a public square, and re-lease the rest to the opera for its theater and associated money-making ventures. "The thought is," the family's public relations man Ivy Lee wrote to Rockefeller, "to make the square and the immediate surroundings the most valuable shopping district in the world." That struck a chord with Rockefeller. During one hectic week in 1928, he said no to Otto Kahn's proposal and made a private deal with Columbia. He may have had in mind a great slum clearance; the area, only a few blocks from his home, was full of fleabag hotels, pawnshops, and speakeasies. Or Rockefeller may have been trying to insure that he'd have the upper hand in contending with the opera's board. Or visions of profit may have danced in his head. Making money had been his father's job, and Junior was supposed to be a philanthropist. But this desirable section of mid-Manhattan presented him with an opportunity to profit in a way his father had never done. Metropolitan Square would be his project; he alone would take the risk and reap the glory.

On September 6, 1928, Rockefeller and Columbia signed a document a foot thick conveying to him power over the property. Columbia insisted that Rockefeller be personally liable for the payment of $3.3 million per year for the next twenty-four years. Plans were shown to the public for what was now to be called Metropolitan Square: a new, wide boulevard from Pennsylvania Station to the opera's new home; the tearing down of the Sixth Avenue El and submerging of a train line that would have a stop at the square;

sunken shopping plazas; huge underground garages; floating sky-walks; great public gardens.

This was all cast into limbo because the opera decided to be dilatory. Maybe they'd remain in their own house until a better location came up. Maybe they'd require more of a percentage of income from the development, as they were the jewel that would attract the crowds to the setting. Maybe Rockefeller should put up half the funding for construction of the building and donate the site, or agree to underwrite the whole project and obligate himself to bankroll the opera from now until the millennium.

An aide recommended to Rockefeller that he develop the square by himself, and to hell with the opera. Rockefeller wanted to compromise — acting as a mediator was one of his dubious pleasures — but the price of keeping the jewel in the setting seemed to be rising as quickly as the 1929 stock market, with the Metropolitan continually asking for more concessions. Two dozen large commercial firms interested in the project all wanted to know if the opera was in or out, and, the aide wrote Junior, "I think it's outrageous that the Opera should be playing us . . . and making us wait on their convenience."

Then came the Crash of 1929. Billions disappeared from the valuation of the country's common stocks in the space of a few days. Ivy Lee persuaded Rockefeller that his ninety-year-old father ought to make a statement to reassure the public about the nation's economy. "Believing that the fundamental conditions of the country are sound, my son and I have been purchasing sound common stocks for some days," announced the elder Rockefeller. The best rejoinder came from comedian Eddie Cantor: "Sure, who else had any money left?" The Rockefellers' losses were counted in the hundreds of millions, but because of their vast reserves it did not make much of a dent in their projects, and none at all in their lifestyle.

The Metropolitan Opera knew a debacle when it saw one, however, and viewed the crash as prelude to a drying-up of its benefactors' charitable impulses. A month after the crash, the opera's board told Rockefeller that the development plans for Metropolitan Square lacked clarity and the assurances that it would be fail-safe (meaning that the Rockefellers would foot the bill if others could no longer do so), and that the opera would stay in its current building. Rockefeller received the opera's note and the same day publicly declared that the opera was out of the project;

from then on, and crash or no crash, the square would be solely a Rockefeller venture.

Otto Kahn's 57th Street purchase lay fallow. An enormously rich man himself, Kahn was not interested in real estate for its own sake and had bought the plot just for the Met. When the opera announced its plans to stay put for a while, an opportunity arose, and someone took advantage of it. One day in early 1930, Kahn was asked by a middle-rank employee of his firm (Kuhn, Loeb) to see a relative, a young real estate broker who might have an interesting proposition for Kahn. His name was William Zeckendorf.

Back in 1925 the large, ruddy-complexioned Zeckendorf, who liked whist, late-night parties with cronies, and large cigars, had entered the real estate business of his uncle, Sam Borchard, who had just purchased an undistinguished building at 32 Broadway. Even in Wall Street's heyday, 32 Broadway was only half occupied, but while Borchard was away in Europe on vacation, through the application of shoe leather and charm, Zeckendorf filled it with tenants. He was then an undergraduate at New York University and so excited at renting out the building that he left school to continue in real estate. When Borchard returned home he offered Zeckendorf only a fifteen-dollar-a-week raise rather than a substantial fraction of the $25,000 commission an outside broker would have charged for filling the building. "I told Sam what he could do with his forty dollars a week," Zeckendorf later recalled, and he went to work for Leonard Gans, the man who had just masterminded the site acquisition for French's Tudor City. Zeckendorf admired people like French, Mandel, and Lefcourt whose visions were larger than individual buildings. He was in love with a young woman from a good Jewish family named Irma Levy. To marry her, he believed he had to have money of his own. His ardor galvanized him. On a mission to gain funds to be a worthy suitor, he convinced an elderly flapper who was a holdout against a new development to sell a key lease to him; this allowed the completion of a series of transactions that brought him $8,000. In Paris for his honeymoon, he made a few thousand more with a flier on a stock, and blew a good deal of it on a six-week high-living tour of the continent.

Not yet twenty-five, Bill Zeckendorf had tasted the heady wine of the good life. Taking stock, he decided he liked best the brokers who made a few large deals and didn't spend their days buying and selling dozens of leases for small markups. This realization impelled him to use Irma's connections to get to Otto Kahn. Just days after obtaining Kahn's agreement to let him represent the property, Zeckendorf sold it to Henry Mandel, who immediately undertook to erect there a 600-apartment complex he dubbed the Parc Vendome. Mandel's new dream would include a swimming pool, interior garden, restaurant, and many other features of the Central Park West or Park Avenue type of apartments for the wealthy; units in the Parc Vendome, however, would be geared to smaller families and have fewer rooms. Zeckendorf walked away from the deal with an immediate $30,000; Mandel stood to make millions — but not right away.

In fact, Mandel was already in trouble on both business and domestic fronts, though as yet he was only aware of his personal problems. Just after Christmas at the end of 1929, he had separated from his wife, Bertha, signing an agreement to pay her $2,500 per month in alimony and an additional few hundred in child support. Leaving the family at 575 Park Avenue, he took up bachelor residence in the Mayfair House, at Park Avenue and 65th Street, and planned to marry Nola Locke as soon as a divorce decree was granted.

In 1930 Mandel seemed breezily oblivious of the dangers that lay ahead. He garbed his doormen at London Terrace in uniforms similar to those worn by London bobbies, delivered on the many amenities promised to the 4,000 people beginning to fill his 1,700 apartments, and seemed on schedule with his leasing. He went on touting his new buildings as if there were still plenty of middle-class people to fill them.

Highly leveraged real estate was riding for a fall even more precipitous and of longer duration than that of stocks. The reasons go to the heart of the way real estaters operated in the 1920s. Standard procedure had been to buy a property with borrowed money, then borrow even more to put up a building. At this point the builder had an edifice whose potential worth was very large, but he was quite heavily in debt. When times were good, he wouldn't even have to obtain a permanent mortgage, for he could sell the building to someone with deep pockets, such as publisher William Randolph Hearst. Mandel had just done that, but even in a rising market there were not buyers for every newly completed office or apartment tower. About 75 percent of the income from a fully occupied building went to pay off the first mortgage, city taxes, and maintenance, even before the owner addressed the issue of substantially paying down that mortgage. How could an ambitious builder go on to bigger projects if his capital was tied up in the present building? Could Mandel, with several successful buildings and lots of plans, sit still until the mortgage was paid off, and wait for his big profits? He could not, and neither could most other builders. To extract some money from his just-completed project he'd sell off part interests, pay down the mortgage a bit, and "roll over" the majority of the money into an even larger project. That made sense, but also irretrievably linked the health of the first project to the second. If one became shaky, say because rents were no longer producing enough income to meet the lower but still extant mortgage payments, the second might also be compromised because money would have to be siphoned from it to keep the first one from slipping into default. If both started to slip, the builder was in double trouble. Another common tactic was to wait until the property had gone up in price, then apply for new loans based on that increased value, pay off the old ones, and plow the difference back into the next project. Here, the linkage was just as tight because new mortgage payments required from the first building would be higher than they were before the refinancing. The first building would have to stay fully rented, at top market rates, to meet the now-larger mortgage payments.

When you came right down to it, whole real estate empires rested on the ability of tenants to pay the landlord regularly. And in the United States in the four years after the stock market crash, each Friday saw 100,000 people thrown out of their jobs, until by late 1933 more than a quarter of the country's work force was unemployed. Many of those who still had jobs had been induced to take voluntary reductions in wages. The steady loss of workers and the ever-shrinking amount of space their truncated employers occupied translated into millions of missed rent payments. Not just blue-collar workers were out of luck; executives of corporations and other white-collar employees lost bonuses, took salary cuts, and received many of the pink slips. New York, where the height of the boom had been most keenly and joyfully felt, became the place where the most profound depths of the depression were plumbed.

So while Henry Mandel was all right through 1930 — many tenants had signed several-year leases before the crash — things began to slip early in 1931, while London Terrace was being rented and the Parc Vendome was being built, and while his Chelsea

Corners buildings were in various stages of development. In April
1931 he opened an expensive showroom on Fifth Avenue at 36th
Street that reproduced in exact detail model apartments in his complexes, wholly furnished, and including miniature versions of their
facing gardens. Since London Terrace's boxes came in thirty-seven
sizes and configurations, and there were more than a dozen layouts
for the Parc Vendome, the showroom was quite large and costly
to maintain. It was also a sign of desperation on the builder's part,
a last grand attempt to get people to rent in his buildings.

Not only Mandel's buildings were in difficulty. Next to a pro-
motional story about The Apartment Shop in the newspaper was
a notice that Rockefeller family members had taken over title to
three large cooperatively owned apartment houses on Park Avenue
because the apartment owners couldn't meet their own mortgage
payments. While $1,000-per-room-per-year apartments for the
upper middle class stood empty, there weren't enough $15-per-
room-per-year flats to accommodate all the newly poor people who
wanted them. Curiously, Vincent Astor still thought there were
enough wealthy people around to go blithely ahead with a huge
building on East End Avenue at 85th Street; its 550 rooms were
to be divided up into forty-one apartments ranging in size from
nine rooms and four baths to nineteen rooms and eight baths.

"Deflation is certain to run its course," Mandel told an inter-
viewer. It was merely a problem of market organization. Why
couldn't the government create a central monetary institution for
real estate akin to the Federal Reserve System, which had helped
the banks continue to operate? Conditions were "serious, but far
from hopeless."

He continued sounding hopeful notes even as the sky was falling.
In December 1931, foreclosure proceedings began against Mandel
for the $45,000 he still owed on a $110,000 mortgage on a building
on Union Square that Mandel had bought in 1926 for very little
money down and a willingness to become the guarantor of the
mortgage. This amount represented about one-eighth of 1 percent
of the $36-million Mandel empire, but when it came due he couldn't
or wouldn't pay it.

It is a bitter but well-known irony in the real estate world that
the smallest creditor is the one most likely to start the rolling snow-
ball that culminates in the avalanche called bankruptcy. Large creditors with a lot at stake are forced by the very size of their
investments or mortgages to let a builder run for a while and hope

that payments on the debt can be resumed; big creditors may even negotiate lower rates to be paid in the interim. But smaller creditors, seeing that a man's total debt is many times that owed them, are apt to insist on immediate payment, reasoning that if he declared bankruptcy, they'd then have to stand in line behind major creditors and wait for payment that might never come. Alarmed, they press for payment or have a court force a sale. Mandel's creditors were probably disturbed by the realization that, as a leading broker stated in an article in the *Times*, "the value of the real estate given as security for [some developers'] mortgages has shrunk . . . [to where it] is actually below the amount of the mortgage." Scared lenders saw no choice but to repossess and sell a defaulted building and obtain from it even the small amount of cash that a sale would yield, and be out from under the continuing obligation to pay its taxes.

Only a Vincent Astor could take money from his private fortune to keep his buildings from entering default, even rescuing the St. Regis Hotel — not his, but built on land his family had owned — when it fell into default in 1934. Mandel did not have the resources for that sort of salvage work, as his fortune was almost entirely tied up in real estate parcels that he owned only so long as he continued to pay their mortgages. Three months after the first foreclosure, Mandel declared personal bankruptcy; his petition listed liabilities of $14 million and assets of $380,602.19. He owed $3 million to his Pershing Square creditors, $5.5 million to those of London Terrace, $1.4 million to those of One Park Avenue, $1 million to those behind 475 Park Avenue, and tens of thousands each to a dozen others. Because his assets could not make much of a dent in his obligations, all those buildings were taken over by the creditors. His empire vanished.

The moment he entered bankruptcy, Mandel stopped paying alimony and child support to his first wife; he had, after all, another wife to support now, and if he wasn't making his business mortgage payments, why should he continue to make payments to a discarded wife? Bertha sued him for seven months' worth of back alimony and child support, a total of $18,958. In the good days, that had been pocket money for him; now, he couldn't pay it. In May 1933 he was arrested at the Mayfair House for nonpayment of these personal obligations and languished for seven weeks in the county jail on West 37th Street in Manhattan. His lawyers convinced a friendly judge to release Mandel and reduce his alimony payments from $32,500 a year to $3,000, because he couldn't pay the greater charge, and so that he would have a chance to "rehabilitate his business." A tall order.

Consider what happened to London Terrace. In the clutches of the depression, many renters moved from larger to smaller apartments, and some who couldn't pay the full amount of their rents were granted rollbacks — but to no avail, as far as the owners were concerned. For the first eight months of 1933, rental income was $160,000 lower than the $440,000 needed to cover the mortgage payments. Mandel defaulted, and London Terrace ownership reverted back to Bishop Clement Moore's estate; shortly, the heirs of the popularizer of Santa Claus discovered that they couldn't pay the interest on the mortgages either, and defaulted in favor of an insurance company, a trust company, and a savings bank, none of which could collect enough money from the property to cover the maintenance and the taxes due on it. Taxes were a critical factor. For generations in Manhattan, taxes had been calculated on the basis of what it cost to put up a building on a property, not on that building's current worth. Despite high rates, the city's income was being eroded because so many owners were unable to pay their bills; that's how the city and state of New York also became victims of the London Terrace collapse. Last but not least among the victims were individual bondholders. Units once worth $1,000 dropped in value to $170 apiece, and that only if a buyer could be found to purchase them. A survey discovered that bondholders of London Terrace lived in each of the United States and in fifteen other countries. In this multiple default game, there were no winners, only large numbers of losers.

Relieved of the burden of paying expensive alimony — and of sitting in jail — Mandel looked for new investors. Few were willing to take chances, even though, as Mandel stoutly proclaimed, there were bargains to be bought. Mandel still had his expertise, though, and on the strength of it in 1935 he put together a syndicate to buy foreclosed properties. He tried to put up a movie theater on the corner of 79th and Madison, but his scheme was opposed by wealthy residents of the area such as Vincent Astor and other members of the Metropolitan Riding Club, which Mandel once had helped form. Bill Zeckendorf sold him a property or two and may even have stuck his "good friend" Mandel with a lemon or two. They remained friends and fellow divorced men. Zeckendorf had "grown apart" from Irma Levy and, like Mandel, had left small children in the care of his first wife. Moreover, Zeckendorf lived after his divorce in the Lombardy Hotel, which Mandel had erected during his more productive years and which remained a frequent haunt.

Mandel's latter investments didn't show much of a profit and his financial condition continued to deteriorate. His second wife, Nola, refused to curtail her spending or conform it to his reduced circumstances. In January 1936 she threw him out of their apartment on Central Park West altogether, and Mandel took refuge in an eleven-dollar-per-week hotel room.

In 1930 poet Michael Gold published a memoir of his downtown childhood, *Jews Without Money*, and gave an insight into what many poor people thought the city had become:

> New York is a devil's dream, the most urbanized city in the world. It is all geometry angles and stone. It is mythical, a city buried by a volcano. No grass is found in this petrified city, no big living trees, no flowers, no bird but the drab little lecherous sparrow, no soil, loam, earth. . . . Just stone. It is the ruins of Pompeii, except that seven million animals full of earth love must dwell in the dead lava streets.

Fred French wanted to change those dreams. He was making fine, secret progress on assembling twenty-five square blocks of Manhattan's worst slums, between the Manhattan and Brooklyn bridges, and by the end of 1930 had 250 parcels, approximately one-third of the total area. But even as he accumulated them, he ran into trouble on other projects. The first piece of the empire to go was the old Hippodrome Theater, on whose site he had planned an eighty-three-story skyscraper. He had bought the land in December 1929 for a reported $7.5 million and taken a mortgage for $2.5 million from Farmers Loan and Trust; now Farmers Loan foreclosed on the property. That was $5 million of French's money gone in a puff of smoke.

French dreamed of giving the residents of the Lower East Side the same sort of gardens and outdoor amenities he had provided for the middle class in Tudor City. He announced his project publicly and sold the first share of stock in it to Al Smith, who told the press he'd played on the Lung Block as a child; there had been more cases of tuberculosis there than at any other location in the city. Some angels anted up, as they had done earlier for French's other projects, but not enough, and he was forced to ask for help. Figuring that 25,000 people would be employed if construction were in full swing, he thought this would be gratifying to the government officials and wealthy men who personally were shouldering some of the burden of providing for the unemployed. He arranged secret meetings with Henry Ford, John D. Rockefeller, Jr., men from the J. P. Morgan Company, Governor Franklin D. Roosevelt, Owen D. Young of General Electric, Colonel Arthur Woods (Junior Rockefeller's trusted aide), and the heads of important labor unions. French suggested that their organizations take part in this monumental project. All turned him down flat. He decided to go ahead on a reduced scale, using his own companies' money, and in the meantime raise $50 million from his small-investor angels to complete the whole thing.

But as the Great Depression became deeper and lasted longer than anyone had thought possible, French's dream project seemed less viable. It shrank from forty-five acres to five — still a considerable chunk of land, but hardly enough to change the entire character of the ghetto. Costs rose, and the first building to go up, replacing part of the old Lung Block, had to be rented to people who had more income than the block's previous occupants. Adding to the indignity, tenants staged a rent strike to protest the low levels of service in the buildings and the absence of promised amenities.

After New York's governor Franklin D. Roosevelt won the presidency and began many new government agencies, French applied for $75 million as a housing loan from the Reconstruction Finance Corporation. Washington thought $8 million would be enough to end the ghetto in Manhattan for all time. It wasn't, and to complete Knickerbocker Village French used a "limited dividend" plan similar to that devised for Sunnyside Gardens and, earlier, for the City and Suburban Homes projects. Uptown, Rockefeller's Dunbar complex ran into difficulties, too, but sought no government help; when Junior couldn't sell the apartments as cooperatives, he rented them out.

A series of newspaper articles uncovered health hazards in tenements owned by several of the old families, such as the Astors. Vincent Astor tried to sell his ghetto properties to the city at a great loss, but the city couldn't afford to buy anything, just then. Astor evicted the tenants, tore down the buildings, and (to the chagrin of other landholders in the area, who were still making money from tenements) all but donated the land to the city for a development called First Houses. Red tape and governmental restrictions merely irked Astor and other old landholders who wished to help, but hamstrung French, who didn't have the cushion of a great fortune. French complained to an audience at Princeton that the government would either have to allow private builders to make reasonable profits on such slum-replacement projects or, if the government wished to take charge, "award contracts in such a manner that the builders need not spend most of their energy in worrying as to whether or not they will be able to make a modest profit on the jobs."

In Tudor City, French's problems were compounded by those of directly competing apartment buildings that had already fallen into receivership. Since court-appointed receivers were not expected to make the building show a profit, only to meet maintenance costs, they usually lowered rents, a practice that in this instance induced tenants in the privately run Tudor City to give up their higher-priced units for comparable space in the defaulted buildings. French's well-run buildings were thus toppled into default. For a while, the only French building making money was the skyscraper on Fifth Avenue with his name on it. Eventually most of his buildings fell to the mortgage holders, so that in 1936, at the time of his sudden death from angina at age fifty-three, French had no property and less than $10,000 in his personal estate. His buildings had all been incorporated as separate corporations, however, and his family had enough stock in them to live reasonably well, for a time.

Just after the October 1929 crash, A. E. Lefcourt attended with joy the opening of the new Temple Emanu-El. As owner of the old site, on which he had erected an office building and affixed his name, Lefcourt had felt enough of a tie to the congregation to join it and contribute to the completion of the largest and most beautiful temple in the New World.

Asked by a friend which building of his he considered the best from the standpoint of architectural elegance and its ability to produce income, he answered, "My next one." Nevertheless, Lefcourt scaled down what was to have been the world's tallest building on the corner of 49th and Broadway, to a twelve-story edifice now known as the Brill Building. He had been forced to complete the Essex House on the site of the old Spanish flats that he had torn down amid controversy. He defaulted on the Essex House, and on a thirty-one-story building he had committed to erect to house the offices of the International Telephone and Telegraph Corporation, on Beaver Street, which was taken over by ITT almost as soon as the building opened. In the end, though, it was a foray into banking that toppled Lefcourt's empire. His real estate ventures had been capped by his founding of the Normandie National Bank in January 1929. That bank's securities affiliate specialized in handling the stocks of banks, a group of securities especially hard hit in the crash; since Normandie held a great many bank stock shares, the bank's own financial underpinning was fatally weakened. Lefcourt understood the concept of leverage on the up side but, like so many others, he never contemplated the disastrous things that could happen, due to leverage, on the down side. He personally lost many millions and also was pressured to repay some outstanding loans to Bank of U.S.; he had to sell even more properties to make good on those loans. Outside stockholders of Normandie Securities brought suit against Lefcourt and his top associates to account for a missing $4,631,000. Despite the man in the street's belief that a historical inevitability had caused the precipitous decline in stocks that threw Normandie and every other financial institution into a tizzy, those who had lost money looked for someone to blame who possessed assets that could be sold to assuage their pain. As they had found Mandel, they found Lefcourt.

The other part of the bear trap that closed on Lefcourt had originally been set by John Jacob Astor. The former shoeshine boy had built expensive structures on land that he didn't own — that he'd only leased for twenty-one years. Had he been patient enough to wait to build until he'd found land he could buy, however, he would not have erected as many edifices. So during the depression, in addition to mortgage holders who wanted to foreclose for missing payments, landowners sought forfeit of Lefcourt's properties for being in arrears on monthly payments for the ground leases. Both mortgage holders and fee holders, when they took back Lefcourt's buildings, also insisted on removing Lefcourt's name from the buildings. His empire was not only taken from him; most of it no longer bore any trace of his name.

On a Tuesday morning in early November 1932, sixty lawyers showed up at the Supreme Court in Brooklyn to begin what was expected to be a sensational suit pitting disgruntled stockholders against Lefcourt. They pressed for a reorganization of Lefcourt's banking companies that would turn over to the stockholders certain securities, some leases, and personal notes of $25,000 each from

Lefcourt and an associate in return for a general release from "all liability incurred by reason of losses" to Normandie National Securities. An entire truckload of documents was to be entered into evidence. On Wednesday morning Lefcourt, now fifty-five, had a heart attack but recovered well enough to go to his offices for the rest of the week. On Saturday evening he suffered another attack at his home in the Savoy-Plaza hotel at 59th and Fifth Avenue, and died after a third attack on Sunday morning.

Lefcourt's funeral was held at Temple Emanu-El and was well attended by politicians, garment center officials, and delegates from the Grand Street Boys, an association of men raised on the Lower East Side who had attained positions of prominence. The trial was called off, of course, and newspapers eulogized Lefcourt as "one of the greatest builders in history since Louis XIV and Sir Christopher Wren," who had "cut New York's brilliant sky into a fretted pattern of terraced battlements." A collage artist assembled drawings of the twenty buildings Lefcourt had erected during his career into a single image that showed his extensive impact on the skyline. A wistful associate recalled that, at the time these buildings were completed, they were worth $75 million. A few weeks after his death, a petition was filed for probate asserting that Lefcourt had no real estate holdings and that the entire value of his estate was "about $2,500."

The crashes of the empires of Lefcourt, Mandel, and French had a tremendously sobering effect on contemporaries such as Sam Rudin, the Rose brothers, and the various Tishmans, Minskoffs, and Urises. One moment, a Lefcourt or a Mandel was sitting by your side at an industry dinner, enjoying the accolades of the community, and the next, they were nearly paupers, or having heart attacks and dying in middle age. Lefcourt, Mandel, and French had built everything within the space of less than a decade and then saw it all vanish in a matter of months. As one piece of their empire fell, it undermined the others, in a slide of reverse leverage. What was an empire in real estate if it did not endure more than a few years?

John R. Todd, managing agent for Metropolitan Square, was delighted when Junior Rockefeller refused to cave in to the Metropolitan Opera's demands, because a contract that gave him a share of the rents encouraged him to make the square into the world's finest shopping and office district. The builder of the successful and attractive Graybar skyscraper near Grand Central Station,

Todd was a teetotaling lawyer whose passions were, he once said, "selling, romance, dog fights and horse trades." All four elements were present in his dealings with Metropolitan Square, where Todd was as important in shaping the complex as the more celebrated architects. A tyrant, Todd belittled the architects' abilities and what he saw as aristocratic pretensions. "For an architect, you show almost human intelligence," he was fond of repeating. Todd forced through his own vision of the final design by riding herd on teams of architects until they made the most use out of the space. L. Andrew Reinhard, Henry Hofmeister, Wallace Harrison, and Raymond Hood were the major designers. Harrison, though relatively junior on the project, was connected to the Rockefellers by his marriage to the sister of Junior's son-in-law, David Milton, and acted as the family's conduit for artistic input. Hood was the most visionary. Contemporaneous with his work on Metropolitan Square, he was designing two anchors of 42nd Street, the sleek, black-lobbied *Daily News* skyscraper between Second and Third avenues, and the turquoise McGraw-Hill Building between Eighth and Ninth avenues. Todd's message seemed to get through to the brilliant Hood, who later wrote:

> Far from being a handicap, this discipline . . . of being obliged to make a project stand on its own financial feet . . . leads to honesty and integrity of design. . . . The cobwebs of whimsy, taste, fashion and vanity are brushed aside, and the architect finds himself face to face with the essentials and elements that go to make real architecture and real beauty.

Instead of a low building in the center of the complex, flanked by tall towers, Todd gave instructions to reverse the design now that the opera was gone — to have a strong, tall, central tower fronted by a plaza and flanked by shorter towers and lower corner buildings. General David Sarnoff's Radio Corporation of America (RCA), recently severed from its corporate parent General Electric, was slated to become the major tenant of the central tower. Perhaps some of RCA's affiliates, such as the new Radio Keith Orpheum (RKO) entertainment concern, headed by Boston investor Joseph P. Kennedy, would also be involved. It grated on purists that the august tones of grand opera would now be replaced by broadcast soap operas and "Amos 'n Andy," but a major tenant could not be denied. Rockefeller had already spent $10 million on the project and would have to spend an estimated $75 million more before a nickel was returned. Vincent Astor could erect a $7.5-million apartment building in which he was able to rent out whole floors even before construction was finished. But could Rockefeller fund by himself an office complex that cost ten times that much? Practicality became the order of the day. With his income reduced from $35 million per year of the 1920s to less than $15 million per year, Rockefeller sought financing for Metropolitan Square not from the Chase Bank, which was like a private Rockefeller fiefdom, but from the Metropolitan Life Insurance Company, a regular bankroller of construction projects. His $45-million construction loan was the largest ever given, and to get it Rockefeller again had to make himself personally liable. The square was bleeding even his huge fortune, and there was no telling when the project would begin to make money.

While still at Dartmouth, Nelson Rockefeller, his second oldest son, had importuned Junior to make him a director of Metropolitan Square, along with his oldest brother John. That was before Nelson's dreams of being an architect were deterred by a B grade in the college's architecture course, but even afterwards his interest in the square continued. Nelson steadily sniped at Todd, trying to gain control of the square back from what he saw as outside hands. His other interest was modern art, his mother's passion; along with two other women, Abby Aldrich Rockefeller had founded the Museum of Modern Art. Junior, enamored of medieval and Oriental art, didn't cotton to such "modernists" as Van Gogh, Gauguin, Cézanne, and Seurat, whose work comprised MoMA's opening exhibit in 1929, in borrowed quarters in August Heckscher's 57th Street skyscraper. A story tells of a dinner Junior gave for Henri Matisse, at which the artist pleaded the cause of modern art. Junior responded, in polite French, that he was stone-set against it, but he was sure that on this subject Mrs. Rockefeller's gifts of persuasion would wear him down to the consistency of jelly.

Nelson's ambition, the battle between the Rockefellers over modern art, and the exigencies of the square came to a head in 1932. Work was proceeding on the construction of the seventy-story central tower, the plaza fronting it, and the mid-level buildings. When holdouts at the 49th and 50th street corners set their prices too high, Junior and Todd had the tower designed and built around them. The British and French were recruited for low buildings on the Fifth Avenue plaza. "Roxy" Rothafel, a burlesque theater and show designer, was involved in his ultimate fantasy, the building that would become Radio City Music Hall. Several thousand union-ized workmen made the site into a center of activity so attractive to passersby that there was even an official sidewalk-superintendents club, with membership cards. Six buildings and two theaters were almost complete and four more were ready to graduate from blue-print to construction stages. Large companies agreed to move their headquarters to the square, and more became interested as it became clear that Metropolitan Square would be the new midtown business center. It was the greatest construction project in New York City and, because of the lack of any others, of tremendous importance to the city.

Critics lined up to condemn it. In *The New Yorker*, Lewis Mum-ford would shortly write that the project "lacks the distinction, the strength, the confidence of good architecture, just because it lacks any solidness of purpose and sincerity of intention. . . . The whole effect . . . is mediocrity — seen through a magnifying glass." "The crux of the matter is that Radio City is ugly," said the *New York Herald Tribune*. "Its exterior is revoltingly dull and dreary." "From every source of intelligent appreciation," wrote the *New York Times*, "has come a perfect stream of objection, protest, and, one may say, wondering malediction."

Perhaps in response to such artistic critiques, Junior felt the need to turn over the decision-making about the last remaining touches on the central building to his aggressive son Nelson. The lobby and entrance decorations had to be modern, Junior understood, and he would yield to those who knew about modern art.

The initial blow to Junior's straitlaced character came from the stylized, nude, bas-relief figures, sculpted by Leo Friedlander, that vaguely represented radio and television and were placed over the north and south entrances. These so offended Junior that he vowed never to enter the building by either of those doorways. He would proceed to his fifty-sixth-floor office from the east, entering un-derneath Lee Lawrie's bas-relief, *Wisdom: A Voice from the Clouds*. But he admitted privately that he hated the inscription; moreover, why did the traditionally feminine goddess of wisdom look like an Art Deco version of Michelangelo's bearded male deity from the Sistine Chapel? And why was that architectural drawing instru-ment (not unlike Junior's four-foot rule that he kept in his back pocket) coming out at right angles from Wisdom's outstretched fingers?

In September 1932, Todd and Hood sailed for Europe to interview great artists from a list chosen by Nelson to design ten panels, each at least seventeen by twenty feet, to grace the walls of what would be the world's largest office building. Matisse turned them down flat and Picasso couldn't be scared out of hiding, but they got agreement on panels by José Maria Sert and, by cable, from the great Mexican muralist Diego Rivera.

The Museum of Modern Art had exhibited Rivera's work in 1931 and 1932; both Nelson Rockefeller and his mother owned Rivera paintings, and Abby Rockefeller had commissioned Rivera to do portraits of her grandchildren. Also, the family had purchased Rivera's Russian sketchbook celebrating the 1917 Communist victory, so Rivera's deep embrace of Communism was well known to the family. During the next year of negotiations on the colors, forms, and materials, Rivera threatened to walk away from the project several times. "The only things these architects like to paste on the walls of their buildings are canvas enlargements of the vulgarist kind of illustration from popular magazines, done in oils and as slick, smooth and shiny as the patent leather pumps which they wear to their evening parties," the muralist later wrote. Several times young Nelson had to intervene to keep him on the mural project, whose formal name and theme was *Man at the Crossroads Looking with Uncertainty but with Hope and High Vision to the Choosing of a Course Leading to a New and Better Future*. Rivera did a sketch and wrote a long note to Hood and the sponsors about his proposed design. It read, in part:

> On the side [of the lobby] where Sert is to represent the development of the Technical Power of man, my panel will show the Workers arriving at a true understanding of their rights regarding the means of production, which has resulted in the planning of the liquidation of Tyranny, personified by a crumbling statue of Caesar whose head has fallen to the ground.

Any newspaper reader of the time would have known that such language echoed the rhetoric and phraseology of Communism. But Junior Rockefeller went ahead and approved a sketch that Rivera later said showed clearly that the figure who would occupy and embody what Rivera called "the median line . . . [of] cosmic energy" would be Lenin. As the huge panel took shape, the Lenin figure emerged very clearly; on the wall Rivera set him apart from the group in which he originally stood. Other parts of the mural also became more politically pronounced: civilizations revolving around nightclubs, microbes given life by poison gases, policemen ominously swinging their clubs. The building was scheduled to open on May 1, 1933, and in early April Nelson was still sending the painter little notes of encouragement. A few days before opening, the *New York World Telegram* made the controversy public with the headline, "Rivera Paints Scenes of Communist Activity and John D., Jr. Foots the Bill." Junior was aghast. The opening was postponed. Nelson asked Rivera to substitute an unknown person's face for Lenin's, and Rivera refused, allowing only that he'd balance V. I. Lenin with Abe Lincoln — Lincoln was much admired in Communist circles for having freed the slaves. That was not an acceptable compromise.

Junior reasserted control. Rivera was paid the remainder due to him for the mural, ordered off his scaffold, and sent packing. The mural was covered over and the building opened with it hidden. Six months later, when the Museum of Modern Art seemed unable to agree to have the mural transferred there, it was destroyed as it was taken down from the walls.

After this fiasco, when Nelson and John Rockefeller next tried to take control of Metropolitan Square away from John Todd, Junior slapped them back so forcefully that they found it imperative to eat quite a bit of crow in their joint Christmas letter to him on December 20, 1934:

> As we express our mingled feelings of pleasure, satisfaction and appreciation, we cannot help wondering just a little what your reaction has been to our relationship these past few years. . . . This subconscious feeling on our part that you may sometimes question the motives which actuate our sayings or doings is our only source of regret. That our relationship should even on occasion be the cause of apprehension and concern to you is something we feel should not and must not exist. The family's responsibilities are too great and the opportunities for accomplishment too challenging to allow anything of this sort to creep in. . . .

Chapter Nine

The Hard Years

IN THE MID-1930s an editorial in a New York newspaper praised the "Two R's" for building projects in New York — the Rockefeller family for Metropolitan Square and the Rose family for 500 units of low-income housing at Clason Point in the Bronx. Of course, the editors were comparing a giant project to a small one, but in the hard years, when there was very little construction going on in the city, even a project that might otherwise have gone unremarked was to be celebrated.

The Rose brothers already had a thousand units of housing to their credit, mostly in the Bronx. Dave Rose was emerging as an energetic leader who loved the business. His desire to know how things worked, and his wish to make them work better, was applied to everything from medicine to masonry. At Clason Point he devised new solutions to old problems — for instance, an on-site plant for "co-generation" of energy, a way of recycling waste heat that enabled the complex to lower its heating costs.

Daniel Rose later recalled that, in good times and bad, his father and uncle "lived out of one pocket." Dave and his wife, Rebecca, were childless, and he seemed always to be at Sam and Belle's home in Scarsdale, sharing the more boisterous family atmosphere. "Dave got the better of the deal," Daniel muses, "because he had the benefits of having a family without bearing all of the actual responsibilities." Sam was more imaginative and reflective, an artist to whom work, while interesting, was secondary to his delight in living in the suburbs, his golf, the drawings with which he amused his sons, his oil paintings, and his willingness to read the books the boys excitedly brought home from school. Sam was fond of quoting the Talmudic saying, "The Sabbath was made for man, not man for the Sabbath," which he interpreted as meaning that work must be for man's edification and pleasure, and that the hiatus of a Sabbath was necessary for man's soul to grow. The brothers and their families had a Sabbath dinner together every Friday night at Sam's home. To further emphasize the differences between the sacred and the profane, Sam, Dave, and their four sisters and families began their annual black-tie Seder.

As with all the great partnerships of the immigrant builder families, the Roses' working arrangement harked back to the relationship of the *luftmensch* and the *arendator* within the Pale. Each respected the other, relied on the other, and knew the other had qualities that he himself lacked.

Through caution and pluck, artful financing, careful cost control, and attention to detail, in the 1930s the Roses continued to build and never lost control of a building. Incomes fell, but there were no defaults, no giving back of the keys to mortgage holders. It might be nice to be as big as the Rockefellers and to build monuments that everyone could applaud, but there was an advantage to having a small, tightly controlled family firm.

From the time he was six, Sam's oldest boy, Frederick Phineas Rose, loved being taken out on the steam shovel at the family's construction sites. Small for his age and athletic, Fred liked what his father and uncle were doing. Mother Belle insisted that he and his younger brothers Daniel and Elihu commute to the Horace Mann School in Riverdale because of its high educational standards. In 1938, when Fred was fifteen, David and Sam were erecting the family's first project in Manhattan, a 400-unit apartment complex near Columbia's Bakers Field; as he recalled years later, he "raced there from school to take part in it, and spent vacations hanging around the project." His father and uncle told him he'd go into the family business, but he needed no urging. The real question was, would he train as an architect or as an engineer? Though he was good with his hands, he couldn't draw, and thought that ruled out architecture. He decided to study engineering at Yale.

In its heyday in the 1920s, Emery Roth & Sons employed fifty men, each so skilled that one draftsman complained because he only got to do renderings for stairwells. When the depression came, Roth was forced to reduce the staff to his two sons, a secretary, and himself. Julian could not draw, so he handled construction and business matters while Richard, trained in architecture at MIT, worked on plans under Emery's direction. Both young men remained firmly in their father's shadow, Richard even more than Julian, because he was also an architect. The situation forced Richard to keep his feelings bottled up. Even after Emery made his sons partners, they continued to receive only salaries and had no share in the profits. Of course, in the hard years, there were no profits. Moreover, Emery had made investments in some of his clients' buildings and could only watch helplessly as the structures were foreclosed and his money was lost along with that of his clients. For instance, the Urises couldn't save the stately, Roth-designed St. Moritz Hotel on the corner of Central Park South and Sixth Avenue. One day Emery found in his mail a notice that Harris Uris had declared bankruptcy. "I played pinochle with him last night," Emery wonderingly told his sons, "and he said nothing about it."

Manhattan real estate men charted the depression by the number of foreclosures and forced sales: in 1935, $250 million in properties were foreclosed and there were twice as many forced sales as unforced ones. The sale of the Ritz-Carlton (owned by Robert Goelet) wasn't a foreclosure, but it fetched only $725,000, including the $100,000 contents of its bars and wine cellars. The $25-million Pierre Hotel was costing so much in taxes that it was sold for $2.5 million. The half-built Hampshire House, on Central Park South near the Urises' St. Moritz, was sold because the mortgage couldn't be paid, then sold again because the mortgage holder couldn't pay his taxes on other buildings.

Such conditions offered opportunities to young men who could figure out how to exploit them. Early in the 1930s, Henry Brakmann Helmsley, an office boy for Dwight, Voorhis & Perry, was promoted to the status of delinquent-rent collector. The son of a notions buyer, Helmsley had gone to work for the firm right out of high school in 1925, a tall, shambling man with bad eyesight and a bright smile. Lack of a college education was not seen by real estaters as a drawback; individual initiative, not extensive training, was the key to success. Helmsley did well in an area appropriately dubbed Hell's Kitchen. Twice a week Helmsley would go to Metropolitan Life to learn what buildings the insurance giant had recently foreclosed and to make deals to manage even more difficult buildings. He became expert at figuring the income that could be obtained from foreclosed buildings and solicited similar work from Chase Bank, where the man in charge had recently been a young rent collector himself.

Helmsley's mother, Minnie, daughter of a small landlord, advised her elder son to buy real estate whenever and wherever he could. She, too, could read the headlines telling how the owner of the New York Yankees, Colonel Jacob Ruppert, was scooping up more important properties than anyone else in the city. Relying on his brewery fortune to pay their monthly bills, and convinced he could eventually resell the buildings for much more than he'd paid, Ruppert plunked down hundreds of thousands for properties that had originally cost millions. Midsize operators who didn't have Ruppert's money could use the same ratios — buying for 2.5 percent of the real value of the building and underlying land, plus assumption of the mortgage. The owner of a loft building not far from Helmsley's Flatiron Building office was in trouble on a $100,000 mortgage and agreed to sell the building for $1,000 in cash if Helmsley would take over the mortgage payments, which amounted to $3,000 per year. Helmsley knew the area very well and was convinced that he could make the building a paying proposition, so he paid out all that he had saved from his job to buy it. He also hired his unemployed father as the building's superintendent. "I was supporting him anyway," Helmsley later recalled. "One of the reasons I wanted to buy the property was so he could get a job."

Helmsley did well enough with this building, and several others purchased for similar songs, that he was able to buy a partnership and have his old firm renamed Dwight, Voorhis & Helmsley. At about the same time, Helmsley met Eve Sherpick Green; she was several years older than he, a widow, and a devout Quaker. She also had a bit of money, and her brother was a well-connected lawyer. On their first date, Harry took her dancing. Within a year, they were married.

Bill Zeckendorf was a freewheeling, recently divorced bachelor living in Henry Mandel's creation, the Hotel Lombardy on East 56th Street, when he met Marion. She was walking her poodle one evening on an Upper East Side street when it was attacked by a bulldog; passerby Zeckendorf leaped to the poodle's defense. The incident resolved, he asked the dog's owner to have a drink with him. She could hardly refuse. Shortly, their courtship was on in earnest.

Zeckendorf, too, had sunk to the level of salvaging properties for insurance companies, though he had enough resources to take more risks than Helmsley. He converted a former bank on 57th Street near Third Avenue into the Sutton Theater, only to see it repossessed by Manufacturers Trust. At times he gambled on the horses; other times played bridge for money. He was getting tired of "scrambling up straight walls" in the brokerage business. His opportunity came after a 1936 transaction in which he sold a building to the Webb & Knapp brokerage and management firm. The next year, when the building lost tenants and slipped into the red, Webb & Knapp requested help from Zeckendorf, implying the he should have told them that its tenants were about to take a powder. He was able to refill it with paying tenants. That impressed Webb & Knapp, who asked him to become a partner at a salary of $9,000 a year, far less than the $20,000 he was spending annually. But this was steady work with a prestigious firm that could further his dreams, so Zeckendorf took the job. The firm had originally been started to handle real estate for the New York Central railroad and the Vanderbilts, and was well regarded among the old-money families. Shortly, a cousin of one of the Webb & Knapp partners came into the firm, bringing with him a stake of $400,000. With that money, and spurred by the ambitious Zeckendorf, Webb & Knapp began to buy buildings.

For the small community of immigrant builders, the most significant collapse of the hard years was not that of an individual, but of the Bank of the United States. Its demise foreshadowed today's collapsing savings and loans institutions. Just before the Crash of 1929, Bank of U.S. had hoped to stave off bankruptcy by obtaining new funding, but negotiations on a stock sale and a merger with a more respected bank ended badly when the Seligman brokerage house found out the bank was being audited by the state. During 1930 Bernie Marcus and Saul Singer continued to borrow from their bank and tried to hold off the examiners. They saw as the bank's major source of security the Beresford and San Remo apartment houses on Central Park West.

In late October 1930, Saul Ravitch received a call from someone who said he was an officer of a branch of Bank of U.S. and wanted to know whether the Beresford had an incinerator the bank could use to burn some old papers. Sure, Ravitch said, and told the janitor. Weeks later, a moving van backed up to the Beresford's service entrance and more than a thousand bundles of ledgers, journals, cash books, and correspondence from the bank's main office on Fifth Avenue were unloaded. No HRH officers were on the premises on that Saturday afternoon — nor did they have any notion that the bundles contained sensitive materials. It took two days to incinerate it all.

Marcus and Singer had almost finalized a plan to merge the Bank of U.S. with Manufacturers Trust and two other banks. On Sunday, December 7, 1930, Irwin Chanin, David Tishman, Joseph Durst, and fifteen other directors waited at the offices of their lawyer for the deal to go through. The three real estaters were a contrast in styles: Chanin was a natty, theatrical sort; Tishman was refined and affable; Durst was most comfortable with figures. As much as Singer and Marcus, they wanted the deal. They would have to resign as directors but at least there would be no public embarrassment. All would be covered over in the absorption of one bank by others. Then word leaked out to the general public that Bank of U.S. was in trouble, and on December 10 depositors made a run on the fifty-seven offices. Fifteen thousand people showed up at one branch; squads of policemen were necessary to control crowds at others. The bank worked assiduously to accommodate ordinary depositors who withdrew more than $10 million in cash that day. It also took special care of directors — the wife of one was allowed to withdraw $25,000, well after closing hours.

Negotiations continued. In the offices of the New York branch of the Federal Reserve System, the state banking superintendent made a last, impassioned plea to the presidents of Chase, Chemical, J. P. Morgan, First National, National City, and several other institutions to save Bank of U.S., because its closing might cause widespread bankruptcy among its 440,000 depositors. The bank presidents refused to agree and the Bank of the United States had to be closed. The banking superintendent was appalled, and many people whispered that the Protestant bankers had deliberately withheld help from the biggest Jewish bank in the country. The extent of the damage to the Jewish immigrant builder fraternity was considerable.

When investigators started looking at the bank's records, it became obvious that two major assets were the Beresford and San Remo apartments. The first was well rented and the second was filling up slowly but decently — and these income-producing properties were desperately required by the bank to pay debts measured in the tens of millions. The Beresford and San Remo were sold, an auction that stunned the HRH firm and its founder, the old iron-maker Joseph Ravitch. He was owed money for construction and management expenses on both buildings and now could not collect. He and his son also had to endure the indignity of being questioned about the burning of the papers, and innuendoes that the Ravitches had possibly taken part in the destruction of vital evidence of bank fraud. HRH had been unwittingly used by the bank's officers and was cleared, but after the debacle Joseph Ravitch was a broken man. To save on rent, several generations of Ravitches moved into a building HRH managed.

The Century apartments on Central Park West, built by the Chanins and nearly as sumptuous as the Beresford and San Remo, were similarly in debt to Bank of U.S. for the relatively trifling amount of $160,000; nonetheless, this mortgage was seized and sold and the Chanins lost the building. Shortly they lost others, and clung to salaries from the management company owned by Irwin's wife and an unmarried sister.

Officers of the Bank of the United States were charged with fraud, and the stockholders were asked to pay its debts. Prosecutorial ire turned toward the directors and focused on those with the highest profile; the most obvious target was a member of the family that boasted their firm was the largest owner-builder in the city. David Tishman was in his early forties, impeccably dressed and exuding a patrician air, and seemed politely puzzled by the actions of Marcus and Singer.

"Didn't you think that [depositors] who were putting their money in the bank relied on you to do your duty?" Tishman was asked in court.

"I believe personally I did [my duty] insofar as getting men we thought excellent bankers, who knew how to run a bank, know how to check up credits," he responded. "I feel that I did everything I could humanly possible have done."

"What did you do?"

"Any questions that came up on matters that pertained to my business I took care of. Problems that came before the board — discussed them in the manner that a director would. After these people [the loan committee of the board] that you trusted came in with the information — "

"You have admitted . . . that they loaned $40,000,000 you did not know to whom it was loaned or anything about it."

"How could I discover about it?" Tishman wondered.

"By asking, by looking," the assistant district attorney answered for him. "They say they put the applications in the center of the table so as to go through the form — to give you an opportunity to look. . . . Did you look?"

"I did not."

As Tishman and others made clear, directors had been lulled into thinking that the bank's affairs had been proper and profitable, and were now being pilloried for their lack of attention to detail. On another, related issue, the sale of stock to the depositors, the prosecutor asked whether the board had requested a report. Tishman replied, "I have an idea that [Marcus and Singer] did report back. How it was it is quite vague. I didn't place much importance on it."

"No, it wasn't your money, Mr. Tishman."

The prosecutor was wrong. Tishman's money was very much at stake, and so was that of Ravitch, Chanin, Durst, and other directors and intimates of the bank. Former depositors of Bank of U.S. eventually received back every single penny they had placed in it, though they were deprived of use of the money during the years it took to amass the necessary repayment. Directors and stockholders were more directly and immediately shattered. They lost those pieces of their dreams that had been backed by Bank of U.S. They were even subject to grand-jury indictments charging them with "misapplication of funds of the bank." These charges were not assiduously pressed, but became the basis for a 1934 suit in which the directors were sued for $60 million in damages by New York State for "approving alleged illegal and improvident loans to affiliates and subsidaries." Chanin, Tishman, and Durst all settled with the authorities before trial, and the charges were later dropped after an appeals court voided one of the bank officers' convictions. Chanin agreed to pay $142,000; he was said to owe another $155,000 personally, an additional $300,000 in conjunction with his brother Henry, and to have "contingent liabilities" — that is, amounts owing on their various properties — in excess of $4 million. Their other properties were sold to pay these debts. Tishman and Durst also settled; their exact indebtedness was not reported but was probably in the area of $100,000 each.

In addition to his director's indebtedness, for David Tishman the bank's collapse meant finding $750,000 in cash — the amount of loans his company had outstanding to the bank, and which were called. To pay, he had to liquidate many of the firm's nonbuilding assets, for example, selling cherished real estate parcels once destined for development, such as the choice plot on 42nd Street between Second and Third avenues. Further damage to the family fortunes came from the Tishmans' interlocked investments in such big losers as the Lefcourt company, and in General Realty & Utilities, the company built out of Thompson-Starrett. David's family, at home, knew little of this mess; Bob Tishman recalls hearing only that their father's "good friend Bob Marcus" was going to prison for a while.

The price of the Tishman company's stock fell so low that there was no market for it; the five brothers' wives tried to save up a few dollars and bought odd-lot shares whenever they could. "Only one of the buildings the Tishmans had erected in the 1920s was permanently lost," David's son Bob remembers, though many were temporarily taken back by the mortgage holders, mainly Metropolitan Life and Equitable Life. Belt-tightening allowed the retention of the bulk of the Tishman holdings; some remained in inventory through a strange but legal form of genteel blackmail. Many buildings had been erected on leased land; the yearly fee for land usually ran about 5 percent of the land's value, say $250,000 on an apartment-building-sized plot along Park Avenue worth $5 million. On top of this land might sit a building valued at an additional several million dollars. When an owner-operator saw that he'd shortly be unable to make his lease payments, he could threaten to give the building back to the landholder, who would then be responsible for the taxes on the completed building as well as on the underlying land. Faced with having to assume such a burden, a landowner might agree to a reduction in lease payments, say, down to $150,000 a year or even less, to avoid having to carry the building himself. Such tactics were used by General Realty & Utilities, whose directors included David Tishman. When times got tough, the big boys played hardball.

Personal troubles intermingled with financial ones. Louis, David's favored brother, died in 1931 of the long-term effects of the poison gas he had inhaled on the battlefields of the Great War; he left a widow and three children, among them John Tishman. "My mother took in David's family in the summers in order for us all to get by," John remembers.

In the middle of the decade, Bob Tishman graduated from Cornell and came to work at the family firm. No choice was involved. Job opportunities were scarce enough during the hard times; moreover, his entry into the firm had been talked about throughout his youth, and he had looked forward to it. Bob was a taller, quieter version of his father. "Dad put me to work managing and collecting from the family's light protectors," he recalls. These were twenty-foot-wide buildings erected at the flanks of some of the large Tishman apartment houses on the Upper West Side, principally to deprive rival builders of the opportunity to put up adjacent buildings that might cut off the light and air in the Tishman structures. Collecting rents from light protectors was an unenviable task, but fundamental to keeping the family's holdings intact in these difficult years.

Other firms, faced with bleak prospects, let executives go, but that could not be done so easily in a family business. As a consequence the Tishmans and their business came under considerable strain. Family businesses often fail, argues John L. Ward, an expert in the field, when they neglect to "prune the family tree," resulting in "sibling rivalry and subsequent managerial conflict." That's what happened to the Tishmans. Father Julius died in 1935, but he had long since given way to David, so continuity and leadership was assured for a while. However, the line of succession after David became a battleground in which Paul and Norman, younger than David by eleven and thirteen years, were the main combatants. These two youngest brothers had been at odds since childhood. Always an iconoclast, Paul found his style stifled within the family company. In the mid-1930s, after a dozen years in the company, he had fully served his apprenticeship and was ready for big projects just at the time when there were none and would be none for some time. Moreover, the tasks of a bad period did not play to Paul's strengths — design sense, construction expertise — but rather to the mundane, difficult business of managing the family's holdings well enough to provide incomes for everyone.

Norman, on the other hand, had an advantage in that his wife was the sister of David's wife, and their families were thus doubly close. David worked hard to keep both his brothers in harness, but things came to a head in the late 1930s. "There was a debate about being able to keep everyone in the company, then," Bob recalls. Things were picking up a bit, especially outside of Manhattan, and Norman and Bob were spun off from the parent company as an independent construction firm. If profits from the new construction had accrued to the larger firm, these might have been seized by the insurance companies to pay off long-standing debts.

This maneuver allowed Norman to have a separate income and to relieve the family firm of the burden of his salary. It also cooled down the potential conflict for a time. Nobody formally asked the dynamite question of who, precisely, would succeed David — because the answer would have split the family immediately. Paul got an upgrade to vice president but continued to chafe at his restrictions.

The late 1930s were a time of renewal for many players in the Manhattan real estate scene, large and small. David and Samuel Rose were constructing their first big Manhattan project, near Columbia University. Sam Rudin commissioned a first Manhattan apartment house from Emery Roth. Leo Bing was completing an Emery Roth project that he had actually begun a decade earlier, six apartment houses on both sides of East 73rd Street between Second and Third avenues, known as East Village. As the depression lifted, the sons of Harris Uris, Percy and Harold — their old firm bankrupt — used personal savings to buy a plot and commission the Roth firm to design a large apartment building at 930 Fifth Avenue.

That completed, the Urises were again doing well enough that Percy sought to buy the venerable Biltmore Hotel from Harold Vanderbilt. The two men regularly played bridge at the Metropolis and other clubs — Percy, like Bill Zeckendorf, was an excellent bridge player — and Percy got ready to pop the question at a game in which he was paired with Vanderbilt. But the cards ran against them, and the team of Uris and Vanderbilt went down badly to defeat. "There goes the Biltmore," Uris thought to himself, and a brief postmortem with Vanderbilt proved him right.

Some property casualties of the depression could not be rescued. In 1940, after a series of owners had defaulted time and again on mortgage and tax payments, the Roth-designed Beresford and San Remo apartment houses were sold, together, for the absurdly small sum of $25,000 and an agreement to take over the mortgages. By that time, however, HRH and Emery Roth were on to new projects. Roth was emboldened to design and even to sink his own money (along with three larger partners) into the biggest residential building put up in Manhattan since the Beresford and San Remo, the 250-unit Normandy Apartments on Riverside Drive, between 86th and 87th streets, on a bluff above the Hudson River. In the Normandy, luxury was redefined; whereas the Beresford and San Remo had boasted maids' quarters, separate dining rooms, and huge entrance halls in their apartments, the Normandy conceived luxury as labor-saving devices and extra terraces. Dining rooms had become dinettes, entrance halls were reduced to foyers, and maids' rooms disappeared. The previous generation's extravagances could no longer be afforded by either the builders or the renters of new apartments.

The Normandy was made feasible, in part, because a government project had covered over the previously open railroad tracks between Riverside Drive and the Hudson. Once residents would not be bothered by trains puffing smoke in their windows, the bluff became suitable for a luxury residential building. Public-works projects under the direction of Robert Moses had absorbed much of the building energies of the 1930s, creating parkways around Manhattan and two key gateways to the city — the Lincoln Tunnel and the George Washington Bridge. In the words of an influential planning report, these highways were to be "a sculptor's armature to serve as infrastructural support for the desired suburbanization and decentralization of the region." The highway system and river crossings sent many families to lower-cost living quarters outside Manhattan, but also provided managerial-class breadwinners access to Manhattan and thereby encouraged the transformation of the island from a center for residences and light manufacturing into an island even more full of business skyscrapers.

The 1933 musical *As Thousands Cheer* included a skit in which Junior Rockefeller begged his father to take his midtown buildings back as a gift, because they were losing so much money and bringing so much ridicule to him. The project was a hotbed of familial intrigue, as well as the source of good jokes for the theater. In 1932 Nelson had finally convinced his father to change the project's name from Metropolitan Square to Rockefeller Center. Junior had earlier said no, as he was not in the habit of splashing his name over buildings or foundations; for example, either the Museum of Modern Art or the Cloisters could easily have been called Rockefeller Museums, since his family provided the lion's share of the funding for each, but they weren't so named. In the matter of the center, however, Junior Rockefeller's other advisers remarked that since he had put more than $100 million into the project, which was supposed to be a business venture, and the Rockefeller family was closely linked with the best of American business, Junior was certainly entitled to name it after his family. Moreover, they said, the Rockefeller name could draw the sort of corporate tenants that the project must attract if it were ever to become profitable. In 1934

Rockefeller Center was still in the red but was earning more respectability, and the producers dropped the skit from the Broadway musical. Nelson firmed up his alliance with brother John over long lunches in the elegant Rainbow Room, an exclusive club by day, a public nightclub in the evenings. He did a creditable job bringing in tenants and had a flair for publicity that everyone considered necessary to bring the project to the point of at least paying its current operating costs and making a dent in the $100 million Junior had already laid out.

An important artistic corner was turned in 1936, when the influential French architect Le Corbusier visited New York. Though generally acerbic about the city's buildings — "The skyscrapers of New York are too small and there are too many of them," — he admired Rockefeller Center, a "machine-age temple [that] affirms to the world the dignity of the new times by its useful and noble halls." Even Lewis Mumford, who had earlier derided the center, now called it "architecturally the most exciting mass of buildings in the city . . . an impressive collection of structures." Other Manhattan builders saw how formidable Rockefeller Center was; all later office skyscraper projects would refer to it as their model for a business city-within-a-city.

In 1938, a year after John D. Rockefeller, Sr., died, Nelson finally succeeded in retiring John Todd with a golden handshake, overcame the last of Junior's objections, and was anointed president of Rockefeller Center. In a move related to Junior Rockefeller's new understanding of the business situation, he had Wallace Harrison, the architect related to the family through marriage, design apartment houses for plots on West 54th and West 55th streets, once bought in the vain attempt to keep the middle class from overwhelming his private enclave. That done, Junior moved at last from his 54th Street home to a forty-room triplex at 740 Park Avenue and traded lots with the Museum of Modern Art (Nelson was pushing for control of that, as well) so MoMA could open a sculpture garden and later build on the land where three generations of Rockefellers had lived.

On November 1, 1939, Nelson Rockefeller was master of ceremonies at a celebration in honor of the completion of Rockefeller Center. Three hundred people sat in the cold, damp, unfinished lobby of the fourteenth building of the complex, its rough concrete walls draped with red, white, and blue bunting. Across the ocean, war was being fought. The United States had still not entirely climbed out of its decade-long depression, but the world's largest business center, one of the glories of Manhattan and the epitome of the cultural mix of the 1930s, was an accomplished fact. Junior, now sixty-five, shared the podium with Mayor Fiorello La Guardia, the president of Columbia University, a labor leader, and General David Sarnoff of NBC, whose radio network carried the proceedings nationwide. After opening speeches, Junior took off his overcoat and donned workman's gloves. Using a riveting hammer ("the machine gun of American industry and peace," the *New York Times* gushed), he drove in the last piece of the center, a two-pound rivet made entirely of silver. During the years of construction, he had given employment to 75,000 unionized workers, and for that, the labor leader said, everyone could be grateful to Mr. Rockefeller. Noting that the project had raised New York's tax base, Mayor La Guardia suggested to Junior, "Look around you and see if you could put up a few more centers in the city." Junior must have gasped inwardly: the once reluctant patron and energizing force was still owed upwards of $100 million by his center, and didn't know when or if he'd recoup his investment, even on the day he was celebrated as the biggest and best builder of the hard years in Manhattan.

PART THREE

EMPIRE BUILDING

Chapter Ten

Making Matches

BALDING, and with his expanding girth only adding to the impression of his size and power, thirty-six-year-old Bill Zeckendorf sat in the penthouse apartment of Vincent Astor at 120 East End Avenue in the wartime spring of 1942 and tried to close the biggest deal of his life. The penthouse was among the most spectacular apartments in Manhattan, twenty rooms constructed to Astor's specifications, filled with antique treasures, and offering broad views out over the East River. It overlooked the Hell's Gate area, where John Jacob Astor had had his summer home, and fronted on Gracie Square, the park that was front lawn to the home of New York's mayor.

Astor, fifty-one, had volunteered to serve in the navy and was now a commander about to leave town to shepherd convoys across the Atlantic, a notion that thrilled him. He was interviewing Webb & Knapp because he wanted his real estate empire looked after while he was on active duty.

In 1912, on his twenty-first birthday, Vincent had stalked into the family office on West 26th Street and begun a revolution in the way the Astors did business. His father, John Jacob Astor IV, had recently gone down with the *Titanic*. The family's real estate was then worth $63 million but young Vincent, who had dropped out of Harvard because of his father's demise, didn't like the way it was being run. Romantic and imbued with the spirit of progressive reform, Vincent took to the streets of Manhattan, knocking personally on the doors of buildings he owned, trying to find out whether any were being operated as brothels. He didn't want to profit from vice, even indirectly, and would evict tenants who used the premises for illegal activities. He began to get the family out of the business of owning tenements and into other construction — an apartment house and an open market on upper Broadway, an office building on the old Astor Hotel block adjacent to the Woolworth tower. Within a year he had to sell the public market at a loss and suffered other reverses. His mind wasn't on business: Vincent wanted to take flying lessons, to improve the country's agriculture, to marry, to uplift the world. Shortly, he began pulling back from real estate except for the occasional venture. Income from his properties plummeted but was still enough to support a grand lifestyle.

The young reformer of 1912 became the archetypal heir and socialite of 1942, spending his life in pursuit of diversions. Connected through marriage to the Roosevelts, he was part of the crowd that entertained the president in Manhattan, upstate at Rhinebeck, and in Washington. Two partners in Webb & Knapp, social acquaintances of Astor's, sat in the room with Zeckendorf, the commander, and two Astor real estate advisers, one a tall and slender former actor, the other, diminutive and red faced. To Zeckendorf, they resembled "the ascender and the dot of an exclamation point." Astor finished the last of several scotches he had drunk during the afternoon, announced it was time for cocktails, switched to martinis, and inquired of Zeckendorf, "Well, what do you think of my properties?"

"For the most part, Commander," replied the brash Zeckendorf, who had done his homework, "they stink. They are outmoded."

Astor's reaction was stark silence, and Zeckendorf thought the sound of someone shifting in his deep leather chair was like gunfire. But he knew he was on target: $50 million in debt-free properties were returning Astor $500,000 in income, only 1 percent a year — they could hardly have been doing any worse. The depression was over, but aside from such winners as the St. Regis Hotel (in which Astor had taken a strong personal interest), very few Astor holdings had returned to profitability. Rather than getting Zeckendorf shown to the door, his straight business talk proved a tonic to Astor, whose properties had for some years been in the hands of drinking buddies whose conviviality had replaced the sixth sense of Southmayd and other early advisers of the Astor clan. Convinced, Astor agreed to give Webb & Knapp a free hand while he was at war. In a single stroke, Zeckendorf became one of the biggest real estate players in town.

The handshake between the last of the Astors and the first modern real estate tycoon was a sign of the changing of the guard. Though the boom of the 1920s had partially displaced the Astors, Rhinelanders, Beekmans, and other great landholders as the builders of Manhattan, it was the surge of the 1940s and 1950s that brought to true dominance the families who created the preponderance of Manhattan's skyscrapers.

Knowing that any Astor property had a cachet attractive to buyers, Zeckendorf sold off the less desirable ones through an ingenious scheme aimed at hiking the value of them all. He proposed very high purchase prices but accepted small cash down payments and made the deals attractive by taking back large second mortgages. Thus a property that previously sold for $400,000 would be noted in the newspapers as having fetched $1 million; the press would not know that the property had been transferred for only $50,000 cash down and that it bore an Astor second mortgage amounting to the difference between the buyer's actual price and $1 million. Because the price of this property had ostensibly risen, prices for Astor's adjacent properties also went up. Zeckendorf bought as much as he sold, using Astor money to buy and lease in an area he'd long coveted but which had been off-limits because he'd lacked purchasing power: Park Avenue from Grand Central north to 59th Street, which he saw as ripe for business development. Within a year, through dozens of deals, he increased the value of Astor's holdings by several million dollars and tripled its annual earnings. He also enriched Webb & Knapp by obtaining a fee of $350,000 (and a bouquet of flowers) from the pleased Vincent Astor.

With the authority to buy, and the weight of $50 million in properties behind him, Zeckendorf had his choice of good deals for Astor and for himself. Although there was always room in the Manhattan skyscraper game for the occasional lone hand who could pull off a spectacular deal, what counted most was sheer size. The larger the mass, the greater its gravitational pull, causing ever more deals to come the way of Astor-Zeckendorf. Earlier, Big Bill had played a good hand of bridge; now he became adroit at multiple buying, selling, swapping, and mortgaging that was akin to an intricate bidding match. He described to *Life* magazine a typical deal of this era:

> We had a property in Detroit that cost $100,000. It didn't look like it was going to make any money. So we swapped it for another piece in Brooklyn and a second one in Camden,

N.J., and took on a $60,000 mortgage. We exchanged the mortgage for a building in Rockland, Mass. Then we sold that for $60,000. We still weren't getting anywhere. So I gave the Camden property and $80,000 for a piece of Trenton, N.J. We raised a $100,000 mortgage on that and about the same time sold the Brooklyn piece for $77,000. Then we got out of the Trenton deal for $30,000 and a building on 161st Street, Manhattan, and sold that for $20,000 and finally we had the Detroit turkey off our hands and $50,000 in the bank. Simple.

Of course it wasn't simple, and Zeckendorf reveled in its complexity; the more Byzantine the deal, the greater its attraction. When he turned the properties back to Astor in 1945, Zeckendorf had completed 152 transactions and had increased the estate by $10 million and the return rate by $2.5 million per year. In the same period, and not incidentally, Webb & Knapp had raised its corporate net worth from minus $127,000 to plus $2 million.

Among the properties Zeckendorf bought for his own account in 1945 was the Swift & Wilson slaughterhouse, center of a district of abattoirs north of Tudor City along the East River. So strong was the odor from these butcheries that one section of Fred French's dream had been built without northern windows to keep out the stench of death. Zeckendorf had been thinking of this area since he had worked for the broker who had assembled the Tudor City site. He wanted to create a complex that would surpass both the residential splendor of French's dream and the commercial distinction of Rockefeller's center. Over the abattoir district he imagined a fourteen-square-block raised platform of the sort that had covered the railroad tracks and created modern Park Avenue. Atop his new platform Zeckendorf envisioned four office towers, a hotel, a convention hall, a new home for the Metropolitan Opera, underground parking for 5,000 cars, and a series of luxury apartment buildings that would reach to Beekman Place.

The price of the Swift & Wilson facility was $6.5 million. Zeckendorf paid out $1 million as an option; the remainder was due in December 1946. In the next year, Zeckendorf quietly bought up adjoining parcels until he controlled the entire area from 42nd to 49th streets, from Second Avenue east to the river. To prevent competitors from learning of his involvement, during the assembly procedure he took a vacation in Rio de Janeiro. Even there, however, he did a little business, for one owner of a small property lived in Rio, and Zeckendorf personally convinced him to sell.

There is an adage that it takes a big man to have a big dream. Zeckendorf's vision refines this presumption. Only a few years earlier, for him to postulate a huge complex would have been merely a theoretical exercise, as he had neither the resources nor the reputation as a big operator necessary to realize such a dream. Now sizable enough, he had a reasonable chance of bringing to fruition a city-within-a-city. Unable to sleep because his idea was so exciting, Zeckendorf called Wallace Harrison, who had first come to prominence with his work on Rockefeller Center, though his roots went back to the last years of McKim, Mead & White. Harrison's most striking recent work had been the trylon and perisphere symbols of the 1939 New York World's Fair. Zeckendorf and Harrison sketched out "X City" and included a floating nightclub and marina on the East River and a heliport, in addition to the elements Zeckendorf already wanted. Their discussions were held in the Monte Carlo nightclub that Zeckendorf had had to repossess, so these X City additions owed as much to the liquid blandishments of the hour as did Zeckendorf's earlier deal with Astor.

Toward the end of the war another heir, Nelson Rockefeller, worked on the founding conference of the United Nations and was appointed to a committee dedicated to convincing the UN to choose New York City as its permanent headquarters. The delegates to the Lake Success conference set December 11, 1946, as a deadline for making a decision on the headquarters site. After twisting family arms, Nelson offered the UN the Rockefeller estate at Pocantico. Robert Moses countered with the suggestion of the 1939 World's Fair site in Flushing Meadows, but as the deadline neared the delegates were reported as leaning toward seating the UN in Philadelphia.

Zeckendorf also had a deadline in early December: in a week, for lack of $5 million to complete his purchase, he'd lose the X City site and his $1-million down payment. On Friday, December 6, he made the obvious connection between his holdings and the current headlines and announced to his wife, Marion, "I'm going to put those bastards on the platform." He would offer the site to the city as a home for the United Nations. Calling Mayor William O'Dwyer on the phone, Zeckendorf obtained his flabbergasted assent and a statement that the UN could buy the site for whatever it wished to pay. Harrison then called Nelson Rockefeller and offered him Zeckendorf's site for $8.5 million. In buying the site and welcoming the UN instead of allowing X City to be built, the Rockefellers could wipe out a potential rival to Rockefeller Center, whose vacancy rate was rising and which was still burdened with tens of millions in debt.

Nelson called Junior, who agreed to donate the entire purchase price — "Why, Pa, that's most generous of you," Nelson thanked him — and then sent Harrison to the Monte Carlo, where Zeckendorf held court at lunchtime and after hours. Bill and Marion were celebrating their wedding anniversary and had had a lot of champagne. On a property map, Zeckendorf drew a line around the area from 42nd to 48th and east of First Avenue and signed an option on it to the United Nations. The next morning, Nelson Rockefeller called to say the deal was all wrapped up, and with charactertistic modesty Zeckendorf told his wife, "We have just moved the capital of the world."

At that moment, Junior Rockefeller, approaching his seventieth birthday, wanted to sell Rockefeller Center, into which he had sunk more than $65 million that had not been repaid. The major obstacle to a sale to his sons was that both landowner Columbia University and mortgage-issuer Metropolitan Life had insisted that Rockefeller be personally liable for the lease and mortgage payments. But Rockefeller had learned to use the weapons of a big player, and now applied one of the best, genteel blackmail. Because Junior's lease expired in 1962, the Rockefellers would be within their rights to simply turn the land and buildings back at that time and let Columbia run Rockefeller Center — a frightening prospect for the university, since there was no assurance that the center would then be profitable, and taxes were rising. Columbia agreed to let Junior out of the personal liability clause of their contract in exchange for the center putting in escrow $30 million earmarked for payments on the lease. That matter solved, Nelson and Junior worked out a sale. If Junior gave the center to his five sons, each might have to pay considerable taxes based on its estimated value. But if he sold it at a loss, the Internal Revenue Service ruled, they wouldn't have to pay. So in 1948, Rockefeller Center was bought by the sons for a mere $442,000 each, plus their agreement to take on a debt of $10.6 million each, payable to Junior's estate only at the time of any future sale to non–family members.

Reprieved from its mountain of debt, and under the direction of Nelson and the third generation, Rockefeller Center expanded along the side streets between Fifth and Sixth avenues north of 51st Street and, most importantly, leaped across Sixth Avenue to make towers for Esso and other former tenants who now required buildings of their own. As the postwar boom hit full stride, Rockefeller Center's value increased astronomically, finally fulfilling the profit potential that Junior had seen for it in the 1920s. It became the single most important money-generator for the Rockefeller family. Indeed, the Rockefellers were no longer rich by virtue of oil; their fortunes now derived from Manhattan real estate.

So did those of the Kennedys. Former ambassador to Great Britain Joseph P. Kennedy's career in New York real estate began innocuously with a call to Manhattan's archbishop, Francis J. Spellman, in 1941, shortly after he returned to the United States. Summoned home in disgrace for his isolationist sentiment, Kennedy wanted to sell his Bronxville home and move his legal residence to Florida, which levied neither income tax nor inheritance taxes. Could Spellman recommend a broker? Spellman suggested John J. Reynolds, who had begun in the Bronx early in the century and become a successful independent broker. The diocese's extensive real estate holdings had been entrusted to Reynolds by Spellman; as Astor's estates had done for Zeckendorf, these had helped make Reynolds a big player.

After Reynolds sold Kennedy's house, he told the investor that together they could both make a lot of money in Manhattan real estate because it was still undervalued. During the previous three decades, in Wall Street and in Hollywood, Kennedy had made $30 million. Though a large fortune, it was far less than the immense holdings of the Rockefellers, Astors, and others of the wealthy Protestant establishment. Believing that hard times would ensue after the war, by the early 1940s Kennedy had extracted his money from other investments and had a substantial cash hoard; he was also well enough known as a successful investor to be able to call on banks to loan him money at favorable rates. This was a perfect combination for investing in real estate. Kennedy researched the investments and let Reynolds act as front man and, occasionally, as a decoy for his purchases.

For instance, Reynolds represented "John J. Ford" of Boston, who bought the Siegel-Cooper loft building, in trust for the children of Joseph P. Kennedy. At a public hearing, Reynolds belligerently testified that Kennedy had never seen the property and that he, Reynolds, operated it for the benefit of the children's trust. Kennedy concentrated his investments between 42nd and 59th streets, and eastward from Sixth Avenue. An old hand at buying stocks on margin, Kennedy quickly became comfortable with the commensurate leveraging of real estate through the use of mortgages. He'd buy a building for $1 million, mortgage it for more than 80 percent of its value at the current low rate of 4 percent per year, reap 6 percent from its rents, turn a profit even before the building appreciated, and use the mortgage dollars as down payments on other properties.

Kennedy's timing and ready access to money combined for profit. A corner of 51st and Lexington, bought for $600,000, sold for $3,970,000; a corner of 46th and Lexington, bought for $1,700,000, sold not much later for $4,975,000; a third corner, 59th and Lexington, bought for $1,900,000 — of which only $100,000 was in cash — sold for $6,000,000. In the space of a single decade, by speculating in New York real estate, Kennedy tripled his fortune. After his spree, he devoted his money and energy to furthering his sons' careers in politics.

His rapid-fire tactics in New York left plenty of casualties. Tenants in the Siegel-Cooper building complained to a New York City panel about unconscionably raised rents during the midst of the war effort. The panel was powerless to force Kennedy to roll back rents, but his angry tenants' testimony inspired legislation that imposed commercial rent control on Manhattan. By the time the controls became law, the Siegel-Cooper building had been sold for a million-dollar profit. Shortly, Kennedy vowed not to buy any other commercial properties in the city so long as rent controls remained in force, and began to liquidate his holdings.

Kennedy's goal was to get in and get out, and he did. His dream had nothing to do with creating a real estate empire through acquisition. But that became the aspiration of a matched pair who benefited as Kennedy and Zeckendorf did from being willing buyers in New York City during the war years. They were Harry Helmsley and Larry Wien.

In his youth in Paterson, New Jersey, at the time of the Great War, Wien was exposed to both sides of the headline-making labor conflict recently played out in that city, the silk capital of the United States. Newspapers trumpeted the plaints of the Wobblies, as the members of the Industrial Workers of the World were called, and made it impossible to ignore the near-servile conditions endured by workers in the mills, one of which Wien's father, Joseph, owned. The young Wien knew his father to be kind and generous, and was also impressed by Mayor Nathan Barner, a Paterson benefactor who stated in his will, "The money I have spent and the money I have given away I have enjoyed. The money I leave behind me I have lost."

After entering Columbia College at age sixteen, Wien earned a bachelor's degree in 1925, and took a law degree in 1927. In a geometry class in high school, Wien had solved a problem in such an ingenious way that the teacher declared that he had produced a new theorem; Wien later liked to claim that this was the only new thing he ever invented, and that everything else he accomplished was due to the application of common sense. His father, wary of the stock market, had put his extra cash into second mortgages on apartment buildings; while at Columbia, Larry specialized in residential real estate law. Shortly after graduation, he formed a firm with several partners. Two years later, reasoning that office buildings would be risky in the depression but that people still had to live somewhere, he and three partners paid $2,000 each to buy a small apartment building in Harlem. As the depression wore on, many of the thirty properties on which his father held second mortgages defaulted, and the buildings came into Larry's hands. He managed these well enough to keep them from further default, and bought others.

Wien applied his intelligence to a recurrent problem in his basic law practice. Many widows and surviving dependents of his clients were frittering away money left to them in the form of lump sums or as property. He wanted to devise a way to protect them — some estate-planning vehicle that could put money into real estate and make sure that the investment would pay off properly for years to come. The key was depreciation. If the depression did anything at all for real estate, it was to highlight the concept of depreciation of an asset. In the 1920s, when the price of a building could double in a year or two, owners had little need to use a building's supposedly deteriorating worth to make money from their investment. But when prices of properties fell and rental income shrank, depreciation became a major device to offset income. Tax law assumed that as a building aged, it lost value and in twenty years would be worthless. Accordingly, each year part of the loss could be used to shelter its rental income from taxes.

Such a tax benefit was available only to the actual owners of rental property, usually corporations. In Fred French's syndications, investors didn't directly reap the benefit of depreciation, and they paid taxes twice — once as shareholders of the corporation and a second time, as individuals, on their dividends. "What I wanted to create," Wien later said, "was a vehicle which could achieve a yield of 12 percent while avoiding the high corporate income tax. . . . If I could create a partnership which isn't engaged in business but merely receives a fixed return on capital investment through a conduit, then the investor would have to pay only on an individual income tax." Also, half the investor's return would be tax-free because of depreciation.

Reading through law books, Wien found an Ohio case that dealt with an arrangement now called a sale-and-leaseback. A property was sold to a group of investors who then immediately leased it back to the seller. The seller obtained cash and continued to operate the property (and to receive rental income from it), while the investor-group buyer also benefited — twice. First, the buyer group avoided corporate taxes on income because its members did not actually *operate* the property; second, since they did *own* the property, they were permitted to depreciate and shelter income from it. Wien extracted from the Internal Revenue Service a ruling that said his sale-and-leaseback activities would indeed be subject only to individual taxes. Now he could form partnerships for groups of investors who could buy units for the reasonable cost of $10,000 apiece.

It was on a deal for such a group, in June 1949, that Wien first met Harry Helmsley. Wien represented a half-dozen investors buying a two-story office building on Columbus Avenue for $165,000; Helmsley was the broker for St. Louis University, which would lease back the property. Both men were in their forties, erect and dignified, modest in their personal habits, somewhat religious, and surpassingly smart in real estate.

In the decade since Helmsley had married Eve Sherpick Green, he had converted from the Lutheran faith and become a Quaker, moved to Gramercy Park (near the Quaker meeting house), and prospered. Kept out of the draft by his poor eyesight, he had continued buying distressed properties for a few percent down — an East 57th Street midsize building, for example, for one year's mortgage payment of $16,000. During the 1940s he bought a dozen others, all unornamented buildings on or near major midtown cross-

A Monopoly game played by real tycoons, for the benefit of Homes for the Homeless. At the Regency Hotel's "ultimate power break-fast" were, *right to left*, Bob Tisch, Leonard Stern, Lew Rudin, architecture critic Paul Goldberger, and, substituting for an-nounced participant Donald Trump, Broad-way star Jackie Mason.

1891: First skyscraper dreams. Architects Daniel Burnham and John Root, *top,* in their office in the Monadnock Building in Chicago. From their atelier came a stream of business-minded architects and construction men who skyscrapered Manhattan. Among these were the five Starrett brothers, *above, left to right,* Paul, Goldwin, Ted, Bill, and Ralph. Burnham's most influential New York skyscraper was the Flatiron Building, seen here under construction in 1902.

Just before World War I, Louis Jay Horowitz, seen here with his fiancée, Mary Decker, elbowed one Starrett out of the way and fought with another. He masterminded the construction of the much-admired Wool-worth Building, *left*, and the much-reviled Equitable Building at 120 Broadway, *above*. The Equitable's imposing bulk triggered zoning restrictions that affected the sky-scrapers of the next fifty years.

The booming 1920s: Reflected in the window of Irwin Chanin's 1929 office tower on 42nd Street, *opposite above,* is a gargoyle from the nearby Chrysler Building. The ultimate residential skyscraper, the San Remo on Central Park West, *opposite left,* was designed by Emery Roth, *opposite right,* and constructed by Joseph Ravitch, *left,* for the ill-fated Bank of U.S. *Above,* Fred F. French let his love of the occult show atop the Fifth Avenue building that bore his name.

The Empire State Building, seen here shortly after its completion, in 1931, replaced the Flatiron as the symbol of New York. It was the last project in which any of the Starretts played a leading role.

Undertaking a grand complex was for "Junior" Rockefeller (*top left*, wearing a bowler in 1927) a way of showing independence from his father (in top hat). The area that would become Rockefeller Center (*above*) was full of speakeasies and boardinghouses. Initially, architecture critics hated the complex. Junior turned the decoration scheme over to his son Nelson, then refused to enter the main building through most of its doorways, crowned with what he considered to be offensive nude bas-reliefs (*top right*). Nonetheless, Junior put in the ceremonial last rivet in the fall of 1939 (*left*).

Vincent Astor, left, fifth-generation scion of his landlord clan, shown on his twenty-first birthday and first day of work in the family office, 1912. A handshake agreement with Astor in 1942 allowed Big Bill Zeckendorf, *above,* to do more than dream up gigantic projects. Behind Zeckendorf, on his wall, is the design for X City, on a parcel that later became the site of the United Nations; at his fingertip is a plan for redeveloping a huge area north of Central Park.

*"Damn the Uris brothers,
damn the Tishmans, damn Zeckendorf ..."*

Members of the club. In the 1950s and 1960s, a small group of families dominated the skyscrapering of Manhattan. The three families circulated copies of this cartoon, signed them, and added a caption of their own: "Damn the pedestrians." The heirs of Emery Roth continued to be the architects for most of the families: *above, left to right,* Julian Roth, Richard Roth, the firm's gray eminence, Mrs. Beale, and, next to a photograph of his grandfather, Richard Junior.

The Tishmans. Grandfather Julius (*above left, opposite*) built his first tenement on the Lower East Side in 1898 (*above right, opposite*). His son David (*opposite left*) led the family firm to the forefront of skyscraper builders, finally putting their own name on a headquarters at 666 Fifth Avenue (*opposite right*). Unable to continue together, the third generation split in three directions. *This page, top:* Robert Tishman (*at left*) formed Tishman-Speyer with his son-in-law, Jerry Speyer (*at right*); among their projects, the tallest building in Europe. Bob's brother Alan, *above*, seen here with his wife, Peggy, is a power in leasing and management. Cousin John Tishman, *left*, the country's foremost construction expert, now heads a rejuvenated version of the old family firm.

Skyscrapers into culture. Top left: Lawrence A. Wien (*left*) with Francis Cardinal Spellman at the 1966 dedication of the archdiocese's educational broadcasting station. Wien used proceeds from the sale of part of the lease of the Empire State to his better-known partner, Harry Helmsley, *top right* (seen here with his second wife, Leona), to help complete the first group of theaters at Lincoln Center. The Rose family, seen here in about 1967 (*from left*, Dan, Fred, and Elihu standing, David Rose seated) became the major donors for the newest building at Lincoln Center, opened in 1990, seen in the center of the photograph at left and named for their father, Samuel, and their uncle David.

On returning from World War II, many sons of this generation of developers joined their fathers in the family firm. *Top left:* Lew, *left*, and Jack Rudin in 1946, when they began an apprenticeship with their father, Sam, *top right*. Lew became one of the city's most visible boosters, and is seen above with David Rockefeller, presenting a humanitarian award to Mayor Abe Beame in 1975. Jack, the builder, remained a more private figure. The Rudin empire's headquarters, 345 Park Avenue, *left*, was designed by Emery Roth & Sons.

Queens comes to Manhattan. The Trumps and
LeFraks made their initial fortunes in the
outer boroughs. Both families were late-
comers to the business of skyscrapering
Manhattan. Sam LeFrak, *above left*, billed
himself as the developer for the common
man, while Donald Trump, *above*, tried to
create luxury in his Trump Tower on Fifth
Avenue, *left*, and in casinos in Atlantic
City.

Quartet of titans. Larry Silverstein, *top left,* and Bernard Mendik, *top right,* once brothers-in-law and partners, had a difficult time separating their interests. Each now heads a major independent firm. Seymour Durst, *left,* was the premier property assembler of his generation. Richard Ravitch, *above,* relinquished skyscraper-building for public service, including several years as head of the MTA. The latter two men tangled over the character of Manhattan Plaza.

End of an era. The party to celebrate the ninetieth anniversary of the founding of the Tishman firm was held in the Rainbow Room of Rockefeller Center in the spring of 1988. *Above left:* Host John Tishman chatted with Mayor Ed Koch, whose administration had fostered the skyscrapering of the city. At the party were many from the club of builder families: *above*, Daniel Rose of Rose Associates traded stories with John Brademas, president of New York University (*left*), and labor lawyer Ted Kheel (*right*). Shortly afterward, new skyscraper construction came crashing to a halt that threatened to last well into the 1990s.

streets, with newsstands and restaurants in the lobbies. His typical partners were his wife, his brother Walter, who worked for him, and Dorothy Schwartz, wife of his associate Alvin Schwartz as well as daughter of longtime friend Leon Spear. (Shortly, Schwartz was asked by Spear to come into his business, and left Helmsley; this was a blow, but not unexpected in the family-dominated arena of Manhattan real estate.) In 1946, Voorhis was forced out and the firm became Dwight-Helmsley. That same year Helmsley sold the first building he'd bought (in 1936), the ten-story loft structure on 23rd Street, for $165,000, after having paid down considerably the $100,000 mortgage and having had it profitably rented all that time.

The Helmsleys had no children. Eve had had a child by her first husband, a son who died one day after she gave birth. Harry devoted his off-work hours to occasional flings at dancing, a week-end round of golf, and some duties for the Quakers, but his main recreation was perusing briefcases full of real estate documents. He seldom attended the theater or concerts and, aside from professional organizations, was uninvolved in his community and city. By contrast, Wien and his wife had two daughters, he was a regular at the theater, opera, and concerts, and already a substantial contributor to Columbia University and to Jewish causes.

One benefit of a complicated real estate deal is that it allows those involved time and circumstances in which to size up one another. As it had been with Bill Zeckendorf and the Webb & Knapp team, this was the case with the Helmsley-Wien Columbus Avenue sale; from the first deal, the participants came away with impressions propelling them toward alliance.

At the closing, Wien, five-foot-nine-inches tall, was surprised by the size of the six-three Harry Helmsley, his six-five brother Walter, and their associate, Jim Early, who at six-six "looked like a lineman for Notre Dame." During the negotiations Wien discovered Harry Helmsley to be "one of the most astute people I ever met." Wien learned that Helmsley could forecast the economic direction in which a neighborhood was heading, knew what improvements (new elevators, more shine to the brass, better windows) would bring in new tenants, and could figure out which rental leases could most easily be renewed at higher rates. That was because Helmsley's business wasn't just sales; unlike most brokers, he made a significant fraction of his income from management, which gave him a broader perspective.

Helmsley understood right away that the sale-and-leaseback

structure the brilliant lawyer had perfected would enhance not only Helmsley's capacity to make deals for buildings but also the fortunes of his property-management firm, which could operate future properties when sellers didn't want to do so. Wien, he saw, was a good persuader: he had already put investors together to acquire fifty buildings, and was itching to expand from residential to large commercial buys. After the deal was closed, Helmsley asked Wien if he was interested in other properties; of course he was.

"At the time," Wien later recalled, "the banks, insurance companies, and investment houses wanted to have nothing to do with real estate." Burned in the depression, they were overreacting by staying completely out of the kitchen. Scarcity of financing translated into fewer groups trying to buy, even though a plethora of attractively priced buildings were available. So there were tremendous opportunities for people with both the money and the acumen to buy. Helmsley found and evaluated the properties, and Wien checked his analyses and provided the cash to buy them: a perfect match.

In acquisition real estate, partnerships are always desirable. What you looked for was someone (preferably a relative) with a body of expertise that overlapped your own but was different, who could follow your logic, correct fallacies or inaccuracies, and then bet with you on a common project and accept the gains or losses from it without breaking stride or quitting the field of play. You tested that partner on one or two transactions; if you were still in tandem after several, you kept going and grew closer together and more bold in your outside reach.

Immediately upon teaming up, Wien and Helmsley bought the Brewster Building in Queens, where chassis frames had once been built for Rolls-Royce cars; Harry found it, and Larry rounded up clients who put in $10,000 a share and incorporated as Brewster Investors. Helmsley quickly found two more, the first in the garment center at 501 Seventh Avenue, the second, which he had coveted for many years and stared at from the Flatiron Building, the headquarters of the toy industry, called the Toy Building at 200 Fifth Avenue, just opposite Madison Square.

In New York real estate, a successful operator later wrote, "Property is appraised according to the return it brings investors, and the effect of the syndicate has been quite simply to double values. A building worth $5 million to a corporation is now worth $10 million to a syndicate." Because the syndicate would pay taxes at an individual rather than a corporate rate, Wien and Helmsley could offer top dollar, spend more to acquire properties than other buyers, and beat out almost any other bidder.

Though Wien invested alongside the other members of the syndicate, Helmsley did not. Harry's income came from his broker's fee and from Wien's allowing him to assign the management of the building to his own subsidiary, which guaranteed him a continued income from the building. Wien and Helmsley pledged investors at least 10 percent annual return for a period of ten years; after that, the building would probably be sold, and investors would then receive 50 percent of any profit — which could be very considerable, as most buildings went up in value. With economics such as these, it was no wonder that after the first three Wien-Helmsley syndicate purchases Harry felt he was doing well enough to buy into the ownership of the Flatiron Building and to purchase a hilltop site in a wealthy Westchester community that overlooked the Hudson River and a nearby golf course, where he began to build a house. Once in a while, at Larry's behest, the Helmsleys and their new best friends, the Wiens, would attend the theater together.

During their honeymoon period, Harry Helmsley and Larry Wien went on a buying tear, using the syndicates and sale-and-leaseback mechanisms to acquire some of New York's better skyscrapers and hotels — including the Shelton Hotel on Lexington Avenue at 49th Street and the Hotel Lexington a block further south, the Fisk Building at 250 West 57th, and the fifty-three-story Lincoln Building at 60 East 42nd Street. "If I was a girl, I'd be pregnant all the time," Helmsley said in a rare moment of public ebullience. "When someone comes in with a good deal, I can't say no."

On each property Helmsley thought ripe for a syndicate deal, he would gather the facts and write Wien a "Dear Larry" letter so concise and insightful that many became texts; copies circulated through the Helmsley brokerage and management offices as models of great real estate thinking. The two men used a common language that was mathematically based. "If you were in a room with them," remembered Alvin Lane, a former law partner of Wien's, "you wouldn't know what the hell they were talking about. It was sort of a volleyball game of numbers."

In 1955, for half a million dollars, Harry bought his old friend Leon Spear's space-management firm, though not solely because of its strength in the garment center; rather, he wanted to return Alvin

Schwartz to the fold. The firms were merged as Helmsley-Spear and took space in the Lincoln Building. Helmsley-Spear couriers in red jackets and black pants seemed to be all over town delivering messages for what had overnight become one of the largest management concerns in the city. With Schwartz and Irving Schneider as his lieutenants, Helmsley was relieved of the day-to-day responsibilities that could hamper his deal-making activities. They, as well as brokers who brought deals to Helmsley, frequently received shares in the acquisitions done for the Helmsley-Wien syndicates.

The syndicators became even more bold, going after the Taft Hotel at Seventh Avenue and 50th Street, three more hotels in the midtown area above Pennsylvania Station, forty parcels in the Union Square area, and the double filing cabinets of 120 Broadway. They bought the most glittering hotel in New York, the Plaza, on Central Park South, for $21 million, the most money ever paid for a hotel to that time. It was bought virtually overnight. On a Friday, Wien wrote one of the "Sincerely, Larry" letters that accompanied an SEC-approved offering to a handful of past investors and received enough money by return post on the following Monday to cover the purchase.

After the transformation of X City into the United Nations, Zeckendorf became a real estate adviser to the Rockefellers; he also rapidly outgrew his conservative partners and soon bought them out. The new, Zeckendorf-owned Webb & Knapp needed a spectacular office. Ieo Ming Pei, a graduate design professor at Harvard, designed a cylinder that sat above the highest floor of the twelve-story building at 383 Madison Avenue and housed an executive dining room at the top. Below, abutting extensive roof terraces with gardens and statuary, was Zeckendorf's office, with many doors leading to side conference rooms. As Zeckendorf later wrote, his raised offices dominated the building — and the real estate industry — "as effectively as the lone turret of that famous Civil War ironclad, the *Monitor*, once dominated its own deck and the water for miles around."

Zeckendorf then decided he needed a public company. Only that, he thought, would make possible the larger ventures he had in mind, projects on the scale of clearing an entire section of Atlanta or Denver. He found an old holding company that was broke but still traded on the American Stock Exchange. In what was styled a reverse merger, Webb & Knapp absorbed American Superpower through an exchange of stock in which, on paper, Zeckendorf appeared to lose $10 million. However, in acquiring the indebted company he also bought enormous tax credits he could offset against other income. Also, since he was now sole owner of a public company, he could issue stock and sell some to wipe out his considerable personal debts and to start new ventures. He bought a limousine and equipped it with a ship-to-shore telephone. He bought a DC-3 airplane. On one trip out west, he was maneuvered into stopping off to see a nudist colony wedding. There, he was confronted by a well-endowed stripper (each breast insured for $50,000) who curled up next to him and waited for the flashes of accompanying photographers to go off. Zeckendorf had a moment of panic when the pictures were printed in the New York newspapers. Returning to his grand circular office in Manhattan, he found two of the most conservative bankers in the nation, the heads of J. P. Morgan and of Morgan Guaranty, waiting to see him. He thought sure they had concluded that he was no longer a good credit risk and were there to call in his loans. But they only wanted some less printable details of the nudist colony encounter.

At around this time, Vincent Astor had grown restless again. After Zeckendorf returned charge of the properties at the end of World War II, the Astor holdings, under less capable managers, had slid back into lassitude. One typically bad lease permitted a shoe-repair parlor to remain on the ground floor of an otherwise vacant tenement, rendering the building unsalable. A new adviser convinced Astor that real estate wasn't paying well enough — this in a boom era — and persuaded him to sell properties and put his money in stocks for long-term appreciation. Forced sales were always obvious to the real estate community, and buyers offered relatively low prices for Astor's parcels; he took most offers, but kept one property that seemed so suitable for a big office skyscraper that he determined to build his own. In 1955 he announced he would erect Astor Plaza on the entire block bounded by Park Avenue, Lexington Avenue, 53rd, and 54th streets; the project would cost $75 million. The site was not precisely his — it belonged to his English cousins — but he took a long lease and began clearing the site, leaving a huge hole in the ground at which onlookers gaped.

Astor was also in the midst of personal turmoil, shedding a wife and courting the recently widowed Brooke Russell Marshall, features editor of *House and Garden*. He was also suffering through the last illness of the only Astor relative to whom he was personally close, his sister, Alice. That was one reason for his difficulties. The other was that he had made his plunge at an inauspicious time; the hole in the ground soon became known as Disaster Plaza. No sizable corporate tenants would agree to sign up just then, and even Astor did not possess funds enough to foot the construction bill. He went to banks and other lending institutions, but these had a general rule of not issuing mortgages on leased land, only on buildings. There may have been some dissembling, here; in another exactly contemporary and notorious instance, an insurance company agreed to join in the construction of a building with a developer, then backed out at the last moment and watched the developer sink deep into debt until he was forced to sell his lease to the insurance company, which then used his plans to put up its own skyscraper there. Astor might have found equity partners among the Jewish builder families, but for the most part his social circle excluded them, and none offered on their own to share the load. The Minskoffs, for example, were having their own problems a block away from Disaster Plaza, in a building under construction on Lexington Avenue.

Having to pay the taxes and lease-fees on the land was costing Astor millions. Hat in hand, he applied to his English cousins, the children of that William Waldorf Astor who had so viciously broken with his father more than sixty years earlier. Vincent proposed that the two branches of Astors put up the building together. The English cousins refused. Distraught, Astor told Brooke that he must have had a hole in his head to have started the hole in the ground. His real estate advisers counseled patience; soon there would be a turnaround in the business climate, and if he held on, his plaza would ultimately be profitable.

This was the moment of truth. Hands-on real estate developers faced this sort of moment with a different mind-set; they knew their markets well, and had learned from experience not to sell when they were losing money if the right sort of odds existed that better days were around the corner. In this instance, Astor's unquestioned size and weight were not enough to continue in the game; he needed the nerves born of experience. He didn't have them. After losing a lot of money, he refused to continue doing so on the chance that he'd eventually make everything back and more. He sold his lease to First National City Bank, which soon put up its own headquarters on the site. After that, Vincent Astor never again developed another building.

Chapter Eleven

Members of the Club

IN NOVEMBER 1941 David Tishman's two sons were on top of the world. Both were recent Ivy League college graduates, newly married, with bright career prospects in the family company. Bob was lanky and thoughtful; Alan, two years his junior, was similarly tall but broader and more outgoing, a born salesman. While working, Alan was taking accounting and law courses at New York University, as his father had done thirty years earlier. Bob had just finished a law course at Columbia. "You don't have to get a law degree," Alan remembers his father advising, even though David had one. "Just take enough courses to know when to hire a lawyer."

Bob had met Phyllis Gordon, a trim and bright young collegian. Once she'd had her sights on being an Olympic swimmer. "But the training would have been too rigorous," she remembered having felt at age thirteen, "so I gave it up when I got interested in boys." After meeting Bob, she attended NYU law school, "with a promise to my family and to myself that all I wanted was the law education — I did not want to become a lawyer." She was a good enough student to be selected to the law review, an academic honor, but never took the bar exam; instead, she married Bob Tishman and in 1940 gave birth to a daughter, Lynne.

Alan met Peggy Westheimer, daughter of a prominent German-Jewish family, at a traditional event for the bringing together of eligible young Jewish men and women, the annual Thanksgiving-eve ball of the Jewish Guild for the Blind. They were teenagers. After Peggy graduated from Wellesley, they were married. Shortly, in November 1941, Alan was called up for duty from the naval reserves. He pleaded with his commander for additional time to enjoy newly married life, but less than a month later the Japanese attack on Pearl Harbor put an end to all such indulgences. Alan was called for active service, and so was Bob, also in the naval reserves. In fact, the navy mixed up the brothers. Bob got a telegram to report to Harvard Business School, which had been taken over by the navy's supply corps. The order had been meant for Alan. Both men eventually ended up in the Pacific, handling millions of dollars worth of supplies and ordnance.

By the time the war was over, the brothers had settled into moderately important positions within the navy supply hierarchy. Then their father called. Nearing sixty and vigorous, David was a commanding, silver-haired presence. But he'd raised his sons as negotiators. "When he said I should come back to the firm and that he'd pay me $100 a week, I turned him down," Alan recalls with a wry smile. "I was a lieutenant commander making $7,500 a year, and with the possibility of a good career in the navy." David called back and told his sons that it would be $7,500 each, "even though we weren't yet worth it. And he wanted no further arguments."

Perhaps that was because the Tishman skyscraper dream was shifting directions. David no longer thought solely about creating an empire, but also about ensuring its future. His sons could have asked any salary, within reason, for what was at stake was the family's continuance in the business.

During the Great Depression, David had become cautious. Even so, tremendous opportunities beckoned in the postwar market, and the family must take advantage of them or be surpassed. David wanted to take the firm out of housing — the basis for its success, to date — and into office towers. With some difficulty, he had landed a site he thought perfect for an office skyscraper. Earlier in his career, he had taken chances on locating new apartments outside established districts. Now he wanted to do the same with a business building, at 57th Street and Park Avenue, then primarily a residential neighborhood. Since potential clients might object to renting there, David decided to include in the first Tishman office skyscraper the latest technology, including central air-conditioning and automatic elevators. Richard Roth, Emery's son, designed adjustable interior offices for the building. When Alan joined the firm, his first task was the renting of 445 Park Avenue. He found that clients loved the possibilities in a scheme that allowed secretaries to have one window, managers two, and higher executives three.

One office skyscraper couldn't keep a whole family of Tishmans

busy for very long, so David accepted commissions for Federal
Housing Administration units in Queens and across the Hudson
River on the palisades of New Jersey. Beyond the four surviving
sons of Julius, plus David's two sons, in the late 1940s the firm
also brought in Louis's son John and two other cousins: nine Tishman to be kept working. Expansion was necessary.

So was an infusion of cash. Comparing ledgers, Alan noted that
"monthly checks from the big Park Avenue apartments were no
greater than those from the FHA apartments we were putting up
in Rego Park." Wartime rent control continued to freeze rents at
depression-era levels. The situation bothered Metropolitan Life
even more than it did the Tishmans. Met Life had taken back from
the Tishmans many residential buildings during the depression,
for which the Tishmans were now acting as managers. David persuaded the insurer to sell the family those classic, prewar Park
Avenue buildings so that they could be converted to cooperatives.
That way, both the Tishmans and Met Life would get their money
out. Alan had to convince Judge Sam Rosenman, former speech-
writer for President Roosevelt and the head of a tenants group, that
it made good sense for the tenants to buy their Park Avenue apartments. "The price was $1500 per room," recalls Alan. "Rosenman
was going to have to pay $15,000 for his ten-room duplex. He was
irked at that. Today, it's worth millions."

After converting a few luxury buildings, the Tishmans decided
that the effort required to overcome tenant resistance was more
trouble than it was worth. They sold their remaining ones to Sam
Weichert, who did eventually convert them all. David retained his
penthouse apartment at 1095 Park Avenue, though he relinquished
the floor below. His children were grown and didn't really want
to move in downstairs. Several other senior members of the firm
had penthouses; it was an expression of style in the builder families.

It also reflected the underlying problem of the Tishman firm —
too many older relatives who felt entitled to the best salaries, though
they might not merit them. A top-heavy structure was a common
burden in family businesses once they were past the first stages of
growth. In an earlier era, with strict laws or customs based on
primogeniture, a similar set of nine related males could have been
configured in such a way as to avoid conflict — but not in America
just after the war.

Now, the bad times behind the firm, David's younger brother
Paul decided to force the family to do what they'd been avoiding

for ten years: choose between himself and Norman for the position of heir apparent. Paul was then in his mid-forties, well trained as a construction chief and with collateral executive experience in every other division of the company. He had become a collector of primitive African art, a breeder of dogs, a maker of furniture. He was a martinet on the construction site — but good construction bosses had to exude authority or else they'd be disobeyed. His principal stumbling block was not of his own making: Paul was becoming the victim of a sort of snobbery. Just as the Tishman priorities were changing, so was the game of being a builder. Earlier, the edge had gone to those who could build well; now, it was enjoyed by those who could handle the financing, the wooing of potential lenders and tenants. As the balance shifted, those responsible for the development and leasing of properties were beginning to look down their noses at those involved in the process of actually erecting buildings. When the structure of a family was small — the brothers Harold and Percy Uris, or David and Samuel Rose — a division of labor was helpful and merely fraternal, because the partners depended on one another in every phase of the business. But when families were larger, and members encouraged to develop specialties, the split could exacerbate natural ability differences and rivalries.

That's what happened to the Tishmans. Though one could not hope to find a more cultured gentleman than Paul Tishman, within the Tishman family the job of head of construction — and its holder — now began to be viewed as covered with a patina of concrete dust. As the financing, deal-making, and leasing arrangements became more complicated, some "developers" came to believe that underlings could be hired to perform the actual construction, promoting the corollary belief that those involved in construction were not able to leave the site, doff their hardhats, and switch to handling the sophisticated tasks of negotiating with banks, insurance companies, and big corporate clients.

Paul was not without allies. He was particularly close to his young nephew John Tishman. John, too, was an iconoclast. Whereas Alan and Bob went to Ivy League schools and immediately entered the family firm, John, after a more plebeian upbringing, studied electrical engineering at the University of Michigan and then became a mathematics teacher at the Walden School, a private school on the Upper West Side where he had once been a student. "I was the only Tishman not forced to join the family business,"

John recalls. But in 1948 Paul asked him to come into the firm, possibly because he needed an ally. John was a scientist, of sorts — a tinkerer, good with his hands; his fellow teachers convinced him this was an opportunity not to be passed by. Still uncertain, he came to work under an alias, a stratagem that lasted precisely four hours, until his mother called and had "John Tishman" paged.

Norman, the other candidate for heir apparent, was two years younger than Paul, and was David's brother-in-law as well as his brother. His specialty was leasing, and he was considered more knowledgeable than Paul at finance, an important factor as the company moved into high-stakes development. He also seemed to have broader horizons; on a trip to Los Angeles, he saw out a hotel window acres of underutilized land, currently held by the big motion picture studios, and convinced the family to buy some and put up buildings there. Alan worked closely with Norman and remembers him as having "a Jekyll and Hyde personality," affable and warm to insiders, but ruthless when facing business competitors (and sometimes suppliers). "He hated to pay commissions to brokers even when they brought deals to him," arguing that they should get their money from the other side. David would invariably pay such commissions to insure that on the next choice piece of property the Tishmans would get the coveted first look.

In late 1948, Paul's question was formally asked and answered. David announced that he would assume the position of chairman and Norman would become president. The battle over, Paul announced his resignation, to take effect on January 1, 1949, precisely twenty-five years after he had joined the company. To finance his own construction firm, Paul sold some of his Tishman Realty stock to non-family members. This was a serious dilution of the family's clear ownership of the corporation. Now they retained less than 50 percent of the stock.

It mattered because the first family of Manhattan builders was not among the very wealthy just then. Alan commuted into the city from Hartford, where he had built a house on land owned by his father-in-law, because he found it too expensive to raise a family in town. For nights when he had to stay in Manhattan, he and Peggy split the cost of a $60-per-month studio with some friends. Tishman Realty & Construction was still a public corporation whose officers (Tishman family members) were permitted to take compensation only in the form of salaries and dividends. While the Urises' and other builders' tax-sheltered incomes were soaring into the stratosphere, the Tishmans were taking home many less dollars from a business that was actually larger than that of any other New York family.

"Those were the days before leveraged buyouts and junk bonds," Bob Tishman points out. In the years after Paul's departure, Bob searched for a way to release the family from the public-company structure. One he chose was to split the stock and sell new shares to raise cash; this allowed the Tishmans' position as controlling stockholders to remain secure even though they now owned only a third of the shares. The sale added to the coffers and enabled slightly larger salaries to be paid to the junior family members.

The three youngest cousins were all pushed toward the hole left by Paul's departure. John remembers being apprenticed in construction, "remote from the family," as assistant to the assistant superintendent on a site in Freeport, Long Island. The two other cousins discovered they didn't like construction. But John soon recognized construction as a way to rise rapidly in the firm. During the depression and war years the Tishman firm had taken work for the FHA in which they constructed buildings that others would eventually manage — the first time they weren't constructing just for themselves. The business of constructing for others grew in the postwar era, which made even more inexplicable to John the gulf widening between development executives and construction experts in the Tishman firm.

"The attitude became apparent on a new office building we were doing at 460 Park Avenue," John remembers. The Tishmans planned to move their corporate offices there, and this occasioned a battle of blueprints. Designs were drawn for two lobbies, each with separate elevators; one would be used by the developers and managers, the other by those Tishman employees "with dirty feet" who had been summoned to headquarters to discuss construction projects with the executives, but who were not to be allowed to muddy up the carpeting of the first lobby and elevator. "The whole idea of two lobbies annoyed me," John says. He understood it as an attempt to deprecate the construction team. The two-lobbies scheme was inked over, but John capitalized on the sentiment behind it; since the other leading executives didn't care for construction, he could take over this lower-status division and encourage its growth into a separate empire. Within five years of joining Tishman Realty, John was able to take over construction completely. One cousin who had come in at about the same time was pushed out to California for projects there, and the other was absorbed into leasing management. John became top dog in construction, Bob was positioned behind Norman in development, and Alan was poised to take over leasing. The triumvirate of the third-generation Tishmans was in place by the early 1950s.

Richard and Julian Roth, the sons of Emery Roth, were both in their forties and had succession problems of a different sort: though Emery was in his seventies, he still had not allowed them to become full partners and share in the profits of the business. After a long illness, their mother, Ella, had died in 1943. During the war, Julian had worked on military housing under the direction of Percy Uris, and Richard for the navy in Providence, Rhode Island. Emery's business was then so slack that he invited other architects to share his offices, so he'd have someone to talk with in between the very occasional jobs; he did all his own drafting for the first time in years. He grew vegetables on the huge terrace of the 101st Street apartment. His grandson Richard, Jr., remembers visiting him there, a cold, stiff, remote, pipe-smoking man. "I liked to go to the apartment to look at his collection of *National Geographic* magazines," says Richard. After Ella's death Emery found the place too large and moved to the Hotel Alden.

As soon as the war ended, Emery was back in business. Percy and Harold Uris asked for plans for a large apartment building at 880 Fifth Avenue, across 69th Street from one Emery had earlier designed at 875 Fifth Avenue. The renderings had already been approved by both the Urises and the bank that would provide the mortgage when Richard Roth arrived home from the service.

In earlier years, Richard had been the dutiful apprentice, kept down by reverse nepotism. Now he had been to war and done well on his own. He made extensive suggestions for changes to the plans for 880 Fifth. If these alterations were accepted, a new set of plans would have to be drawn, and that would eat up the Roth firm's entire fee for the job. Father and son had a face-off over this. Emery asked, "Why redraw them?"

"Father, was that the way you made your reputation?" replied Richard.

Stung, Emery soon came to "cherish that reprimand more than any praise," because it demonstrated that his tradition of excellence would be carried on by his sons. The new plans made the building considerably more modern than any he had attempted before. Still, he refused to grant Richard and Julian the status of true partners until the following year, when throat cancer forced him into semi-retirement. As he recuperated from surgery and radiation treatment, he wrote a memoir. He relived the excitement of the great Columbian Exposition of 1893; the heady days at the turn of the century when he'd cadged commissions from Hungarians along Second Avenue; his four-decade association with the Bings. He lamented the passing of good builders who were not quite tough enough; all had been supplanted now, by the ruthless. Harris Uris passed away in 1945, and others of the old breed were failing. Modernism — even the design predilections of his sons — was openly rejecting the fanciful cartouches and decorative embellishments that had made his buildings so vibrant.

After a lifetime of very little testimonial attention from his peers, in April 1948 the cancer-ridden Emery Roth received the Apartment House Medal from the New York Chapter of the American Institute of Architects for the best high-rise residential structure designed for the city since 1940. The building that won the award was his very last, a nineteen-story residence currently being completed at 300 East 57th Street — a building more modern though less visually eclectic than most of the 250 others he had helped to create. A few months later, Roth died at Mount Sinai Hospital.

After their father's death, Julian and Richard had as much design business as they could handle. Both were modest men, as if in reaction to the baronial touches liked by their father. Richard was the artist; Julian, who had not gone to architecture school, was the construction and technology expert — the classic pairing. Julian even collected images of turtles. They were not close personal friends, though; "Julian could let off steam, while my father bottled up his emotions," Dick recalls. They had different sets of friends. Richard grew close to his neighbors in Purchase, New York: the Urises, the Fishers, and Erwin Wolfson. The Roths had a small plot, while those of the builder families measured thirty acres or so. Julian, meanwhile, was good friends with Sam Rudin.

During this key period, the Roths were in the thick of the building boom as the firm's traditional clients — the Tishmans, Urises, Rudins, Minskoffs, and other old families who had survived the depression — became a virtual club of builders, skyscrapering every corner of Manhattan. After Emery died, these families relied even more on his sons, knowing they were imbued with his sense of care about the "belly" of the building. Richard and Julian developed the Roth firm into a great resource for the builders. Their role as common designer to the club mandated tremendous discretion on their part, and their reputation for diplomacy was exceeded in importance only by their speed.

Julian remembers, "Percy Uris would call me and say, 'Julian, I've just bought a plot of land. How soon can Richard have the plans ready?' "

The Urises probably hadn't really bought the plot yet, but needed the Roths' plans to correctly fashion a bid. The Urises sent over the specifications — the plot size, the building's purpose and possible clients, the zoning requirements — and the Roths responded quickly enough. The first of a series of such phone calls, for a building on a piece of land on Madison just north of St. Patrick's Cathedral, gave rise to one of Richard Roth's most striking designs, a white-concrete, multiple-setback structure whose exterior featured many windows and right-angle curved corners.

Though admirably efficient, most buildings commissioned by the Urises and designed by the Roth firm were not as striking as the *Look* tower; they were considered utilitarian and rather drab. But with a business based on the speed with which the architect could respond to a call, there was little incentive to go for the artistically unique design. And when they did try flights with more fancy, as often as not Richard and Julian were asked to scale back the more extravagant touches. Years later, when asked why he did not design more interesting buildings, Richard was heard to mutter that if he'd had more innovative clients he'd have produced more innovative designs. This was more humble than necessary: the designs were better than critics suggested. And perhaps the forelock-tugging inherent in the statement was subtly encouraged by the Roths' developer clients, to reinforce awareness of the minor place of the architect in the builder's grand scheme. In a period in which beauty was no longer perceived a great sales tool, artistry in buildings was not assiduously cultivated.

Past troubles put behind them, the Uris brothers began a march that soon took them to the forefront of the builder-owners of Manhattan. Timing, luck, connections, the ability to make quick decisions, and the willingness to take risks all figured in their success. Of the buildings that the Urises had completed in the 1920s, only Two Lafayette had stuck with them through the depression. Their first postwar office building was a big gamble that almost didn't pay off. The first hurdle was obtaining a lease on the land at 505

Park Avenue; to do so, they used an attorney who was also close to the Vanderbilt family, owners of the site. While the building was under construction, a sudden slowdown in rentals threatened them with too many vacancies. Shortly before completion, however, a savior came along in the form of the oil company Aramco, which had been looking for an entire building to rent. The success of 505 Park (no matter how close it had come to disaster) gave the Urises a reputation as smart builders, and there was no stopping them. They aggressively bought land and leases, mostly in midtown Manhattan, mostly on plate 78 of the New York City land book, and began to put up office towers. They considered erecting more apartment buildings, but residential tenants always wanted to see the top men about their problems, even if the difficulty could be handled by a plumber. Such a tenant braced Percy in his office one day and gave him a hard time; Percy vowed that as soon as practicable he'd sell the Uris apartment holdings and from then on concentrate solely on office buildings.

Indicative of their single-mindedness was how they viewed the Ritz-Carlton Hotel. In the real estate game, hotels were expensive jewels, often owned for prestige as much as for profit. Originally erected by the Goelets, the Ritz-Carlton had earlier evaded Percy in a bridge game with Vanderbilt, but when it came into the hands of Harvard University after the war he was able to buy it. The hotel was in need of major, expensive repairs. Its original value had come mostly from being near Grand Central Station, but by the late 1940s train travel was beginning to be eclipsed by the airplane, and people arriving in New York by air didn't have to stay in the Grand Central area. The Urises tore down the Ritz-Carlton and put up an office tower at 380 Madison, then one at 300 Park Avenue, and a third on Lexington Avenue.

Richard brought his son Richard, Jr., a recent graduate of architectural school, up to the Uris office. "I looked out the window and saw the new Seagram's Building," Dick remembers. The tower at 375 Park Avenue, between 52nd and 53rd streets, had been designed by Mies van der Rohe in bronze and bronzed-glass with a spacious, invitingly proportioned plaza in front; it was a triumph of the international style Dick had learned to revere in school. A member of the Bronfman family that controlled Seagram's had sought out the greatest artist-architect of his day, and had had the wherewithal to turn van der Rohe's imagination loose on a magnificent site. The result was stunning, but most commercial builders didn't have the resources to indulge in such enterprises. "I said something about the Seagram's Building being beautiful," Dick recalls, "and Percy retorted that 'The only beautiful building is the one that's fully rented.' "

It wasn't that the Urises cared nothing for art — both brothers were interested, sensitive collectors of twentieth-century paintings, prints, and sculpture — but they refused to equate erecting buildings with making art. In this postwar period Percy's main interest was in applying the interlocking elements of the tax structure, which made profiting from reasonable-cost buildings easier than ever before. When land was leased and then built upon, tax laws allowed the builder to deduct from taxable income the rent paid to the ground-holder and, over the terms of the first lease, the entire cost of erecting the building. Beyond that, an astounding loophole called accelerated depreciation permitted the builder to deduct from income not only all the cash he'd invested but also the mortgage money he'd borrowed to erect the building. The Urises (and other developers) could deduct about 30 percent of what they'd invested in each of the first several years of a lease and pay off their investment entirely within three or four years. After that time, they'd completely own the building and have a continuing annual return from it. No wonder there was such a rush to construct office towers during the postwar years.

The Urises, the Tishmans, and Bill Zeckendorf were so busy during this era that a cartoon in *The New Yorker* by Stevenson showed pedestrians picking their way through a maze of Manhattan construction sites saying, "Damn the Uris brothers, damn the Tishmans, damn Zeckendorf." The three families sent copies of the cartoon around among their offices, with a space underneath where they affixed the signatures of the leaders of each clan, along with an additional caption: "Damn the pedestrians!"

Percy and Harold were in their forties, their red heads balding rapidly. Percy was the deep thinker, a man who took calculated risks based as much on his considered opinion of the strength and direction of the economy as on his sixth sense for property. An athlete in his youth, he played tennis and golf regularly, as well as bridge. Harold was quieter as well as younger, larger and more stolid — the construction man through and through. "In meetings, Percy would do nearly all of the talking, but he wouldn't proceed without Harold's agreement," says a man who sat in on their meetings. Harold's assent was often indicated by nothing more than a nod: the strong emotional bond between them, friends thought, permitted Percy to be as daring as he was in business.

"Percy and his wife had had no children, but during the depression they took in two daughters of his wife's sister whom they raised as their own," one of Harold's daughters remembers. Those girls had had a brother, another family member said, but Percy did not raise or adopt him; family lore had it that this boy stayed with his mother to help support her, though Uris intimates later came to believe that Percy hadn't taken the boy in because he had never really wanted a successor in the business. Harold also had a house full of daughters, two from Ruth's earlier marriage and two from their own union. The all-female households were another bond between the brothers. The Uris families lived in penthouses in Park Avenue buildings erected by the brothers, and the daughters went to private schools, several to the Brearley School for girls at 83rd Street just off Gracie Square.

"Daddy," one of his daughters said to Harold after her first few days at Brearley, "one of the other girls' father is a builder, too."

"Oh, yes? Who is that?"

"Lindsey Rockefeller," was the answer.

The laughs that Harold garnered when he told this favorite story stemmed from the understanding on the part of those who heard it that if the sons of an immigrant ironworker were not yet really up with the Rockefellers, they certainly were in the process of getting there.

Part and parcel of the dream in the postwar years was the creation of a lifestyle of comfort, a position of power commensurate with being major players in the building of the city and its future. The Uris brothers were members of the emerging set of *Yidn* real estate families whose social and business lives were converging as they shook off the hard years and began to amass substantial wealth and influence. They shared the same architects, lawyers, and mortgage lenders, and in the social arena their lives continually brushed against one another. "I remember walking down the aisle at Temple Emanu-El for confirmation, stirring a bit of conversation because I was directly behind one of the Tishman girls," another of Harold's daughters recalls. The congregation thought it a clustering of builders; she knew it was just alphabetical order.

Emanu-El, that great Fifth Avenue edifice, the largest temple in the New World, was no longer the sole bastion of the *Yehudim*, many of whom were falling away from Judaism as they entered their fourth and fifth generations in the United States. *Yidn* families were embracing the reform branch of American Jewry, and Emanu-El was its apotheosis. Some complained that new members had bought their way into respectability, but old ones had done the same, in their time. Emanu-El was joined in effacing the distinctions between older and newer crowds by a brace of private clubs. The Harmonie, a social landmark at 4 East 60th, had once recorded its minutes in German and was nearly the scene of a revolution when a member suggested they change to English; the Harmonie fought off the *Yidn* for years, until it needed them to maintain a satisfactory level of membership. Together, *Yehudim* and *Yidn* men had formed the City Athletic Club, at 50 West 54th, because the New York Athletic Club on Central Park South would not accept Jewish members. All the Urises joined the temple, Harold used the Harmonie as a second home, and Percy was a fixture at the CAC.

The *Yidn* builder families had followed the *Yehudim* financier families along similar paths to wealth and community standing partly out of admiration for their style and partly out of necessity because some institutions and enclaves were still closed to Jews. But in the postwar years, when some *Yehudim* families, already intermarried with non-Jews, became completely assimilated and left Judaism behind, many *Yidn* families reaffirmed rather than sidestepped their Jewish identity.

The Urises and other builder families with roots in the Pale experienced no confusion in claiming and celebrating their Jewishness. The persecution and difficulties of their own fathers had informed their childhoods, and the plight of the Jews under Nazi rule echoed and underscored the importance of those memories. Also, the suffering endured in the death camps and the fact that, though six million died, the race of Jews had survived gave to many American Jews a sense of pride in their people's strength and creed, and drew them to close sympathy with the emerging state of Israel. The postwar years were a good time to be upwardly mobile and Jewish in Manhattan. There were pockets of obdurate anti-Semitism, to be sure, and the *Yidn* builders did not want to be as obviously Jewish as the *Hasidim* in caftans and uncut sideburns who dominated the diamond trade, but the builder families embraced their religious and ethnic background and did not strain to obscure it. Jews were not only in the majority — they were becoming part of the ruling oligarchy, the upper class.

Had the Urises had sons, those boys would probably have attended the Horace Mann School in the Bronx or its rival, Fieldston, both situated on the 246th Street transverse, a bluff overlooking Van Cortland Park. At Horace Mann one found Dursts, Tishmans, and Roses; at Fieldston, Roths, Ravitches, and scions of other builder families. Horace Mann was not a particularly Jewish school; had it been so, it would probably have been less attractive to these families, who sought a challenging yet decidedly upper-class training for their sons. In its early days as an adjunct to Columbia University, it boasted such students as William Carlos Williams and Heywood Broun. Since the 1920s the school had been the beneficiary of the Pforzheimers, a leading *Yehudim* family, and in sending their sons there the *Yidn* families were following the *Yehudim* once more. All admired Horace Mann's headmaster for what alumnus Dan Rose described as his "muscular Christianity," and were pleased that other teachers' strong points were Greek, Latin, and classical studies. Horace Mann was proper competition for Andover, Exeter, and similar boarding schools that prepared the sons of non-Jewish families for Ivy League college careers; it was said that one of the reasons Jewish families didn't send their sons to those preparatory boarding schools, aside from a fear of discrimination against Jews, was that they preferred their boys to live at home during the formative teenage years.

During a population crunch at the time of the early school years of the baby boomers, Temple Emanu-El temporarily provided quarters for Horace Mann's lower school; the boards of the temple, the Harmonie and City Athletic Clubs, and the Fieldston and Horace Mann schools often listed the same men. In the summers, the sons and daughters of the emerging builder families often attended the same camps — the boys at Takajo and Androscoggin in Maine, their sisters at Red Wing on Schroon Lake in the Adirondacks or at Tripp Lake or Truda in Maine. In an era when baseball reigned alone and supreme as the national game, the boys' camps stressed what were considered upper-class sports, tennis and swimming. One song at Red Wing, "I Am a New Little Girl," poked fun at the camp's lack of a Rolls-Royce to bring newcomers onto its grounds. The boys' and girls' camps held "socials" with one another; supervised dancing kept partners at least six inches away from the opposite sex. In that age, the stratagem worked.

Chapter Twelve

Learning to Love the Cow

L EW AND JACK RUDIN, the sons of Sam Rudin, had worked for the family firm during summers and vacations ever since they were young. At New York University each took courses in real estate. Upon graduation, first Jack and then Lew went to work for the family concern. In training for it all their lives, they seemed not to be making any decisions in entering the firm: it was what dutiful sons did. Both found that what they had learned in college was "kindergarten stuff" compared to what they absorbed on the job — Jack in planning buildings and letting contracts, Lew as a rental agent trying to fill the new buildings. It was a fitting division of labor, one brother in construction, the other in a position that required salesmanship. Lew was a talker and a joiner, Jack more reclusive. Sam's brothers Henry and Edward were also in the business in the late 1940s, having left behind careers in law and the garment center. Both were childless. "Though there were lots of Rudins in the firm," Lew remembers, "Dad was the sole boss."

That last, award-winning building Emery Roth had designed, 300 East 57th Street, had been for Sam Rudin. The Rudins and Roths were friends as well as mutual clients. After Emery's death, Sam transferred his allegiance to Richard and Julian Roth, who served in part as tutors to Lew and Jack Rudin.

Sam signed every lease, figured out the financing, and made all major decisions. He wanted to hold on to every property he bought; the family still owned the plot on 54th Street that Sam's father had bought in 1904, for instance, and Sam was assembling others around it toward the day when he'd build on the site. Most of his projects didn't take that long, though. As with the Urises, he'd buy a plot of land, go to the Roth firm and get an architectural plan, then take that plan and the land deed to the bank and obtain a loan commitment enabling him to build. Lew believes Sam's strength "lay in his ability to convince each person in the equation — the architect, the loan officer, the construction superintendent, the man who made the decision for the big tenant — that they had a special relationship with him. In return, he tried to live up to his promises." Those promises and their potential consequences were on view in early January 1950, when the *New York Times* announced on its front page that Rudin had bought the Rhinelander buildings at the foot of Fifth Avenue, on Washington Square, and would replace them with a skyscraper.

It was a call to battle. The eleven old Rhinelander brownstones that fronted on Washington Square North and along Fifth Avenue to Eighth Street had been an obvious target for development since the 1920s, but had occasioned several defaults and the defeat of a thirty-story tower planned by another developer. Richard Roth's original drawings showed a twelve-story frontage on the square with a larger building behind. Rudin knew there might be opposition, and in the announcement said that "we recognize and respect the sentiment of the neighborhood with respect to preservation of the old-time atmosphere, and our plans are in keeping with that feeling." Sam had underestimated at least one opponent. The Rhinelander buildings contained a church, several clubs, a former stable, and a handful of choice residential apartments, one occupied by an editor of the *Herald Tribune* who spearheaded a campaign to prevent development.

The *Tribune* editor recruited the Washington Square Association, the Municipal Art Society, the City Planning Commission, and every other group that could express outrage over the idea. "The clout of the *Herald Tribune* reached Senator Herbert Lehman," Lew recalls. Lehman agreed to introduce legislation to designate the Washington Square buildings as national landmarks. Opposition swelled when it was learned that the Roses and the Minskoffs had bought nearby sites and made plans that might transform the small-scale residential character of the area.

Sam Rudin, who had sunk a lot of money into the project and was not used to being called names in the newspapers, had a heart attack. But he didn't use that as an excuse to give up, because there was more at stake than just one building — the family empire had been challenged, and Sam's sons must be set an example of tenacity.

Recovering, Sam moved to alter the design. Richard Roth sought compromise solutions from the chairman of the Municipal Art Society's architectural committee and from city hall. Sam wanted to attend the community protest meetings. "We told him he'd only be exposing himself to more vilification, but he was uncomfortable having other people represent him on the front lines." So Sam went to defend the new design, which would replace the Washington Square frontage with a five-story structure whose height and red-brick color would be of a piece with the neighboring townhouses; this structure would connect to a larger white-brick and concrete building on Fifth Avenue, whose nineteen-story bulk would seem only a backdrop when viewed from the square. To nearly everyone's surprise, the changes and the personal lobbying helped. Senator Lehman dropped his bill, construction went forward, and the Greenwich Village Chamber of Commerce, including several former critics of Two Fifth Avenue, honored Sam Rudin at a quiet luncheon in February 1952 as its man of the month.

Fred Rose was in the Seabees and on Guam in early 1946. The war was over, and so was most of the construction work to be done on the naval base and airstrips of the South Pacific island. "I'd get letters from my father and uncle about their new projects, and I longed to take part in them," he recalls. On obtaining his release papers, Rose hurried to New York; his mother advised him to take a vacation before joining the firm. "I told her that being on Guam with nothing to do had been a vacation" and — like Harold Uris a generation earlier, who went to his father's office straight from graduation — Fred, still in his khakis, headed to a Rose Associates construction site.

Welcomed, he was put to work at 215 East 79th Street in the traditional entry job of assistant to the construction superintendent, the same one given to Paul Starrett sixty years earlier, to Fred French forty years earlier, to Paul Tishman twenty years earlier. Through the hands of the superintendent pass all the important documents that go into erecting a building. As his assistant, Fred learned everything "from how to check shop drawings to how to coordinate the work of contractors and schedule the arrival of materials." There were other sites to build, in those hectic years, and Fred's responsibilities advanced on each one.

"I had two fathers," he recalls, "but only one spiritual tutor," and that was his Uncle Dave, whose apprentice Fred became after getting his feet properly wet in concrete. What that meant, in real terms, was learning from your own mistakes. On an apartment house to go up in Queens, Fred argued with Dave for including some three-and-a-half-bedroom apartments; Dave said they'd be too luxurious for the area, and recommended two bedrooms; the final design included half of the larger and half of the smaller size. The two-bedroom units rented more quickly, giving credence to a lesson Fred would not have learned as effectively in school: Never overbuild for a neighborhood. On a second apartment house near Washington Square, uncle and nephew had another set-to, over kitchens. The sort of tenants Dave knew liked kitchens with exterior windows, but Fred thought modern housewives didn't need or require them; rental contracts proved Fred more astute on that matter. Fred learned ingenuity by watching his uncle wrestle with a design problem: Dave thought inelegant the window air conditioners that stuck out into the street and dripped on passersby, but no other kinds of units were available. He eventually found a manufacturer that would listen, and proposed that they jointly design a unit no thicker than the wall of an apartment house, no higher than from floor to window, and able to exhaust through a grill or grate flush with the outside line of the building. He offered to pay all development and manufacturing costs for machining enough such units for two of his buildings currently under construction, with the proviso that if the "under-window" units became popular and an assembly line was begun to produce them, Dave would have the privilege of retroactively paying the lowest production price available. That's how Chrysler's under-window air conditioners became a standard feature of postwar apartment houses.

On a skiing trip with a friend, Fred stopped off at Vassar College in Poughkeepsie, New York, and met Sandra Priest, a freshman. Seemingly in a hurry with love as with the business he had longed to join, Fred married her in 1948, and Sandra left college to start a family.

In 1950, a realtor came to the young man with a deal on a property at 22nd Street and Lexington. "My father and uncle approved the terms, and I was allowed to personally let most of the contracts and to supervise construction," he recalls. Fred learned to be tough in negotiating with contractors but to keep personal matters out of the bargain, because on the next building he'd have to deal with the same contractors. "After this, they told me to 'go find yourself a job,' by which they meant a property I could develop on my own." He chose one in White Plains, handled all the contracts, financing, and supervising of the construction himself, and "had the satisfaction of not having my father or uncle show up at the site until we were in possession of the C-of-O," the certificate of occupancy. Now he was a full partner.

Eight years flew by, and it was time for Fred's next youngest brother, Daniel, to come into the company. Fred was enthusiastic, Dan no less so, but more reflective. After Yale, graduate work at the Sorbonne, and a stint in the air force at the end of the Korean conflict, "I caught a plane and came home unexpectedly on a Friday," Dan recalls. On Monday, when he first went to the office, "my father, Sam, was out of town, speechifying, and Dave pronounced himself upset. He said I ought to have a proper formal and celebratory welcoming into the firm." Instead, Dave allowed, he'd simply inform Dan as to what had evolved over the past thirty years into the four cardinal principles of Rose Associates.

"Most people in the business think of real estate as a cow to be milked," Dave began his lecture to Dan. "You'll have more fun at it — and get more cream — if you learn to love the cow." By this he meant that Dan must learn to be a professional, to understand what he was doing in business and how to make money out of it. "You're a bright boy," Dave allowed, "but what you already know about real estate is wrong and the things you think you know will get in your way." Since it was impossible to learn to swim by reading a book on the subject or just watching others, Dave and Sam (and Fred) were going to throw Dan into the water and see what happened. "We hope you'll make relatively few mistakes, and that if you make beauts, you'll make them only once. We view your making these inevitable mistakes as a capital investment." Learning to love the cow was Principle Number One.

Principle Number Two was a house rule: "No one is ever to do your work for you. Oh, you can ask questions of us and our associates about other projects, or about history, but you have to do your work yourself. Take all the time you need; judgment comes not only from knowing what you've done wrong, but also from knowing what you've done right."

Number Three: "There's only one signature on a check, and it's 'Rose.' " Inquiring further about this, Dan was given bank signature cards to fill out, and was told that anybody with the name of Rose could sign a check on the Rose accounts. That meant that he could come into the offices on a Saturday, sell out everything the firm owned, and no one could stop him from doing so; but it also meant that any other member of the family could do the same, and so it followed that all must be actively involved and communicating with one another constantly so that none would get discouraged, sell out all the buildings, take the proceeds, and go and live in splendor in Brazil.

Principle Four: "French peasants, at the moment of harvest, toast and pour a little wine onto the soil, a ceremony returning something to the earth for what it has given them. The counterpart at Rose Associates — tempered with moderation, of course — is that some portion of your day must go into pouring back. Take your time and find charities that interest you; if you don't find some within a reasonable amount of time, one will be found for you."

So simple but so all-encompassing and so obviously the product of concentrated thought were these principles that the philosopher of the family could do little else but sit back, contemplate what had been decreed for him, and rub his hands in anticipation at working in such an environment. And that may well have been the goal of Dave Rose's speech.

The young sons who came to work for their builder fathers and uncles in the late 1940s and 1950s were thunderstruck to discover, if they had not already realized it, the extent of the older men's knowledge, salesmanship, audacity, and sheer personal force. For Mel and Robert Kaufman, Burt Resnick, Bob and Alan Tishman, and Fred and Dan Rose, the immediate sensation was of tremendously enhanced respect for the father or uncle as a businessman and creator. Because of his puissance — inspirational as well as dominant — they bent their minds to willing apprenticeships of a sort that other young men fresh from the responsibilities of war refused to consider. Giant companies were then ascendant; into them funneled many returning soldiers who became "organization men," managers who shuffled paper and made no product, interchangeable cogs in machines that afforded them sustenance and safety even as the organizations robbed them of individuality.

The young builder scions were bright and canny enough to realize that in the family firms they could use their own creativity, enhance an empire, and — if things broke reasonably well — make fortunes. It was exciting to help birth a building; to be able to walk or drive by it and say, "I made that"; to feel the solidity of the ultimate end-product of their work, a skyscraper that would endure through their own lifetimes and beyond. No other profession rewarded practitioners with such tangible proofs of accomplishment. They weren't shuffling papers; they were creating icons of intrinsic worth.

They knew full well, however, that in agreeing to enter these family firms they were accepting attendant restrictions — mainly the necessity to work for an unspecified number of years in the shadow of a father or uncle, chafing at restraints and always junior to the founders. Also, they were entering their apprenticeships at a time when a family firm was far from a safe harbor. A second thunderclap was produced by the sons' growing awareness of the daunting challenge for builders hanging in the air of postwar Manhattan. The time of great opportunity was also a time of immense risk. David Rose, William Kaufman, Sam Minskoff, and Sam Rudin were mustering every ounce of their talent and hard-won expertise — and practically all of their fledgling fortunes — to take tremendous business gambles. A boom was on but, unlike the boom of the 1920s, it was possible to go very badly wrong if you built in the wrong location, or built in a manner inappropriate to changing tastes and technologies, or got held up by government or neighborhood forces. Two Fifth Avenue was a calculated roll of the dice for Sam Rudin; he could easily have lost more than he had paid for the old Rhinelander properties and never been able to erect the apartment house. William Kaufman's first skyscraper went up before the Third Avenue El came down, and industry insiders actually wagered money on whether it would still be open when the El was razed. Any new project was a risk for the Roses but the family could no longer rely solely for income on their old properties such as the 1935 building called 1000 Grand Concourse, whose worth was evaporating with each passing year of rapid shifts in the Bronx; flight to the suburbs was undercutting the value of aging assets. The Minskoffs could not wait forever for proper financing on 575 Lexington Avenue and were forced to start construction even without all their loans in place — the most risky of circumstances — to prevent competing buildings from being completed first and stealing away potential tenants. When the young sons joined their elders in this era, they breathed the heady air of a business climate in which deliberate risks had to be taken to ensure the family empire's survival, and in which their own livelihoods were hazarded into each and every gamble their fathers took.

In such a climate of excitement, the years passed quickly. When the sons had been in the firms about ten years, the fathers began to admit to being a little tired. They had worked hard all their lives and risen from near poverty to considerable comfort. Of course, most of them didn't like the idea of letting go — empire builders never do, regardless of their field — but ten years of apprenticeship had made the sons nearly as wise as they in the ways of real estate. The sons had weathered good and not-so-good years, seen projects through from inception to completion, and been present at transactions involving the most important of the elder generation's partners, those key people in banks and insurance companies who made construction and mortgage loan decisions. "The big moments of transfer from father to son often have a lot to do with a golf foursome that includes a bank president," says Fred Rose. "Deeding over the physical real estate from father to son isn't what kept the builder families going," Seymour Durst contends. "Expertise and contacts, those are the essentials passed from generation to generation of the builder families."

Years of increasing responsibilities had given the sons confidence; they understood that if they became blocked inside, they could leave the family firms to become independent builders. The fathers also recognized this. Rather than have a clear and open clash of wills with their sons, the building-empire founders — in contrast to the founders of other empires — chose to ease themselves out of absolute leadership in favor of their sons, and they did so by making the pleasant discovery that their outside interests had pyramided to the point where they took up a great deal of time. The fathers could now yield to well-trained sons and be assured of stability in the firms' management. This was crucial. As students of family businesses have shown, those family firms that fail once the founder has aged out do so principally because they lack adequate second- or third-generation leadership.

The pattern of transfer was seen first in the Durst family because Joseph Durst's sons had entered the firm in the 1930s, a decade earlier than the sons of the other families. In 1945, Joseph became president of the Hebrew Free Loan Society, an agency of the Federation of Jewish Philanthropies. His presidency had been preceded by more than thirty years of work in Hebrew Free Loan and was symbolized by a story he liked to tell. A few years earlier, he'd taken a taxi ride with an immigrant driver who had complained that he was working three shifts to pay off an exorbitant interest loan; Joseph suggested that he apply to Hebrew Free Loan for help, and the cabdriver did, obtaining a no-interest loan that wiped out his earlier indebtedness. In gratitude, the man offered to drive Durst to the office every day. "But I take the bus," Durst protested. "The cabbie wouldn't take no for an answer," Joseph's son Seymour remembers, "and insisted on showing up to drive my father to work every day that it rained." Taking his new presidency of Hebrew Free Loan as an opportunity to say he had other things to do, in the late 1940s Joe Durst carved up the responsibility for his accumulated holdings among Seymour, Royal, and David. "He just divided up the properties and turned the firm over to us," Seymour recalls. Joe felt that if he didn't formally and all at once yield to his sons, succession would never be graceful or complete; rather than go through the pain of intergenerational fights later, he chose to abdicate sooner and remain available for consultation, if needed. After the transfer, "he'd still come into the office every day, but go and sit in the back room and play pinochle, or have a long lunch with old friends."

Other aging pillars of the builder families found similar focuses — the needs of the nascent state of Israel, of a particular college one had once attended, or of a hospital then in formation.

Charitable endeavors also began to absorb the women of the builder families. For the most part, the college students or recent graduates who married the sons of the builders in the 1940s and 1950s became homemakers and did not go into professions or businesses of their own. Precedent and sentiment effectively precluded the women from participation in the family business. It was assumed that men at construction sites would not take direction from a woman, and that the boardroom struggles and clashes of big-time property development required a toughness that excluded the so-called weaker sex. Looking to use their intelligence and energy, the wives of the young builders found charitable endeavors, generally connected with Jewish causes. Rita Valentine Tishman, Norman's wife, was older than the wives of Bob and Alan and served as a model for them in her volunteer work. During the war Rita took a leading role in the sale of war bonds, and after the war was active in the Anti-Defamation League of B'nai B'rith; she also rose through the ranks toward the presidency of the National Council of Jewish Women. For a few years Bob Tishman's wife, Phyllis, concentrated wholly on raising her two daughters, and took up golf, her husband's game, "a great relaxer." The former Olympic swimming hopeful became a golf club champion at the Century of Westchester. When her daughters were well settled into the Dalton School, around the corner from the Tishman penthouse at 89th and Park Avenue, Phyllis volunteered for the Federation of Jewish Philanthropies and began to climb the charity ladder. By the late 1950s her organizational abilities had brought her near the top of what was then permitted for women in the organization, a directorship of one of its 116 affiliates, the Grand Street Settlement House, and the campaign chairmanship of the women's division. In this latter post, she had charge of 5,000 volunteers pledged to extract $2.5 million in contributions from other women through "dial-a-thon" phone calls and "person-to-person" letters. In the final stages of the annual drives, sixteen-hour days were the norm.

Peggy Westheimer, married to Alan Tishman, followed much the same route, though a few years later, delayed in her step onto Federation's ladder by her long residence in suburban Connecticut, where she raised her son and two daughters. But Peggy had been a member of the young Jewish elite in her teens, and on her return from exile started a steady climb that would eventually take her to even higher positions than those filled by her sister-in-law. She discerned that in the arena of the charities, being social — giving dinner parties and attending testimonials even when you would rather be somewhere else — was a key to advancement.

The wives of Fred and Dan Rose, and those of the sons of other prominent builder families, pursued similar charitable paths, though their major focus continued to be in the home. Divorce proved rare among this generation of builder families, a fact which most attribute to luck, but which perhaps also has to do with their sense of long-term investment. Great emphasis was placed on continuity, tradition, and a stable home life.

This set of values and feelings made all the more disastrous the death of Seymour Durst's young wife. Seymour, the eldest of the Durst sons, was a small, dapper, intense man, and became the leader among the second generation. In 1950, just when he was taking control of the family firm, his wife, the mother of two small sons and a daughter, climbed out onto the roof of their Scarsdale home. She was, the press later reported, disoriented by too great a dose of an asthma medication. The fire department arrived with ladders but was unable to rescue her before she slipped on wet autumn leaves and fell to her death. It was labeled an accident, but many friends of the Dursts understood the death to have been a suicide.

After this tragedy, Durst became more secretive in his professional dealings and more eccentric in his personal life. He never remarried, but began a collection of New York City memorabilia that grew to be the most important in private hands. In business, he became the premier site assembler of his generation, cagily buying properties that could be sold at just the right moment to a developer who needed a key piece to complete a large site. Durst developed to a high art the use of distractive tactics, decoy brokers, and dummy corporations, and took pride in the battle of wits.

The Dursts had never been builders. Through the 1920s and 1930s, Joseph worked in real estate principally as an investor and began to manage properties only because he wanted to maximize income while waiting to sell them to someone else for actual development. But in the 1950s, the erection of 711 Third Avenue by the Kaufmans created a crisis for the Durst family, now headed by Seymour. In anticipation of the El's demise, the Dursts had bought up many properties. If these were not developed immediately, they might prove worthless as the area filled up with other new office towers. His hand forced, Seymour decided that the family should do what it had never done before: erect a building.

Perhaps knowing how many problems construction could bring, the Dursts turned to Emery Roth & Sons for a design. At just that time the elder Dursts were about to embark on a previously arranged vacation in Europe; Joseph called up Julian Roth and asked him to "take care of the boys" while he was away. "He said he could afford to bail them out if they made a mistake, but not if it was a really large mistake," Julian remembers. Joseph needn't have worried; the experiment was so successful that Seymour announced the Dursts were selling their other holdings in order to erect skyscrapers along Third Avenue. Brother David, a sculptor, became interested in construction, and a third brother, Roy, took over management and leasing. For the next seven years, the Dursts put up a skyscraper a year and changed from being operators to being one of the major builders of Manhattan, along with the Urises, Rudins, Roses, Kaufmans, Minskoffs, Fishers, Zeckendorf, and the Tishmans.

Although the Tishmans did not usually build for New York's competing developer families, their construction expertise was increasingly being sought by out-of-town developers. John was excited about the possibilities. A construction firm that put up its own buildings and did jobs for others could swing quite a bit of weight. For instance, it could command the first use of innovative materials and techniques, so that the Tishman company's new skyscrapers could offer advantages over those of other builders. John's personal tinkering produced a new wrinkle in fluorescent lighting. The norm was four lights in a one-foot strip, but these often burned out or got too hot; John wanted to try a two-foot strip, but these wouldn't fit with the usual dimensions of ceiling tiles. Because of the Tishman company's growing clout in construction, John was able to convince a large ceiling-tile manufacturer to work with him on designing a smaller fluorescent strip and to alter his tiles so that such a strip could be easily installed in a building Tishman had under construction. Others liked it, and a new standard was adopted. John then saw that similar cooperative ventures were possible with other materials manufacturers, and regularized the practice in a separate research division of the company.

As the building boom continued, the Tishmans became a national company. They opened offices in Chicago and Los Angeles, and erected and managed skyscrapers in half a dozen major cities. By the mid-1950s, David Tishman was in his late sixties and growing deaf. He sometimes turned off his hearing aid in the middle of negotiations when he didn't want to hear someone say no to a deal. Because of the company's public structure, the Tishmans were not keeping up with the other families in terms of wealth, but David conceived a passion to keep up with them in another way. The family was the most visible of the builders in this era, its red-girder T logo distinctive and ubiquitous on new construction. After Lefcourt and French, New York builders had generally not affixed their names to buildings, preferring to reserve the encomium for the use of their clients. Even Junior Rockefeller had fought a battle to keep his name off what had been Metropolitan Square. But David Tishman wanted the family name on a structure, despite some reticence from his relatives. "I never would have had the nerve to call it the Tishman Building," Bob recalls.

David searched for some time before being able to assemble a near-perfect site for his dream. The plot lay along Fifth Avenue between 52nd and 53rd streets, and had the added advantage of a subway stop that could be incorporated into the building. There was a beautiful church across the corner, and the Museum of Modern Art halfway down 53rd toward Sixth Avenue. This was a highly visible location for a building, and the Tishmans planned to erect on it the largest skyscraper north of Rockefeller Center, nearly sixty stories. In the manner of the Tishmans themselves, 666 Fifth Avenue would be distinguished, not outlandishly modern but with a contemporary feel. It would feature a whitish, stippled metallic skin and clean, vertical lines, and an open lobby dotted with stores in front of its recessed office entrance. This lobby would have a patterned, stylized ceiling and a waterfall designed by sculptor Isamu Noguchi.

Tishman's dream involved more than a building: it was a statement of the family's tastes, aspirations, and values. As with 30 Rockefeller Plaza, 666 would have a restaurant on the penthouse floor. This one, called Top of the Sixes, would be the last word in 1950s elegance. Directly below the restaurant would be two floors of Tishman company offices, including one suite each for David and Norman that would boast working fireplaces similar to those installed for Junior Rockefeller on the fifty-sixth floor of 30 Rockefeller Plaza. David and the other chieftains (except John) chose offices with southern exposures that would allow them to look down Fifth Avenue toward the other statements of identity: Rockefeller Center, the towers of Lefcourt and French along Fifth Avenue, the Chrysler and Chanin buildings to the east. The Tishmans were more than Park Avenue residential landlords now, and this building would sum up their power.

David wanted his imprint on the skyline, and he wanted to begin it immediately. There was a tight market for loans in 1956, however, and to bring 666 to fruition, he had to make compromises that spoke of the family's strengths and weaknesses. Still hampered by the public structure, David determined that he must not put too much of the family fortune at risk in this one building. The Tishmans formed an alliance with the Crowns of Chicago, through Corky Goodman, son-in-law and real estate adviser to the elder Crown brothers. With the Crowns on board, construction commenced. But before 666 Fifth Avenue was completed, David was forced to make a sale-and-leaseback arrangement with Prudential Life. This safeguarded both the Tishman and Crown investments, but meant that David's dream, the Tishman Building, was actually owned by someone other than the Tishmans.

Chapter Thirteen

Sizable and Dubious Pleasures

IN 1959, Percy and Harold Uris contemplated a difficult move: taking their company public. The real estate community of New York understood from the Tishman example that there were major drawbacks to being public. Wall Street evaluated companies by their bottom lines: a good one meant a good stock; a bad one, a loser. A private real estate company might show only an extremely modest annual rental income — that is, a lousy bottom line — that still allowed its principals to take home millions of dollars annually thanks to depreciation and other tax-code allowances, while a public company with equivalent real estate holdings would pay only modest dividends. The fact that a real estate concern's properties were also appreciating in value was similarly discounted by stock buyers. Wall Street analysts would compare the earnings of apples (real estate companies) to those of oranges (traditional manufacturing or service companies) and invariably conclude that apples weren't good investments.

Since the days of Fred French, however, real estaters contemplating major expansion had had a desperate need for large amounts of new capital. If you weren't pals with the Crowns, the best way to obtain money was to make a stock offering. That was why the Tishmans had gone public in 1928; thirty years later the results were still hampering them. But the current times and circumstances were different, Percy and Harold Uris became convinced.

The Urises' dreams were changing. They now wanted to create an entity of grand size, perhaps to become the General Motors of builders. By some measures, they already were doing better than GM. They had been turning out products (buildings) at an extremely rapid rate and had a spectacular cash flow. On rents of five or six dollars per square foot — a dollar below the going price in most areas of the city — the Urises were realizing an average of eighty-three cents per square foot in profits before taxes; on Two Broadway, recently completed, the net was $1.13 per foot before taxes. This meant the Urises were keeping about 25 percent of their gross income; in contrast, General Motors could only manage to hang on to 7 percent of gross income. Such an obvious success gave Percy, and the Wall Street salesmen, a rationale to which investors have always responded: the Urises were hot and needed cash. Brokers were continually bringing them terrific deals, not only in Manhattan but all up and down the northeastern industrial corridor. They had to take advantage of these great opportunities! They projected that, on a $12 stock price, in the first year a shareholder might reap a dividend of $1.20 or more. "Private companies are often asked for audit statements, but these can conceal as much as they reveal," a Uris associate remembers. "Percy also thought that being public — and having open books — would make the company more attractive to institutional lenders." Also, money begat money: if the Urises had $20 million, that was all the more reason for a bank or an insurance company to loan them an additional $100 million.

In 1959, then, the Uris Properties Corporation was transformed into the Uris Buildings Corporation. UBC offered both stock and bonds to the public, raising about $40 million, half in long-term debt. Percy and Harold retained 62 percent of the stock and absolute control, along with ownership of several buildings not included in the sale. The stock rose to $30 a share, then settled back to a respectable $18.

"Part of the reason the Urises wanted the new money," Harold's former son-in-law John Halpern recalls, "was to play in the same sandbox as the Rockefellers." Here was the not-quite-hidden agenda: the Rockefeller family was being dilatory about entering into joint ventures that abutted Rockefeller Center, where the Urises had two projects in mind. With enough money in the bank to start these buildings themselves, the Urises were in a better bargaining position, and the Rockefeller interests soon agreed to come in on the Sperry-Rand office tower and the Hilton Hotel, both on Sixth Avenue in the Fifties. The Urises also used their new money for two office buildings in Philadelphia's Penn Center (designed by Richard Roth), and their connection with Hilton Hotels to erect the Washington Hilton.

To service their growing empire they took on new staff, among them young Halpern, son of a suburban home builder. Halpern's father had once asked Percy to join in a venture and "was dazzled by what Percy told him about sheltering money, using tax laws, and other financial stratagems." The deal didn't go through, but the elder Halpern sent John to apprentice with the wizard. John was attracted to one of Harold's daughters; in business, though, he grew close to Percy. They'd play tennis together, often against a team consisting of a chairman of the board of two insurance companies and the chairman of a steel company. After one match and its attendant chatter, John observed to Percy, "These two guys aren't as smart as the real estate operators we deal with every day."

"That's right," Percy agreed, "but they represent more combined economic power than some nations."

For that matter, so did the Urises. From 1947 to 1962, they developed 8.7 million square feet of commercial space, twice as much as constructed in Chicago during the same period and about 15 percent of everything that went up in New York. Their new millions occasioned a few changes in the Uris lifestyle. The public corporation's logo was a U with the second shank extended in an upward fillip, as of a skyward-reaching building; Harold wore the logo in place of a monogram on custom-made shirts. Other gestures were grander: the Urises had a foundation that made grants to educational institutions, hospitals, and the performing arts; now, with greater wealth, they began to give millions to Percy's alma mater, Columbia University, to Harold's, Cornell, and to Lenox Hill Hospital.

In an important move, Columbia University asked Percy to join its board; the university was about to begin a major building program. He started having breakfast one morning each week with Columbia's president to review plans. Intrigued by the problems, he soon raised his commitment by many more dollars for a science hall, a building for the graduate business school, and a swimming center. He accepted the position of head of the board's finance committee, and the one breakfast a week became a morning spent on Columbia matters, then a whole day out of each week, and then two.

As the 1950s drew toward a close, competition made the syndication game somewhat less lopsided, and Larry Wien began to wonder how much longer he and Harry Helmsley could lead the pack.

Following the Wien-Helmsley lead, other syndicates were formed and bid up the price of buildings. This competition effectively lowered the rates of return that could be offered to investors. Adding to syndicators' difficulties, Congress and the Securities and Exchange Commission enfranchised a new form of investment, a cross between a stock and a syndicate, the Real Estate Investment Trust (REIT). REITs were beginning to out-bid all private syndicates because their investors would accept a 9 percent return on a building, whereas Wien and Helmsley would want to guarantee 10 to 12 percent. Rounding up thousands of investors for each purchase was also a burden; it was far easier to go to a small group, as they had for the Plaza Hotel. Wien cultivated such major investors as David Schwartz, chairman of the Jonathan Logan dress firm; Lester and Alfred Morse of Morse Shoe (Wien's daughter Enid had married a Morse); Albert Warner, a director of Warner Pictures; and John L. Loeb and Clifford W. Michel of Loeb, Rhoades.

Although never shy, Wien did not have the need, as Helmsley did, to express himself in grandiose gestures. While the Wien law firm took offices on a high floor of the Lincoln Building, Helmsley's real estate firm took the top floor. The building that figured most prominently in Helmsley's magnificent view of the skyline was the Empire State. "There it stands," he said later, "and every morning you would look out the window and the building is staring you in the face. So, you'd say, 'Well, I gotta buy it.' "

The Empire State Building, once a dream of accomplishment, had become the foremost prize in a dream of acquisition. In 1951, the Crowns of Chicago had bought the symbol of New York for $51 million from John J. Raskob's estate, a record price for a building, while Prudential Insurance bought the underlying land for $17 million. The Crowns didn't achieve complete control until 1954, then put in a $10-million central air-conditioning system. Modernization made the tallest building in the world also one of the most profitable — it had a $10-million-a-year rent roll, drew $2 million from the observation tower, and brought in $600,000 for allowing television and radio stations to use the antenna. Out of this income, the Crowns paid operating expenses and more than a million dollars each year to Prudential, but they still netted hefty profits.

Helmsley began his courtship of the Crowns in 1957. To be of utmost value to a buyer, a deal had to include the land, or a long-term lease on it, as well as the Empire State Building and the right to manage it. So Wien evolved the most complicated sale-and-leaseback scheme of all time, one that allowed the parties to have their cake and eat it, too. A typical investment syndicate would be the lynchpin, while Wien, Helmsley, and shipping magnate Daniel K. Ludwig would be the equity partners. The syndicate would buy the building from the Crowns for $65 million and the land from Prudential for $17 million. Some $46 million for the purchase would be loaned to them by Prudential. Then the syndicate would sell everything to Prudential for an artificially deflated price of $29 million. Finally, Prudential would lease the building back to Helmsley and Wien for four successive terms of twenty-one years each, at an annual rate of $3.2 million during the initial term; that would give Prudential a 7 percent return on its money where before it was only obtaining 6 percent. The added 1 percent a year finally convinced Prudential to assent to the complicated deal.

Then it began to fall apart. Prudential's lawyers didn't like the idea of selling the land, Ludwig decided to opt out, and the Crowns' lawyer fought the sale. Wien told Helmsley, "You can't do it. These people are impossible. Look, there's no sense killing yourself. Let's forget it." But Helmsley kept on talking to them. Wien believed the deal had been killed five times before it was eventually agreed to by all sides. More than 3,000 syndicate units of $10,000 each made up the $36 million required for the purchase above the Prudential loan and went to pay legal and brokerage fees of over $3 million. The syndicate's prospectus promised $900 per year on each $10,000 unit.

The closing, in late December 1961 at Prudential's corporate headquarters in Newark, New Jersey, was a massive endeavor that involved about 150 people around the largest conference table Wien had ever seen. It had to be rehearsed twice in full and many times in part before the actual signing of documents, which took more than two hours. One lease was more than 400 pages long. Everyone tripped over the cables of the television lights. Afterwards, Helmsley and Wien vowed never to do such a massive public offering again; from here on in, they'd stick with their circle of big investors. Multi-investor syndication had climaxed and come undone in this largest deal of them all.

The most profitable part of the Empire State Building compact was the operating lease. Helmsley-Spear cut overhead expenses for the building to maximize return on investment; for example, the number of bookkeepers was reduced drastically, and elevator service was minimized during off-peak hours. Shortly, return on investment for the syndicate investors and the holders of the operating lease went up, and estimates ran that Helmsley and Wien personally took home several hundred thousand dollars each year from the Empire State Building.

What does one do after realizing the ultimate acquisitive dream? For Wien, an opportunity arose to consolidate in a new direction. At the urging of Wien, both men had set up personal foundations; Helmsley's didn't do very much and was just a tax shelter, but Wien's was a serious endeavor. His son-in-law Peter Malkin remembers Wien arguing to Helmsley that making money was not in itself significant; what counted was the "enlightened selfishness" of giving it away. Wien's first large contributions, both of money and time, went to Jewish causes. Wien was one of the earliest supporters of Brandeis University; in 1956 he became national chairman of a special fund that raised several million dollars for the university; in 1958 he made a permanent endowment worth $7.5 million for annual scholarships for students from fifty foreign nations. The size of the gift, and the obvious thought behind it, brought him to the attention of the Federation of Jewish Philanthropies in New York City.

Federation was the largest private philanthropic organization in the United States, administering almost as many hospitals and community and welfare agencies as did a half-dozen of the smaller states in the country, combined. Its annual budget had reached $20 million a year. People such as Harold and Percy Uris, whose father had been helped by Federation agencies in his days as a penniless immigrant, gave sizable contributions annually, as did members of other builder families. These men displayed a streak of toughness in business that seemed to exist in tandem with a charitable urge and a nostalgic bent, as if these three were in balance and together made a whole. Federation was the ideal repository for their urges, and in the 1940s and 1950s the aging immigrant builders and their sons gave tens of millions of dollars for Mount Sinai, Beth Israel, the Hospital for Joint Diseases in Manhattan, a half-dozen other area hospitals, and more than 100 summer camps, homes for the aged, and welfare clinics.

Federation's focus was local, which the builders liked; they had obviously benefited from New York's growth and believed in returning something to the city that had given them so much. And Federation's activities succored the Jewish needy. Although secure in the idea that their own intelligence and fortitude had made them winners, the builders also knew they'd been lucky and felt a responsibility to those who came from similar backgrounds but hadn't been so fortunate.

Federation was tough, too. It insisted on commitments of time and energy as well as money from aspirants for its leadership. Other Jewish charitable groups were known to award a presidency on the basis of a one-time donation, but you couldn't buy a top post at Federation, where offices were reserved for those who had toiled within its ranks. Some grumbled that the very top posts were also the sole province of the *Yehudim*, a canard balanced by an acknowledgment of how hard the Schiffs, Buttenweisers, and Leidesdorfs had worked to build Federation during its formative decades.

Although Wien had been a steady contributor, until the mid-1950s he had spent his energies elsewhere. Ordinarily this would have disqualified him from high office at Federation, but it was decided to fast-track him. In 1957, he was made assistant to the head of fund-raising; in 1958 he took the head job himself; in 1959 he advanced to president-elect; in 1960 he became president.

Maurice Hexter, who had been with Federation since the 1920s, was pleased. During Wien's three-year term — a time in which, for instance, he negotiated to buy the Empire State Building — Hexter remembered that Wien "did what no other previous president had done, spent an entire day each week on Federation business," and was always available for the near-continuous round of early breakfast and late dinner meetings. Moreover, Hexter recalled, Wien "thought about us when he wasn't there," pushing the board to set up health and retirement plans for the professional staff. "Federation had never before had such an active president," says Malkin. Wien championed a building campaign for the "City of Life," and made many reforms to the organization.

Wien's only defeat during this period was an attempt to interweave the interests of his two charitable groups by trying to have Mount Sinai Hospital designated as the medical school for Brandeis University. Jewish doctors in Boston, concerned that their own hospital in that city would be slighted, combined to force the Brandeis board to reject Wien's proposal.

Though Columbia University had graduated many Jews, and many of its graduates had gone into real estate, Wien's alma mater had been mainly governed by men who were neither Jewish nor from the real estate field. Selected to the Columbia board, he became the first trustee to donate a million dollars to a $200-million campaign that made Columbia, per capita, the best-endowed educational institution in the United States. Percy Uris's election to the board followed Wien's. From Columbia, it was a small step for Wien to the boards of other cultural institutions that had traditionally overlooked both Jews and those in real estate. Wien liked to insist that he was not *in* real estate, but just a lawyer who looked out for his client's investments in that field. That helped make him acceptable to the boards. Also, his style in his charitable endeavors was deliberately low-key and self-effacing. One Federation summer camp offered to give him a testimonial dinner; once Wien found out what they needed — funds to put up buildings on a 500-acre tract on Butler Lake in New Jersey — he refused to be the honoree, and turned the tables. At his own expense, he rented the Grand Ballroom at the Waldorf-Astoria, induced George Jessel to be the toastmaster, and invited 800 guests to pay $200,000 to honor a camp that enabled poor inner-city children to enjoy a summer month in the country. Years later, when he went to visit the new facility, he discovered it had been renamed "Camp Vacamas on Lake Larriwien," and that visitors assumed the lake's name was of American Indian origin.

In 1958, at a closing on 305 East 47th Street, a small loft building near the United Nations owned by one of the Helmsley and Wien syndicates, Wien met twenty-seven-year-old lawyer Bernie Mendik, who along with his equally young brother-in-law Larry Silverstein and Silverstein's father, Harry, were buying the building. A week later, Wien called Mendik and asked if he could take him to lunch. Mendik thought the meeting might be about other buildings for sale, or problems that had come up after the closing, but it wasn't. "I could tell by watching you," Wien said over lunch, "that you're going to make a great deal of money some day, and I want you to think about how you're going to give it away."

Mendik was flattered and flabbergasted. Wien described his own method: after making sure his family would be comfortable, he looked for areas or institutions that meant something to him and concentrated on those. Plenty of people, Wien said, would want money from Mendik, and it was hard to refuse friends — but he should pick his own charities and stand by them; that was the only way to make a really useful commitment.

Bernie Mendik and Larry Silverstein were a matched pair of brothers-in-law, both Bronx-born, tall, skinny, intense night students at New York Law School. They were just starting to articulate and pursue their dreams — which, for the moment, focused on acquisition. Like many sons of immigrants, Harry Silverstein had been brought up to be passionate about artistic endeavors, but in the 1920s had reluctantly concluded that, despite talent and love of music, he was not going to be able to make a living as a classical pianist. In the public library he found a book that identified the source of all wealth as real estate, so he decided to try to make his living that way, selling some of his precious sheet music to obtain some starting capital. "He would still play Chopin nocturnes to lull us to sleep," Larry remembers, but real estate became his livelihood. For nearly thirty years Harry eked out a living as a broker in the downtown loft districts. Larry graduated from the Washington Heights campus of New York University and came into the firm. "It soon became apparent to me," Larry says, "that if we stayed in brokerage we'd starve to death." He met Mendik, the son of a handyman and a graduate of Bronx Science and City College, at New York Law, and introduced him to his sister Annette, whom Mendik shortly married. Then Bernie, too, joined the firm. Harry G. Silverstein & Sons, the shingle now read, a bit of a misnomer in a sign that reflected an invigorated partnership. Harry was the steady hand, the arbiter; Larry and Bernie — best friends — were the live wires, full of energy, poring over second-hand copies of the Wien-Helmsley prospectuses, putting together mock syndicates of their own on the weekends. They were like two future basketball stars practicing give-and-go patterns at a backyard hoop under the watchful eye and urging of the coach.

In 1957, they found a building that was perfect for their purposes, a thirteen-story loft building on East 23rd Street. Though rundown, it was in a good district, the rents were low, and leases were shortly due to be renewed. The three men obtained a personal loan of $25,000, used it as a down payment, convinced some of Harry's regular clients to take $10,000 units that promised a 12 percent annual return, then put an ad in the papers to find the rest. "The last of the twenty investors we needed to cover the entire purchase price came in on the day we closed the deal," Mendik remembers. "On nights and weekends we painted the corridors, refitted the lobby, went down to Canal Street to buy fixtures." Soon new tenants (and some old ones) were paying substantially higher prices for the now more attractive space. The project was a success.

The second building they bought was 305 East 47th, from their heroes Helmsley and Wien. Both Bernie and Larry were smitten with Helmsley's firmness and rectitude in the negotiations, as well as with the brilliance of Wien, and consciously tried to slipstream their own operations behind those of their models. They became close to the older men, close enough to know that Helmsley, though always honest, was often cheap: his buildings were on a regimen of subsistence maintenance and slowly sliding toward deterioration. In their own buildings, Silverstein and Mendik were more lavish with money, believing that a dollar spent on upgrading and maintenance was easily worth ten in future rent increases.

Harry G. Silverstein & Sons bought a building every six months. Bernie and Larry spent sixteen-hour days working on them, taking more night courses in law and real estate, purloining copies of leases so they could copy the more interesting clauses, and inventing some clauses to cover unusual situations. Mendik recalls that he knew his "home life was suffering, that I was hardly spending any time with my children" — but the work was thrilling. He could see the portfolio growing with each passing month, its growth directly attributable to what he, Larry, and Harry were doing. "I hated to go home at night and couldn't wait to return to the office in the morning."

They already owned a handful of buildings when they tried to buy one from Bill Zeckendorf. Accompanied by an old Jewish woman broker named Sadie, they sat in the circular office with the legend. They negotiated for a while, and then Zeckendorf's phone buzzed. He answered it, went out a door to the left, and was gone for ten minutes. Then Bill came back in, worked some more, and another call took him out a door to the right. Upon his return, Sadie upbraided him, saying that while he was flitting about they'd been cooling their heels and their time was important, too.

"Do you think this is the only deal I'm negotiating right now?" Zeckendorf asked rhetorically. In the two adjoining rooms, he said, he was making deals concerning the Graybar and Chrysler skyscrapers.

"*Oi*, Bill," Sadie said in her thick Yiddish accent, "you're too big for this business. You should be dealing with whole countries!"

Perhaps he should have been, because everyone acknowledged that Zeckendorf was smarter than anyone else in real estate. His ideas were so large and visionary that the ordinary mechanisms of business moved too slowly for him — but at that moment he was also teetering on the edge of bankruptcy.

Casting for fish on a Hawaiian beach in 1953, with the surf swirling around his bare feet, Zeckendorf had conjured an idea. Someone who wanted to buy a $10-million industrial business, he reasoned, had many ways of carving up the risk and the profit — bonds, secondary debentures, bonds convertible to stock, preferred shares, common stock, and accounts receivable on which money might be advanced by a factoring concern. Why couldn't he similarly partition off and apportion out the various parts of a real estate property? He had recently acquired One Park Avenue, which his friend Henry Mandel had erected in the 1920s, and proceeded in his mind (and later that day, on the telephone) to divide it into pieces — a mortgage on the ground rent, the sale of the actual land, an inner lease that would own the building and an outer or operating lease to manage it, as well as mortgages on both leases. By creating multiple slices a $10-million property and its annual income could be sold for $15 million, and while Zeckendorf made money, so did those who bought slices from him. Earlier schemes had leveraged buildings by taking cash out with mortgages; Zeckendorf's Hawaiian maneuver would be the ultimate use of a property's inherent value and money-making potential to swing deals.

Zeckendorf employed the technique to squeeze cash out of One and Two Park Avenue, 1407 Broadway, the Graybar and Chrysler buildings, the old Equitable Building at 120 Broadway, and dozens of others around the country, so that he could buy and develop more properties. His dream, too, had become one of size. The problem was that with each fractional sale, he encumbered his properties with mortgages and decreased his income from them. Yes, he had more money to play with, but he also had much more debt and many less dollars coming in to cover expenses.

Soon, Zeckendorf seemed to have accomplished his objectives. He controlled more diverse urban and suburban properties than anyone else on the North American continent. He held, for example, more hotel rooms in Manhattan than anyone else, 7,000 of them. But he began to think that his touch was magic, and ranged beyond real estate. Trading one asset for another, he became the owner of a played-out copper company, then discovered that its slag heaps were potentially worth hundreds of millions. Unfortunately, the process for turning slag into profits took too long to perfect and he lost a good deal of money. Similarly, he exchanged ownership of the land under a store on 34th Street for 360 acres in Baychester, then leased that to people who wanted to open an amusement park. When Freedomland's operators went belly up, he decided to operate the park himself until the land could find a good new use — and that meant huge annual losses. Interest charges on his various kinds of debt kept mounting.

The Zeckendorf style continued unabated: the great black limousine, the foot-long cigars, the headline grabbing that he insisted was only an inexpensive way of passing information to the public. Once he interrupted a phone chat with President Dwight Eisenhower to take a business call. He owned dozens of suits, some for when he was stout, others for when he had gone on one of his periodic diets and lost forty pounds — which he would soon regain. If he was unabashedly aggressive, he was also hugely sentimental, once buying a bad building simply so an old broker who'd fallen on hard times could make a commission, and closing the Monte Carlo nightclub with a bash for the employees so extravagant that they almost forgot they had planned to go on strike for higher wages. A colleague suggested that Zeckendorf had "the memory of a bull elephant, the heart of a baby, and the guts of a brass monkey."

Zeckendorf seemed to draw into himself and embody all that was flamboyant and excessive about his profession, so that any other man who wore a ten-gallon hat, or dramatically pulled a drape off a model of a fabulous city-within-a-city, or smoked a foot-long cigar, or consumed by the barrel the most expensive wines, would be accused (to their detriment) of aping Zeckendorf. He was addicted to risk, knowledgeable competitors said of him, shaking their heads; you could see it in the extent of his staggering indebtedness: in 1960 he needed to pay back $100 million in three months and owed four times that on projects under construction. For high-priced, short-term financing to keep everything going, Zeckendorf was forced to turn to what he called "my Shylock moneylenders." He didn't seem to mind; not for him an Astor-like style of sitting on assets and counting rent receipts. "I'd rather be alive at eighteen percent than dead at the prime rate," he bragged.

If detractors later decided that his brash overleveraging was a fatal flaw, it must be judged a classically tragic one, for he could not have done otherwise and still remained Zeckendorf. To realize his grand schemes, he needed a million here for a down payment on a spectacular site, a million there for I. M. Pei and his minions to create designs for projects so huge they had no precedent. He was turning a former airfield, Roosevelt Field on Long Island, site of Lindbergh's takeoff for Paris, into an industrial park and shopping mall complex; he was almost outdoing Robert Moses in urban renewal projects in New York, Chicago, Washington, and Denver; he had a contract on hundreds of acres of old studio land in Los Angeles; he was becoming the largest developer in Canada, with shopping malls and office complexes under way from Vancouver to Montreal. Nearly a billion dollars in Zeckendorf construction projects were ongoing. Now he was a chess grand master: the world was watching him play fifty games at once against as many opponents, and expected him to win them all.

Every three months or so he'd mount the steps of Gracie Mansion to publicly announce a new project that would, he'd say, be the world's most spectacular. He introduced (as if it were already a fact) the world's tallest skyscraper over Grand Central Terminal; over Pennsylvania Station would soon rise the $200-million Palace of Progress with more than twice the space of the Pentagon and housing a permanent world's fair as well as a shopping mall and offices. When the Palace of Progress scheme fell for lack of financing, he trumpeted the $500-million Atomic City above the freight yards from 24th to 71st streets, to include (in addition to the permanent world's fair, shopping mall, and offices) Television City, a heliport, and a hotel. Because Atomic City would take some time to realize, in the interim he'd build the first new hotel in Manhattan since the 1920s, to be called the Zeckendorf, on Sixth Avenue between 51st and 52nd streets. With a flourish, he paid a small fortune to restaurateur Toots Shor to relieve him of a lease on part of that site, then donned a hard hat and used a pneumatic drill to start tearing down the buildings. Shortly, he had a hole in the ground that drained money at a rate even faster than his friend Vincent Astor's Disaster Plaza. But in Zeckendorf's mind, it was already a hotel.

All but one of Zeckendorf's big latter-day projects were completed, though not by him. He never made money on Roosevelt Field, though fortunes were made by those to whom he sold it. He created Century City in Los Angeles, but not in time to gain much from its success. He cleared slums and made plans for what became L'Enfant Plaza in Washington, DC, only to see it slip from his grasp because he didn't have the resources to wait out the delays imposed by opponents. Similarly, he built but did not reap great profit from three urban-renewal projects in Manhattan: Park West Village between 97th and 100th streets at Central Park West, Kips Bay Plaza near the United Nations, and Lincoln Towers near Lincoln Center; together, they housed 10,000 families. Erwin Wolfson and his partners erected the Pan Am building on the Grand Central site (not the world's tallest office building, but big enough); Madison Square Garden and the buildings of Penn Plaza replaced the above-ground portions of Pennsylvania Station. Zeckendorf's most elaborate project, envisioning a new city over the rail yards on the Upper West Side (Atomic City, including Television City), did not come to fruition in his lifetime, but as of 1991 it was still being pursued by Donald Trump.

Zeckendorf's loss of the site where he wished to build his name-sake hotel illustrated the rough tactics of the big players. The hole in the ground sat unoccupied, draining money from Zeckendorf, and was a source of wonder even to his friends. Daily, Dave Tish-man would look out the window of his office, see the hole, and exclaim, "He's still there!" But he was trying to get out. Zeckendorf held discussions with the Rockefeller interests, but they dragged on, and some said it was Bill's flamboyance that deterred an agreement with the Rockefellers. Simultaneously, he pursued extensive negotiations with Hilton Hotels and with the Crowns, major investors in the chain, but these players, too, would not give him a straight yes or no. All waited until the site became a near-mortal wound that had to be addressed. Only then did the Urises offer to buy the site from Zeckendorf, at quite a loss. Shortly, with agreements and participation from Rockefeller Center and Hilton Hotels, the Urises built both the Sperry-Rand office tower on that 52nd Street site, and a hotel — a Hilton — a few blocks north, where they already owned land and where all three players agreed it would be better placed.

Part of the reason Zeckendorf was unable to realize all his projects was his inability to believe that others would not see things his way and help him turn his dreams into skyscrapers. The other part was his refusal to go along with the sort of political trading increasingly necessary to develop properties in cities from Montreal to Washington, and especially in New York City. In the 1950s he'd understood political dealing well enough to take a floundering urban renewal project on the edge of Central Park between 97th and 100th streets off the city's hands and turn it into Park West Village, but by the 1960s he had become impatient with political processes, demanding, for instance, that he be allowed to circumvent the new zoning laws.

It was not as if he reached a precipice and didn't know enough to pull back. He wasn't blind; as early as 1957 — five years after he'd begun the public company — Zeckendorf began major sell-offs to pay down his debt, many to the other big players. In these years, when other buyers faded, Zeckendorf would often call Harry Helmsley from his car phone and invite him to take a ride in the limousine with him. As they toured Central Park, Zeckendorf would unburden himself about his troubles and then get around to discussing one or two little properties he might sell. For these titans of acquisition, paper wasn't necessary — they knew each property well from their continuous study of Manhattan buildings and sites, and they trusted one another not to dissemble about rental income and encumbrances. They'd sometimes shake hands on a purchase even before Harry stepped out of Bill's car again in front of the Lincoln Building. "I bought a lot of buildings that way," Helmsley later recalled.

Maybe Helmsley and old survivors such as Dave Tishman were the only ones left who could understand and sympathize with the scope of Zeckendorf's problems. His wife, Marion, had tired of the fray and stopped accompanying him to his early morning break-fasts with the rich and powerful. Bill, Jr., who had earlier worked for the company as a messenger boy, joined Webb & Knapp for-mally after his service in Korea. He had the unenviable task of reining in his father to help him survive. To his son, Zeckendorf delegated the difficult detail work of closing Webb & Knapp offices, paring down the overhead. I. M. Pei, who supervised the design of hundreds of projects in his dozen years with Zeckendorf, and who credited Zeckendorf with inculcating in him the understanding of how a developer must work and think, started to do projects for other people, as Zeckendorf could no longer afford to initiate many new ones of his own.

In 1960, when *Fortune* magazine prepared a devastating feature on Zeckendorf's finances, Big Bill acknowledged difficulties but nevertheless said, "If we work out our problems, we'll be one of the greatest companies in the world." That was his goal — not wonderful buildings, but an enormous company. Through the big sales and cost-cutting Zeckendorf had pushed down his short-term debt to a mere $40 million, on which he was paying 20 percent a year, three times the prime rate. Financial analysts announced his imminent end, but in December 1961 he pulled off what *Business Week* referred to as "the supreme coup of his career," inducing his partners in his Canadian operations to supply that $40 million in exchange for a half interest in the three Manhattan urban-development projects, Roosevelt Field, Century City, and other Zeckendorf dreams.

For a while longer, he thought this new money would enable him to start over, but it only got rid of his immediate creditors; he still had to deal with long-term debt of ten to fifteen times the amount he'd received from his new partners. More forced sales, shuffling of assets, and abandoning of projects made for what Zeckendorf later described as "a tale of conferences, exchanges, and minor ventures devised to stave off disaster while we prayed to put together one or more major projects" to prevent financial ruin. When notes came due, he personally cosigned new ones, throwing his own fortune into the maelstrom. He had bet on one sure thing in the postwar period — an inflationary spiral — but had been caught by progress of a sort he hadn't imagined, such as the increased efficiency and speed of jet planes which made it possible for businessmen to come to New York for a day and fly home without having to stay overnight; this lowered occupancy rates for the nine Zeckendorf hotels in Manhattan, which began hemorrhaging money. He disposed of a large portfolio to Alcoa, then other pieces of the empire to the partners who'd brought in the $40 million. Twenty years earlier, he had sold properties for more money than they were worth because they bore the Astor name; now people offered him less than market prices for properties just because they were associated with the beleaguered name of Zeckendorf.

Alan Tishman, who had known Bill since childhood, was in the bathroom during a charitable event when Zeckendorf came in and stood at the next urinal. In tuxedos, they exchanged greetings, and then Zeckendorf wondered to Alan, "How can they say I'm broke? I owe a *billion* dollars."

On Friday, May 7, 1965, as he was being driven in his limousine toward Wall Street for a meeting with creditors in which he planned to restructure his debt, Big Bill received a phone call from a *New York Times* reporter inquiring if Webb & Knapp was going into bankruptcy; he denied it, and then took a similar call from the *Wall Street Journal*. Two conversations with his office were required before he learned what had actually happened. Under a standard clause in certain debenture contracts, a bank could demand full payment of a note before its maturity date if the mortgagee was known to have missed payments to other creditors. On just this basis, because Webb & Knapp had obviously missed other payments and was trying to borrow more from Peter to pay Paul, Marine Midland Bank was calling in an old $8.5-million note on 120 Broadway. This was a minor fraction of a billion dollars, but the bank believed that if it did not now press for the money, it might be vulnerable to stockholder suits that could allege that they hadn't acted promptly enough to obtain their money from the crumbling Zeckendorf empire. Zeckendorf couldn't pay the $8.5 million when it was demanded, so his company was now technically forced into involuntary bankruptcy. When he learned the facts and realized their implications, Zeckendorf told his chauffeur to turn the car around and head back to his turret office, for there was no longer any use meeting with his major creditors. The rest of his empire, he knew, would now be taken from him and sold to pay his debts.

In 1957, newspapers carried the announcement that two men whose names were not generally known were purchasing from the floundering Zeckendorf the prestigious Chrysler Building, for $42 million. The sale was emblematic of the restless, continual shifting that marked the purely acquisitive dream. Zeckendorf was exciting to watch in his flamboyance, but scrutiny of those who bought the Chrysler from him yielded a sense of sadness that the grand icons of Manhattan could be reduced to commodities. Sol Goldman and Alex DiLorenzo, Jr., were outer-borough acquirers who had amassed fortunes without ever entering the arena of the Manhattan skyscrapers. Rumors circulated that the pair were connected with the Mafia, especially after DiLorenzo attended the funeral of Albert Anastasia, a mob boss executed by other mobsters while he sat in a hotel barber chair.

Selig Usher Goldman, called Sol, and Alex DiLorenzo, Jr., had been childhood friends in Brooklyn in the 1930s. Cementing their friendship was the first building Sol bought, the one housing his father's grocery store, with money saved from his bar mitzvah, more from odd jobs, and the remainder borrowed from Alex's father. "Never leave the store, Sol," his mother had told the red-haired teenager. "It's a gold mine." But Sol did just that, dropping out of Brooklyn College and buying distressed properties in Brooklyn for as little as $500 and no mortgage. Even then "a scoundrel and a charmer" (his wife's later phrase), he was able to convince owners to let him take properties off their hands. In the five years after the war, Goldman amassed forty-four Brooklyn buildings.

Alex was quieter and darker, unprepossessing in looks, abrupt in his conversations; his mother had died when he was an infant, and in his studies of pharmacy at St. John's University he seemed oriented toward an ordinary, humdrum life. But he, too, bought a building at age eighteen in 1934, sold it for three times what he'd paid for it, and was soon more interested in properties than prescriptions. "By the time I was twenty-two," he later said, "I didn't need to worry [about money]."

DiLorenzo left pharmacy to study at Brooklyn Law School, passing the bar in 1950; Goldman was one of his first clients. In 1951 the old friends recognized the practicality of becoming partners and shook hands on it; they never got around to making a written contract. As they prospered, they moved from Brooklyn to the Kings Point area of Great Neck, where they had homes around the corner from one another and sent their children to the same schools. Soon they were millionaires lusting after a "trophy" building in Manhattan. Goldman and DiLorenzo moved into offices on East 42nd Street in 1955. It was convenient to subway lines, and Alex liked to walk to services at St. Agnes Roman Catholic Church on 43rd Street.

There were allegations that the purchases of the Chrysler and Graybar buildings were financed by money from the longshoremen's and teamsters' unions, both riddled with corruption and shown to be under the control of organized crime. Those allegations were disproven, but the pair's actions always had the taint of skirting the edge of legitimacy. During a strike in the Chrysler Building just after DiLorenzo and Goldman bought it, DiLorenzo hired a labor-consultants firm that had ties to the Gambino crime family; he fired the firm as soon as he (and the newspapers) discovered the connection. No mob links were ever proved, but stories kept circulating, and the pair took advantage of them. People in the industry were afraid of Goldman-DiLorenzo. Brokers wouldn't press too hard for payment; property sellers would accept a Goldman offer because it might be dangerous to refuse. Adding to the aura of unsavory involvement was DiLorenzo's propensity for small duplicities. When callers asked for him, he'd say that Mr. DiLorenzo was out and then talk to them as if he were an underling in the firm.

They were acquirers, insiders said, but without the style of a Zeckendorf. They were what Helmsley might have become had he not teamed up with Wien.

Within three years of the Chrysler Building's purchase, Goldman and DiLorenzo had reduced the mortgage substantially. They were eventually able to pry out of the Chrysler, through second mortgages and bonds, a total of $23 million with which to make other investments. Using the tactics they'd practiced with $500 down payments on tenements in Brooklyn, in the 1960s Goldman and DiLorenzo amassed an empire of 1,000 buildings in the United States and Canada, half of them in New York. They became the largest holders of property along Fifth Avenue, landlords of such prestigious hotels as the Gotham and Stanhope, which they bought after foreclosures. Goldman and his wife later took the penthouse of the Stanhope as their primary residence. Another trophy was the building at Park Avenue and 42nd Street originally constructed by Henry Mandel, also bought from Zeckendorf. Many times millionaires, in interviews Goldman and DiLorenzo wrung their hands about the potentially deleterious effect of their wealth on their children.

Chapter Fourteen

The Changing of the Guard

IN 1969, the six buildings of the Lincoln Center for the Performing Arts were nearing completion, the result of a compelling dream. As with many projects in Manhattan, the complex began with the landowning elite — in this instance, their wish to move the Metropolitan Opera out of the garment center in the 1920s. Lincoln Center's location and spaciousness owed much to the plans Benjamin Wistar Morris had made for the site Otto Kahn had bought at the intersection of Broadway and Columbus Avenue near 63rd Street. After Robert Moses swung the wrecker's ball, opening several blocks through slum clearance in the 1950s, John D. Rockefeller III provided seed money and became chairman of the project. Rockefeller brought in Wally Harrison to oversee the design of all the buildings and convinced several family members to make large donations. Regular supporters of the opera such as the Goelets, Vanderbilts, and Vincent Astor also made substantial gifts. The buildings were designed by distinguished architects: Harrison himself, his partner Max Abramowitz, and such luminaries as Philip Johnson, Eero Saarinen, and the firm of Skidmore, Owings & Merrill. Lincoln Center grew into grandly proportioned performance halls of travertine, grouped around an elegant plaza dominated by a fountain that looked especially attractive as audiences gathered to enter the various edifices in the early evening. Huge paintings by Marc Chagall, a larger-than-life-size reclining figure by Henry Moore, and Elie Nadelman's white marble figures of the proportions of ancient Egyptian temple statuary added to the sense of the monumental. Here was culture, writ as large, as beautiful — and almost as overwhelming — as New York itself.

Through the nearly two decades that it took to complete Lincoln

Center, the wealth and influence of the builders of Manhattan had been growing. Larry Wien became involved with the complex at an early stage, at a time when he began to give money away in chunks that, his son-in-law Peter Malkin recalls, "amounted to as much as fifty percent of current income and part of his capital." For Lincoln Center, Wien also solicited contributions from the real estate community, such as his predecessor and successors as head of Federation, his partner, Helmsley, and old builder families such as the Dursts, Urises, and Roses. By the late 1960s the $184-million physical setting of the center was almost complete and almost all paid for — but the performing troupes were having difficulty raising operating funds. Potential donors felt they'd already been squeezed dry to build the culture palaces.

This impasse was the occasion for a decided transition in the character and participants of philanthropy in the city. To prevent the situation from further hurting the troupes, Wien and Rockefeller agreed to match one another and give $1.25 million each in a big splash to pay off the remaining capital debt. Rockefeller could rather easily write such a check, but Wien had to sell something to raise his part of the gift. What he sold, to Harry Helmsley, and for a fairly low price, was the majority of his portion of the operating lease for the Empire State Building.

This transaction was tangible evidence of the divergence of the two friends. While Wien had been devoting more time to charitable affairs and less to business, Helmsley had done just the opposite, snapping up properties in a half-dozen major cities. He also bought, for $1 million each, two major brokerage and management firms, the Charles F. Noyes company, strong in the Wall Street area, and Brown, Harris, Stevens, Inc., a specialist in cooperative apartments. Now he was large enough to squeeze other brokerages to the point that they had to sell out to him; that's what happened to the firm of John J. Reynolds, the broker for Joe Kennedy. And Helmsley made another leap, one Wien considered too risky for his clients: he started developing — the Pfizer Building at 42nd and Third Avenue, 140 Broadway near Wall Street, and One Penn Plaza. Though some operators had difficulty crossing into development, Helmsley had the sense to know what he didn't know, and hired experts to help avoid major blunders.

Helmsley didn't get the same thrill as Wien did from donations. He had few charities other than Eve's Quaker Meeting House and a small welfare organization in Harlem she also patronized. "Real estate is the best game around," he told a reporter, "and when you're ahead in a game you like to keep playing," continually plowing back profits to buy more properties.

Wien and Helmsley had already come near the end of their string as partners and close friends, but they put philosophic differences aside when their interests coincided. When the World Trade Center project was proposed, Wien and Helmsley became alarmed. Their cash cow, the Empire State Building, would no longer be the world's tallest building; more important, each twin tower would have more rentable space than the Empire State and would draw tenants away. Also, broadcasters would have to move their antennas from the Empire State Building to the World Trade Center in order to have a clear broadcast range. Nothing seems to galvanize real estaters to action quite as much as a threat to private enterprise. Normally a quiet man averse to publicity, Wien spoke out at thirty community and legislative hearings. He wasn't opposed to a center for world trade; he just objected to the enormous size of the building. He argued that the Port Authority, using its special tax status, was going to erect enormous buildings that would be able to charge substantially less for space than could competing buildings owned by private investors. The $3 million that the Port Authority would pay in lieu of annual taxes on the site, Wien pointed out, was $12 million less than private developers would have had to pay on the same acreage. Wien's legal challenges were finally struck down by New York State's Supreme Court.

Helmsley, on the other hand, became more upset by a deal that went sour. In mid-1965, Wien and Helmsley agreed to buy all the properties held by J. Myer Schine, sixty motion-picture theaters scattered around the country, a dozen hotels, and 3,000 acres of ocean beach frontage in Florida. The price of the deal, $64.4 million, found its way onto the front page of the *New York Times*. Helmsley and Wien then went to work on the details of a 200-page contract. But Schine used the announced Helmsley-Wien deal to extract a higher bid from a rival buyer, to whom he sold for $69.5 million on the very morning when the completed Helmsley-Wien contract was to be signed. Wien seemed philosophical about this defeat, but Helmsley was incensed, for it hurt deeply his pride in his professional integrity. He sued Schine for his brokerage fee and obtained a partial settlement. After the Schine fiasco, an associate recalled, "He got harder and tougher. He didn't trust people the way he used to. And he got a lot more demanding of the people who worked for him, and a lot less forgiving of mistakes."

It was after these blows that Helmsley shifted more into development and experienced the satisfaction of creating new structures from the ground up. Perhaps in consequence of taking on added responsibilities, he spent even more time at the office. Associates sensed that his marriage was disintegrating — not being torn apart, just tailing off to the point where the participants arranged matters so they saw very little of one another.

When it came time for Helmsley to make the single largest deal of his life thus far, buying the holdings of the Furman-Wolfson real estate trust for $165 million in 1969, he did it without Wien, and in a most spectacular way. One afternoon Helmsley went to Chase Manhattan Bank and was permitted to borrow $78 million based on nothing more tangible than his signature — in effect, a huge, unsecured personal loan. This tremendous expression of confidence in Harry Helmsley staggered those hardest to impress, his fellow real estate men. To replace the loan, Helmsley and Irving Schneider made a syndicate offering that was well subscribed. With its proceeds, Helmsley paid off the loan and became the owner of thirty major buildings in New York, Chicago, Los Angeles, Des Moines, and Newark. He no longer needed Wien to make a syndicate, and with Zeckendorf in eclipse Helmsley considered himself Manhattan's leading real estate magnate. Increasingly, the press spoke of Helmsley in these terms, too. Earlier, when the Empire State Building had been bought, newspaper stories had focused more on Wien than on Helmsley; now the building became known as Helmsley's and, retroactively, was referred to as his greatest negotiating triumph.

Soon after the Furman-Wolfson declaration of independence, Helmsley met Leona Mindy Roberts, a broker specialist in the sales of cooperatives and condominiums. Leona, a young-looking forty-nine, had ingratiated herself with Leon Spear, who made the introduction. She was offered a position at Brown, Harris, Stevens and began an affair with Harry, then sixty. Leona was enough of a real estater to appreciate Harry's exploits, and among the many ways she endeared herself the most effective may have been to tell him, as one who knew, that he was a magnificent businessman.

*　　　*　　　*

Just then, players on the outer fringes of Manhattan who had earlier limited their horizons began to enlarge them. A newspaper squib reported that the busiest architect in Manhattan was a graying, portly, unpretentious man who favored casual clothes and went by the name of Philip Birnbaum. His usual clients were in Queens, and his work was considered pedestrian by the architectural fraternity. Birnbaum was a direct disciple of Leo Bing, for whom he began work while still a student at Stuyvesant High School in the 1920s. "My family was so poor that I made my own roller skates," he recalls. For nine years, Birnbaum worked for Bing & Bing as an on-site inspector; during the last six he attended Columbia's architecture school at night. When the architecture school at Princeton told him to withdraw his application because "they didn't accept 'Hebrews,' " that forced him to begin his own practice at the height of the depression. Emery Roth designed 250 buildings in his life; Phil Birnbaum designed more, mostly apartments for the middle class in Queens, Riverdale, and other nearby suburbs. A social observer, his basic architectural innovations included putting garages beneath apartment houses ("safety and comfort"); a pool on the roof ("you look at the sky and think you're on the beach, and it's a good baby-sitter for the kids"); and lots of balconies ("an older woman, unable to get out on her own, can at least take the air"). Once introduced by Birnbaum, these features came to be required even by tenants of competing buildings.

Beginning in the 1950s, some of Birnbaum's major clients began to apply their outer-borough style in Manhattan. In the island's history, mass had followed class when reaching for luxury; now, as Queens came to Manhattan, mass brought along its own style. Second and Third avenues on the Upper East Side became what an architecture critic disparaged as "Birnbaum Country," lined with new apartment houses replete with small balconies, underground garages, circular driveways, canopied entrances, and flashy lobbies.

Not all suburban builders viewed Manhattan as a Mecca for developers. The Muss family, though it possessed enough resources, thought the stakes in Manhattan unnecessarily high and chose to keep developing in the outer boroughs. But some Birnbaum clients who had made considerable fortunes kept thinking about Manhattan. The Trump family was one of them.

Working for the Federal Housing Administration (FHA) during depression and war, Fred Trump completed 2,500 homes and after the war parlayed his knowledge of government contracts into subsidized complexes in Bensonhurst and Brighton Beach. Trump cultivated such young city officials as housing commissioner Robert Wagner, lawyer Abraham Lindenbaum, city budget officer Abe Beame, and Hugh Carey, the latter men stalwarts of the Brooklyn Democratic club. Such ties were even more imperative for outer-borough builders than for Manhattan developers. In many ways, the boroughs were still small towns.

In the mid-1950s Fred Trump was a target of an FHA investigation. He had borrowed more from the FHA to erect the two complexes than it had cost to build them, and auditors discovered that Trump had been paid $1.6 million in dividends without prior FHA approval. Trump was not alone — the problem was widespread. For instance, Norman Tishman was similarly investigated for $1.7 million in extra payments on two developments in Rego Park. In the case of the Tishmans, this "windfall" was blamed on shoddy administration from Washington, and the Tishmans were allowed to collect land rent from the complex for the next ninety-nine years. Trump, however, was replaced as manager of the FHA complexes and his permission to build new ones was withdrawn. Even so, a few years later Trump had gotten back far enough into the government's good graces to be allowed to develop a $65-million project in Coney Island. It was a sweet deal. Land was cleared by the city, then sold to developers below cost. Developers also enjoyed financing provided by the state and hefty tax abatements.

In 1961, when Republican mayoral candidate Louis Lefkowitz railed against a fund-raising dinner given by Abe Lindenbaum at a Brooklyn restaurant, Trump was again spotlit. At the dinner, contributions were pledged to Mayor Robert Wagner's reelection campaign by forty-three developers, principal among them Fred Trump, whose donation led the list. Charging that the developers were too cozy with the city, Lefkowitz cited Trump's Coney Island project as evidence. The contributions were legal, but Lindenbaum was forced to resign from the city planning commission; a few years later, it was revealed that the lawyer had been working with Trump at the same time that he billed the state $520,000 for evicting slum-clearance-area tenants so that Trump Village could be built. Lindenbaum's bills were questioned but eventually paid. The focus turned to Fred Trump; after audits showed that he had made a windfall of $1.8 million, a New York State investigation asked, "Is there any way to prevent a man who does business like that from getting another contract with the state?" A state auditor replied, "I don't think so, under our present laws." Trump's profits became the main impetus to alter those laws.

Donald and Robert Trump, Fred's fourth and fifth children, grew up in a large house on Midland Parkway, went to Kew Forest prep school in the WASP enclave of Kew Gardens, and attended services at Norman Vincent Peale's church, Marble Collegiate in Manhattan. Tall, blond, and athletic, Donald was a discipline problem whose antics led to a transfer to the New York Military Academy. His background (outer boroughs, Protestant, military academy school) made for an experience distant from that of the sons of the Jewish builder families. Like those young men, however, Donald worked on construction sites and in the family office during school vacations.

Fred Trump's public raking over the coals solidified young Donald's determination to get his father out of the subsidized housing business and into something more prestigious, larger, and less subject to public auditing. In the mid-1960s, while at Wharton, the business school of the University of Pennsylvania, Donald began to talk to classmates of changing the skyline. He could remortgage the 24,000 units of housing that Fred controlled in the outer boroughs and use the resulting millions to start skyscrapers in Manhattan. If this meant a clash with his father, so be it. He told his friend and contemporary Richard Lefrak, "Don't let Sam run over you. Get out from under his thumb." He planned to follow that advice himself.

Sam Lefrak had quickly escaped his own father's thumb. At the University of Maryland in the late 1930s he studied engineering, then completed graduate work in finance and business at Columbia and Harvard, taking time off to build his first apartment house. He joined his father, Harry, in 1940, but not in the usual way. Harry insisted that Sam put $5,000 in the organization. Sam did so and took charge. The firm had been going from project to project; Sam standardized procedures and mechanized operations where possible. In 1948 Harry called him into his office and made a farm analogy: "Most of the time you see the horse running and the colt following. Here the colt is running and the horse is following." Harry offered to step down. Sam asked him to stay on for five years, during which "I'll make the money and you spend it." Shortly, Harry departed to build medical centers in Israel.

While Fred Trump liked to keep out of the public eye, Sam

Lefrak cultivated publicity, though not as brilliantly as Zeckendorf did. In an early interview, the ebullient Lefrak claimed that he was going to build big projects by himself, with no help — and no interference — from government entities. Toward that end he bought a huge parcel of swampy land in Queens that had been owned for generations by the Astor estate; he convinced the executors to sell it for four dollars a square foot. By 1959 he'd put up 4,600 apartments in Brooklyn and Queens, and begun the 6,000-apartment Lefrak City on the Astor swamp. When Harry died in 1963, the Lefrak Organization was among the largest owners in the city, renting to a quarter-million people. He confided to *Architectural Forum*, "I want people to say about me, 'There's a human being' . . . a landlord with a heart."

If tenants said that, it was because rents were low. What Lefrak called his "supermarket approach to apartment planning and building" was founded on a philosophy of cutting costs. He'd buy trainloads of distressed merchandise, such as unused bricks, storing them in warehouses until he had a building to construct, or buy land that he'd similarly stockpile until the right moment. His dream was to cater to the common man.

Although Lefrak consistently denied wanting to join the skyscraper builders of what he called "the isle of Capri," or that he sought acceptance into the circle of Jewish families who dominated the scene, he made forays into their territory. Using government subsidies, he built West Side Manor and the Floyd Gibbons Houses in upper Manhattan. He erected a business skyscraper at 40 West 57th Street. He also competed in charitable matters. Lefrak joined with several Manhattan developers as a founder of the Albert Einstein College of Medicine, but in his other Jewish charities he tried to pick causes and institutions somewhat distinct from theirs, for instance leaping regional bounds to sustain the Jewish Hospital in Denver.

Becoming close to Brooklyn and Queens Democratic organizations, Lefrak accepted nonpaying public jobs with high-sounding titles: he was a commissioner for public works for Manhattan under Wagner; a commissioner for the Interstate Sanitation Commission encompassing New York, New Jersey, and Connecticut; a member of Governor Rockefeller's finance and advisory committee of the State Traffic Safety Council; and a commissioner of the Landmarks Preservation Commission of New York City. These positions kept him in the public eye, and he also grabbed headlines with a proposal to keep the Brooklyn Dodgers in Flatbush by offering to build a stadium at low cost, and another in which he sought to buy the decaying Ellis Island and make it into a monument. No one took him up on either offer, so he wasn't out any cash.

Larry Silverstein and Bernie Mendik, the young brothers-in-law who had consciously slipstreamed behind Wien and Helmsley in their syndications, tried to acquire more expensive buildings each time they made a purchase. Respect in real estate came in direct proportion to the price of your buildings; the man who could play in a poker game that used five-dollar chips was considered more worthy than the man in a one-dollar-chip game. To obtain these larger chips — and $100,000-per-unit rather than $10,000-per-unit investors — required sophistication. No longer doing the painting and polishing themselves, Silverstein and Mendik still took guidance from Harry Silverstein. Though the elder Silversteins had more money now, like many seared by the depression who later came to wealth they wouldn't move from their modest lodgings on Cabrini Boulevard in the Bronx.

Harry Silverstein died in June 1966. "Harry was the glue that held us together," Mendik knew; after his father-in-law's death, it became more evident that Mendik's marriage was in serious disarray and that he and Larry had real differences. Larry wanted to take more and bigger risks, to edge over into actual development. Bernie simply wanted to be the best at acquiring and retrofitting buildings. As Bernie's marriage to Annette continued to deteriorate, his deep personal connection to Larry — that trust so necessary to working partnerships in high-stakes real estate — eroded, too. Yet the intertwinings of business and personal matters was so complex that both Mendik's marriage and the real estate partnership continued to exist.

Perhaps that was because they didn't want to rock the boat when things were going well and they were being encouraged to enter the club in terms of philanthropy as well as business. Silverstein had been a student leader at New York University in his undergraduate days, and had been called upon after graduation to work in alumni matters, then to join the board. "I found I was crossing paths often with David Tishman — at NYU dinners, on business matters, and in REBNY meetings," Silverstein recalls. Another charitable focus was the Anti-Defamation League of B'nai B'rith, where Norman Tishman was a big wheel. When it occurred to

Silverstein that real estate was not being taught on a professional enough level, he discussed the idea of an institute with David Tishman and Harry Helmsley. Shortly, these three teamed to convince the board of NYU to begin a real estate institute for which the trio provided seed money and brought in as occasional lecturers the biggest names in the field.

After David's wife, Ann, died in 1962, the patriarch of the Tishman clan decided to make fundamental changes in his life. His son Bob was advancing the same arguments for the presidency that Norman had used in 1948: it was time for a change, time to let the younger men have their moment in the sun. David ceded the title of chairman to Norman, and Bob became president. David yielded the penthouse to his other son, Alan, on the occasion of his own remarriage to Beatrice Levinson Rosenthal. Alan and Peggy found the penthouse "too stuffy and old-fashioned" and in their redecorating covered over many of the Art Deco details, an action they came to regret when such period touches again came into vogue; still, the large dining room was suitable for the social events in which Peggy was increasingly involved.

Norman Tishman's reign as chairman was short and so filled with charitable doings that he didn't spend very much time in his wood-paneled office with the fireplace. In the manner of the earlier heads of the builder clans, his calendar filled with endless meetings of the Anti-Defamation League, the Federation of Jewish Philanthropies, the United Jewish Appeal, the Boy Scouts, and the Citizens Tax Council. In early February 1967 he died at the age of sixty-five.

Time healed some wounds; Paul, the outsider brother who had lost out to Norman in the 1940s, convened family parties after the latter's death and invited all the Tishmans. They came to Paul's Sutton Place apartment and admired his latest purchases of African art, or looked at the home movies of his trips to meet with tribal chieftains in exotic places. The younger relatives didn't know all their cousins and cousins-once-removed, as had been the norm in those earlier days when several generations of Tishmans had gathered every Saturday night at the command of Julius or, later, of his widow. Paul wondered privately if he should give out name tags.

In the driver's seat, Bob Tishman felt the responsibilities of his leadership keenly, and with these in mind put a proposition to his son-in-law in 1966. His daughter Lynne had married Jerry Speyer, the soft-spoken, broad-shouldered son of a family of German Jewish builders who had fled Hitler in the 1930s. Speyer had been in the Tishmans' social set all his life, having attended Horace Mann and then Columbia, where he graduated with an MBA; he had gone to work as assistant to the vice president and treasurer of the new Madison Square Garden. "I'd hoped to work in real estate with the Garden," Speyer remembers, "but 80 percent of my time was spent on the Rangers and the Knicks." He landed another position, with the largest builder-owner of post offices in the country, but didn't feel fulfilled there, either. Then Tishman approached him. They differed in appearance but were otherwise much alike — quiet, courteous, and well versed in finance. "Smart and decent, a rare combination," Speyer recalls of his early impression of his father-in-law. For his part, Tishman promised Speyer "tremendous opportunities," including the sort of resources he wouldn't find elsewhere. Speyer had qualms. He wanted to run his own show, and there were quite a few Tishmans in the firm, though none of his generation. But he felt that Bob would be an able and sensitive mentor; he took the job. "I believe in nepotism," Tishman told reporters, "so long as the son-in-law you're bringing in is smart."

Shortly after Speyer's arrival, Norman died. Just then, Norman's son Peter was a vice president. With his father gone, Peter had no rabbi to assure further upward progress in the company, and Bob was obviously grooming Speyer for the future leadership. So, as Paul had done twenty years earlier when he saw his route to the top blocked, Peter decided the time had come to leave the family firm and form his own.

Bob's attention to the long term required two basic changes in strategy. The first was voluntary. "I'd rather deal with twenty corporate presidents than with three hundred crazy women tenants," he quipped, sold even more apartments, and pursued office-tower projects such as a twenty-story building in Chicago. The second change was forced by the IRS, which questioned the sale-and-leaseback technique. In response, Tishman had the company retain title to the new buildings it was completing. On this basis the company's assets rose from $77 million in 1962 to $169 million in 1967, and rental income also increased. However, the new full-ownership positions meant increased mortgage costs and operating expenses that actually caused rental profits to fall 29 percent over the same period. Bob Tishman continued to be haunted by the difficulty of realizing money from the family's properties. They were sitting on a mountain of gold but were unable to mine it properly. Although Tishman assets per share were at $100, the stock was mired in the low thirties. Cash flow doubled, but with profits low Tishman executives still did not make as much as their counterparts in private real estate companies did. Harry Helmsley, insiders estimated, took home a half-million tax-sheltered dollars each month. The Tishmans, the largest owner-builders in the country, didn't realize anywhere near that amount.

In the 1920s and even in the immediate post–World War II years, builders had been admired as positive forces in the community and celebrated for contributing to the city's progress. But the slum clearance and redevelopment projects of the 1950s (as administered by the heavy hand of Robert Moses) and the steady increase in rental prices of most New York City property combined to produce a continuing stream of newspaper stories in which builders were depicted in the role of villains bent on evicting the poor from their homes in the pursuit of excessive profits.

Adding to the mix was the public outcry surrounding the destruction of the old Pennsylvania Railroad Station in 1963. The death of one of the city's last horizontal monuments made apparent to many New Yorkers that development ought not to proceed unchecked by government. The Landmarks Preservation Commission was chartered in 1965; its powers included that of denying permission to raze or alter architecturally or historically important older buildings.

Now anti–urban-renewal sentiment combined with a new awareness of the plight of the poor brought about by the "war on poverty." Landlords had always been a target for vitriol because tenants were reminded monthly of their existence and their demands for payment. In a climate highlighting the problems of the poor, landlords were raised in the public mind several steps closer to the embodiment of capitalist greed.

The 1961 revision of the zoning codes inserted city government forcefully into the business of shaping the skyline. As fashioned by longtime realtor James Felt, chairman of the City Planning Commission, the new code replaced Ernest Flagg's idea with a different basis on which buildings could be erected. Rather than having the limiting factor be the relationship of the building's size to the adjacent streets, the new code was based on the floor area ratio — FAR — of a building. If a skyscraper was allowed a FAR of 20, it could have floor space equal to twenty times the area of the plot on which it sat. How the building achieved that ratio was largely left up to the builder. You could construct a very tall edifice set back from the street, or a lower one that took up the entire site, or some other configuration. The new code encouraged the addition of extra stories to office towers by permitting a larger FAR if the building was placed well inside the sidewalk line, and semipublic plazas separated the building from surrounding ones. What the 1916 zoning code had expressly sought to prevent — domination of light and air by a new skyscraper that looked like the old Equitable file cabinets — the revised zoning code of the 1960s allowed. Freed from the wedding-cake, multiple-setback requirements, new buildings approached the sky as large, unsegmented blocks, only some of which bore distinguished crowns.

Government also lured builders by making attractive the construction of projects for low- and middle-income residents. Under the Mitchell-Lama law, a builder could count on help with the financing and guaranteed rates of return, and retained the right to sell the buildings for profit after twenty years.

Dave Rose didn't like anything that depended so heavily on government involvement, but Fred, Dan, and Elihu wanted to do Mitchell-Lama buildings, for these fit in well with the social agenda they also espoused in work for Federation welfare agencies, civic organizations, and institutions such as the New School for Social Research. The new generation won out and the Roses erected more than 2,000 Mitchell-Lama middle-income apartments. The old guard was giving way at Rose Associates. Uncle Dave spent a great deal of the 1950s in Israel, constructing an entire village (200 homes, shopping center, synagogue) that he and his wife had underwritten, as well as a vocational school in Jerusalem; they were on their fifteenth trip to Israel when Rebecca died there in 1959. After her death, Dave continued his efforts in Israel and in a new direction, medical technology. He helped engineer the first hyperbaric chamber, installed at Mount Sinai; another related project was a portable artificial kidney, developed in association with Dr. Willem Kolff; a third involved electronic suppression of pain. His construction and medical interests were combined when he became a consultant to the building of Dr. Jonas Salk's new laboratories in La Jolla, California.

In 1960, a broker had approached Fred Rose about the corner of Park Avenue at 48th Street. Fred thought it suitable for the company's first office tower, and on the golf course he talked a high official of Bankers Trust into siting its headquarters at 280 Park. The building received an award for the design (by Emery Roth & Sons and interior designer Henry Dreyfuss), and Sam Rose drily observed, "I'm happy to see that the ink on the certificate is as black as the ink on Rose Associates' corporate ledger."

Sam Rose died in 1964 at age seventy-four. He had been the dreamer, the artist, the intellect that David had always consulted. Sam's sons had looked up to him for the creativity and gusto he brought to the pursuit of culture and the good life, and after his death collected letters he had written to them and to other correspondents, ranging from Winston Churchill to the groundskeeper at a local golf club, in a volume they privately printed.

After Sam's death, Dave devoted himself even more to his outside interests, and the second generation of Roses settled into a smooth-running, tripartite division of the work of the business. Fred was the builder, the leader and developer of Manhattan and Westchester projects. "Elly originally wanted to build, too," Fred recalls of his youngest brother. "He did one building and hated the work so much he said he'd never do another." Discovering that he didn't like the concrete-on-the-shoes environment in which Fred thrived, Elihu opted for the more orderly pursuits of managing and leasing, a task that played to his strengths. Dan — the philosopher of the firm — believed the future lay outside New York and wanted to take the company national. Fred argued that this would overextend them, but the brothers had arranged matters so that each could, in the parlance of the day, do his own thing. Dan started office and multiple-use projects in downtown Boston, then looked to Washington, DC, and Florida for others. "Soon I was traveling so much that I decided to put the time in the air to good use," he recalls. Rather than perusing magazines, he read classical Greek and Roman authors. Quotations from them started showing up in his conversation and speeches. He likened "the feasibility studies that a developer shows to a potential mortgage-lender or investor to the opinions offered by the Delphic oracle in support of Greek colonization expeditions."

Richard Ravitch's social agenda was much on his mind as he and architect Lew Davis walked out onto the East 23rd Street pier in 1961, carrying paper-bag lunches. In Ravitch's pocket was a letter from Adlai Stevenson, ambassador to the United Nations, decrying the lack of housing available for UN delegates and staffers who were nonwhite, and asking members of the real estate community if they could do anything about this need. The letter had reached a sympathetic recipient. Ravitch was then in his late twenties, had recently entered the family firm, and was trying to put into practice the idealistic, liberal principles he had been forming since his youth. After graduating from Fieldston, Columbia, and Yale Law, Ravitch had worked in Washington as counsel to a Senate subcommittee on housing and then decided to come into HRH. Currently, the family business was in a bit of turmoil. Ravitch's father and grandfather were both dead, and Saul Horowitz, Sr., was in sole charge, seconded by the cousins with whom Dick had grown up, Saul, Jr., and Alan Horowitz. "There were problems getting Saul, Sr., to give up control," onetime subordinate Irving Fischer recalls, suggesting that the elder Horowitz was "a difficult man." Moreover, running the business was like rolling the dice. HRH was then a general contractor, bidding for construction work on both private and government-assisted projects; if they guessed properly, HRH could make a bundle, and if not, the company could lose a lot. It was losing with greater frequency than Fischer thought warranted, even as HRH expanded through work in Puerto Rico and California while the senior Horowitz built charitable projects in Jerusalem.

Ravitch had seen his entry into the family firm as an opportunity to do something worthwhile in housing. While sitting on the pier, he and Davis looked north to the United Nations complex, a short way up the river, and thought their lunch spot and the piers reaching to 30th Street the ideal place for a waterside housing complex for delegates and other middle-income people. With Mitchell-Lama and federal subsidies, it could be done. The setting for their dreaming wasn't the Monte Carlo nightclub used by Zeckendorf and Harrison to formulate X City fifteen years earlier, but Davis and Ravitch soon had in mind a striking design that included features of the sort Zeckendorf and Harrison had once conjured — riverside walks, shopping promenades, a floating restaurant nightclub — amenities not usually found in publicly assisted housing.

Galvanized, Ravitch returned to the office and researched the idea. Problems included a federal law dating back to the War of 1812 that gave the United States government the right to expropriate every part of a property that lay outside the bulkhead line, and a city administration that was lukewarm to the idea. It took several years to get title and generate enthusiasm from the city planners. By then, in 1964, HRH was in serious trouble. After a divorce, Alan had moved to California and taken charge of an HRH office there; the fixed-bid practices on general contracting had been losing money rapidly, especially in California but also in New York. Moreover, Horowitz, Sr., remained chairman of the company. In 1965, Ravitch and Saul, Jr., known as J. R., took over the company, buying out the others' shares and refinancing to put HRH on a more sound basis. The "retirement" of Saul, Sr., was announced.

J. R. was a West Point graduate, a combat veteran, an engineer, and a Republican suburbanite. "He didn't look like a Horowitz," says Fred Rose, who became J. R.'s best friend in Scarsdale, where they both lived; "he looked like a parachutist, which he was — rugged, military, crew-cut." Ravitch remembers of his cousin, "We couldn't have been more unalike. It was a forced marriage, but one that worked out serendipitously." Dick and J. R. discovered that they liked one another and functioned well together, J. R. handling the institutional contracting and construction, Dick taking care of financing and developing. To cut their risks, they began to take mostly "cost-plus" contracts in which they were paid a fixed percentage over the actual expenses. A company couldn't make a killing doing that sort of contracting, but it could provide a living.

Ravitch recalls, "I was asked by a friend to present the Waterside project proposal to Laurance Rockefeller, who was interested in building a school to serve the United Nations delegates." Ravitch suggested to Rockefeller that they develop the site jointly, but heard nothing more from him. Months later, the chairman of the City Planning Commission called to alert Ravitch that the pier site was on the next agenda of the Board of Estimate. Investigating, Ravitch discovered that "Rockefeller was trying an end run," appealing to the city to deed the piers from 25th to 30th streets to the United Nations for the school he wished to underwrite. Had HRH been a bigger player, Rockefeller might not have tried to exercise his power in quite so arrogant a fashion. Only by stressing the project's commitment to low- and middle-income housing could Ravitch get around Rockefeller's attempt to take the site from him.

This scare was followed by more delays, financing difficulties, and fights with groups that claimed Waterside would not provide enough housing for the poor; these matters carried through the first administration to Mayor John Lindsay. A liberal Manhattan Republican, Lindsay was running for reelection in 1969, and Ravitch hoped that if Lindsay won the Waterside project would finally receive all the permissions and help needed to begin construction.

Then a reporter whom Ravitch had met at a social event called for a comment on the mayoral race. Ravitch very candidly said that he didn't like the Democratic candidate and as a lifelong member of the Democratic party wasn't too crazy about Lindsay, but would support the mayor because "in a democracy, sometimes you have only limited choices." This became the quote of the day in the *Times;* it was the first time Ravitch had ever been quoted in the newspapers, and the remark managed to irk everyone, especially Lindsay. It was possible that Ravitch would never get his social-agenda project off the ground.

Sam Rudin was annoyed in the fall of 1963. The British government had agreed to move some of its offices out of Rockefeller Center and into a new Rudin building on Third Avenue that Richard Roth had designed; Rockefeller Center wanted a payment of $100,000 to let the tenants out of their lease, and the Rudins were being forced to pay it. Sam fulminated and tried to call David or Nelson to complain. They were unavailable. So one bright, brisk October afternoon, Sam, his son Lew, and a lawyer started to walk from their offices on East 48th Street to Rockefeller Center. Lew reminded Sam of the old story of how his own namesake had asked John D. Rockefeller where he lived, and how the answer had led to the Rudins' first purchase of real estate in Manhattan; now the Rudins were millionaires in their own right. "It's a beautiful day," Lew remarked to his father, "and a beautiful country. Think of it: the Rudins, only one generation from the ghetto, have the opportunity to give the Rockefellers a check for $100,000. It's a sign of our triumph." Sam agreed, walked happily into Rockefeller Center, and handed over the check.

More than an individual triumph and a passing of the torch to a new generation of Rudins, this was a sign of the arrival at full power of those builder-owner families whose forefathers had come to this country from the Pale. The family who could hand over a $100,000 check and smile while doing so was not to be trifled with; the members of the club all now could play in the same sandbox as the Rockefellers. The dominant families got first look at all the best properties, relegating outsiders to the unenviable position of being able to buy only what the families had seen and rejected. They held enough properties overall that in any attempted assemblage they were likely to already control a key piece. They enjoyed such long-established relationships with the largest mortgage-lending institutions that they effectively tied up most of the money these institutions were willing to commit to Manhattan projects.

In 1965 the Tishman output slackened, the Dursts stopped their tremendous spurt of development, and in the next few years the Rudins, Minskoffs, Roses, Kaufmans, and even the Urises slowed down the frantic production of the postwar era to one building a year, or two every three years in Manhattan. That seemed a comfortable rate of growth for firms that were still, despite their monetary size, basically small family enterprises; it allowed a brother or son to personally supervise the projects on which the family's livelihood depended. One skyscraper a year was more than enough to create a base of wealth that now seemed close to invincible. The position of these families astride the industry was so strong, and their inventory of buildings so large, that if care was taken, the third and fourth generations could now be assured of having thriving empires — each estimated in the neighborhood of $100 million to $300 million — to manage and augment when they came of age.

Such a family enterprise could be seriously compromised only by making a wrong bet on new construction. As inflation began to take hold, costs rose dramatically and the demands of labor increased. To put up a big new building was now a matter of $100 million — an enormous sum in anybody's terms. So most of the families looked to equity partners to share the start-up costs and the risks involved. And they usually didn't proceed without a major tenant in tow. This steadiness of production, lack of overreaching, lining up of all elements in advance, and risk sharing with equity partners showed that these second- and third-generation builders were trying to take as much speculation as possible out of the profession that had once been called speculative building.

Their fathers and uncles had been great risk-takers, often throwing into the construction of a new building a tremendous fraction of their personal resources. These founders gambled so heavily because they had not that much to lose — many of the builder families did not achieve personal millionaire status until the late 1950s, though their buildings were valued in the millions. The succeeding generation, coming to full power in the late 1960s, could not be so reckless as their fathers. Now the families had a great deal to lose. To spread their resources too thin — as Zeckendorf had done — in a rush to construct, say, half a dozen buildings at once, might result in familial disaster. Steady accumulation was best, these sons seemed to agree, and if in their steadiness they seemed less daring and colorful than their fathers, they accepted drabness because they were conserving their resources to insure the future of the family empire; to pursue any other course would be folly.

PART FOUR

THE CITY AND ITS SYMBOLS

Chapter Fifteen

1166 and All That

RICHARD AND JULIAN ROTH were conferring over the single largest project with which they'd ever been confronted: the World Trade Center. Should they take it, or not? To accept would mean hiring a great many people, and what would happen if they had to carry the added staff should political or other delays halt payments for a while? They'd be paid by the Port Authority on a "time-card" basis — a fixed percentage above the actual costs billed — but even so the twin towers represented a large commitment for what was still a small firm. Julian finally convinced his brother by pointing out that the contract was in the millions and that surely "some of it will stick to us."

The building of skyscrapers in New York in the late 1960s and early 1970s was dominated, as the city's skyline itself would soon be, by the two gigantic towers designed by Minoru Yamasaki in association with Emery Roth & Sons. Though there was a great deal of work to do in terms of the interior, the exterior of the buildings and their silhouette against the sky were excruciatingly stark, or dull, depending on the viewer's frame of mind. Almost no one found them beautiful. Their attraction, such as it might be, lay solely in their size. That seemed fitting, as the conceivers of the trade center were not individuals but an institution, the Port Authority of New York and New Jersey. Monumental public projects didn't have to be faceless — those of Robert Moses bore the stamp of his personality boldly imposed — but these gigantic tombstones seemed merely practical.

They also represented an entirely new construction mountain to conquer. One can walk around a floor of the Empire State Building in a minute or so; it's tall, but compact. In contrast, each floor of the World Trade's twin towers was to be larger than a football field, an accomplishment made possible by a new technology of load-bearing walls (and a generous FAR allowance). For years, growing Wall Street firms had wanted such huge floors on which to concentrate and streamline their operations. To take the project from the drawing board to completed buildings, the Roth firm was joined by Tishman Realty & Construction when John Tishman's division won the contract to do the actual construction work. During the seven years of construction on the World Trade Center, there were allegations of irregularities on building sites all over the city; contractors and subcontractors were paying off workers and foremen — and city inspectors and policemen who could delay work for real or imagined causes — to the tune of $25 million a year. Because the World Trade Center was the largest project, investigation focused on it, but all that could be proved definitively was that a lot of overtime provisions had been larded into union contracts and that the unions and the near-monopolies, such as concrete suppliers, were completely intertwined, an arrangement that also added to costs.

The World Trade Center dream was good for John Tishman. Because his firm was being sustained in large measure by the millions paid for its construction, Tishman's strength within the company increased apace. While John was gearing up to deal with the World Trade Center, in the late 1960s his cousins Bob and Alan had found an ideal site for a new office tower: the east block front of Sixth Avenue between 45th and 46th streets. Parts of the site were controlled by various other major players, among them Goldman-DiLorenzo. By swapping properties and making cooperative deals with these firms, Tishman Realty came into possession of most of the plot for 1166 Sixth Avenue. A few holdouts remained. "One small old brownstone was being operated as a house of ill repute," Alan recalls, "and we tried everything to get it out of there. We even had someone call up and pretend he was a potential buyer who was mob-connected, and say that [the holdout] would be well advised to sell. That ruse didn't work, either." Eventually, the firm of Skidmore, Owings & Merrill designed a black-toned, forty-four-story building around the problem. Alan signed a letter of intent with General Telephone & Electric (GTE) to lease more than a third of the building, a consortium of four banks came in with loans, and construction began. Because the new building showed promise, the Tishman company's stock rose slightly — part of the reason Bob, Alan, and others in the hierarchy had been so keen on doing the building.

Negotiations with GTE to convert its letter into a lease went slowly, possibly because Alan had unwittingly scheduled early morning meetings and the GTE executives were out of sorts at having to start their commutes from suburbia earlier than usual. Then GTE's Lexington Avenue offices were bombed to protest its involvement in the Vietnam War, and the company abruptly decided to relocate entirely to Connecticut. "You're a defense contractor," Alan tried to tell the rattled executives; "you'll get bombed anywhere you go." Logic notwithstanding, GTE relocated and left the Tishmans with a half-completed building and no major tenant, in a city about to be glutted with office space by the World Trade Center.

To own an empty building was worse than possessing the sort of gaping holes that had damaged Vincent Astor and Bill Zeckendorf. Construction could not be halted, so the Tishmans had to bear the costs of completion and of paying back the short-term construction loans; they began to lose money on 1166 Sixth Avenue at the rate of more than $10 million a year. This absorbed the profits from their other buildings — a year earlier, the company's net profits had been only $7 million — and sent the Tishman stock again into decline. Second-guessers in the industry analyzed the Tishmans' every move and concluded, to their dread, that the Tishmans had done nothing wrong. Forces larger than any individual or family could control were at work in the disaster of 1166. That was frightening.

Alan called Lew Rudin, with whom he'd just begun a civic booster organization, the Association for a Better New York. He told Rudin of GTE's decision and quipped, "Now we don't have to worry any more about sleazy operators who are pushing the city toward commercial rent control. Now we have to worry about all the big tenants leaving the city."

In ordinary times, for a Tishman to tell a Rudin something that might give him a competitive edge would be unthinkable — a New York phrase encapsulated this philosophy as "Does Macy's tell Gimbel's?" — but both families were then being hurt by big towers that they could not rent.

Lew Rudin was of a similar age and as tall and likable as Alan Tishman; he differed in being more inclined than Alan to make his presence known in public. After he and his father handed that check to the Rockefellers and reminded themselves of their good fortune and their roots, the Rudins had increased their support for the city in ways both substantial and sentimental. Several Rudin foundations were devoted to hospitals and educational institutions. Shortly, they commissioned a monument near the site of Castle Garden, commemorating the immigrants who'd come to America before the turn of the century.

At the time of Alan Tishman's call, the Rudins had just completed their own headquarters, 345 Park Avenue. This was the culmination of a dream that had been a long time forming. In his youth, Sam Rudin had attended a public school on this site. He had spent decades assembling the entire block from Lexington Avenue up an incline to Park and from 51st to 52nd streets. It was flanked by masterpieces. Directly to the south was the ornate St. Bartholomew's Church and to the north was the Seagram's Building, as much a monument to the international style as St. Bart's was to the era of the Great War (when it was conceived) and to its Renaissance models. One of Richard Roth's most cohesive designs, the modern, building-block tower took advantage of the adjacent landmarks by not crowding them: it sits back as far on the site as the Seagram's Building, and is squeezed onto the north side of the plot so it doesn't unduly compete with the low-lying church. Its plazas on Park Avenue, with carefully aligned benches, encourage people to sit and admire the surroundings. Entrances on several levels, mandated by the sloping ground, give on to marbled lobbies that feel open even though a large tower sits above them. As the 1960s ended, Lew Rudin knew the family was fortunate to have already completed and leased out 345 Park; had it opened a year later, it, too, might have been as empty as the Tishmans' 1166 Sixth Avenue. Pride in the success of 345 Park was balanced by the upsetting knowledge that another Rudin building nearing completion, on Madison Square, might have to open without a single tenant signed to a lease.

"GTE, Union Carbide, General Foods, and other giant companies were fleeing Manhattan in droves," Rudin recalls of this era. The number of *Fortune* 500 companies with headquarters in New York dropped from 140 to 90. To explain their exodus, they cited crime in the streets, overcrowding, a scarcity of housing for middle managers and schooling for their children, not enough office help, and rising taxes. But one study concluded that companies were simply moving their headquarters to places that were considerably more green — suburbs that just happened to be down the road from the golf courses or the homes of their chairmen and CEOs.

When the Tishmans lose a big tenant, Rudin reasoned, the city also loses a chunk of its tax base. It was axiomatic in the industry that real estate's fortunes were intertwined with those of the city but, Rudin felt, insiders had never tried to help the city — by lobbying, contributing to its policing, or touting its attractions — with the understanding that this would also help their industry. That's why he conceived the Association for a Better New York (ABNY). "This didn't sit well with many people in real estate," Lew remembers, "including my father. It started the only real argument we ever had." Sam saw that Lew's neck would be sticking out and warned him that people would see a landlord's neck as a target and make attacks that could do the Rudin company no good.

For years, like most other builder families, the Rudins had quietly contributed money to the candidates for the city government's top slots, usually those of both major parties. So in the early 1970s Lew Rudin had standing to talk to Mayor John Lindsay and Controller Abe Beame about the exodus of big tenants, which was, the elected officials agreed, hurting the city's tax base. But neither the government nor the Better Business Bureau thought they could do much about the situation. Out of frustration Rudin formed ABNY, at its inception composed mostly of midtown property owners. In company with Alton Marshall, a close aide to Governor Nelson Rockefeller who had recently been appointed head of Rockefeller Center, and the president of a midtown bank, Rudin went to Wall Street to ask thirteen bank and financial-institution presidents for $5,000 each to fund ABNY; they refused, telling Rudin that his group was "too Jewish and too real estate."

Rudin swallowed the insult and ABNY raised its own money. The organization bought better streetlights and walkie-talkies to connect midtown-building doormen and elevator operators with police precincts, and took other steps to ameliorate the conditions that GTE and General Foods cited as reasons for leaving the city. Rudin lost no opportunity to pin ABNY golden apples on the lapels of foreign visitors. In one important outreach, he invited John Sawhill, chancellor of New York University, to join ABNY's board. In return for the new access to some of the city's wealthiest men, whom the association represented, Sawhill made introductions in Washington, where he had prior political connections. Official Washington wasn't terribly interested in the problems of large corporations leaving Manhattan, either. Didn't these apple-polishers understand that there was a war on in Vietnam?

No one seemed to comprehend the real estaters' troubles. One evening in 1972, the man who was NYU chancellor before Sawhill, James Hester, invited Rudin up to the top of Bobst Library on Washington Square to see his new office and to ask the Rudin family for a million-dollar donation. Rudin pointed out the window to the Madison Square Merchandise Mart and told Hester that it had been recently opened but was dark because there wasn't a single tenant in it. "When you can stand here at this time of day and see it lit up, I'll give you the money," Rudin said grimly.

Exacerbating the troubles of the Madison Avenue Merchandise Mart were Larry Wien and Harry Helmsley. The new Rudin building was attempting to siphon tenants from their own property, the Toy Building, across Madison Square, and Wien wrote restrictive covenants into the leases of tenants to try to prevent any further desertions. This tactic added to the difficulty the Rudins experienced in signing up new tenants. The underutilized building began draining money from the Rudin empire faster than patriarch Sam could believe, several million dollars a year, with no end in sight. Approaching eighty, Sam was afraid that this last dream was going to ruin everything for his children and grandchildren.

Leona Roberts's heavy-pressure techniques in trying to convert rental housing to cooperatives were on display to tenants in several buildings on which she worked in the late 1960s and early 1970s, and her pressurized pursuit of Harry Helmsley was equally obvious to colleagues, especially after Harry installed her in a penthouse of a building he owned. Her flattery, sexiness, and passionate enjoyment of the things money could buy were tonic for Helmsley. A man more used to wealth might have resisted these blandishments or enjoyed them clandestinely — but Helmsley was not accustomed to the trappings of a great fortune and not inured to the sort of sycophants and adventurers who often pursue aging, wealthy men.

Perhaps sensing the pressure, Eve Helmsley at last took a slightly more active interest in his business. Through purchases, Helmsley had become the owner-operator of a number of hotels around the country, and Eve suggested he build one on a narrow frontage on Central Park South. Harry said he was too busy, and she told him she'd get involved with the designers, Emery Roth & Sons. Julian was informed that there was to be a pool in a penthouse atop the hotel, a penthouse the Helmsleys could use as their primary residence when they were in Manhattan.

There seemed to be no restrictions on luxurious features. "I didn't know why, at first," Julian Roth says, but told Helmsley that the added comforts would substantially raise costs. To make the hotel economic, Helmsley would need four more stories than the zoning laws would permit, and Julian offered to argue Harry's "hardship" case before the Board of Standards. He did so, successfully. Toward the end of construction, in early 1971, Julian stood with Helmsley in the empty expanse of what would be the penthouse. "I asked Harry what paintings were going to hang on which walls, so we'd know how to place the lighting fixtures. He told me he had no paintings to hang." A few months later, Julian Roth was back in the now-completed thirteen-room penthouse duplex for the opening party of the Park Lane Hotel. Nearly everyone of importance in the real estate community attended; most of them had never met Eve Helmsley. Julian chatted with her. "She told me that the penthouse was as beautiful as she'd hoped, but that she would never live there, because she and Harry were getting a divorce."

The settlement was amicable, a recognition of the couple having grown apart. According to one estimate, Eve received more than $7 million and the penthouse of another Helmsley hotel in Manhattan.

While the settlement was being shaped by attorneys, Harry announced to his closest associates his desire to marry Leona; Leon Spear and Larry Wien, among others, advised him against doing so. Part of their concern was that Leona was under New York State indictment for illegal practices in connection with converting a rental building to a coop. Alarmed, Helmsley asked Al Marshall if he could intercede with State Attorney General Louis Lefkowitz; Harry's major concern was the embarrassment that would ensue if he married someone who was convicted of a real estate–related crime. In a business based on trust — he hadn't even looked at the bill Julian Roth sent him for Park Lane, certain the Roths would never overcharge him — Harry could not afford to be associated with someone whose business practices were adjudged illegal.

Marshall called Lefkowitz, who said he'd look more closely into the matter, which a subordinate was handling. That was as much pressure as was applied; in the interlinked worlds of big business and big politics, the sort of overt importuning and heavy-handed assurances of quid pro quo seen in popular movies are not employed. Just as one developer would never overtly ask an elected city official to push through a particular Mitchell-Lama project, nor would a second plead baldly for the rollback of an assessment, a third would never directly ask to have a prosecutor look the other way. Rather, senior officials would be requested to examine more closely the underpinning of the serious charges — the assessment, the zoning-variance request, the need for speed in an application review process — to see if everything was absolutely as it should be. Charges against Leona were quietly dropped in exchange for a plea in which Leona and two associates agreed never again to engage in the sort of practices they had used on that particular conversion, and Leona's voluntary return of her real estate broker's license. Only after this agreement had been reached did Helmsley's remarriage proceed, in early 1972.

After that, Helmsley's life changed dramatically. Old friends of Harry's found themselves eased out of social contact with him: Leona wanted him all to herself. The new couple attended charity balls and dances two or more nights a week and invited the big players in the real estate community, and many famous people whom they knew more as acquaintances than as friends to lavish affairs at the Park Lane on Harry's birthday. Guests wore buttons saying "I'm Just Wild About Harry," and Harry wore a big one saying "I'm Harry." Garish themes were the norm. One party featured dolls in the shape of famous couples in history and fiction, though with the faces of the host and hostess: Tarzan and Jane, Antony and Cleopatra, King Kong and Fay Wray. At these parties, Leona's bad manners were noticed. For instance, she would invite to the party several unattached men so she could dance with them and show herself off. When one such bachelor showed up with a fiancée, he was taken off the list for the following year. Leona was tolerated as Helmsley's wife, but in private roundly disparaged.

That was a shame, because, albeit in a heavy-handed way, she was just trying to induce what she saw as an industry full of old fogies — her husband included — to have some fun. Under Leona's influence, Harry purchased a corporate jet and other amenities of chief executives of billion-dollar concerns. The Helmsleys commissioned hotels, extravagant real estate baubles that observers thought would be less responsive to the miserly Helmsley business techniques than the properties Harry had bought and developed in the past. Little noticed at the time, Leona set up her son Jay Panzirer as a general purchasing agent for the Helmsley hotels, which encouraged purchasing and billing practices that would eventually come under scrutiny by prosecutors.

Seymour Durst had been assembling properties in the area north and west of Times Square for years when he bought Eastern Pork Products, which had a storehouse on one of the blocks, and then used the company's name as a dummy acquirer of other parcels. A friend phoned him to say, "Seymour — pork? Shame on you!" Durst accepted the good-natured ribbing about pork, which Jews were prohibited from eating, as he learned that what he'd thought was a secret ploy wasn't so secret after all.

Assemblage was a difficult game. When you dealt with one of the other big families, you could at least be straightforward and obtain an option to buy at a good, fair price. But visions of instant wealth were common among small owners and strange operators. Albert King loved to frustrate Durst by buying corner lots or buildings, then advertising on them that he was King For Corners. Durst had had to negotiate with him many times; they'd sit and talk all day, and only in late afternoon would King say, "I want the big one," by which he always meant a million dollars, a price usually far above even the extortion value of a particular site. Once, during such a negotiation, the two men took a walk to smoke cigars, and Durst narrowly saved King from being killed by a truck — then mused that if he hadn't pulled King back it would have been far easier to deal with his estate.

For years Durst had also been nourishing a dream for a development even larger than Rockefeller Center, in a five-block area bounded by 42nd and 47th streets, Sixth Avenue, Broadway, and Seventh Avenue. There he hoped to site ten large office towers, most on the avenues. Between the towers would be plazas providing midblock walkways approaching the old theaters in the district. This complex might revitalize New York's commercial theater, then in one of its periodic doldrums. He already had a hold on the properties.

Continuing to pay out on many diverse parcels, often when these were not making money, was an expensive game, and one that an operator or a family had to play personally, for no bank would lend money to keep idle the basis of a dream a dozen years away from realization. The Dursts had been willing to foot the bill in the past. Now, in the early 1970s, Seymour's vision of a new center to rival

Rockefeller's started coming apart. One major reason was the Tishmans' empty black sentinel, 1166 Sixth Avenue, which stood across
the street from Seymour's assemblage and warned against anyone else trying to erect a large office tower in the area —
let alone ten of them.

Durst tried to sell some parcels to raise cash to carry the others.
One candidate was the entire block bounded by Ninth and Tenth
avenues and 42nd and 43rd streets. By any developer's lights, the
block was a gem, for its small commercial buildings (including one
fleabag hotel) were old and decrepit enough to be of no great loss
to the city if demolished. It had taken Durst years to assemble its
eighty-two separate units.

Friends suggested that he try to get government subsidies for
housing on the block. But Durst's dislike for government involvement had transmuted into a major tenet of his philosophy. It had
begun in the 1940s, when he made the decision to get out of apartment buildings because he saw that rent controls would never be
lifted, and was solidified by 1961 when, in the process of putting
up a building, he was given the choice of adhering to old or new
zoning laws, and chose the old because he wouldn't put in what
he knew would be a useless public plaza, even if that won him extra
stories on the skyscraper. In 1973, Durst decided not to consider
changing the focus of the block. Instead, he sold it to Dick Ravitch
for $10 million.

This looked like a simple business transaction. Durst didn't care
what Ravitch did with the block, so long as his plans would not
adversely affect the other properties Durst controlled. The $10
million would help keep the larger assemblage (Sixth to Seventh
avenues, 42nd to 47th streets) in the Dursts' hands for a while
longer. But the master assembler hadn't taken into account the
nature of Ravitch's vision.

Ravitch had the money to plunk down for the site because he'd
finally completed Waterside. Just recently he, John Lindsay, Robert
Wagner, and a clutch of reporters had boarded a former city fireboat
for the opening ceremonies of the Waterside development; construction was still being finished, and ashore the hardhatted men
ate most of the hors d'oeuvres that had been spread out for the
visiting dignitaries. Years of delays had translated into increased
rental costs for three of the four apartment towers and twenty
duplex townhouses on the site, spread out along five blocks at the

edge of the East River, though apartments in the fourth tower would rent for as little as twenty-two dollars a room per month. It wasn't all that Ravitch had hoped for in terms of a social agenda, but it provided good housing to families whose annual income was about six or seven times their annual rent.

Durst's West 42nd Street block would be perfect, Ravitch thought, for another dream within his context of socially helpful housing. "I hoped it would do for the area what Fred French's Tudor City had done for East 42nd Street thirty years earlier," Ravitch told reporters. He and architects David Todd and Robert Cabrera planned large towers at either end of the block, low-rise commercial and recreational entities in between, and a huge garage underneath to help pay for it all. What Durst had seen as impossible Ravitch saw as feasible because he planned to get the government involved — first, through Mitchell-Lama guarantees for middle-income housing, and second, through his ties to the Lindsay administration, which he hoped to convince to condemn every building on the block so he could begin construction right away. Ravitch's last project had taken a dozen years; this one, he vowed, would move more quickly.

Percy Uris steered Columbia University's real estate through difficult times in the 1960s, counseling the buying of brownstones and apartment buildings bordering the campus to prevent them from slipping into the category of slum housing. In 1966 he championed the acquisition by the university of two choice building sites in the Wall Street area; one was immediately sold for a good profit, and the Uris Buildings Corporation leased the other at $400,000 a year, a rate low enough to engender an accusation that Percy was hoodwinking Columbia into warehousing the site for his own public company. By 1971, after years of campus riots, no one seemed interested any longer in whether a trustee had helped himself while helping the university.

The value of the Uris Buildings Corporation's buildings had recently been estimated at $350 million to $400 million. UBC ranked just behind the city itself, Consolidated Edison, and the Penn Central railroad as holders of the largest aggregation of valuable properties in the city — and ahead of Columbia University and Rockefeller Center. UBC dividends were being paid quarterly, though the stock price was down. Brother Harold had recently welcomed back to the fold son-in-law John Halpern, who had been out on his own for three years, during which time the family corporation had grown to 140 employees.

The major project at hand was the completion of a fifty-six-story skyscraper at 55 Water Street, which would bring the company's total to 13 million square feet of office space developed in New York since 1946, more than all the office space built during that same era in Boston or Philadelphia. This Wall Street–area tower was said to be the largest-ever privately built skyscraper, for it carried a mortgage of $150 million. That money had been very hard to find, for Percy had been ahead of the curve with 55 Water Street. Traditional lenders such as banks didn't favor the Wall Street area for new skyscrapers. They liked buildings that catered to manufacturing tenants rather than to service industries, reasoning that the former would be less able to leave rented premises during a temporary economic downturn. What the banks didn't seem to understand, but Percy Uris did, was how rapidly Manhattan's economy was changing. Manufacturing jobs were being drained out of the city at a rate of 50,000 per year, but service jobs were on the increase, though in the early 1970s that trend was still modest; 55 Water Street offered a home for the growing financial-services firms. The building opened formally in June 1971, and though it was not fully rented — the World Trade Center was in direct and proximate competition — there was hope that it would be full in the near future. From his vacation home in Boca Raton, that fall, seventy-two-year-old Percy Uris directed the company's business by telephone, usually in a relatively short conversation during the morning before he went out to play tennis or golf. Two more projects were under construction — a sprawling suburban office complex called Blue Hills, and 1633 Broadway, in midtown, an office tower that would contain a new theater to be named after the Urises.

In November 1971, Percy Uris died of a sudden heart attack. Harold was especially bereft; relatives and associates watched helplessly as the heart seemed to go out of Harold when his brother died.

"If Percy had been in ill health for some time before death," John Halpern believes, "he would have made provisions for attacking the three big problems — the rental situation at 55 Water Street, the escalating costs and lack of tenants for Blue Hill and 1633 Broadway." But his unexpected departure from the scene was traumatic because Harold had left the initiative on all matters other than construction to Percy. As a result, Harold had neither the specialized knowledge of finance nor the mind-set to deal well with the current difficulties. "When someone has gangrene in a toe," Halpern reasons, "you cut off the toe and get rid of the problem, then take measures to make the rest of the body healthy." Such measures in regards to the Uris holdings were obvious to Halpern — laying off staff, selling bad properties even at a loss, temporarily stopping dividend payments. Retrenchment actions are more often applauded than decried by Wall Street. After Percy's death, Harold "called everyone together and made a speech saying that Uris would go on forever," another staff member recalled. But it was only a brave front. With Percy gone, the business was no longer fun and the difficulties seemed insurmountable. Harold had no sons and evidently didn't consider his daughters worthy successors, though one was a competent lawyer and another a knowledgeable real estate broker. With no personal reason to keep fighting to get the company back into the black, six weeks after his speech to the employees he decided to sell.

Although a foreign offer had been made, it was taking too long to complete, and Harold became nervous. He accepted an offer from National Kinney for $14.50 a share, or a total of $63 million in cash over the mortgages for the Urises' 54 percent interest in the company. As was usual in these transactions, National Kinney agreed to take over all indebtedness, most importantly the current construction loans on 1633 Broadway, and the mortgage on the recently completed Blue Hill in Rockland County, which stood virtually empty.

Trouble over financing of the deal embroiled the principals on the National Kinney side — the experienced developers Paul and Seymour Milstein, and Steve Ross, the young dynamo who had built National Kinney and then used it to take over Warner Communications. They had an agreement that, after the Milsteins started the turnaround, Ross would resell both National Kinney and the Uris empire to the Milsteins at a reasonable price. But National Kinney had a fearsome ninety-day note to pay off — the money that had allowed the company to make the UBC purchase — and the old Uris buildings were losing money at the rate of tens of millions a year. Vacancy rates were soaring and inflation made matters worse as interest rates rose from 6 to 10 percent, driving the company deeper into the red.

The Milsteins still saw the Uris empire as a bargain that they could manage back to profitability. They aggressively sold off properties to raise cash — the Urises' half of the New York Hilton, the Washington Hilton, and the Rye (New York) Hilton went to Prudential for $40 million, less than a third of their value in the last UBC annual report. The Milsteins also fired Halpern and other executives and cut the staff. But just like the inexperienced Vincent Astor, Steve Ross couldn't wait for the turnaround to take hold, because the Uris drain (a loss of $17 million in two quarters) was affecting the profits and stock of National Kinney and of Warner. A week after they fired the other executives, Seymour and Paul Milstein were forced to resign by Steve Ross.

Ross let the mortgage holders have the burden of renting out Blue Hill and was glad to see it go. Even that radical surgery was not enough to save the Uris holdings, and Ross came to the conclusion that he absolutely had to sell them before a deadline arrived to buy out the minority stockholders. Most big players on the Manhattan scene had a shot at the Uris empire. But Harry Helmsley said he couldn't even fill One Penn Plaza, the huge building atop Penn Station that was almost as bad a money drain as the empty Tishman and Rudin skyscrapers. Sam Lefrak would only agree to buy if the loans were all renegotiated to long-term status, a cure for the ailment that the banks found unacceptable. With no buyers in sight for 1633 Broadway, in December 1973 Irving Trust, the leading bank of four that had loans outstanding on the building, initiated an action not taken against a major property in Manhattan since the end of the depression: foreclosure.

Chapter Sixteen

The Shadow of Default

DURING THE ERA of New York City's near-default, many real estate empires were subject to the most relentless pressures they had encountered since the Great Depression. While their survival hung in the balance, the complex interplay between the health of the city and the fortunes of the real estate magnates became highly visible. Ownership of certain Manhattan properties had already become burdensome by 1971. To hold a vacant lot where Madison Square Garden had been, between 50th and 51st streets and Eighth and Ninth avenues, required $1 million in taxes each year, an assessment based on its potential, not its current use. *Forbes* magazine suggested, "The question isn't who owns New York. It's who the hell wants to?"

Since the depression — when the city had defaulted and yielded control to a financial-control board for a time — New York had been among the most generous of cities, supporting public hospitals and welfare and school systems; Chicago, by contrast, had no public hospitals and spent considerably less per pupil. As a magnet for emigrants from the rural South and Puerto Rico, New York also housed a disproportionate share of the country's welfare recipients; sustaining them took more than a quarter of the municipal budget. The city's agreements with its employees were overly bountiful, too, particularly after 1965, when incoming mayor John Lindsay gave in to a large wage increase to end a crippling subway strike. Sanitation and clerical employees won the right, already enjoyed by police and firefighters, to retire on half pay after twenty years; actual retirement pay was also redefined upward. Governor Nelson Rockefeller, who needed the unions' continued political support, made sure that these agreements were all ratified by the New York State Legislature.

Disastrous dependence on federal money evolved from the requirement that the city match or forfeit funds to carry out the ambitious societal-improvement programs championed by the Kennedy, Johnson, and Nixon administrations. As Mayor Robert Wagner put it, "I do not propose to permit our fiscal problems to set the limits of our commitments to meet the essential needs of the people." Translation: to match federal funds, the city would pledge money it didn't have, even if that meant going into debt. The budget ballooned at an annual rate of 9 percent under Wagner and nearly 16 percent during Lindsay's first administration.

To pay for this expansion, the city taxed a source that couldn't say no: the sort of big office buildings owned by the old families and large corporations. Their assessments rose from 13 percent of all property taxes to 17 percent. This didn't produce enough money, however, so mayors and state officials resorted to a series of fiscal gimmicks to which the public paid little attention. Current expenses such as the cost of stationery were buried in the capital budget. The amount anticipated from the federal government was inflated, as were the estimates on what property taxes would bring in, but spending was predicated on these higher estimates. Begun as temporary expedients, these tactics soon rose to the level of financial chicanery; had the same maneuvers been employed in private enterprise, lawyers said, they would have been cited as evidence of criminal fraud.

These problems were compounded by the nature of the short-term debt to which the city became addicted. Years earlier, to fund the state's housing program, Governor Rockefeller had used "moral obligation" bonds on which the promise to pay back was not absolute. Rockefeller liked them because they could be issued without first asking voters for permission. Using the moral obligation bond as a model, New York City introduced Revenue Anticipation Notes, or RANs, short-term bonds issued in anticipation of receiving federal and state money. Acceptance of these notes as a legitimate financing tool, another disaster, required the collaboration of executives from major Wall Street banks and brokerages, who sat on city advisory boards. These men well knew the deteriorating state of the city's finances, but they touted the RANs to buyers. In 1965, New York's short-term debt was $526 million, or

10 percent of its total debt; ten years later, it was $4.5 billion, nearly 37 percent of total debt.

The distinction between short-term and long-term debt was a muddle to most people, and part of the reason the public didn't wake to the danger of default until it was almost too late. But real estaters lived with short-term debt. It was akin to a construction loan, the money you were forced to borrow — and for which you paid very high rates — while erecting a building. At completion, you scrambled to replace the construction loan with a mortgage, a long-term debt instrument that carried a considerably lower interest rate and could be paid back over a period of decades, not months. Only then could you breathe easier. The warning sentinels — 1166 Sixth Avenue, 1633 Broadway, the Madison Avenue Merchandise Mart — were testimony to the maxim that builders were most at risk before the permanent financing took over; before that desired moment, short-term debt could swiftly drain your resources.

Through the early 1970s, New York City ignored the developer's nightmare, the counterpart to the high-priced construction loan that you couldn't pay off. The city chose instead to echo the old cry of Bill Zeckendorf: "I'd rather be alive at eighteen percent than dead at the prime rate."

Before long, more than 30 percent of the city's annual revenues were being used to pay down — they couldn't make a dent in paying off — short-term debt. It had become quite clear that the Empire City could collapse just as readily and completely as Zeckendorf's empire had. By mid-1974, when Mayor Lindsay fashioned his last budget in conjunction with his probable successor, Controller Abe Beame, the city's problems were visible to everyone. There was more garbage in the streets and more perceived criminal activity. A dearth of jobs in the private sector forced more people to apply for welfare at a time when the new president, Gerald Ford, had begun to slash federal dollars for assistance programs. Mirroring the budgetary woes were the problems of real estate. Hundreds of brownstones and small apartment houses were abandoned by their owners in the marginal areas of the city because income from them was not enough to pay taxes or the higher fuel costs stemming from Middle Eastern politics. Big office buildings gaped empty. Thirty million square feet of office space stood completely unoccupied, and tenant corporations were trying unsuccessfully to sublet fifteen million more. Private owners complained bitterly that the huge

World Trade Center (with its six million square feet of space and its lower rents and taxes) was undercutting their ability to attract tenants to privately owned office buildings.

The first real estate magnates to experience repercussions from the city's problems were those who had bought into a dream, the acquirers. Early among them were Sol Goldman and Alex DiLorenzo, Jr. Underscoring the many-layered relationship of real estate to the city, they were contributors to the city's deficits as early as 1969, when their properties, assessed at $845 million, were delinquent on $4.7 million in back taxes. Then they became victims of the city's problems.

For instance, hotel occupancy rates in the city plummeted drastically — and Goldman-DiLorenzo's half a dozen hotels turned into money-losers. Goldman-DiLorenzo owned the land under the Tishman albatross, 1166 Sixth Avenue, and when the construction lender defaulted and dropped the costs (and its debt obligations) back on them, they were staggered. Fuel costs for the Chrysler Building jumped from $300,000 to $1 million a year. They tried to control maintenance costs by cutting back on upkeep and delaying repairs, especially in marginal areas. Some buildings of theirs could have been saved from becoming slums, but not after Goldman-DiLorenzo "walked away" from them.

Their troubles were exacerbated by personal problems with their children and their own health. Sol developed kidney trouble that would shortly force him to begin twice-weekly dialysis, and the fifty-seven-year-old Alex required open heart surgery in 1974. After an extended convalescence DiLorenzo returned to his desk in the Chrysler Building, in the spacious office that he enjoyed because he could practice his golf putting on its great expanse of carpet — only to find that Texaco was announcing its intent to leave the Chrysler Building. Unable to replace the oil company, in September 1975 the partners declared they couldn't pay what they owed on the second mortgage. Default proceedings were begun to return the Chrysler to Massachusetts Mutual Life Insurance. A week later, DiLorenzo keeled over at his desk and died.

Their thousand properties had been owned jointly by DiLorenzo and Goldman, so it was impossible to determine which ones belonged to Alex's heirs. A will left his share in a trust for his children, to be administered by his son, Alex DiLorenzo, III, then twenty-five, until teenager Marc came of age. Alex III, a gawky child of the 1960s with horn-rimmed glasses and a ready grin, stepped into the picture; he had studied city planning at Fordham, but nothing had prepared him for dealing with an overleveraged, property-heavy, money-draining empire. Goldman moaned that they owed $30 million to Chase Manhattan and now $18 million in back taxes. Forced sales became necessary. In short order, the Goldman-DiLorenzo empire lost through such sales or foreclosures the McAlpin, St. Regis, and Gotham hotels; two choice blockfronts on Fifth Avenue, including the old Bank of U.S. building; and many other properties, until about 200 of their 500 New York holdings were gone. Sol and his old friend's son screamed at one another about the disposition of the remaining 300 until Sol convinced young Alex that to dump those on the market in the midst of a financial crisis would be the worst possible action. They'd have to hold on until the city turned around.

In late 1972, a scandal broke: certain large and prominent landlords were identified as the owners of property in the Times Square area catering to peep-shows, pornographic book stores, massage parlors, and prostitution. Indicted along with Goldman-DiLorenzo — the most notorious offender — the press also named Rockefeller Center, a relative of President Nixon's son-in-law, and the Durst family. Professing himself surprised at the nature of some of his tenants and subtenants (many premises had been sublet to businesses less savory than the original renters), Seymour Durst promised to work with the city in ejecting undesirables from his buildings. Durst's real problem was that an assembler often must make purchases in marginal areas in the hope of reaping profits when those areas are redeveloped. Once Durst and the other owners had made public their determination to oust the bad tenants, the controversy died down.

During the next few years, and as a consequence of the worsening financial climate, Durst scaled back his plans for ten towers in the district just south and west of Rockefeller Center. This was when he sold the block along Eighth and Ninth avenues and 42nd and 43rd streets to Ravitch. Thus, as the frantic days of near-default approached, the stage was set for a classic confrontation between two differing dreams.

In early 1975, Durst was appointed by incoming mayor Abe Beame as a member of a task force on cleaning up Times Square. This governmental appointment raised Durst's public profile as years of developing had not done; soon newspapers were calling him for comments on matters having to do with midtown, and even for statements on what to do about the increasing number of welfare recipients. He offered solutions for cleaning up the pornographic district in "Degomorrahization," a signed article in the *New York Times*. In September 1975 the Times-Square-as-vice-capital story, which had lain dormant, suddenly showed up again on front pages. The Durst-owned Luxor Baths was named as the most notorious massage parlor in the city. Durst's position on the mayor's task force was considered an outrage and he was forced to resign. To escape the immediate focus of attention, he sold the Luxor Baths property at a loss to the massage parlor's operators and let the city have the headache of evicting them. Afterwards, he worked hard at slipping out of the public eye.

This pattern was followed by several real estaters. Years of contributions to political organizations would culminate in an appointment to a committee or an advisory board, on the basis of which the developer would be treated to a flirtation with the media. A hint of a public profile emerged — and then, without warning, the real estater's name would surface in some connection the press considered scandalous. The story would be just onerous enough to engender a flurry of unwanted scrutiny, after which the real estater yearned for anonymity. After his debacle, Durst transformed a small room in his townhouse, opposite his bedchamber, into a Times Square memorial featuring items salvaged from establishments that he had closed — a ten-foot-tall woman with a chain around her ankle, a sign with oversized letters spelling EXPLICIT, a warning message about oral sex — all illuminated by a green strobe light.

Meanwhile, Ravitch's profile was rising. "A lot of people say I'm nuts to be doing this," Ravitch told reporters in late 1974, when Manhattan Plaza was being built. It was the largest real estate gamble then being tried in a city beset by economic doldrums, and it was being done in a rush: sidewalk superintendents could see all three phases of construction going on concurrently — demolition of the remaining older buildings (condemned by the city, as Ravitch had hoped), the pouring of foundations, and emplacement of the steel superstructure. Two forty-five-story towers would rise at the east and west ends of the block; in between would be gardens and low buildings for an athletics complex, restaurants, small shops, a supermarket, and a large parking garage.

Why the rush? Because times were difficult, and Ravitch had a new agenda. In the years after Ravitch and his cousin J. R. Horowitz had taken over HRH, the company had profited from constructing Citicorp Plaza at 53rd and Lexington, the downtown headquarters of New York Telephone, the Gulf & Western Building at Columbus Circle, as well as hospitals and apartments all over town and in other cities. Horowitz handled these construction projects while Ravitch developed Waterside and the Riverhead complex in East Harlem, and began Manhattan Plaza. Each cousin had also been making his mark in charitable and civic endeavors. Horowitz was mayor of Scarsdale and vice chairman of the Mount Sinai Hospital board of trustees; Ravitch was involved in community housing, Federation, and other civic work.

Part of the reason for the rush in the construction of Manhattan Plaza was that Ravitch and Horowitz had made a deal about their outside obligations. Horowitz was spending 1974 principally as national president of the Association of General Contractors of the United States, while Ravitch handled HRH. The following year, 1975, was to be Ravitch's time out of the firm: Hugh Carey, Democratic candidate for governor, wanted Ravitch to join his administration as soon as he won and assumed office. The plan was for Horowitz to finish his term with the Contractors, then return to take full charge of HRH so that Ravitch could accept the chairmanship of new York State's troubled Urban Development Corporation (UDC).

The UDC and its moral obligation bonds were a terrible mess when Ravitch took office as a first appointee of Carey, in January 1975. Even though Ravitch was an expert at refinancing — he'd done it for Waterside, for instance — he couldn't work fast enough to prevent the UDC from defaulting on $104.5 million in notes due on February 25, 1975. The very next day, the banks and the state's legislators agreed to a refinancing plan, and within the month the state made good on the missed payment. In terms of preventing the demise of a state agency and the loss of hundreds of millions of dollars, the refinancing was a tremendous accomplishment for Ravitch and Carey. But the ripples from the UDC default caused public authority bonds from all over the country to fall precipitously in price, and bankers to question the solidity of the new debt notes New York City was about to offer. A month after the UDC debacle, the city found it impossible to sell its new securities, a circumstance that accelerated New York's slide toward bankruptcy.

One very likely victim of the slide was going to be Manhattan

Plaza. The UDC default caused a rise in the interest rates on New York City's bonds — notes being used to finance $90 million of the $95-million project. The rising rates would force the expected rents Ravitch would have to charge up to $125 per room, a price beyond the reach of precisely those middle-class tenants needed to make Manhattan Plaza practical. While tending to the UDC, Ravitch searched for a way to make his dream project viable again.

Just at this moment, Horowitz went to New Orleans for his farewell address as president of the Association of General Contractors. The jet in which he was returning to New York crashed at La Guardia Airport, killing him as well as scores of other passengers in the worst air disaster in the city's history.

This was a personal and professional tragedy for the HRH family, and for Horowitz's friends in the real estate community. Ravitch was naturally wounded by the loss of his cousin and friend. But there were further ramifications of J. R.'s untimely death: it also meant the loss of the senior partner who could have run the firm in Ravitch's absence. Ravitch struggled to keep the firm whole and at the same time work with the UDC and the Municipal Assistance Corporation, to which the task fell of regularizing and refinancing New York City's obligations. And, of course, he had to do something about Manhattan Plaza.

To keep the rents down, Roger Starr, the city's housing administrator, decided that Manhattan Plaza would have to ask for federal subsidies for low-rent housing, called Section Eight monies. Ravitch didn't initially embrace the idea, but the threat of foreclosure if no additional subsidies were found quelled his resistance. Washington shortly agreed to a whopping $11.5 million a year for the next forty years, a solution that occasioned a storm of protest. If Manhattan Plaza were designated as a low-income project, Seymour Durst fumed, it would attract only the poor and vitiate any real efforts to change the character of West 42nd Street. A "40-year, $400-million mistake," Durst called the Section Eight solution, an unjustified bailout of the developers. Durst was crying foul because he believed that a low-income project would lower the value of his extensive property holdings in the area, a contention backed by other businesses, by the League of New York Theaters and Producers, and even by local community and antipoverty groups. If subsidies were the only way to prevent the project from falling into default, Durst said that it ought to default, since it was no good as it was.

There was an impasse. "Something had to be done," Dan Rose recalls. Rose Associates was to be the rental agent for Manhattan Plaza, so the problem of how to get it rented, and to whom, had been much on his mind. He remembered a saying attributed to theatrical impresario Mike Todd in a discussion of his show-business youth: "We were broke, but never poor." Dan's interpretation: those associated with the arts might not have much money, but they were intellectually alive and would always manage to stay afloat. They would be good tenants; moreover, they would bring creative excitement to the neighborhood. He proposed that the two forty-five-story towers keep the federal subsidies and be designated as residences for performing artists. To make this happen, the government would have to raise slightly the income permitted tenants under Section Eight, just enough so that renters could be drawn from the lower middle class. Seventy percent of the renters would be drawn from members of Actors' Equity, the Screen Actors Guild, and similar unions, and the next largest group from the local community. Durst grumbled that the plan was "a glamorous distraction to cover the misuse of low-income subsidies." He was outgunned, for a home for performing artists was a happy solution. Manhattan Plaza quickly filled with actors, dancers, and members of other guilds, and opposite it, across 42nd Street, repertory and community theaters moved in, contributing to area renewal. In time, everyone would forget Seymour Durst's point, that the bill-payer for this happiness was the federal government.

By the spring of 1977, with the debate over Manhattan Plaza's fate still in the balance, Ravitch found himself at a crossroads. What had earlier seemed a viable dream, to be a developer of good housing for the middle class, seemed a chord from a song now out of date. Times had changed, and so had Ravitch and his aspirations. HRH was only marginally profitable; his main partner was gone. Unless Ravitch was willing to forgo public service in appointed roles and the possibility of an elective public career — his name was being mentioned as a Liberal party candidate for mayor — and devote himself wholly to business, the family firm would not survive. For the past several years the Starrett Housing Corporation had been interested in buying HRH, but Ravitch had fended off Starrett's feelers; now he sought to sell the company. However, Starrett knew how to play hardball. Recognizing Ravitch's difficult position, Starrett offered only to keep HRH's employees on the payroll, to wrap up the final details on Manhattan Plaza, and to continue the firm's name as a division of Starrett Housing. Dick Ravitch was thus forced to sell his family's firm and not get a penny for it. There were no Starretts left in Starrett Housing, and there would now be no Horowitzes or Ravitches in Starrett's HRH division.

"Finding some way to make Manhattan Plaza viable was an exercise in management ingenuity," Dan Rose recalls of the mid-1970s; he looked upon that side of the business as one to be creatively enhanced at a time when it was impossible to build in New York City. Uncle Dave was in his mideighties, remarried, and still hearty though less active in the business. The Roses managed 15,000 apartments and eight million square feet of office space. Other developers had problems in this era with their Mitchell-Lama projects, some of which had been built as tax shelters. When the city clamped a ceiling on annual rent increases, all the developers groaned. Many Mitchell-Lama projects fell in this era, at a combined cost to the city estimated by one expert as more than $1 billion, a major contributing factor to the city's woes. None of the Roses' Mitchell-Lama projects defaulted. "We evaluated ours better before building them," Dan concludes.

In a 1973 speech at the New School, Dan took aim at rent control, terming it as harmful to New York "as the fire bombing of Dresden" in World War II, causing the abandonment of tens of thousands of occupied housing units by their owners "because the economic value fell to zero." Over the previous two decades, the suburbs had absorbed many members of the city's middle class, who had been replaced by "members of the rural poor who tend to lack the skills, attitudes, and lifestyles that make for successful adaptation to a Northeastern urban environment." Blacks had replaced whites, but race was not the crux of the matter, Rose said, because New York's blacks were entering the middle class rapidly and would be "the white-collar clerical force of the 1980s"; the problem was how long New York would survive while continuing to lose its middle class. Seymour Durst had said as much himself, many times, but after his difficulties in the public eye his outbursts were looked on only as eccentricity and the public lost the full benefit of his curmudgeonly critiques.

Dan's analyses convinced him to look outside New York for development opportunities, and what Fred Rose labeled Dan's "greater supply of patience" allowed Dan in the mid-1970s to make a deal to buy what an industry executive termed "the choicest piece of sizeable, underdeveloped real estate on the East Coast," more than a hundred acres just across from the Pentagon in Arlington, Virginia. No one in Washington wanted it, and Fred passed on it, too, believing he didn't have the patience to nurture it for ten years or more. Dan applied his long-term view to staging the financing, site acquisition, and construction so that the right parts would come into use only at the appropriate time. Pentagon City would have apartment houses, a shopping center, a hotel, office buildings, its own subway stop, a theater, and other community amenities. The largest project Rose Associates had ever undertaken, it was the one Dan believed would ultimately be the most profitable.

During the doldrums in New York, Fred Rose followed the example of earlier builder-family chieftains after they had worked steadily for a quarter-century — he devoted a good deal of his time to climbing the ladder at the Federation of Jewish Philanthropies. In 1970, he took what insiders knew as the crucial appointment at Federation: campaign chairman of that year's fund-raising activities. Hard work in that job usually led to presidency of the organization within a few years.

Posting over his desk a quotation from the eight steps of charity laid down in the twelfth century by Moses Maimonides, Fred started raising $30 million, the year's quota. Federation's 116 agencies had grown to serve 1.5 million people in the metropolitan area. He convened a dinner to honor Larry Wien and two other former presidents. There was a bit of unexpected activity from members of the Jewish Defense League who tried to force their way into fund-raising dinners that year; the JDL contended that Federation was helping too many non-Jews, a notion the courts soon decided was ludicrous.

Four years later, when Fred reached the presidency of Federation, circumstances had changed, and so had Federation. The Middle East war in the fall of 1973 had altered the usual alignment of the major Jewish charitable organizations. There had always been two fund-raising seasons a year, in the fall for the United Jewish Appeal (which sent money to support the state of Israel) and in the spring for Federation, whose focus was local. The war mandated a combined solicitation in 1974, and UJA and Federation merged their fund-raising for that effort. Fred concentrated on the social-service side of the organization, and after his term returned to similar work for Yale. He was soon asked to take responsible positions for the Metropolitan Museum of Art and for Lincoln Center.

He'd still be a builder, but the edifices he now created would be for these institutions.

Lew Rudin had been publicly linking the health of the city and the real estate community for years when, in the late spring of 1975, he gave a birthday party for his mother, May. Among the guests was Mayor Beame; the Rudins had made one of the larger donations — $15,000 — to his campaign. This night the mayor looked ashen, and Rudin asked why. Beame showed him a response from President Gerald Ford to a request by the mayor and governor "for Federal legislation which would enable the City of New York to use the credit of the United States for a period of ninety days and in the amount of $1 billion." Unable to sell its new bonds, the city needed money to stay afloat, and Beame had turned to Washington. Ford's answer, which Beame had in hand, was a harsh no.

Rudin felt the real estate community ought to do something, and the next day he quietly telephoned the city's largest taxpayers, among them Consolidated Edison, New York Telephone Company, Rockefeller Center, and Helmsley-Spear. His notion was to have big businesses (including his own) prepay their quarterly real estate taxes to help the city over a cash crunch. He arranged $195 million in pledges. Beame was heartened.

In the ensuing weeks of fiscal crisis, Rudin worked on committees addressing the problem and appeared often at Beame's side during news conferences that dealt with matters affecting the business community. Though not an elected official, he had become involved in politics and was now somewhat of a public figure. Then, as with Seymour Durst in the Times Square controversies, a sudden flare-up occurred in which Rudin drew fire because of his connection to the mayor. In August, a report surfaced showing that several large real estate contributors to Beame had received what the Social Service Employees Union charged was excessively kind treatment of requests for reductions in assessments on their properties. Helmsley-Spear and Goldman-DiLorenzo were mentioned, but the union made a specific study only of the Rudin holdings. In the previous six years, the report said, the Rudins had been granted $32 million in reductions; moreover, the Rudins won two-thirds of their assessment appeals while property owners in the same blocks as those in which the Rudins held parcels won only 16 percent of their requests.

Incensed, Rudin told reporters that all he had done was protest a boost in a building's assessment from $5 million to $6 million, and get it reduced to $5.5 million when he showed the proper official that it was half empty. He insisted that "our skirts are clean," and that it was any owner's right to file for a reduction. Rudin contended that the city often arbitrarily raised its valuation of a property and owners often tried to have the raise knocked back. Recently, the utility companies, the city's largest landholders, had had their assessments lowered by nearly a billion dollars, due to changing economic conditions. He challenged the *New York Times* to pick any Rudin building at random and trace its assessment history. The newspaper's reporter found that for a building on Fifth Avenue, "after bobbing up and down wildly over the years, the final assessment figure settled upon for 1976 was $6.7 million — only $50,000 more than it was 20 years ago." Rudin's counterattack deflected further press inquiry, but his appearances at the mayor's side became less frequent. He continued to make his counsel heard — but behind the scenes.

That August, President Ford categorically said he'd refuse to sign any bills bailing out New York; the *Daily News* interpreted this in a classic headline: "FORD TO CITY: DROP DEAD." Two months later, enough power had been marshalled to convince Ford that it was political suicide to let New York default, and he agreed to a loan to tide the city over until its fiscal house was more in order. The corner had been turned for the city, but the consequences for the real estate empires had not yet come to their conclusions.

Part of the reason that builders took body blows during the near-default years was because their holdings had become heavily weighted with office towers at a time when there were the equivalent of sixty twenty-five-story skyscrapers unoccupied. Families who had extensive apartment holdings, though they screamed about rent control, were actually cushioned from the full impact of the space glut and assured of receiving some income from their fully rented apartments. They didn't lose as much as those who relied solely on office-rental income. "Rent control was a disaster for everyone *but* the old dynastic families," Roger Starr remembers.

Nearing Christmas in 1975, Sam Rudin took Lew's twenty-year-old son, Billy, in a limousine with him to visit the Rudin empire's buildings, more than thirty of them (mostly apartment houses) scattered through Manhattan and the Bronx. It was a time of transition for the family, as well as for the city. Sam was still heartsick over the drain being caused by the Madison Avenue Merchandise Mart, though Lew and Jack assured him that business indicators were becoming positive and that the family would eventually regain what it had lost. Billy had been out west, flirting with a career in films, as had his sister Beth. Their mother had divorced Lew and remarried a man who had been Lew's close friend, film industry executive David Begelman. Now Billy was thinking about transferring to New York University and entering the family business. For fifty years, Sam had personally handed out Christmas bonuses. After accompanying Sam, Billy told Lew, "I couldn't get over how the doormen and supers and other employees seemed to love Grampa," and not only because he arrived bearing gifts. The experience solidified Billy's determination to join the family business. A few days later, on Christmas eve, Sam Rudin died; within the month his surviving brother, who succeeded to the chairmanship, also died.

Soon afterward, ostensibly because of a relatively minor dispute over some building costs, the Rudins severed their long relationship with Emery Roth & Sons. They were in the midst of a new project, and plans had already been drawn by the Roths; despite the obvious cost, the plans were shelved, and a new set was commissioned from another architectural firm. Julian had been a close friend of the elder Rudin, but Jack had long felt that the Roths had slighted his own burgeoning talents and control of the building process, and he now wanted architects who would be more closely linked to him.

While still in college, Donald John Trump discovered for himself a principle espoused by those who conduct weekend seminar and mail-order courses on real estate: buy from "don't-wanters," people or organizations who are desperate to get rid of their properties. As a student, he bought a run-down apartment complex in Cincinnati on which the FHA had foreclosed and, as he reported in his first memoir, "got rid of the bad tenants." Because Cincinnati did not have the same sort of rent controls as New York, Trump was able to raise rents substantially after renovations, and then to sell the project for a profit he reports as $6 million, though this figure does not seem to carry over into his contention that his net worth at the time he graduated from Wharton in 1968 was $200,000. On entering the family business, he convinced his father, Fred, to remortgage his 24,000 apartments to realize cash for expansion. During the next few years, he bought and sold apartment complexes in Florida and California, and attracted attention with a chauffeured Cadillac that seemed ostentatious when parked in the drab Avenue Z area of the Trump family's headquarters in Brooklyn. He lived in an expensive Birnbaum Country building on the Upper East Side, wore monogrammed shirts and cufflinks engraved with his initials, and bought memberships in trendy private clubs so he could meet other wealthy people. But he continued to look outside Manhattan for development possibilities.

One day in the early 1970s Donald Trump telephoned Lew Rudin. Rudin knew the Trump name, though not Donald, and took the call. Donald said he had an option on a good property in Brooklyn, and brashly asked if the Rudins would be interested in codeveloping it with him. Rudin, who received dozens of similar calls each week, was pleasant but turned him down. "In this family we have two rules," he told young Trump. "First, we only develop in Manhattan. Second, we don't develop with partners."

Trump thought about what Rudin had said. He had worked with his father for five years and still thought in terms of the outer boroughs. Now he resolved that for his dreams he should, as Burnham once suggested, "make no little plans." For Trump, that meant taking the plunge in Manhattan, and doing so as much as possible without development partners. Shortly thereafter, in 1973, Donald and Fred announced that they'd build a luxury rental apartment house on Third Avenue, much in the style and manner of other outer-borough developers making the transition to the higher-stakes arena of Manhattan.

Abe Beame, whom the Trumps had befriended early in his career, was just then favored in the mayoral race; a win by Beame would give the Trumps access to city hall of the sort already enjoyed by the Rudins and other Manhattan-based families. Late in the campaign, however, an allegation surfaced that, if not beaten back, could compromise the Trump access: they were accused of discrimination against blacks in 16,000 of their apartments, because only 700 of the occupants were black. The Lefraks, hit with a similar suit, settled with the government by quietly promising to revamp rental procedures. Donald Trump hired famed attorney Roy Cohn, whom he had met at the private Le Club, to countersue the government for a headline-grabbing $100 million in damages incurred by "irresponsible and baseless charges." No amount of government harassment, Trump insisted, would force him to rent to "welfare clients . . . unless they have guaranteed income levels, because otherwise, everyone immediately starts leaving the building." As soon as the suit reached court, it was dismissed by a federal judge as "wasting time and paper." Eventually a version of the Lefrak compromise was reached that allowed Trump the moral victory of not having to rent to anyone unable to prove he had an income — no private owner could be forced to do that, anyhow — and satisfied the government by making Trump supply a weekly list of vacancies for which the Urban League could provide, in return, lists of appropriately monied black potential tenants. But Donald Trump had been established as belligerent — and present on the scene.

During 1974 the Trumps firmed up close ties with Hugh Carey, the front-runner for governor, contributing $135,000 to his campaign, the largest single contribution after that of Carey's brother. The money was funneled through fund-raiser Louise Sunshine, who later had an official position in the Carey administration as well as a salary from Trump. Though other developers contributed to both Beame and Carey, none did so in as open-handed a way as the Trumps. Donald would later complain that a new law limiting large political contributions was "a terrible thing. You should be able to give as much as you want and can afford." His political alliances well established, Trump looked for deals that depended for their completion on political elements.

As all developers knew, the time to make the best deals is when things are bad, and New York City was a disaster area in 1974. The Penn Central Railroad was in receivership and under a mandate to quickly realize money from its vast holdings in New York, where it was the third-largest property owner. Penn Central's clunkers included unused railroad yards (nine acres in the West Thirties, and seventy-six acres between 59th and 72nd streets) and the Commodore Hotel, adjacent to Grand Central Station, whose occupancy rate of 40 percent meant an annual loss of $1.5 million and back taxes in arrears of $6 million. Here was a perfect situation for a man who already knew that a "don't-want" owner often consented to deals to which a savvy landlord would never agree. Because the Trump empire consisted almost entirely of apartments, it was weathering the economic downturn better than that of builder families who had put up office towers, a factor that gave Donald additional credibility in the eyes of Victor Palmieri, the liquidator of Penn Central. In July 1974, the two men announced that Trump was taking an option on the Penn Central yards and would eventually pay $62 million for the sites. In a Zeckendorfian flourish, Trump promised to erect a new city of 20,000 luxury apartments on the Upper West Side parcel.

This was a bad deal for Penn Central. Trump was putting no money down, and two better bids had been circumvented. Starrett Housing's $150-million bid had been withdrawn after a meeting in which Trump exerted heavy pressure on Starrett by citing his family's large equity position in Starrett City. Dick Ravitch's HRH bid, contingent on using the site for Mitchell-Lama–supported middle-income apartments, would have doubled the money Penn Central could have obtained from a subsequent sale of the land under the Trump proposal. But Penn Central chose the Trump bid. Later the lawyer who on behalf of Penn Central stockholders had opposed Trump's bid in court, then changed his mind and supported it, was hired by the Trumps to handle their challenge of the major oil companies on recent price increases in heating oil. Palmieri's own company benefited from a deal partially arranged and brokered by Trump in which the Levitt Company was bought by Starrett.

The Penn Central lease announcement marked both Donald's arrival on the scene in a big way and his eclipse of his father, who had opposed the deal on the grounds that the parcels could not be developed for apartments. Fred was right, a fact Donald recognized as he quietly let his option on the upper parcel expire — but perhaps, as later events showed, Donald had not intended to develop the parcels at all, only to use the announcement to attract interest in his deals. Fred Trump had striven to stay out of the limelight; now Donald courted it as the route to big development. Donald's stratagem seemed to work, so maybe it was time for Fred to step aside. Unlike the transition from Harris to Percy Uris in the 1920s, or from David to Fred and Dan Rose in the late 1950s, the change in leadership of the Trump family firm marked a whole new way of doing business, and was abrupt and unsettling.

Trump next convinced Palmieri to let him have the Commodore Hotel, and the city and state governments to make the purchase feasible through a combination of tax abatements and condemnation proceedings by the UDC. At the time, the Chrysler and Graybar buildings next door were in receivership, other hotels in the Grand Central area stood almost as empty as the Commodore, and the economic outlook remained grim. The deal called for Trump to buy the Commodore for $10 million, but to pay *no* property taxes for the next forty years, and initially only $250,000 a year in lieu of taxes to the city, an amount Larry Tisch disparaged as equivalent to that paid in taxes by a budget motel on the fringes of the theater district. Trump's payments to the city on the property would eventually rise to $2.27 million a year, still well below the $4 million the Commodore had previously paid.

The Commodore project was still hanging fire when, in December 1975, Trump announced that instead of building luxury apartments on the lower Penn Central railyards, he now wanted to use the site for a convention center. With Beame as mayor and Carey as governor, Trump believed he could win the designation for his site, and for himself as its developer. Two other locations were then in contention for such a center, one in the West Forties, owned by the Tisches, and Battery Park, which was already owned by public agencies. Seymour Durst and the head of the Shubert Organization joined Trump to lobby for the Penn Central site, but this project, too, shortly stalled.

In the spring of 1976, Penn Central and Trump announced that the Commodore would be closed instantly unless the city agreed to Trump's deal. This was a challenge to a shoot-out, a face-off between private desire and public weal. The huge tax abatement had been made public, and citizens' groups were even more outraged than rival hoteliers. Other real estate owners had recently paid taxes early to help the city, and here was Trump trying to get out of paying taxes on his new project. Beame attempted to renegotiate, but Trump said he'd back out if he didn't get the entire abatement; Palmieri said nobody else was interested in the property. Your move, Mr. Mayor.

Beame blinked, and acceded to Trump's demands. Trump won the day because he had managed through adroit publicity to convince the public (to whom the politicians listened) that his dream was theirs, that what was good for Trump was good for the city. Criticized roundly, Beame said the deal was an important spur to turning around the city's depressed economy, and no one could disagree with the need to do that. So that Trump wouldn't be the only beneficiary, his tax abatement became the first award under the city's new Business Investment Incentive Policy; shortly, others queued up to receive abatements easing the burden of their new construction projects. Trump brought in the Pritzker family as equity partners — his tax abatement made it a virtual certainty that the Grand Hyatt would make money, if it was done well; after all, the previous building had been reported as only $1.5 million in the red per year, an amount eclipsed by the tax abatement. By the time construction of the hotel began, Trump was established as a master manipulator of the public mind, if not yet as a builder of significance.

Astor bought many properties fresh from the catastrophes of chancery court; Trump similarly made capital from the bankruptcy of Penn Central and the floundering of New York City. Often, in the history of Manhattan, the death of one real estate empire is the birth of another. The largest such transfer to come out of the years of near-default was about to occur. In 1976, Steve Ross was still trying desperately to get out from under the crush of the Uris Buildings Corporation. Blue Hill, 1633 Broadway, and 1301 Sixth Avenue had been sold or taken over by mortgage holders — but 55 Water Street was losing more than $2 million a year, and other former Uris buildings such as Two Broadway were also in the red.

Harold Uris was aghast at the way the properties were being maintained, but they were Ross's headache now. His own was more personal: his daughter Susan and John Halpern were divorcing, and Halpern still worked with him and knew everything about his finances. It was difficult for all of them. "After the divorce," Uris later recalled, "I could not tell him my business," and this connection, too, was severed. The four buildings the family still owned provided a continuing income in the millions, above what had been realized by the sale of the public company to National Kinney.

Edward Minskoff, who had been involved in New York real estate all his life as a member of one of the old families, knew the real value of National Kinney's Uris holdings and touted them to Albert, Paul, and Ralph Reichmann of Toronto. These were out-of-towners, but not unknowns. Their first sizable deal had come during the downfall of Bill Zeckendorf, when they bought his 500 acres of Toronto, sold 100 acres for more than they'd paid for all 500, and began an empire. Ten years later, the orthodox Jewish immigrants from North Africa, whose firm was known as Olympia & York, were among the largest developers in Canada. Minskoff convinced them that, though the rents on the former Uris properties were inordinately low — half the going market price — when they came up for renewal in two or three years, they could be substantially raised. Furthermore, these were sound buildings in very good locations that could be acquired for one-third the "replacement

costs," the figure used by real estaters to denote what it would cost
to build new skyscrapers in place of the old ones. In 1977 the
Reichmanns purchased eight former UBC Manhattan skyscrapers
by paying $50 million in cash and taking over $288 million in
mortgages. "The Milsteins and I figured that National Kinney
would lose about $50 million before they were through with the
Uris buildings," John Halpern remembers, "and they did."

If the entire empire of Henry Mandel or A. E. Lefcourt or Bill
Zeckendorf had survived the depression in the hands of a single
owner, within ten years it would have become extremely valuable.
None of those remained intact, but the former Uris empire was
conveyed almost whole, and as soon as the bad times were over its
worth soared into the billions. Tenants at 55 Water Street included
Merrill Lynch, Lehman Brothers, Bear Stearns, and Dean Witter.
As the financial services industry grew (just as Percy Uris had
predicted it would), within two years of the building's purchase
these tenants rented out the quarter of 55 Water Street that had
been dark and took even more space in another former Uris property, Two Broadway. Leases ran out in the uptown buildings and
were renewed at triple the previous price. The Reichmanns became
a power in Manhattan rivalling that of the old families.

At the same time that the Uris buildings fell to the Canadians,
the Tishman empire entered its final phase. Each of the three senior
officers of the family had become a formidable real estate man in
his own right. Tall, thin, and patrician in bearing, Bob Tishman
was acknowledged as one of the premier developers in the country,
especially in tandem with his right-hand man, son-in-law Jerry
Speyer. During the past ten years they had tripled the amount of
rentable space owned by the company. Alan Tishman was one of
the more successful leasing managers in the country, able to deal
on a high level. For instance, when he lost out on a sale of space
to a large advertising-agency client in Manhattan, he quickly came
back and sold the same client four times as much space in Chicago
and Los Angeles. John Tishman was a rarity in construction circles,
a man tough-minded enough to be effective on building sites, yet
equally comfortable dealing with those in the executive suites who
commissioned big jobs. John had almost single-handedly invented
the field of construction management, in which the Tishman staff
worked to facilitate and insure the feasibility of the conjoint work
of the architect, owner, and contractors, often beginning their con-
sultancy before designs were finished. John flew his own plane,

sometimes paying surprise visits to construction sites around the country where Tishman was active.

These efforts notwithstanding, the bulk of the Tishman empire was still in trouble, and the main wound was coming from the $100-million empty black sentinel of 1166 Sixth Avenue. Leasing expert Alan had been able to let about a third of its space, but, as Bob complained in the clipped, carefully phrased 1973 annual report, "these [leases] are being withheld and rent negotiations are still in progress in an effort to achieve higher rents." Operating a one-third-full building could cost even more money then letting it stand empty. The drain continued at more than $10 million for the year, and highlighted their other problems. Over the previous ten years, Tishman Realty had become the largest owner-builder of high-rise office buildings in the country, the possessor and operator of twenty-four major towers in New York, Chicago, Rochester, Cleveland, Cincinnati, Los Angeles, San Francisco, and San Diego. Now the fact that they owned so much, especially in New York, had become a burden. All that new space was hurting rentals. The corporation's bottom line was way down: in 1973, despite years of prosperity, Tishman Realty & Construction paid out only $1.06 a share on six million shares; that meant about $2 million divided up among the Tishman family members, who together held a 35 percent stake in the company.

Desperate times called for radical measures. During the depression, the firm hadn't sold off buildings, but now Bob felt it was necessary to get rid of assets in Manhattan — an uncompleted building on Third Avenue, for instance. Across town, Seymour Durst was dismantling and auctioning off an assemblage that had taken him fifteen years to accumulate. Harry Helmsley later admitted to giving back to lenders four or five buildings in 1974–75. Tishman reported to stockholders that he was prepared to dispose of five of the seven major land parcels he had carefully amassed in the past decade. If that didn't rankle enough, the Tishman company was under attack from raiders who thought they could make a killing on its stock.

"I invited some of those who had bought big blocs of stock onto the board, and let them help take the hard decisions," Bob recalls. One was the really big decision in 1974: to walk away from 1166 Sixth Avenue. Tishman Realty defaulted on Citibank's construction loan and let the bank become the owner of the building. "In retrospect, we held on to it three years too long," Bob recently recalled;

"We didn't want a Tishman building going under." They lost $30 million in equity and wrote down another $75 million in debt. Citibank's own losses on 1166 quickly mounted into the $20-million to $30-million range. Bob Tishman and the new directors, faced with a deficit of $6.10 a share, quietly asked Morgan Stanley to begin work on a plan to dissolve the company and sell off its remaining assets.

The next year, 1975, was better, but only slightly. No dividends were paid out, and frustration seeped through the dry tones of the annual report: "Management decided to dispose of this assemblage because of the City's financial crisis and the City's continued refusal to direct the relocation of the eight remaining residents in a 1,200-room hotel." For Donald Trump, that same year, the city and state rushed to relocate people from the Commodore Hotel, but the clearing of an equal-size hotel a few blocks away dragged on. Rather than helping this developer, the city used its power on the other side. There were only a few individual inhabitants of the old hotel, but when Bob tried to save a few dollars by eliminating a bellboy, city authorities forced him to put the man back on; anything less, they said, would be a diminution of service. Finally, the major tenant whom the Tishmans had once interested in the site gave up and rented elsewhere.

Gulf Oil came close to buying the company, and so did Metropolitan Life and New York Life. All backed away, not wanting to own a construction firm and hundreds of employees along with the real estate. It became obvious to Bob Tishman and the other executives in early 1976 that the right buyer would want the buildings that Tishman owned but not the construction company, even though it was a proven money-maker. It was equally clear that family pressures also required something to happen. John didn't like reporting to Bob and yearned to have his division independent. Jerry Speyer had been in the business for ten years and was itching for more power, too. "If the company had remained public," he recalls, "I would have left it." Bob didn't want that to happen and involved Jerry intimately in trying to get out from under the public configuration. The company could not be liquidated unless all the Tishmans could realize the millions of dollars in equities that had been amassed in the form of the company's buildings. The Securities and Exchange Commission was looking askance at schemes that allowed insiders to buy a company cheaply and take it private. But if a sell-off of the buildings could be arranged, the various

Tishman family members would benefit, the SEC wouldn't mind, and the three chieftains could each pursue their separate dreams.

Equitable Life provided the key to unlock the puzzle. Equitable agreed to buy the Tishman holdings for prices that were too low, but were all that could be gotten under the circumstances. Equally important, Equitable wanted to retain Alan to manage the New York buildings and Equitable's other properties around the country, through the Tishman offices in New York, Chicago, and Los Angeles. So the entire management division could stay intact, and Bob and Jerry could go out on their own as developers.

All that remained was to shake clear the construction arm. John recalls, he "called up Al Marshall [the head of Rockefeller Center], walked a few blocks to Room 5600 and made a quick handshake deal for them to buy the construction division, and the Tishman Realty & Construction name and logo," for $9.5 million. "I didn't even have to move offices," John says with a smile; Rockefeller Center was happy to have its new division stay at 666 Fifth Avenue. Marshall insisted on buying the company name so that Alan or Bob couldn't use it in their new entities, which would undoubtedly be competitors. Having recently purchased Cushman & Wakefield, one of the city's oldest brokerages, and with a construction arm, Rockefeller Center was well positioned for development in a New York that was expected to boom again soon. By any lights, this purchase was a friendly steal, as the construction division was doing hundreds of millions in projects annually. Even so, the Rockefeller interests drove a hard bargain, eventually bringing the price down to $7.5 million.

Equitable's purchase of most of the major buildings that the Tishmans owned outright, and Lazard Realty's purchase of the remaining properties, enabled Tishman Realty to pay its shareholders a total of $180 million, more than $60 million directly to Tishman family members. At last David Tishman, now nearing ninety, and the three cousins, all middle-aged, possessed riches approaching the same order of magnitude as those of the Rudins, Roses, Dursts, and other old families. It was sad to see the most visible and respected of the old builder firms unable to survive New York's near-default — but the death of one Tishman empire was also the birth of three new ones, each under the direction of a strong-willed cousin.

Chapter Seventeen

The Great Leap Forward

EDWARD I. KOCH believed that the absence of new buildings was very bad for New York City. Construction meant jobs and potential increases in the tax base, as well as more revenues from sales and employment taxes. Mayor Beame had started an incentive program in 1977; on taking office in January 1978, Koch did even more to assist developers, reaffirming the Beame incentives, adding new ones, and calling builders' attention to subsidies enacted earlier, such as the J-51 program to rehabilitate apartment houses and convert warehouses and lofts to residential use. By November 1978, more than thirty new skyscrapers were under construction, among them a headquarters for AT&T on Madison Avenue that would enjoy $20 million in abatements. Because it seemed that all the corporate giants who threatened to leave Manhattan had already gone, critics charged that abatements were unnecessary for companies such as AT&T, which had profits in the billions and were well able to pay to remain in New York.

Those thirty skyscrapers also owed their genesis to a pent-up demand for space, a demand of the magnitude that had produced the booms of the 1920s and the postwar period. It was so strong that the backlog of space that had haunted builders through the 1970s was soon completely absorbed. Even 1166 Sixth Avenue was fully rented, as valuable to its new owners as the Tishmans had hoped it would be to themselves. The combination of incentives, political encouragements, and that large appetite for space created a golden time for the skyscraper builders of New York.

In early 1978 Sol Goldman believed that the business climate had turned around sufficiently so that the Goldman-DiLorenzo empire could now be dismantled. He had just begun dialysis treatment and wanted to make sure that if he died his family would get full value for his lifetime of acquisitions. He and Alex III started flipping coins to determine which buildings each family would own. They put the names or addresses of fifty buildings each in two envelopes and tossed a quarter; the winner got to pick the envelope. The process was repeated three times over the next eighteen months.

While Sol sold off buildings to pay down the $30 million he owed to the banks to $5 million, his son Allan and daughter Jane took over the day-to-day management of his empire. And because the climate was so good, for the first time the crafty old acquirer began to think about making skyscrapers instead of trading them. Maybe, before he died, he'd erect a monument for himself. He owned a series of properties on West 44th Street for which he'd paid half a million dollars; some contained massage parlors and other sex-industry businesses that, as of old, he tried half-heartedly to evict. Canadian developer Robert Campeau offered him $6 million for the properties — a huge profit — and Goldman agreed to sell. A tangle ensued as Campeau tried to back out, then to reassert control and sell it to New York developer Harry Macklowe for $9 million; the three men settled their differences in a way that allowed Macklowe to take title for a $6-million payment to Goldman and $3 million to Campeau.

More than property was being transferred in this transaction. Macklowe was currently attempting in his other projects to erase the memory of his early, crass methods — in 1971 he had been banned from selling partnerships for three months and received a fine for "false and misleading statements." After that, working in a careful way, he financed and erected River Tower, a luxury apartment building at First Avenue and 53rd Street, and developed River Terrace on East 72nd, both considered in good taste. His artistic decisions were made in conjunction with his wife, a curator of modern art, and his buildings were designed in-house by a team of bright young people recruited from respected architectural partnerships. Macklowe had become the very model of a modern major developer — a contributor to Ed Koch, on the board of the Municipal Arts Society — whose work was praised for artistic merit and profitability.

Koch was about to propose a regulation that would make it impossible to tear down single-room-occupancy (SRO) hotels. Goldman had promised to deliver the West 44th Street site cleared of tenants, and had agreed with Macklowe that its SRO hotel could be demolished quickly, before Koch introduced his measure. But Macklowe didn't have the requisite permit, and it was of a type that normally took sixty days to vet. Macklowe was faced with a delay that could leave him sitting on an unoccupied property, one that could possibly lose considerable value if the Koch proposal was passed.

A man more at ease with his newfound wealth, or subject to the advice of a father or uncle in the business, might have proceeded with due propriety even if it meant losing money for a time. But Macklowe was in a hurry, and perhaps his recent successes made him believe that corners could be cut and problems tidied up afterwards. Then, too, Goldman had a sordid history of shoddy maintenance and disregard for municipal rules. The evening after these two spoke, the demolition was done — without city permits and without safety guards to prevent injury. A crane wielding a saw-toothed scoop bucket ripped through the hotel and adjoining buildings. Gas and water mains had not been turned off; only luck prevented an explosion.

There was a firestorm, however, when the story became public. Goldman was indicted, Macklowe was indicted along with his vice president, and so was the demolition boss. Koch returned Macklowe's most recent campaign contribution and the Real Estate Board of New York met to consider censuring Macklowe. Goldman was soon excused; the vice president resigned and pled guilty to a charge of "reckless endangerment"; the demolition boss refused to say who had hired him (though his company was also working for Macklowe on another site) and was fined. Macklowe's indictment was quashed when he agreed to a $2-million out-of-court settlement earmarked for the homeless. The city continued to hold up permits to develop the site, however, forcing Macklowe to lose money on it for the next several years. In a single stroke, Harry Macklowe had succeeded in transferring to himself the bad-boy reputation of Goldman-DiLorenzo.

The enormous size of the Goldman fortune ripped the family apart. Lillian and Sol Goldman moved into separate residences; when Lillian applied for temporary alimony, Sol's daughters filed affidavits that their mother was emotionally ill; a court granted $700,000 a year pending a divorce. Lillian hired Roy Cohn while Sol engaged matrimonial lawyer Raoul Felder, and the foursome sat down and made an arrangement for Lillian to get $6 million in cash and a $4-million apartment, plus a third of Sol's properties in the event of his death.

Lillian may have been unaware of the true worth of the Goldman holdings. Just a few years earlier, the amount had been in the tens of millions, but now estimates ran as high as a billion dollars. Lillian signed the agreement and thought herself well off until, a few weeks later, she discovered a note from Cohn to Felder in Sol's coat pocket. "After the job we did for the Goldmans," it read, "including saving Sol's exposure of 3 or 4 hundred million dollars equitable distribution . . . I was shocked and deeply hurt that he would offer me $100,000 for all these months of hard work. . . . When I put myself in your hands and his, I thought I was dealing with friends who would recognize what my friendship had meant." Lillian thought this note evidence of an attempt to defraud her, sued Cohn, and tried to have the agreement with Sol overturned. By the time her case against Cohn came up in court, Cohn had been disbarred on other charges, and this one was dismissed. The separation agreement was upheld in another court and the divorce granted; less than a month later, Goldman died, and the wrangling over his estate shifted to a battle between Lillian and her children.

Those more experienced in the handling of wealth and the cycles of creating skyscrapers and filling them fared better in the great leap forward in values. In 1978, Jerry Speyer and Bob Tishman, newly released from the old public company, began to erect their first new building under the Tishman-Speyer banner. At the time of its conception, Speyer considered 520 Madison Avenue, the first stone skyscraper to be erected in Manhattan in many years, "an entrepreneurial gamble." One reason was that they were doing it "as of right," without zoning bonuses or abatements. Their timing was impeccable. During construction, the great thirst for space took hold and the uncompleted building's worth soared; it became the equivalent of a gold mine, assuring the new company's success.

Speyer had another task in this period: to dismantle the empire acquired jointly by his friends Bernie Mendik and Larry Silverstein. In the years since Mendik's divorce from Silverstein's sister Annette, the former brothers-in-law had been operating what amounted to separate companies under a single roof. But they owned the properties in common. Matters reached an impasse in which the men hardly spoke to one another. Speyer kept telling them that once they split they'd both be better off, but to separate them while making the division of property equitable was as Speyer recalls, "a nightmare" in which he was forced to be a "Henry Kissinger, shuttling between adversaries." When the task was complete, the former brothers-in-law had separate companies and offices, a block apart — Silverstein atop 521 Fifth at 43rd Street, facing west, and Mendik near the top floor of 330 Madison at 43rd, facing east. It was as if they had their backs to one another.

In the aftermath of the split, and as a consequence of the surge in prices between 1979 and 1981, both former partners changed their definition of the dream. Silverstein (and Tishman-Speyer) bought and rehabilitated the handsome 11 West 42nd Street building facing the New York Public Library. "In replacing virtually everything but the core," Silverstein remembers, he "went a long way toward developing an entirely new building." Silverstein's biggest trophy was 120 Broadway, the old Equitable filing cabinets that had been the focus of real estate dreams in Manhattan since Louis Jay Horowitz, and which had been previously owned by Zeckendorf and Helmsley. In it he discovered architectural treasures hidden or underutilized for years, and set out to renew the building's 1916 elegance. With fresh millions in his coffers, in 1980 Silverstein finally made the plunge into development. He wasn't entirely sure he wanted to do it, but the site called 7 World Trade Center was irresistible, covered only by a small Con Ed substation; he outbid all others for the site and tried to start construction. But clashes among Con Ed, the Port Authority, and other agencies kept delaying the project.

Mendik's first post-partnership purchase was the Sperry & Hutchinson Building on the corner of 42nd Street and Madison Avenue; he bought it from the Catholic church and started to refurbish it. The S&H building had been renting at $9.50 per square foot. By the time Mendik was finished renovating, the market would support double that, and he found he could quadruple the cash flow to over $8 million a year. Within a few years, Mendik and his investors took more than $30 million out of that one building.

Mendik changed his vision, as well, but not toward new development. That he considered too risky. He perfected the craft of finding, rebuilding, and vigorously managing old structures. What Helmsley had done in a cost-conscious manner, Mendik did with an eye toward making things sparkle. Mendik's employees toured buildings daily, inspecting all public areas and asking tenants what they needed in the way of repairs and assistance. On Two Park

Avenue he had the satisfaction of outbidding his friend Speyer by just enough to win the Jazz Age trophy. He proceeded to reinvigorate it with as much enthusiasm for beauty as Silverstein had done with 120 Broadway. By the mid-1980s Mendik controlled more than ten million square feet of office space, as much as contained in the twin towers. Mendik made so many old buildings shine and took so much pride in their efficient management that he characterized himself, the son of a Bronx handyman, as the "most successful janitor in the city."

Each former partner was worth more than $150 million. Silverstein commissioned a yacht; Mendik, a new dwelling for his new wife and child. "The money wasn't really the point," Mendik asserts. "It was just a way of keeping score." Where was there to go? Only up the borrowing ladder. For a while, both men borrowed money for their purchases from the discretionary funds of Equitable and Prudential. But insurance companies began making more of their own decisions on which buildings to buy, and Mendik reasoned, "If they could do my job, which was to find buildings that were good buys, and then manage them, then I could certainly do theirs, which was to raise the money." He formed a joint venture with a brokerage house, E. F. Hutton, that would offer limited partnerships and deal with the investors; Silverstein entered a joint venture too, with the investment banking firm of J. P. Morgan.

Silverstein's mother asked him, "Is that *the* J. P. Morgan?" Larry nodded. "Oh," his mother responded, "what your father would say!"

Indeed, the implied understanding — that Silverstein was up there in the stratosphere of wealth with the likes of the old robber barons — was not far from the mark. As the value of everything a developer or operator had in inventory, and all that was about to come on line, shot upwards, the phenomenon was reflected in *Forbes* magazine's first annual list of the 400 wealthiest individuals in the United States, published in 1981. Reading it, the real estaters learned — some with quite a bit of surprise — that they were worth not the tens of millions that they had heretofore assumed but, in the estimation of the magazine, hundreds of millions of dollars. Relative newcomers such as Mendik and Silverstein could lay claim to being authentic barons, and their contemporaries among the Roses, Rudins, Tishmans, Dursts, Helmsleys, and Trumps could take pride in having accomplished what heirs seldom were able to do — vastly increase the size of their holdings over what had been left to them by their fathers. On this scale, the second- and third-generation men in the old builder families had outstripped the equivalent generation of Astors, Morgans, and Rockefellers.

The suddenness of the real estaters' escalation into great wealth — and its positive meaning for them and for the city — was on display in a lunch between two old friends in early 1981. Fred Rose made it a point to lunch quarterly with a series of men who were a half-generation ahead of him, about fifteen years older than he, and who had been mentors to him. One was Larry Wien, who helped set the mold for many people in real estate in regard to charitable and civic endeavors; another was Jack Felt, former chairman of the City Planning Commission; a third was Harold Uris. Rose Associates rented office space from Uris in the same 380 Madison building where the older man maintained his offices. Uris and Rose liked one another; both were concrete-on-the-shoes men.

"Freddy," Uris asked over a lunch at the Century Club, "what are you up to, these days?" Rose knew Uris didn't mean what buildings were being erected by Rose Associates, but, rather, what sort of outside work had he undertaken. Rose had been director of the quixotic losing campaign of Jacob Javits for reelection to the Senate, but that adventure was over. Nor would Uris want to hear about Yale, as he was such a big Cornell man. He told Harold about the beautiful building he was erecting for the Asia Society, designed by Edward Larrabee Barnes, the architect of the IBM headquarters on Madison Avenue. Thanks to the Rockefellers, they were almost finished with it.

"I won't give you a dime for the Asia Society," Uris grumbled in a good-natured way.

"I didn't ask you for it," Rose responded quickly. Then the light went on over his head, just as in the comic books: Uris was trying to tell him something. Harold was seventy-five, his empire had been sold, his fortune was in excess of $100 million, and he was a dyed-in-the-wool New Yorker. Rose had just joined the board of the Metropolitan Museum of Art, where the president was his former Yale classmate William "Bud" Macomber.

"How would you and Ruth like to have lunch with me next week at the Metropolitan Museum?" asked Rose.

"Oho, you're at it again."

Rose admitted that he was, of course, at it, but thought they'd like the result. He then phoned Macomber and asked if he could free his calendar for a date next week, to meet Harold and Ruth Uris.

"Uris?" Macomber said. "I don't know the name."

Rose groaned. One of the wealthiest families in New York, and the president of the Met didn't know them! He waited to see if the light might go on over his old classmate's head, as well.

"Wait a minute. Is that the guy who fixed up the jogging track around Central Park? I use it every morning before coming to work."

"That's him." Fred grinned.

"Then I'll be there."

At the lunch, Harold and Ruth Uris pledged $10 million for a new education building and to endow a renovation fund. It would be the largest donation in the museum's recent history, eclipsed only by the Rockefeller funding for the Cloisters. At a press conference, Harold recalled that in his youth he'd attended P.S. 6, just a block away from the Met, and had been an admirer of the museum all his life. "Met Museum Aiming to Tap Real-Estate Industry," a *Times* headline trumpeted a few months later. "It's one of the most important industries in New York, with which we haven't been in touch," Met board chairman Douglas Dillon said delicately. Soon Lew Rudin and Charles B. Benenson (an investor and frequent partner of the Roses in buildings) were cochairmen, and Rose the honorary chairman, of a committee formed to put the bite on their colleagues. A few months later, Harold Uris died while at his winter home in Florida.

With the Uris gift and the recognition that many more could be realized from the mostly Jewish real estate community, the last barrier to the real estaters' involvement in the city's major civic and cultural institutions vanished. Before long, every board in town actively sought members of the real estate dynasties; within a few years, the developers became major forces on these boards, just as they had a quarter-century earlier when they had first reached the upper levels at the Federation of Jewish Philanthropies. Tishmans, Roses, Rudins, and other developers sat on the boards of the Museum of Natural History, the Philharmonic, the Museum of Modern Art, and the New York Public Library, mingling with Astors, Goelets, and descendants of other families originally made wealthy through their holdings in Manhattan real estate.

Of course, it had to be the right sort of Jewish real estate man.

The ebullient Sam Lefrak, now calling himself LeFrak and in the process of amassing a stellar collection of impressionist and old master artworks, let it be known that he would like to be on the board of the Metropolitan Museum. Sam's fortune was triple that of most directors, but his reputation in philanthropic circles was as a man who put conditions on his donations — demands for testimonial dinners, for inclusion in invitations of his three-page résumé, for a larger share of the dais than the size of the gift might warrant. He was not offered a seat on the museum's board. Believing he had been turned down because he was Jewish, he donated his money elsewhere.

New York University, alma mater to many of the real estate men, was a particular beneficiary of their energy and largesse. Founded in 1832, it had been the recipient of real estate fortunes since the 1930s, when Louis Jay Horowitz left to the university's hospitals the bulk of his earnings. In the 1940s and 1950s NYU had been a commuter college. Many alumni had not gone there by choice — Larry Tisch had attended because "My parents thought I was too young to go away," Lew Rudin because "My brother was already in the army, and I didn't want to leave my parents at home alone." Leonard Stern hated commuting but his father "thought we shouldn't waste money on dormitory costs when we had perfectly good beds at home."

By the late 1960s, New York University's endowment had dwindled and its student base had declined to the point where the possibility existed that the school would have to declare bankruptcy. Selling off the Washington Heights campus was among the first decisions of John Sawhill, installed as chancellor in 1972. Shortly, Sawhill began to rely heavily on the advice of the alumni real estate men on the board: the aging David Tishman and the men of the next-younger generation, Lew Rudin and Larry Silverstein. Bob Tisch was appointed to the board at about the time Congressman John Brademas took over from Sawhill. On the real estaters' advice, the university aggressively began to buy property, especially in the vicinity of its campus.

By 1978, both the city and its real estate were on the upswing, and that meant better times for NYU. It was then that Rudin finally made the $1-million donation requested in 1971. In 1980, Bob Tisch became chairman of the board and NYU set out to raise a million a week for the next hundred weeks. The Tisches started the campaign with a $7.5-million gift, Stern pledged $3 million, Silverstein

$1 million, and the goal of $100 million was soon exceeded. NYU built dormitories, hired new staff, and aggressively increased enrollment. The Tisch School of the Arts, the Silverstein-sponsored Real Estate Institute, and what would later become the Stern School of Business rose to positions of eminence in their respective fields. By the late 1980s, New York University had raised its standards of admission, become the largest private university in the country and one of the largest private employers in New York City, and (like Columbia University) the owner of more than a billion dollars' worth of Manhattan real estate.

Larry Wien reached beyond schools and individual institutions in his philanthropy. Even he and other wealthy individuals were limited in what they could contribute; the real reserves of wealth in the country, Wien knew, were in the hands of the corporations — the *Fortune* 500, not the *Forbes* 400. For years, he and John D. Rockefeller III, the men who had pushed through the last phase of Lincoln Center, had been discussing the fact that American corporations were quite lax in supporting nonprofit institutions, even though tax laws allowed corporations to contribute up to 5 percent of earnings and deduct this sum from their taxable incomes. Three-quarters of the nation's corporations gave nothing at all, and the ones that did contribute were pikers in real percentage terms — most gave away one half of 1 percent of earnings. Wien set out on a campaign to double that. "I hope to be able to make some of these guys feel ashamed of themselves," he said. "Corporations have an obligation to help maintain a healthy society." Wien bought batches of 100 shares each in 135 companies that had reported recent profit increases, and filed shareholder proposals with eighty of them to raise the level of their contributions. Board after board voted down the proposals, but a handful took them to heart even though officially disdaining them. Under Wien's goad AT&T raised its contributions from $28 million, one-third of 1 percent of profits, to $85 million. That amount, a trifle to the corporate giant, was more than what many of the big real estate men could give, combined. By attending annual meetings, writing letters, and talking to a wide circle of acquaintances that included many corporate directors, Wien wielded considerable influence. Often, his proposals helped management to be magnanimous when it had wanted to be so but feared adverse stockholder reaction. A few years later, not wishing to institutionalize the prodding process, Wien declared the corporate gadfly campaign over. He estimated that he'd stimulated 400

American corporations to give $400 million a year more than they had prior to the program. For Larry Wien, that was the ultimate demonstration of leverage.

The fact of the big new money made some small real estate investors wonder if the major players had made all their money legally, or if those who had backed them were getting their fair share. After nearly thirty years, 100 syndications, 15,000 investors, and $3 billion worth of buildings, there were a handful of suits against Larry Wien's syndications. In the early years of the syndicates truly large amounts of money had not been at stake. Now they were, and smaller investors thought it well worth their while to go to the trouble of a lawsuit. In 1980 Wien advised investors that he and Helmsley wanted to sell one of their early syndicate purchases, which had produced dividends for twenty-seven years but now needed major renovations they didn't want to undertake. Each $10,000 investor would receive $70,588; that seemed to most like an impressive figure, but one investor didn't like the idea that the Wien law firm was to receive 25 percent from the deal above Wien's and Helmsley's other portions, and sued. He was joined by a few other investors. Wien, then going through a bout of ill health, settled by offering to return $2 million to the syndicate. Two similar and larger cases were brought, one on the sale of the old Equitable Building to Larry Silverstein, another on the sale of the St. Moritz Hotel to Donald Trump. In both of these, courts ruled in favor of Wien.

These few cases of dissatisfied Wien syndicate investors in the early 1980s paled before Helmsley's headaches with higher-stakes investors in his most grandiose undertaking, the Helmsley Palace Hotel. The project had begun in 1974, when Helmsley convinced the Catholic diocese, then the owner of the Villard Houses directly to the east of St. Patrick's Cathedral, to give him a ninety-nine-year lease on the property for $1 million. He told Richard Roth to design a very large hotel that saved the Madison Avenue courtyard facade of the connected houses, but little else. Modeled by McKim, Mead & White after the Palazzo della Cancellaria in Rome, these five houses in the shape of a U around a courtyard had been a center of monied society since they were built in 1884. The interiors were filled with gold-leaf ceilings, marble fireplaces, and other decorative touches. Helmsley's original plan would have destroyed these. Outrage from the Landmarks Preservation Commission and influential architectural critics forced several redrawings of the plans until it was agreed to save more of the Villard Houses, especially the Gold Room, considered a masterpiece of Gilded Age design. Even so, the result looked as if the silver-sheathed knife of the hotel had cut through the earth-colored flesh of the old buildings and kept going until it disappeared in the clouds. Had the Helmsley Palace been proposed a few years later, when the city's fiscal crisis had eased, it might never have been built because the Villard Houses were a treasure that could have been maintained intact. But with the city still desperate for revenue, Helmsley conceived a canny way to win the tax abatement. He convinced the diocese to apply to the city for relief on the grounds that financial hardship would ensue if the abatement was not given. The New York City Industrial and Commercial Incentives Board had grown wiser since Abe Beame's first award of a forty-year abatement; the Palace's was only for ten years and for fewer millions.

Harry's dream was to create a monument to the woman who had made his life more enjoyable. This shrine, the Helmsley Palace, was supposed to cost $73 million; $50 million of that was pledged to Helmsley by Metropolitan Life, and the rest by investors willing to put up at least $1 million apiece, including the wife of Frank Sinatra, former mayor Robert Wagner and his wife, a Saudi oil sheik, the owner of Kentucky Fried Chicken, and others who were bundled together under the banner of a small investment firm known as Leperq, deNeuflize and Company. They agreed to invest if Helmsley would guarantee the construction cost (and the attendant construction loan) and agree to bear any additional costs. The crunch began when Leona started to take charge of every detail — such as replacing plastic light switches in the ballroom with brass ones, for $2,750. It escalated as she insisted on $112,714 for better chandeliers in three dining rooms. Cost overruns eventually brought the construction total to $110 million.

In earlier syndicates, Helmsley the great authority had simply written to his small-fry investors and demanded they come up with a few more dollars to cover such overruns. They always did. But now when he wrote to his investors to insist they pay $20 million more to cover the additional costs, the sophisticated group assembled by Leperq objected, investigated, and soon happened upon expensive decorating schemes, purchases that went well beyond the original designs, a set of interlocking Helmsley subsidiary companies that charged more than the partners thought proper for services such as the leasing of television sets. They also found that Helmsley had charged himself less than market prices to lease space in the hotel. Queried about these matters, he immediately withdrew $5 million of his request, but still asked for $15 million.

The syndicators took him to arbitration, during which Helmsley was personally grilled. "You are not supposed to be in my books!" he shouted. "What are you doing in Deco, anyhow?" Deco was the company nominally headed by Jay Panzirer, Leona's son. But they were in all Helmsley's books, and discovered why that $5-million request had been so quickly withdrawn: double billing for charges. Costs on the Palace and on the Harley Hotel being built simultaneously were intermingled, with bills pertaining to the Harley charged to the Palace. They next discovered that the Jay Panzirer firm was charging a 20 percent commission on all its work, twice the going rate. "I think what has concerned the limited partners," said a Leperq lawyer to Harry during the arbitration, "is that you may be using Deco as one means of gaining income from Helmsley Enterprises, and taking a profit there, at the expense of a profit in the hotels or in your . . . "

"You have to make [a] supposition then," Helmsley snapped back. "You have to suppose that I'm a crook, which I am not."

The arbitrators ruled that Helmsley would have to foot the bill for the $20 million in overruns himself. A second judgment ordered the Helmsleys to repay the partnership for all the excesses. When the details of the shenanigans were made public, other major developers shuddered. They had known a Harry Helmsley who was personally honest; they abjured the sort of practices he had used on the Palace and wondered why he'd bothered. Yes, the Palace cost Helmsley personally $50 million, but his pocket was now enormously deep and he was easily able to recoup because his share of profits was $4 mllion to $5 million each year. Why stoop to subterfuge and double-billing? Evidently, extreme wealth could take the old operator out of the realm in which it was necessary to shave expenses, but it couldn't change his old barbering habits.

Another embarrassment was the advertising campaign designed by Joyce Beber featuring Leona as the Queen of the Palace, who kept her eagle eye on the details for the benefit of overnight guests. In advertising terms it worked, helping to fill the hotel. But if Leona's image brought in money, her personal quirks helped keep it away. "We lost at least 10,000 room nights a year," a former Helmsley hotel marketing expert said, because Leona refused to give free rooms to travel agents or to those who booked rooms for large corporate customers, a refusal that cost the hotel $1.2 million in profits yearly.

The Queen-of-the-Palace campaign led to Leona's prominence in the public eye. In turn, this engendered a feeling of invincibility and a sense on the part of both Helmsleys of existing beyond the constraints that hampered the lives of ordinary people. Harry fumed to a friend over the investor furor, "Well, I had to try it. Right is right, and I shouldn't have to follow the rules here." When an applicant for a domestic position at Dunellen Hall, the Helmsleys' country residence, marveled at the huge taxes that must be due on such an opulent home, Leona imperiously announced that rich people like her didn't pay taxes, "only little people do." Deceptive billing for the renovation and furnishing of Dunellen Hall — practices similar to those brought to light in the Palace Hotel arbitration — formed the core of the tax case in which Leona was convicted in 1989.

Before that case was brought, though, Leona and Harry overreached in a direction that caused many in the family-oriented world of Manhattan real estate to shake their heads in amazed disgust. Those old families tried very hard to avoid internecine difficulties and to resolve all familial problems before they could ever be glimpsed by outsiders. Not the Helmsleys. After the death of Leona's son Jay Panzirer, in 1982, she told his wife, Mimi, "I will destroy you," and said to his teenage son Craig, "You killed your father." Though later reconciled with Craig, Leona did attempt to destroy Mimi Panzirer, repossessing her house, owned by Deco, and launching a half-dozen lawsuits that included an attempt to obtain repayment for the transportation of Jay's casket to New York. Harry's acquiescence in these venal pursuits shocked those who had known him in better days and marked a near-total change in the power structure of the Helmsley enterprises. Though Harry remained nominally in charge, the important decisions came from Leona.

After a while it became clear that, under Leona, the dream of acquisition that Harry had evolved into a builder's accomplishments had been further altered. Leona's vision involved spending, not creating, and her business decisions were principally negative. Once she took the empire in hand, there were no purchases of outstanding properties, but a considerable decline in the maintenance of those Helmsley properties in New York and Miami that were not her main focus, and a steady exodus of competent middle-rank employees from Helmsley-Spear who felt that the organization Harry Helmsley had created no longer had a future.

The developer who personified the transformations of the era of the great leap forward — both in business and in his personal style — was Donald Trump. In early 1978, recently elected mayor Ed Koch and Governor Hugh Carey agreed to locate New York's new convention center on the land in the West Thirties that Donald Trump had leased from Penn Central. The state bought the land for $12 million, a fairly low price considering that Trump's original purchase price for the two parcels (never paid) had been $62 million, and one considered by real estate insiders to be a defeat for Trump. He had hoped for designation as developer of the center, but that was denied him, too. Trump then claimed he was owed a $4.4-million broker's fee, which he would forgo if the convention center was named for his father. Deputy Mayor Peter J. Solomon considered doing so, but then discovered that Trump was only entitled by contract to a $500,000 fee. That was paid, and Trump had no further involvement in the center, though he claimed its siting as a triumph in his autobiography.

His attention turned to a building site next to Tiffany's, on Fifth Avenue at 56th Street. The losses incurred there by the Bonwit Teller store placed a strain on its corporate parent, Genesco, whose lease with the owner of the site and the building, the Equitable Life Assurance Company, had many years to run. "Donald has the uncanny ability to smell blood in the water," a Genesco executive said when Trump offered Genesco $10 million to buy out the lease. Equitable, already a partner in the Grand Hyatt, agreed to bet with Trump on a skyscraper, but only if it was tall enough to make money. That required Trump's purchase of air rights above the Tiffany building, a zoning change, and tax abatements. His case before the city agencies was presented by Sandy Lindenbaum, son of his father's friend, while Trump himself bullied the public. "Do you want Bonwit Teller to come back to Fifth Avenue?" he asked rhetorically. "It's as simple as this: if I don't get a zone change, I don't rent to Bonwit's."

Three city agencies agreed to the zoning changes but not the abatement, which they pointed out was earmarked for underutilized land. A parcel next to Tiffany's did not qualify. After calling Mayor

Koch at home and telling him that he'd never forget this slight, Trump sued the city for $138 million in damages, and Commissioner for Housing Preservation and Development Anthony Gliedman personally for $10 million more. The suits were later withdrawn, the abatements granted, and Trump hired Gliedman. In clearing the site, Trump ordered the demolition of Art Deco bas-reliefs and grillwork. There was anger from preservation groups, but there was no hope of raising the "artworks" from the dead.

During construction, Fred Trump visited the site with Donald, looked at the expensive bronze solar glass of the sheath, and said to his son, "Why don't you forget about the damn glass? Give them four or five stories of it and use common brick for the rest. Nobody is going to look up anyway."

"It was a classic," Donald recalled in his first autobiography, "Fred Trump standing there on 57th Street and Fifth Avenue and trying to save a few bucks. I was touched, and . . . understood where he was coming from — but also exactly why I'd decided to leave [his father's company]." The implication was that his father had neither the taste nor the vision to compete in the Manhattan arena.

Trump Tower, designed by Der Scutt, became a striking, multi-angled skyscraper whose many glass-sheathed facets glittered with the reflections of nearby buildings. The lower floors held a promenade and atrium open to the public, and shops that featured extremely expensive merchandise; above were apartments, Trump's office, and his living quarters. Trump's mixed-use skyscraper was full of pink marble, gold trim, and theatrical costumes for the doormen. His vision of opulence was also touted as an investment opportunity. Many critics thought the style overblown, more rhinestone than diamond, but Trump's exclamations of its superiority helped market the tower's apartments for some of the highest prices ever paid in Manhattan, enough for Equitable and Trump to realize a profit estimated at $100 million even before the building opened.

The new definition of luxury that Trump was evolving did not have to do with taste, but rather was an expression of the consumption of expensive materials and objects. The more gilding on the lily, the better. Publisher John Fairchild, frequently an arbiter of taste, visited Trump in his lair and later described how the developer led him from his office through a "secret passage" toward his living quarters, separated by two heavily embossed gold doors, large enough for his stretch limousine to go through. Trump uses all his force to unlock the doors. Before us is a panoramic view of Manhattan. The room, including the floor, is all marble and alabaster, and there are gold-filigreed, fluted marble columns. Above, painted cupids fly through a painted sky. On the left of the room, against the wall, is a fountain large enough for a small square in Paris. Trump goes to a back panel, pushes four buttons, and water spurts into the fountain from all directions, falling into its marble basin. In a corner of the room is a bar with Louis XVI chairs, the legs of which have been elongated to raise the seats to the proper level.

To support this imperial style, ruthless business practices were employed. While Trump Tower was still under construction, Trump commissioned his father's old friend Phil Birnbaum's architectural firm to make an updated, more expensive version of their Queens-comes-to-Manhattan buildings on Third Avenue at 61st Street, which he would call Trump Plaza. Birnbaum's architectural firm had become one of the busiest in the city in the late 1970s, with projects for the Milsteins, Joseph Giffuni, Jack Goodstein, and other developers who had started in the outer boroughs. He even had the satisfaction of having outsiders acknowledge an old slight. While designing a building on Park Avenue that would replace the old Princeton Club, Birnbaum mentioned to some Princetonians that he had been denied admission to the architectural graduate school because he was Jewish. They didn't believe him, so he showed them the original letter from the school's dean; they prevailed upon the college to make a formal apology. By the 1980s, the Birnbaum firm had completed almost 500 buildings in the metropolitan area, more than any other partnership had ever done. Costos Kondylis had developed into a star in his own right within the firm; it was the younger man who designed Trump Plaza. When Trump learned that Birnbaum's firm was designing a building diagonally across the street that was of virtually the same exterior shape as the one Kondylis had done for him, he sued both Birnbaum and developer Morton Olshan, obtaining an injunction preventing them from continuing construction.

Birnbaum, mortified, managed to get a call through to Fred Trump, for whom he had designed buildings in the past. How could Fred let his son sue an old friend? "I can't control him," Fred confessed. Olshan agreed to alter the exterior cladding of the building and its color. Trump dropped the suit, but not until it had cost Olshan several months of delays.

Trump adroitly translated controversy surrounding his projects into a high public profile. His image was burnished through attendance at social events where the press trolled for celebrities, and by continued chest-thumping. Trump became the only developer whom people could name. Atlantic City seemed a proper outlet for his showmanship, and he constructed and purchased casinos there. In terms of cash flow, casinos were much more profitable than Manhattan skyscrapers. Flush, he again gained control of the West Side railyards, acquired a large condominium building in Florida, and began ventures that would eventually drain huge amounts of money from him when his cash flow slowed. For the moment, though, most of the public lionized him as the developer hero.

What one thought of Trump depended on one's definition of the acceptable use of fortunes of staggering size. Nearly alone among the big-time real estate winners in this era, Trump and Helmsley stayed aloof from grand commitments to the major cultural, civic, and educational institutions of Manhattan. Through the mid-1980s, the private foundations of Trump and Helmsley were proportionately less well funded than those of the other families and contributed less to charitable endeavors. The old families noted this but said little to Trump and Helmsley, hoping that they, too, would eventually realize that the city had given them great riches and that more than token gestures were required in return.

The capstone of Trump's public image as hero was his challenge to the city to let him take over the long-delayed completion of the Wollman skating rink in Central Park. His solution was to call Irv Fischer of HRH and have Fischer send an engineer to investigate the reason for the delay, which turned out to be a rather simple one — the wrong chemicals had been used, and this had prevented the correct solidifying of the concrete. Knowing this, Trump could easily direct the rapid completion of the task, and reaped public-relations benefits from having done what he said the city itself could not do. Other developers knew that any private firm could always do construction work more quickly and efficiently than a governmental entity. They shook their heads in helpless recognition at how much positive publicity Trump seemed able to garner from activities that had cost him, in terms of dollars, very little.

Trump bought the fabled Mar A Lago estate in Florida and flew down several dozen friends and relatives for an opening party, among them Lew Rudin, Rudin's fiancée, and his mother. At the dinner, Trump toasted "my good friend" Lew and said that, fifteen years earlier, he had phoned him with a proposition. Rudin said he hoped that he'd been nice to the wunderkind, because he had no memory of the conversation. Trump assured him that he had, and told the guests how he had been spurred toward greatness. On top of the world, Trump could even afford to be magnanimous.

Like the Helmsleys, the more recognizable Trump became, the more he embraced the belief that he was beyond the constraints applicable to ordinary mortals. He told *Playboy* magazine that the tower, casinos, and the world's most luxurious yacht were but "props for the show," and "the show is 'Trump' and it is sold-out performances everywhere. . . . Most people enjoy it."

The economic consequences of this escalation into wealth for New York as a city were not all salutary. When rents in office skyscrapers jumped as a reflection of great demand, every foot of space in town became more valuable. Small retail tenants on the ground floors of all sorts of buildings, not just of big office towers, were hit with substantial rent increases when their leases came due. If the tenant refused to renew, demand was such that his shop could be replaced by another that could pay the higher rates. Even if the shop could not immediately be replaced, the owner could afford to keep the space vacant until he found someone willing to pay the new, higher rates, because the incoming tenant's rent would easily offset the owner's losses while awaiting his arrival. Emboldened by the leap in value, many owners bought back the leases of existing tenants that had been signed in the bad days of the 1970s and rerented the space, at much higher rates, to new tenants.

To pay the stiff rents retailers had to ring up a greater volume of sales, or have a business in which each sale was more lucrative. With what seemed like inordinate speed, in the 1980s small, individually owned neighborhood service establishments were replaced by high-volume chains or upscale retailers. Along Columbus and Amsterdam avenues north of Lincoln Center, shoe-repair shops closed and pricey boutiques and restaurants opened: gentrification. The printing industry, which needed a lot of space but didn't produce a high volume of sales, was forced out of Manhattan by spiraling rents. Businesses that had to remain, such as those associated with the Broadway theaters — costume shops, places that built scenery, rehearsal halls, restaurants next to the theater district, parking lots — were forced to charge higher prices, which were eventually added to the cost of an evening at the theater. Manhattan itself was forced upscale.

New construction of middle-class housing ceased, though luxury skyscrapers continued to rise. The demarcations between rich and poor seemed sharper than at the turn of the twentieth century, when the rich lived on Fifth Avenue and the poor were barely a stone's throw away, on Sixth. Now the poor seemed to be physically pushed out of the skyscrapered part of Manhattan island, relegated to Harlem, the Lower East Side, or, more often, to the outer boroughs where rents were lower and so was everything that was rent-related — the price of food in the markets, the clothes in the stores, and the services offered by neighborhood establishments. Developers were blamed for all the city's troubles. Their greed was absorbing all of the inhabitants' money; their power was making the city kneel. Two New Yorks were rapidly being shaped, one for the rich and comfortable who lived in luxurious buildings and could afford to shop at the boutiques and eat at the restaurants that paid the higher rents, and another for those who could not. Soon there would be no space, services, or amenities for anyone else. Apocalyptic visions began to be voiced, of a twenty-first century metropolis in which the rich lived in a high-walled, armed camp and the poor were an envious, angry rabble at the gates.

Chapter Eighteen

Replacement Costs

IN 1983 Larry Silverstein became chairman of the Real Estate Board of New York for a three-year term. When a "redeveloper" such as Silverstein considered whether to build a new skyscraper or buy and retrofit an old one, the key numerical figure was the replacement cost — what it would cost to replace the old structure with a new one. In his work with REBNY, Silverstein personified the change from old families to new and defined how the new ruling members of the oligarchy would replace old institutions, principally by transforming them from within. Silverstein's recharging of REBNY turned it from a rather old-fashioned fraternal club of space salesmen into a well-financed, activist organization willing to use its size, weight, and members' money to aggressively lobby for its own causes. Dues had been low; they were raised so that large shops such as Silverstein's own had to pay up to $10,000 a year for the privilege of membership, though a small broker could still join REBNY for a few hundred dollars. An enhanced professional staff was hired; political contributions totalling several hundred thousand dollars annually were made in the board's name, and individual members followed these donations with sizable ones of their own. "Every week we have a breakfast, lunch or dinner with the Mayor or members of his administration or members of the City Council or the Governor and his staff," Silverstein told a reporter, to "talk about legislative and regulatory proposals and to help in framing them." As the board and its governors made themselves known to public officials, their power increased.

The largest fight that REBNY joined with New York's public officials was on the 1986 revision of the federal income-tax codes.

The Reagan administration's initial package contained a proposal to eliminate the deduction for state and local taxes. Many people in New York City, and many businesses, too, could rationalize living and working there only so long as they could deduct what they paid in state and local taxes (the highest in the nation) from their federal incomes. Loss of the deductions might drive businesses out of the city or, as Senator Alfonse D'Amato suggested, "take the city back to the bad old days of fiscal crisis."

Banker David Rockefeller was as alarmed as anyone about the potential loss of the deduction, and at a dinner with Senator D'Amato asked Lew Rudin, then head of the Association for a Better New York as well as a governor of REBNY, to accept the leadership of the newly formed Coalition Against Double Taxation. It was obvious that Rockefeller wouldn't chair the organization himself, for he did not want to be seen as taking on the president. Rudin refused, on the basis that he was "too Jewish, too New York, too real estate."

Rockefeller was offended by this statement until he learned of the rebuff Rudin and Al Marshall had received when they sought Wall Street funding for ABNY in 1971. The old slight avenged, Rudin agreed to chair the coalition if the head of the upstate firm of Corning Glass was the cochair. The group hired former senator Jacob Javits, then in a wheelchair and in the last months of a terminal illness, to help them lobby in Washington. Treasury Secretary James Baker, Attorney General Edwin Meese, and Vice President George Bush were sympathetic, though unwilling to offend the president by open opposition to the tax proposal. But partly through New York's well-financed efforts, a ground swell of Congressional dissent was coaxed into existence and the deduction for state and local taxes stayed in place. The deduction for sales taxes did not.

Moreover, in a part of the tax-reform bill that did not attract wide attention at the time, but had tremendous implications for Manhattan skyscrapers, the transfer of accumulated depreciation credits from one asset to offset the profits of another was discontinued. This meant that real estate as a tax shelter for other income lost its appeal, narrowing a developer's sources for financing. The game itself was changing.

Because of their obvious wealth and their inability to move their assets from where they were rooted, the large owners became an ever more inviting target. In his first reelection campaign, Mayor Koch came under fire for being too cozy with the city's real estate interests; the Rudins, Donald Trump, and George Klein, Koch wrote later in his memoir, "were at the very top of my list of campaign contributors." But Koch knew that unless these real estaters united against him to find a replacement as mayor someday, they'd have to stick by him. In response to public pressure, Koch started closing down the lavish abatement and incentives programs in 1982. On the morning of a Board of Estimate vote on limiting tax breaks and the type of skyscrapers that would be allowed in certain districts, Jack Rudin came to see Koch, "very much excited and said that in effect, we were taking his property," Koch wrote. The Rudins then had an East Side skyscraper on the boards, along with an understanding with city officials that this building would be granted an exception if the new regulations took effect. They had gone ahead with the plans only after reaching such an understanding, and were now going to be penalized. Koch told Rudin that he could sue the city, if he thought it proper, and that he wouldn't consider it an attack on their friendship. The Rudins sued and lost.

Perhaps it was this incident that finally caused the Rudins to change their focus and brought them to the realization many other landlords had already reached: on some real estate matters, governmental entities could not be budged. The prime examples were rent control and stabilization, which had become the sacred cows of New York politics. The Trumps, LeFraks, and Helmsley had earlier begun converting to cooperative ownership their tens of thousands of apartments — older rental buildings squeezed to the point where the owners considered them unprofitable, even though these buildings had been lucrative in the past. Now the Rudins, who cherished being considered among the best-liked residential landlords of the city, began the co-op conversion process in their apartment buildings, starting with the old symbol of continuity, Two Fifth Avenue.

Lew's son Billy, his daughter Beth DeWoody, and Jack's son Eric had entered the firm. Billy learned quickly; in a short time, Lew remembers, "He knew more than I had at a comparable age." Beth's presence in the office, and that of other bright women in his own and other family real estate companies, became the subject of conversation at a private lunch for Rudin, DeWoody, Sam LeFrak, and Sam's daughters. At this meal, the Rudins tried to persuade LeFrak that his daughters ought to take up high positions in the Lefrak firm and be groomed for succession, along with their brother

Richard. The LeFrak women were bright and obviously capable: Francine LeFrak was a successful Broadway-show producer who was already involved with Sam's music and entertainment companies; Denise LeFrak worked for an independent real estate broker. These accomplishments were pointed out, but the crux of the Rudin argument was the replacement cost. In the future, when Sam was gone and Richard was in sole charge, there could be serious inter-familial friction if the women in the family were not participants in the decision-making process. Including the women in the company could avoid that sort of disaster. Sam didn't agree, and his daughters remained outside the real estate concern.

LeFrak's old-fashioned thinking may have contributed to his being shut out of the new phase of the development of Battery Park City. He had begun work at the site when there was little money to be made, in 1973, doing tasks for the state — filling in the land, developing the infrastructure, building 2,200 apartments, making a waterfront esplanade. Battery Park City was almost an entire new city, in the shadow of the World Trade Center and a short walk from Wall Street. LeFrak's apartments there produced only a modest income; the big returns were expected to come from office towers, the second phase of development. Then, according to LeFrak, the political climate changed. "They started dealing from the bottom of the deck, and we said *arrivederci*." LeFrak refocused his considerable energies to begin an entirely new city, a 600-acre development on the New Jersey side of the Hudson, just a tube stop from Wall Street. The largest mixed-use project in the country, Newport City was slated to eventually house 35,000 people, shopping malls, office towers, and an oceanographic center. If to replace its dwindling housing stock New York needed affordable apartments for the middle class, Sam LeFrak vowed, those would now be found across the river.

Meanwhile, the rest of Battery Park City's landfill lay waiting, and not only LeFrak was found wanting when it came to evaluating applicants for its future development. Eleven major developers, including many from the oligarchy such as Jerry Speyer, Harry Helmsley, and Paul Milstein, made bids to construct office towers in the ninety-three-acre Battery Park City, but most were reluctant to erect all the office space quickly, reasoning that it would be hard to lease, and promised only to phase it in over ten years or longer. Paul Reichmann said he'd develop it all in five years and offered to put up $50 million of Olympia & York's money to guarantee the

Battery Park Authority's bond payments (just coming due) from then to the year 2014, even if his firm later failed to properly develop the properties. On hearing this, the head of the authority later said, "I really wanted to . . . jump up from behind my desk and kiss the man on both cheeks. He was the only one in the procession of developers who understood my primary worry — paying off the bonds." The Reichmanns won the bid. Similarly, Mort Zuckerman, who had made his mark principally in Boston, was able to win the designation as developer of the property owned by the city at Columbus Circle. The bids from the long-established families were low, perhaps out of a feeling that the project, entangled in governmental red tape and opposed by powerful community groups, might take forever.

Newer entrants to the Manhattan game seemed to be more supple in their financial thinking than the multigenerational families, who had been very successful at erecting structures in a particular way and were less inclined to shift from tactics that had always proven viable. Another reason for the shift was that the older families were overly cautious in the wake of the disasters of the 1970s. As the value of properties climbed ever higher, the amounts of money developers were required to invest to initiate a new building grew proportionately. Even for families whose wealth was stupendous, the cost of a single building — upwards of $150 million — mandated multiple partners, limitations on risks and gains, and a hefty dose of caution.

Was this to be the end of the great families, reduced to caution, collecting rent payments? No, but the configuration of development had to change. Now, one had to dream with partners. Bill Zeckendorf, Jr., emerged as preeminent in this regard. The middle-aged Zeckendorf uncannily resembled his late father in appearance — full-bodied, balding, an intelligent gaze. But the replacement was of a different mold. Whereas his father had plunged into new projects on his own, Bill, Jr., who had watched his father's painful decline, refused to be trapped by too-rapid starts or too-high leverage. Instead, he took many partners, sometimes a different set on each project, even though that meant cutting down his equity, sometimes to as low as 10 or 20 percent of a proposed building. His dreams, though not as grandiose as his father's had been, were sufficiently large: the redevelopment of the Union Square area, and of the old Madison Square Garden site along Eighth and Ninth avenues that became WorldWide Plaza. Each was a multiuse project containing office space as well as middle-income and luxury apartments; each also became the focus for further gentrification of its neighborhood in a way that his father would have found gratifying.

Zeckendorf's frequent partners were a mix of those who had also been burned, and of new blood. On WorldWide Plaza, for instance, they included the Stanton and Elmaleh families, who had initially made money in such other enterprises as automobile dealerships; a Japanese company; and Arthur Cohen. The Japanese were interested — as were many foreigners — because New York was a safe haven for their wealth, and the United States was a place where capitalism was less hampered by governmental strictures than almost anywhere else in the world. Cohen's billion-dollar Arlen Realty company, whose holdings once included Olympic Tower across from St. Patrick's Cathedral and the E. J. Korvette chain, had made one of the more spectacular nosedives in the late 1970s, his difficulties exacerbated by participation with the Tishmans on 1166 Sixth Avenue, and with Goldman-DiLorenzo on other properties. Cohen had wandered in the desert — paid off his debts by means of a series of co-op conversions in the outer boroughs — and returned to development, but with a difference. Now he took what he described as "solid, functional partners" who could keep their eye on properties in his stead. In his alliances with Zeckendorf, sometimes Cohen would take the lead-developer position and sometimes Bill would; often, they were joined by other scarred warriors, such as Zev Wolfson, son of the man who'd developed the Pan Am building. In meetings, one consultant observed, "these guys argue over architectural models and plans as if they are boys fighting over how to arrange toy building blocks, and as little willing to listen to reasons why they can't make their structures fantastically high."

Partnerships were a terrific way to allow the next generation to learn how to take risks while providing them with a safety net. On a new luxury apartment building on West 72nd Street and Broadway, the Zeckendorf organization joined forces with one headed by Peter Malkin, Larry Wien's son-in-law; this arrangement permitted the third generation of each family to oversee the project. Bill's son William Lie Zeckendorf and Peter's son Tony donned hardhats and rode up the shaky construction elevator to stand atop the highest concrete floor when it was still open to the sky. Their fathers' organizational names were on the project, but it belonged to them. A broker on the project tried to go around Tony and reach his father directly about a minor matter; learning about the call,

Tony phoned the broker from an airplane to squelch the attempt at finessing him.

Intergenerational transitions were in process all over town. While Lincoln Center was mounting a tribute to Fred Rose for his work with the cultural institution — he now spent three-quarters of his time on charitable and civic endeavors — his son Jonathan was picking up the social-agenda torch and transforming it to reflect his own passions. Jonathan championed a mixed-use project called Atlantic Center in downtown Brooklyn, 643 condominium townhouses for moderate-income families, and 1.9 million square feet of office space to help underwrite the homes. His other projects included housing sponsored by the Educational Alliance for homeless elderly people and drug abusers, and Tibbett Gardens, a showcase for a partnership of REBNY and the city's housing department. Both the latter and the Atlantic Center project became bogged down with bureaucracy and cost overruns and seemed as if they would take forever to come to fruition.

Maybe development was becoming a game open only to the young or to those who didn't know the meaning of delay. A project that would take a dozen years to complete instead of a dozen months no longer appealed to men in late middle age. The lead time for all new projects grew, especially where they involved the government or were seen as potentially destructive of Manhattan's heritage. Peter Kalikow's attempt to remove one of the old City and Suburban Homes projects and put up a new apartment skyscraper seemed as if it would be sidetracked permanently by community opposition and by the Landmarks Preservation Commission. Jeffrey Glick's project for a large multiuse development near the 59th Street bridge in Manhattan was similarly stalled, but he was a young man, industry wags said, and emotionally as well as financially could afford to wait. With each design change, the projects seemed to become less daring and innovative. A horse designed by committee is a camel; many feared that a skyscraper designed by community boards, city agencies, and nervous financial lenders would be mediocre, at best.

As developing skyscrapers in Manhattan became ever more difficult, some of the established powers turned their energies and resources away from the builder's dream. Though blocked in one arena, they were nonetheless energetic and among the very wealthiest people in the country, and could use the skills they had acquired in pursuit of skyscrapers to advantage in other fields. Sam LeFrak had been in various businesses for years, including entertainment; he was fond of saying, "A song is easier to manage than a building, and it doesn't have to be painted every two years." He was also in gas and oil, and by the 1980s made as much money from his non-building projects as he did from his properties. The Fishers, another old-line builder family, bid successfully with the Getty heirs for control of a midwestern manufacturing firm; Donald Trump bought an airline, the former Eastern Shuttle; the Milsteins took over the United Fruit company and the Emigrant Savings Bank in New York; Dick Ravitch teamed with the Tisches and investor Warren Buffett to buy the Bowery Savings Bank in New York for $100 million, and sold it two years later for $200 million. Such investments seemed more immediately lucrative and a lot easier than fighting the city bureaucracy, community opposition, and all the other factors that made it so arduous to erect new skyscrapers in Manhattan. For the past hundred years, due to the seemingly continual nature of skyscraper construction, there had been a saying in New York: "This will be a great city if they ever get it finished." Maybe that ending day was approaching, because the skyscraper dreamers were looking elsewhere for fulfillment.

Friday, May 13, 1988, was the deadline for the most frantic burst of construction Manhattan had seen for quite some time. On that day, the last of the Koch-era bonuses came to an end. Only those midtown skyscrapers whose foundations had been poured by Friday the Thirteenth would be allowed 20 percent more bulk than usually permitted under the zoning laws, a bonus that could enormously enhance the new structures. The area west of Rockefeller Center, from 42nd Street and Times Square to 57th Street, became an endless traffic jam of cranes, flatbed trucks, concrete mixers, pedestrian bridges, and construction trailers. There were going to be eleven new office buildings and four hotels, more office space than in the entire city of Pittsburgh. Since the stock-market debacle of October 1987, two buildings originally conceived as office towers had been redesigned as hotels — but were too far along in the development process to be entirely scrapped.

City inspectors toting cameras and notebooks visited the major construction sites on that day. There was the twenty-four-story new headquarters of United States Trust building at 114 West 47th Street, done by the Durst family, mostly to enable Douglas Durst and other third-generation members of the family to get their feet wet. The inspectors didn't have to bother with that one; following Seymour's precepts, it was built "as of right," without benefit of incentives, and as a result of not having to go through applications for variances was further ahead in the race for completion than the others — and smaller. Seymour himself was preoccupied with plans to erect atop one of the smaller properties on 42nd Street and Sixth Avenue a huge "national debt clock" that would inform each American precisely how much of the country's enormous debt his family owed, an effective way of making passersby think about an important issue. There was the new Rudin building, at the corner of Broadway and 52nd Street; Billy Rudin, in his early thirties, was point man for this one. "It's so successful it's dull," Lew told inquiring reporters.

Several of the fifteen buildings — though not the Rudin one — had been designed by Emery Roth & Sons, the firm now under the direction of Richard Roth, Jr., and including members of the fourth generation of Roths. The young Roths wished to design a building for the fourth corner of 57th Street and Park Avenue, because the first three generations had each done a building on the other corners. The firm was now ninety years old and Dick Roth was involved in skyscraper projects all around the world, including one close to his heart, in Budapest. The commission on that one "wouldn't buy me a meal at Lutèce," he admitted, but it did take the Roths back to the family's roots; shortly, Dick Roth would have under contract a dozen of the largest buildings ever constructed in Hungary. Several more of the fifteen buildings in midtown were designed by men who had worked for Emery Roth & Sons and gone on to form successful architectural practices of their own.

Bill Zeckendorf, Jr., had several partners on what was billed as New York's tallest hotel, the Royal Concordia, to go up at 154 West 54th Street. Who, now, remembered that his father had once pledged to build Manhattan's tallest hostelry? Zeckendorf also had three other projects in the area, including a second hotel on Broadway and 49th Street, and the mixed-use WorldWide Plaza project further west, on the site of the old Madison Square Garden. The Rockefeller Center project on the corner of 49th Street and Seventh Avenue deliberately did not pass; without a major tenant in tow, the center's management had decided not to rush to make the deadline, and the site was kept cleared though vacant. Larry Silverstein's hotel, intended to rise over the landmarked Palace Theater at Broadway and 47th Street, did not pass, but was given an extension; in a power move less than a month earlier, a special resolution had been passed by the Board of Estimate providing a one-year extension of the bonus to anyone building on a site on which a landmarked theater took up more than half the space. So far, Silverstein was the sole beneficiary of that measure.

There was Harry Macklowe's hotel, finally getting built after years of punctilious delays by the city. Macklowe had recently completed the tallest apartment building in town, Metropolitan Tower, which dwarfed Carnegie Hall, and was doing another, smaller apartment building on West 55th Street. Macklowe had mounted a large public relations effort to demonstrate how wonderful his new projects were — and to erase from the public's mind his association with the demolition disaster on 44th Street that was now receding into the past. Across the street from Macklowe's tower, and not as outwardly extravagant, was Burt Resnick's equally luxurious mixed-use building, where separate entrances served office and apartment tenants.

After this rush of midtown foundation-pouring, very few new building projects were begun in Manhattan. As the current ones were completed and searched for tenants, the outcry again rose that Manhattan was glutted with too much office space, too many hotel rooms, and too many luxury apartments. Once again, as at the end of the 1920s and the end of the 1960s, supply had outpaced demand. Maybe the down part of the cycle would be short, and there would soon be another boom. But some people wondered: How many skyscrapers could New York City support?

At about the same time, in the spring of 1988, several hundred guests in tuxedos and ball gowns rode the special elevators at 30 Rockefeller Center to the Rainbow Room on the sixty-fifth floor to take part in a quiet though festive event that, as with the certification of fifteen skyscrapers on a single day, similarly marked an end and a beginning. Walking through the corridor with its startling glass-and-mahogany columns, guests headed for the grand ballroom and the ninetieth-anniversary celebration of Tishman Realty & Construction. Ninety years ago, the young immigrant Julius Tishman had built his first tenement on the Lower East Side. Tonight, his grandson John Tishman was giving a party.

The Rainbow Room had recently been restored to its Art Deco glory. The two-story-high, domed ceiling gleamed; muted blue, green, red, and amber lights played off an enormous crystal teardrop chandelier and the gold leaf that edged the room. New additions were faithful to the style of 1934, the year when the room had first opened: etched-glass friezes of Bakelite radios on the walls, architect Hugh Hardy's highly stylized geometric abstractions woven into the carpets and other furnishings, hand-crafted cabinetry and inlaid woods. The sons and grandsons of some of the original craftsmen had worked under the overall direction of the Tishman construction firm to make the room a nostalgic jewel.

Some of the guests stepped outside or to the windows, because this was one of the best places from which to view the city's skyline. Craning a neck downward, one could see immediately north some mostly dark and low spots, the places where Tishman was serving as construction manager for six of the fifteen new skyscraper projects. In a year there would be fifteen giants nearby. Larry Silverstein could point out his, David Durst his, Bill Zeckendorf his, Bruce Eichner his; all were guests at the event, chatting with one another over cocktails and dinner.

A congratulatory tribute about the anniversary had been read into the *Congressional Record,* and there were echoing proclamations from the city and state governments. Mayor Ed Koch and City Council president Andrew Stein came by to shake hands with host John Tishman, as did Manhattan Borough President David Dinkins. Former mayor Robert Wagner and his wife, old acquaintances of John Tishman's, stayed through dinner. Though there were many politicians and a great many wealthy people in attendance, along with plenty of newspaper and magazine writers, very little publicity surrounded the event; photographer Steve Friedman snapped everyone in sight. There was Dan Rose chatting with labor consultant Ted Kheel, perhaps joshing him about recently catching the development bug; Kheel was building a resort in Costa Rica. Both Dan and Bob Tisch could only stay for cocktails. Peter Malkin was there with his wife and his current partner in development, Bruce Warwick. There were the Elmalehs and Stantons at one table, smiling for the photographer with their wives and sons and daughters-in-law; as World Wide Holdings, the two families did everything together.

Chancellors and presidents of New York University, Barnard, Carnegie Hall, the New School, the YMHA and YWHA, Sloan-Kettering Memorial Hospital, and other institutions ate and drank and danced through the evening. Tishman was personally involved in these organizations and had done construction and redevelopment work for them, as well. Morgan Stanley, Bankers Trust, Metropolitan Life, Equitable Life, Merrill Lynch, J. P. Morgan, First Boston, Goldman Sachs, and Lazard Frères were all represented by high officials. A sprinkling of distinguished architects (James Stewart Polshek, Shelly Fox and Gene Kohn, Donald Smith of Skidmore, Owings & Merrill) mingled with the developers and bankrollers of their new commissions. It was a convivial crowd, people who knew one another through their dozens of overlapping relationships in business, cultural, educational, charitable, and political endeavors. All understood how to behave and were not inclined to upstage the man of the hour.

The event was a triumph for John Tishman, a vindication of the course he had chosen. Ten years earlier, from the chaos of the dissolving old company, he had engineered the sale of his own division to Rockefeller Center. He had never been happy under the Rockefeller Center, Inc., umbrella; for one thing, the Cushman & Wakefield brokerage people had had the effrontery to tell him that they knew as much about construction as he did (shades of the last argument between Paul and Ted Starrett, a half-century earlier); for another, the Rockefeller Center managers would not let Tishman and his fellow construction executives participate monetarily in the center's development projects, as Tishman had been used to doing in the old family firm. By 1980, John Tishman and three other executives had bought back the firm and its old name and logo, and their enterprise was now many times larger than it had been during the few years with Rockefeller Center.

John had more than justified his release from Rockefeller bondage; he had obtained great satisfaction in reinventing the old family firm after its previous principals, his cousins Alan and John, had left it in the dust. It was a delightful resolution to the old two-lobbies separation. John and his construction-company partners had become as successful as his cousins, and in some of the same fields. In areas outside of New York, the construction firm was a developer, just as Bob and Alan were; John's partners in development included the Disney Company and the Aoki Company of Japan, both also represented here tonight. If John developed nothing in New York City, it was out of deference to the Dursts, Zeckendorfs, Roses, and Silverstein, who frequently hired his firm to do their construction work.

Although relations between Bob and John Tishman had not always been smooth, Bob had come to the anniversary tonight, together with his secretary of many years, Marie Mose, who still had many friends at Tishman Realty. John's firm had built the first new Tishman-Speyer skyscraper, at 520 Madison, but, as one family member recalls, "there had been a sufficient level of heads knocking against one another" on that job that after it there were no further collaborations. Another consequence of the separate growth of the three new firms was that Bob Tishman and Jerry Speyer had employed Alan's firm to manage their properties at first, then later, as the Tishman-Speyer empire expanded, terminated that arrangement and managed their own buildings. Tishman-Speyer was now in the very top rank of American developers, with projects from New York to Beijing, their buildings worth many billions of dollars; next week they would publicly announce their purchase (with Trammell Crow) of the building that the Urises had once erected, the J. C. Penney skyscraper on Sixth Avenue. Speyer had the personal satisfaction of beginning what would be the tallest skyscraper in Europe, the Messeturm, in Frankfurt; his father had been forced to flee Frankfurt fifty years earlier. The elder Speyer was too ill to travel with Jerry to the ground-breaking ceremonies, but Jerry brought him back a videotape of the proceedings, including effusive tributes from city officials. Jerry, who had succeeded his friend Silverstein as chairman of REBNY, was out of town on the night of John's party, and so was Alan Tishman. Alan was in the process of completing the sale of one of his four companies to a division of the Shearson Lehman Hutton Group of $20 million; he had earlier sold another for a similar price.

Like Daniel Burnham a hundred years earlier, these family chieftains made no little plans, and if at this celebration they were not surrounded by the greatest artisans of the age and they did not quaff champagne from massive loving cups of silver, as had the titans of the Gilded Age in their long-ago dinner atop the first Madison Square Garden, they still reveled in the best that Manhattan had to offer. The Rainbow Room was a citadel of nostalgia, the elegance of New York made new once more, a fitting setting for this quiet celebration. Waiters in burgundy-colored suits and captains in champagne-toned tuxedos served the room. The china on the silver-lamé tablecloths was designed by Milton Glaser and architect Robert A. M. Stern; Glaser's were more colorful and Stern's were gray, black, and white. Cigars and cigarettes were offered by two young women in pink pillbox hats, sailor blouses, and mesh stockings.

John's old mentor, Paul Tishman, was there with his wife; at eighty-six Paul was the last surviving brother of the older generation, deaf now, and very frail. Norman's two daughters and their husbands were separated from their father's old competitor, sitting at a table full of bankers, but John's son Dan and his wife sat with Paul. Dan was a small contractor in Maine, and despite his choice of business, "I don't think he wants to come into the firm," John confides. Well, the younger generation valued independence. "It's nearly impossible to keep a family firm going for more than two generations," Bob opines. "Centrifugal force eventually whirls the youngsters away," giving them new and different interests that elders could counter only to the detriment of their personal ties to their children and grandchildren. In the old days, the patriarch called the tune and the younger generation danced; now, Bob muses, "I have to telephone my grandchildren myself and make arrangements" for outings and family celebrations.

Each of the three Tishman cousins' companies were worth twenty or thirty times what the family's net wealth had been a decade earlier, when they had split up the empire. What an enormous company they might have now, if it had been possible for them all to grow together! But, of course, it hadn't been possible. A glance around the room showed that families such as the Tishmans were no longer solely dominant on the Manhattan skyscraper scene, though they were still major forces. Pension funds, huge insurance companies, and consortiums of institutions with great financial resources were the most important elements in development now, and many of the families — including the three Tishman organizations — had become what Dan Rose calls "the development arms of large institutions."

Broadway pianist Michael Feinstein played the melodies of the hard years while the thirty-two-foot-diameter, raised dance floor with its inlaid compass-rose pattern of maple and fumed oak revolved slowly to give dancers an ever-changing view of Manhattan's nighttime skyline. Floor-to-ceiling mirrors and windows combined to bring all the skyscrapers into focus from the very best angle — near their crested tops. From here you could see the gleaming lights of the newest spires, Metropolitan Tower, Trump Tower, and Olympic Tower; the many skyscrapers of the World Trade Center and the World Financial Center downtown; the Empire State Building; the Chrysler Building; and other familiar midtown colossi.

The skyscrapers seemed close enough to touch, and from this

vantage point and in this company you could feel the aspirations to beauty and the compromises to hard-headed business sense that had combined to create those luminous points of the city's crown. A mile to the south of the Empire State Building lay St. Vincent's Hospital, one wing built with gifts from the profits of the Empire State, donated by Al Smith and John J. Raskob. East toward the East River was a bedpan alley of hospitals similarly linked to the skyscrapers through generations of donors from Louis Jay Horowitz to Harry Helmsley; to the north shone the glitter of Lincoln Center, also a particular beneficiary of builder largesse. Viewed through the long lens of time, it was clear that the business skyscrapers that symbolized New York City were the main conduit by which wealth flowed from the inhabitants of the apartments and offices to the institutions that humanized and civilized the city.

The creators of so many of the skyscrapers, the dynastic families represented by the Tishmans and their friends and clients who were celebrating this night, maintained their sway in New York not alone through ownership of property, but because they had evolved into a respected elite. Elected officials sought their counsel; civic and charitable institutions had been given into their care. Billions of dollars from millions of people in the form of pension funds, insurance premiums, and college endowments were entrusted to their instincts and expertise. The symbols of the city depended on their taste and vision. The growth and transfiguration of their family businesses set the pattern for newer empires, while their standards of ethics, decorum, philanthropy, and commitment to the metropolis became the measure of new aspirants to the oligarchy of those who build and control Manhattan's skyscraper dreams.

Epilogue

Waiting for Good Times

MANY NEW SKYSCRAPERS were in the last stages of construction as David Dinkins took office as mayor of New York, in January of 1990, but the clutter of blocked sidewalks and rising superstructures belied the state of health of New York and its skyscraper dreams. In an action little noticed at the time, that January the dying investment banking firm of Drexel Burnham Lambert gave back the keys to a hundred thousand square feet in a Brooklyn building and then did the same with several hundred thousand more square feet of space near Wall Street. The purveyor of junk bonds and the employer of indicted financier Michael Milken, Drexel Burnham Lambert was one of the earliest casualties of the October 1987 stock market crash.

In retrospect, New York's skyscraper builders understood that crash as the beginning of the end of the good times of the 1980s. For a while, they had simply refused to believe that. The huge, shiny, costly skyscrapers of Manhattan seemed so solid and desirable that everyone had a hard time believing these structures would not soon shrug off the effects of a temporary dip in the Dow Jones average and return to economic health.

As with the crash of 1929, whose full effects were not felt until 1931 and later, the consequences of the smaller though still significant crash of 1987 took a while to reverberate through the economy. Yes, the Dursts had to scrap plans for a new headquarters for Morgan Stanley, but in 1988 and 1989, many leases had just been signed, loans arranged, and contracts for construction of those fifteen skyscrapers in west midtown let. As 1990 wore on and the nation slipped into recession, real estaters experienced setback after setback: a major tenant did not renew a lease; a source of funding dried up or made demands that could not be met; the prices of apartments fell as Wall Street firms fired or cut the salaries of their employees.

The growth of the financial-services industry had been the main engine of the boom; now its decline crippled the city's real estate industry. Initially, the savings and loan crisis that engulfed the rest of the country had left New York City virtually intact; as the new decade wore on, however, that crisis and its attendant credit crunch came to compromise the value of the city's icons. A man whose buildings were worth $500 million one month shortly discovered that because of a countrywide decline in prices he could not sell those buildings for $350 million. The city itself was in jeopardy, needing more income lest it slide into the sort of fiscal crisis that had characterized the bad days of near-default — and so increased property taxes were announced, an action that raised the cost of owning buildings. Beneficiaries of past tax breaks, such as AT&T, announced their intention of moving out of part of their midtown headquarters, calling into question the viability of tax breaks to encourage development just as the Real Estate Board of New York proposed new incentives to recharge the city's economy. The value of all the buildings in the city slipped more than 7 percent in a year by official count, and industry count put the figure at double that amount.

Skyscraper builders were in a slough of despond and could not reasonably predict when they or their buildings would emerge from it. Back in the bad days of the mid-1970s, one empty building each had nearly sunk the Tishman and Rudin empires. Of the fifteen buildings whose foundations were finished by Friday the Thirteenth in May of 1988, four stood empty in 1990, and others in the Wall Street area were also vacant. Sixty-one million square feet of office space was unoccupied, the equivalent of six "twin towers" of the World Trade Center, of 120 half-million-square-foot buildings, of all the office towers constructed in Manhattan in the previous decade. "At 175 square feet of space per office worker, that means the city needs more than 300,000 new jobs to fill that vacant office space," Dan Rose observed. Where would those come from, he wondered, when unemployment was on the rise, and New York as a region had already lost one-quarter of all the jobs that had recently disappeared in the whole country?

As the value of the real estate fell, the most notable descent was that of the man who had been the most visible of the developers:

Donald Trump. For the high-flying Trump, disasters came in pairs. His marriage and his empire crumbled at the same time. Both had been in trouble for a while, and the public nature of the disasters — divorce and a change in the ownership structure of his properties — was only the final acknowledgment of the irreversibility of the decline.

It was all a matter of perception. "Cash is king," Trump said to interviewers when the first reports of his difficulties surfaced. But in real estate, leverage, not cash, was of the essence. That was what had allowed Trump to put up his buildings, to buy an airline and a yacht. Now leverage came back to haunt him, as it had done to Bill Zeckendorf, Sr., in his time. Trump had bought properties by convincing the banks and insurance companies that the properties would increase in value because the Trump name was associated with them. It spoke volumes about the gullibility of lenders that they had gone along with Trump's belief — but when the income from his properties could not service the debts, and no buyers could be found because actual values had decreased, the banks demanded what they were owed. Hardheaded industry experts put the true current value of the Plaza Hotel in the $400–$500 million range (the amount of the hotel's indebtedness); Trump listed it as an asset of $800 million. When a gambling-industry analyst dared to say that Trump's Taj Mahal casino in Atlantic City would lose money, Trump's furor served to force the analyst's company to fire him, though his predictions were soon borne out by the casino's operating figures. Trump threatened to sue anyone who said that his new luxury apartments at Trump Plaza on the Upper East Side were in trouble, but New York State's attorney general soon forbade him to sell further units in the building. Trump had crowed that people would fly his shuttle airline because of the amenities that the public knew would be associated with the Trump name; a year after purchasing the Eastern Shuttle, however, Trump admitted that even his magic could not raise the airline's share of passenger traffic past the level of that of the nearest competitor. Trump said he was worth several billions; *Forbes* magazine first wrote that his fortune was under a billion dollars, and then downgraded that into the negative column, saying that Trump's debts were larger than his assets.

In restructuring actions that lasted through 1990, banks agreed to loan Trump extra money in exchange for fiscal control of his empire; henceforth, until his debts were paid down, he would make no decisions without the counsel of bank-appointed financial advisers. Indignity was added to public indignity: Trump was put on a budget for personal expenses; the yacht would have to go; the Mar A Lago estate in Florida would have to be partitioned off and sold for development. Trump was still in charge — but only in the sense that the Queen of England was that country's leader: Trump was a figurehead without any real power over his own enterprises.

In March 1991, a compromise between Trump and community groups was announced, under the terms of which the proposed Trump City over the West Side railyards would be scaled back to half the size earlier envisioned. The 150-story tower disappeared from the plan, and so did the Trump name. Henceforth, the development would be known as Riverside South, and Trump said that rather than developing the entire parcel himself, he would sell parts of it to others.

All over the country, megadevelopers were hurting. Atlanta's John Portman met with his creditors; the Reichmann empire — New York's largest commercial landlord — was reorganized; the Trammel Crow partnerships of Dallas experienced difficulties; Daniel Galbreath of Columbus, Ohio, saw the empire that had been built by his father come apart. "The parade of major developers through our offices is continuous," says a lawyer in a New York firm that specializes in "work-outs," or arrangements in which a property owner and his mortgage holders renegotiate their agreements. "Every week, another man on the *Forbes* 400 list shows up." Also in March 1991, third-generation developer Peter Kalikow was reported in negotiations to restructure nearly a billion dollars' worth of skyscraper debt. And in April it was the Helmsleys who were "downsizing." As the downtown lingered on and on, the evidence about who was hurting and who would be able to survive began to show patterns.

In the Great Depression, the most active builders of the 1920s — French, Mandel, Lefcourt, Chanin — became the biggest casualties. In 1990, those in New York who had been the most active in the latter part of the 1980s, and who were the most recent aspirants to the oligarchy, were reported to be hurting the most. Bill Zeckendorf, Jr.'s current projects included several of the fifteen big midtown buildings. Financial problems overtook one of the hotels and curtailed the leasing of other properties; he sold his interest in the hotel and negotiated to sell portions of his other properties to the Japanese. He would survive the downturn, insiders said, but they pointed out a curious irony. Zeckendorf, Sr., a big plunger, had paid the price of overleveraging. The son was more cautious; he was said to have avoided the big mistakes of his father by the technique of participating in projects only with partners — but he was also reputed to have avoided the sort of big successes that his father had once had, because this Zeckendorf took his money out of profitable ventures too soon and therefore did not realize maximum profits from them.

Zeckendorf and Larry Silverstein were allied (with shopping center developer Mel Simon) in the reconstruction of a big department store at the former site of Gimbel's at Herald Square, and in the construction of stores, offices, and apartments on the site of another former Gimbel's store, at 86th Street and Lexington Avenue. Cost overruns and bad timing compromised both projects. Articles about Zeckendorf blamed the difficulties on Silverstein's supervision of the construction; the men were said not to be speaking to one another. Silverstein's largest gamble, 7 World Trade Center, in the vicinity of Wall Street, was 20 percent vacant in the aftermath of the stock market crash, and Silverstein and his prime lender, the General Electric Pension Fund, tried to sell the midtown Embassy Suites hotel just before it opened, in the late fall of 1990, but failed to receive an acceptable bid. While Silverstein denied rumors that his cash flow had diminished to the point that he was hurting, the characteristically ebullient redhead was not as visible in public as he once had been.

Silverstein and his former brother-in-law, Bernard Mendik, had pursued different paths since their parting. Mendik did not develop new buildings but rather redeveloped old buildings. Near the end of the decade, Mendik bought Lincoln Towers and eleven other buildings in the city in a partnership with Equitable Life and Martin Raynes, head of a very successful co-op conversion and management firm and one of the great success stories of the 1980s. As the market for co-ops fell precipitously, major converters such as Raynes and Time Equities got into difficulties: they held far too many apartments that they could not sell and would not permit to be sold at distressed prices lest those sales force the market down even further. Raynes's empire all but disappeared. Mendik took over Raynes's portion of Lincoln Towers, the complex built by Bill Zeckendorf, Sr., and the Raynes management firm was absorbed by developer Harry Macklowe.

In retrospect, the disaster that had befallen Macklowe in the wake of his tearing down the SRO hotel on 44th Street in 1985 could even be seen as salutary. Although it had transferred to Macklowe the "bad boy" label that Sol Goldman had previously worn, this debacle also seemed to impress on Macklowe the need to rein in his more reckless impulses. In 1990, he had one problem — a medium-sized building on West 55th Street that was only 20 percent full — but because of his change of focus, as the bad times overtook the real estate industry of New York, Macklowe's fortunes took a curious upswing. At long last the courts ruled that the city had been derelict in its actions in regard to his too-quick demolition of the 44th Street site and forced it to return $3.2 million that he had paid as compensation for the SRO. This happened at just about the time when the new Hotel Macklowe was opening to praise from architectural critics. With a firm income stream from twenty buildings nationwide, Macklowe was able to pick up a faltering management concern for a very low price. Testament to his refurbished image came at the final meeting of New York's Board of Estimate, when a longtime foe of skyscraper development, Manhattan Borough President Ruth Messinger, championed a new Macklowe project on the West Side, helping it to win approval by the board.

That last Board of Estimate meeting in the late summer of 1990 featured a face-off between preservationists and a developer who knew his way around city politics. At stake was the City and Suburban Homes complex at 79th Street, close to the East River. For more than a decade the site had been controlled by *New York Post* owner Peter Kalikow, who wanted to tear down the old buildings and erect residential skyscrapers. The Landmarks Preservation Commission had designated the site a landmark because of its historical importance: at the turn of the century, it had been the largest complex of low-income housing in the world. The Board of Estimate had never overturned and only seldom modified a Landmarks recommendation, but Kalikow relentlessly lobbied the politicians to have the designation quashed. At three in the morning of August 23, 1990, the borough presidents of Queens, Brooklyn, the Bronx, and Staten Island carried the board's vote over the objections of Mayor Dinkins and Manhattan officials, for a compromise to permit four of the fourteen buildings to be demolished.

The chairwoman of the Landmarks Preservation Commission said this ruling sent "a very bad signal to the City Council that our designations can be negotiated." But actually, developers' projects in all sections of Manhattan were being attacked and delayed by community groups and preservationists almost as much as they were being hampered by the glut of available space and other depressed market conditions.

The Milsteins complained of being hampered in just such a way on a project they had redesigned a half-dozen times for a site near the South Street Seaport. But were the wealthy Milsteins really hurting from such setbacks, or not? One day there was a notice that the Milsteins had defaulted on the $100 million mortgage for the Normandie Court residential complex on the Upper East Side. The strange thing was that the Normandie Court was 97 percent rented, usually a sign of health; the difficulty was that rents had been lowered to prevent tenants from leaving in droves. A month later, the Milsteins acquired two failing real estate brokerage and management concerns, just as Macklowe had. How could they buy when they were "walking away" from some properties? In a time of difficulties, the Milsteins were doing for themselves what they had attempted to do with the falling Uris empire: getting out from under failing properties in order to maintain and enhance the health of the rest of the family's holdings.

Mentioned along with the Milsteins' troubles were those of the LeFraks, in Newport City, across the Hudson River from Wall Street. The LeFraks defaulted on a mortgage of $150 million that covered four residential towers. Comment from the company came not from Sam, the habitual announcer of good news, but from his son Richard, who placed the blame for the debacle on the "loss of jobs in the financial community." LeFrak also emphasized that this was an isolated problem, and that those projects personally financed by the LeFrak family or by the corporate entity remained unaffected.

It was more evidence that the longest-lived of the empires were surviving the terribly depressed market by being tough and by relying on their great resources. If not exactly thriving, they were suffering their losses and hunkering down. "Dave Rose started in this business with a work-out for a mortgage holder," Dan Rose recalls, "and that's what we're doing today." Because of their longevity and track record of never defaulting on a building, the Roses started receiving management contracts from banks and other lenders on other developers' foreclosed properties. As in previous downturns, the Roses shelved development plans in order to concentrate on the management side of the business. They pulled back on the conversion of the Sheffield on West 57th Street into a condominium building, but continued with similar conversions of their other apartment towers. "Dan's more optimistic than I am," Fred muses, "but that's because he's at a different point in the life cycle."

The fates were not being kind to the Rudins. Drexel Burnham Lambert failed while it was the sole tenant in a Rudin building near Wall Street, and no new tenant for that building could be found until asbestos-insulation removal had been completed, at a cost of $70 million, five times what it had to cost to erect the building in the first place. But a family whose resources amounted to more than a billion dollars could make such a renovation. Among the midtown skyscrapers that were gaping empty or only half-tenanted, the Rudins' new one was well rented. During the downturn, the Rudin family called in their markers. At a time when leases were being broken and large companies were considering leaving the city, Lew Rudin persuaded Mayor Dinkins, whom he had long supported, to attend a ceremony for the renewal of two long-term leases for big companies at the Rudin headquarters at 345 Park Avenue. When a spate of articles in the *New York Times* suggested that these were tough times for all developers, Rudin denounced this conclusion as bad for the city and called for a more balanced reportorial approach; shortly thereafter, an article with just such a balance was published.

For Bob Tishman, the fact that the newer developers were more affected by the downturn than the older families was evidence of the distinction he drew between those who "did it by the numbers" — that is, those who put up buildings because it was possible to finance them — and "the real builders," who committed their resources to a new building only when they were convinced that it would be economically viable in the long term. There had been entirely too many skyscrapers erected in the 1980s because the money had been available; now they had glutted the market, and everyone was suffering. Tishman-Speyer shut down most of its development plans for the New York area, but continued to look for opportunities elsewhere. A crisis loomed in the fall of 1990 when Equitable Life, one of Tishman's oldest partners, made plans to abandon 1515 Broadway.

Even though the building was close to fully rented, and even though Equitable itself had more than $12 billion in real estate assets, Equitable told Tishman-Speyer that it was going to file for bankruptcy on 1515 Broadway. The building was losing money each year — but that had been expected. Contrary to Bob's principles, this one had been done by the numbers in the early days of Tishman-Speyer. It had been designed as a tax shelter. The problem was that shortly after it opened, a change in the tax laws somewhat compromised its viability. In 1990, remembering the time when the Tishmans had defaulted on 1166 Sixth Avenue, an action that had led to the splitting up of the old family firm, both Bob Tishman and Jerry Speyer refused to be associated with the failure of this new building. They sold their 20-percent portion of it back to Equitable for just ten dollars and considered themselves lucky. A few weeks later, in a move that stunned the smaller, limited partners, Equitable filed for bankruptcy. The smaller fry stood to lose most of the $77 million they had invested in the building and were bitter that Equitable seemed to have shown no interest in trying to renegotiate the mortgage on the project. Shortly, the prime lender, Manufacturers Hanover, filed a suit against Equitable that was eventually settled out of court. There were no winners on 1515 Broadway, only a lot of losers.

John Tishman's construction company, active nationwide and also overseas, was so affected by the downturn that it aggressively sought the sort of contracts it had earlier let pass — prisons, public buildings, renovations. While most private developers put off ambitious plans, Tishman Realty & Construction firmed up its alliances with the Disney Company and the Aoki Company of Japan on joint projects including hotels in Puerto Rico, Florida, Chicago, California, and Osaka.

Other nonfamily Tishman employees began talking to John's son Dan about his entering the firm. Dan had been a teacher and then had joined the man who had constructed his house in a small contracting business in Maine. But Dan wanted to continue his outdoors life-style and did not want to work in an office dominated by his father. "I refused to become involved in the negotiations," John says, because he felt that if he asked Dan directly, Dan might say no. John was mindful of his own youth, when he had prided himself on being the only Tishman son not pushed to enter the firm. After a year of talking, the employees persuaded Dan that he could continue to live in Maine and work for Tishman Realty & Construction in the Boston office — which pleased John as much as did the firm's ability to stay healthy in a depressed market. It provided even more of an incentive for working to see that the firm and the family survived until the good times returned.

The old dynasties understood more than ever the reasons behind the caution with which they approached the erecting of new buildings even in the best of times, behind the unostentatious life-styles they embraced, behind their deep commitment to the health of the city as well as to their own fortunes, behind the emphasis on family and continuity that had carried an earlier generation through the hard years of the 1930s and seasoned the current generation of family leaders in the near-default years of the 1970s. They held long-term views and had the resources and the obligations necessary to sustain such views. In five years, or surely in ten, the towers of New York would regain and even enhance their value, and developers and owners would look back on the bad years of the early 1990s as a rite of passage and a maturation experience for their heirs. The perpetuation of the dynasty required not only realizing structures in concrete, but also insuring the next generation's right to imagine and create ever greater skyscraper dreams.

Acknowledgments

Research for this book was conducted at the Avery Library of Columbia University, various Harvard University libraries, the New-York Historical Society, the New York Public Library, New York University's Bobst Library and its Real Estate Institute's Jack Brause Library, and the library of the Real Estate Board of New York, all of which institutions I thank for their cooperation.

I received gracious help from agents Mel Berger and Pam Bernstein, research associate Laura Buckley, editors Frederica Friedman and Perdita Burlingame, and especially from my wife, Harriet Shelare, and my two sons, Noah and Daniel, all of whom suffered through my obsession with the city and its builders for the past several years.

This book could not have been written without the cooperation of many of the families, for there are relatively few written materials or records of their accomplishments and travails. From 1988 to 1991, I conducted interviews with Jane Uris Bayard, Philip Birnbaum, Seymour Durst, Irving Fischer, Jay Gould, Fred Gould, John Halpern, Maurice Hexter, Melvyn and Robert Kaufman, Sam LeFrak, Peter Malkin, Bernard Mendik, V. J. "Jimmy" Peters, Richard Ravitch, Burt Resnick, Daniel Rose, Frederick Rose, Jonathan Rose, Julian Roth, Richard Roth, Jr., Lewis Rudin, Larry Silverstein, Jerry Speyer, Roger Starr, Alan Tishman, John Tishman, Robert Tishman, and Charles Urstadt. I wish to express my thanks to them for their candor and assistance, and to the many other people in the field whom I interviewed but who preferred anonymity.

Index

Horowitz, Saul (J. R.), Jr., 249, 250, 277, 278
Horowitz family, 56, 280
Hotel Belleclaire, 79
Hotel Macklowe, 334
House and Garden, 187
housing:
  low-income, 23, 31, 77, 121, 144, 148–149, 157, 242, 247, 250, 278, 279
  luxury, 18–19, 23, 40, 77, 102, 107, 108, 110–111, 112, 122, 131–132, 142, 144, 295, 309, 313, 318–319, 323
  middle-income, 23, 31, 239, 247, 250, 266–267, 278, 313, 317, 318–319, 320
  residential, 102–105, 196, 228–229, 294
  slum, 10, 63, 65, 148–149, 198, 228, 246, 267, 274
  see also apartments, apartment houses
Howells, John Mead, 133
Howells, William Dean, 53
HRH, 105, 130–131, 161, 162–163, 167, 249–250, 277, 278, 279–280, 287, 311
Humphrey, Burt, 111
Hunt, Richard Morris, 42, 52, 53, 78

IBM, 300
immigrants:
  as cheap labor, 83, 85–86
  Italian, 69–70, 81
  Jewish, 56, 61–73, 81, 101
  self-education of, 44, 67–68
  upward mobility of, 68–69
Industrial Workers of the World (IWW), 180–181
Internal Revenue Service (IRS), 178, 182, 245
international style, 198
International Telephone and Telegraph Corporation (ITT), 150
Irving Trust, 270
Israel, 201, 211, 241, 247, 281

James, Henry, 87
Javits, Jacob, 300, 315
Jay, John, 32
Jefferson, Thomas, 33, 34

Jenney, William LeBaron, 47
Jewish Defense League (JDL), 281
Jews, Judaism:
  assimilation of, 60, 66, 70–71, 201
  charitable institutions of, 113–115, 211–212, 221–222, 242, 281
  continuity in family businesses of, 105–106, 107, 210
  as emergent capitalists, 84–86
  immigration of, 56, 61–73, 81, 101
  Orthodox, 59, 60–61, 114, 289
  postwar family life of, 200–202
  prejudice against, 42, 64–65, 68, 85, 111–112, 201, 239
  Reform, 112–113, 201
  Russian pogroms against, 54–56, 61, 62
  see also Pale of Settlement; *Yehudim; Yidn*
Jews Without Money (Gold), 147
Johnson, Philip, 235
J. P. Morgan Company, 148, 162, 187, 299, 325
Julius Tishman & Sons, 106–107, 115–116

Kahn, Ely Jacques, 134
Kahn, Otto, 138–139, 141–142, 235
Kalikow, Peter, 11, 320, 332, 334
Kaufman, Mel, 12–13, 208
Kaufman, Robert, 208
Kaufman, William, 13, 209
Kaufman family, 213, 252
kehillah, 113
Kelsey, Clarence H., 86, 89, 91
Kennedy, Joseph, Sr., 9, 152, 179–180, 236
Kennedy family, 9
Kessner, Thomas, 69
Khazar Mark, 64
Kheel, Ted, 324
King, Albert, 265
Klein, George, 316
Knickerbocker Village, 148
Koch, Edward I., 18–21, 23, 294–296, 308–309, 315–316, 321, 325
Kohn, Gene, 325
Kondylis, Costos, 310
Koolhaas, Rem, 34
Kuhn, Loeb & Co., 141